The Legacy of Tiananmen

The Legacy of Tiananmen

China in Disarray

James A. R. Miles

Ann Arbor
THE UNIVERSITY OF MICHIGAN PRESS

1999   1998   1997   1996   4   3

A CIP catalog record for this book is available from the British Library

Library of Congress Cataloging-in-Publication Data

Miles, James A. R., 1961–
    The legacy of Tiananmen / James A. R. Miles.
        p.   cm.
    Includes bibliographical references and index.
    ISBN 0-472-10731-3 (hardcover : alk. paper)
    1. China—History—Tiananmen Square Incident, 1989. 2. China—
Politics and government—1976-   3. China—Social conditions—1976-
I. Title.
DS779.32.M54   1996
951.05'8—dc20   95-52804
                                                                  CIP

For Catherine

Acknowledgments

I am deeply grateful to several people without whose help this book could not have been written. Charles Eisendrath granted me a Journalism Fellowship at the University of Michigan, which gave me the time and the resources necessary to undertake the project. Charles's encouragement, advice, and friendship during an idyllic academic year in Ann Arbor from 1994 to 1995 were invaluable. I would also like to thank my managers at the BBC, especially Chris Wyld, for allowing me a leave of absence.

My wife, fellow journalist and China-watcher Catherine cast an expert eye over every draft of the book. Without her criticisms it would never have evolved into a publishable form. My mother Jean devoted much of her time and computer expertise to the preparation of the index. My brother Alexander provided some of the photographs. Thanks to you all, as well as to Michel Oksenberg of Stanford University, Andrew Higgins of the *Guardian,* Jan Wong of the *Toronto Globe and Mail,* and several anonymous readers who offered many useful suggestions on ways to improve the manuscript.

I am very grateful to Adrian Bradshaw, a friend and photojournalist with many years' experience in China, for supplying most of the photographs used in this book.

In Beijing, Meng Fanwei and Zhang Ying helped me find Chinese language books and clippings from the official press, which constitute an important part of the source material for this work. I am fortunate to have worked with expert colleagues in the BBC's Beijing bureau over the years, namely, Tim Luard, Simon Long, and Carrie Gracie, from whom I learned a lot about China. Other friends and fellow journalists in Beijing gave valuable help and information, especially David Schlesinger and Jane Macartney. The views expressed in this book, however, do not necessarily coincide with the thinking of those named on this page. Any errors are entirely my responsibility.

This book is the product of a passion for things Chinese that began at about the age of 10 when I started learning the language. My parents nurtured what began as a childhood obsession and has since become the focus of a fascinating career. To them I am particularly indebted.

Contents

Introduction

Shortly after I arrived in Beijing in 1986, a cocktail bar opened on a trial basis. It was the brainchild of the Beijing Number 2 Cake Factory, an entrepreneurial experiment. In most capital cities the opening of a bar might not be an exciting event, but in Beijing it was the first. In China's capital city the restaurants, most of which were then state-run, closed by eight in the evening, and nightlife began and ended with propaganda movies. Crowds would congregate to gaze in awe at the neon lights of the hotels reserved for foreigners in the otherwise dark and desolate streets. So the opening of a bar, any bar, was news. Optimistically, the bar was called "New Times," a name apparently signifying the owners' hope that their rather down-at-the-heels establishment far out in the western suburbs might herald the start of a new era in the cultural life of Beijing. It closed down a few months later for lack of customers.

Much as the locals would have liked to spend their evenings gossiping over a drink, they simply could not afford such luxuries on their barely adequate state salaries. The little cash they had, and a lot of their energy, was spent on necessities such as bicycles. An aspiring cyclist had to obtain an official permit to buy one and then wait months for the shop to obtain the bicycle from a lethargic state-run factory. Getting around meant bicycling, busing, or using a rudimentary two-line underground.

By the time I left China in 1994, having worked two years with United Press International and thereafter as the bureau chief of the British Broadcasting Corporation (BBC), the city's appearance had undergone an astonishing transformation. From my ground-floor office window I could see a row of private restaurants offering cuisine ranging from Beijing roast duck to Korean barbecue to the roast lamb and kebabs of central Asia. At night their facades were illuminated with neon signs and strings of fairy lights. And if the palate tired of delicate Cantonese dim sum and the fiery fare of Sichuan, there were five branches of McDonald's.[1] State-run restaurants had become almost a thing of the past. The streets were jammed with yellow taxicabs. There were more of them than in Hong Kong, Tokyo, or Taipei, and many Chinese thought nothing of waving one down.

I left behind a city where karaoke bars and high-tech discos stayed open until the small hours, their dance floors packed with youngsters dressed in Western designer clothes, dancing to the latest Western pop videos displayed on massive screens amid dry ice and strobe lights. Brash, expensively dressed men with mobile telephones and beepers filled the restaurants and bars, their girlfriends or mistresses sipping cocktails with apparent disregard for the cost and with an air of confidence that the once longed-for "New Times" had at last arrived. Visiting foreign businesspeople had only to look out of the window of their airplane at Beijing's Capital Airport and see the huge advertisement for a Chinese stomach tonic emblazoned on the air traffic control tower to know that old style Maoism was dead. To the overseas investor, one of the few negative aspects of this transformation was that Beijing had become the world's third most expensive office location after Hong Kong and Tokyo.[2]

During my eight years in China as a journalist I witnessed changes that few other countries on earth have undergone in such a short space of time. I came to a China that still felt austere, Stalinist, and backward and departed from what some foreign observers believed was an emerging economic superpower. Its system of government, they believed, was drifting gradually away from its totalitarian moorings toward an Asian-style democracy in the mold of South Korea, Taiwan, or Japan. China had become the buzzword of international commerce in the 1990s. No Western corporation with global ambitions could afford to ignore its booming market, corrupt, chaotic, and snarled in red tape though it was. Many analysts in the West, and some in Moscow, thought that China had got it right by pursuing economic reform before political reform. Among its smaller Asian neighbors it was a country increasingly feared, a military colossus with nuclear weapons and an army of growing technological sophistication that threatened to dominate the region as American power waned.

Yet in between my arrival in 1986 and my departure in 1994, the Communist Party had confronted and crushed the most powerful challenge to its authority since 1949. The Tiananmen Square demonstrations of 1989 and the subsequent crackdown were events of immense historical importance and would leave their mark indelibly on China's political and social landscape.

It is easy enough now for Chinese leaders to say that any unrest should be nipped in the bud and crushed without mercy. Failure to do so could, after all, mean the end of their careers or even of their lives. In 1989, however, the unexpected confluence of the late party leader Hu Yaobang's death, the sensitive 70th anniversary of the May 4th, 1919, student movement, and the unprecedented May 16th summit between Deng Xiaoping and President Mikhail Gorbachev put more stress on China's political fabric than it could bear. Seven weeks of demonstrations in Tiananmen Square and in cities throughout China left the party dangerously divided. A night and a day of bloodshed, as the army opened fire in central Beijing, left the party's reputation in tatters. The arrests and recriminations continued for more than a year.

Most foreign observers, looking at a country that had achieved a remarkable 9.4 percent average annual growth in gross national product (GNP) during the previous decade of reform, had badly overestimated the country's stability. It was not the first time that the West had turned a blind eye to the instability of China. The horrors of the Cultural Revolution were largely unreported until it was over. By 1989 the West had all but forgotten the Cultural Revolution, as well as the capacity of the country's rulers—not just Mao Zedong but Deng too—to suppress unrest with ruthless determination. Deng was virtually adored by Western leaders and was twice named Man of the Year by *Time* magazine (in 1978 and 1985).

There had been a bad bout of inflation and a run on banks a few months before the student protests erupted in April 1989. But there were many Beijing-based diplomats who believed that China's economic and political problems in late 1988 and early 1989 were not nearly as serious as depicted by some foreign journalists. In September 1988 a senior British diplomat approached me at a reception in Beijing and confidently informed me that he had it on "the best authority" that widespread rumors of a major split between reformers and conservatives during a recent leadership conclave at the seaside resort town of Beidaihe were untrue. He said his source, a senior Chinese official whom he had reason to trust, had told him the position of the reform-minded party leader Zhao Ziyang was completely secure. Less than nine months later, Zhao was stripped of all his posts for allegedly splitting the party and supporting the demonstrators in Tiananmen Square.

Some Chinese intellectuals I met in late 1988 and early 1989 predicted that "big chaos" was likely to erupt in the coming months, but it was impossible to know whether this was mere wishful thinking on the part of a long disgruntled sector of society. With the benefit of hindsight, Deng Xiaoping, the then 84-year-old paramount leader of China, said afterward that the upheaval "was bound to happen" because of the "little and big climate," a phrase that referred to what was happening domestically and internationally. But even if Deng and the rest of the Chinese leadership had indeed accurately predicted that an uprising was bound to occur, they kept quiet about it until after the event.

The events of 1989 gave us a rare glimpse of crucial aspects of China that had long been only dimly perceived. The mood of the public, the workings of one of the most secretive political parties in the world, and the personalities of Chinese leaders were briefly illuminated before the veil was once again drawn. But what happened so unexpectedly in 1989 should alert us to the fact that an economic boom does not necessarily bring stability in its wake.

For its part the Chinese leadership did not underestimate the significance of 1989 even if it was divided over how to prevent such turmoil happening again. Deng Xiaoping's endorsement of capitalist transformation of the economy in 1992 was a high-risk gamble that increased prosperity would lessen the threat of renewed unrest.

Hard-liners, who in many cases opposed the economic reforms that had already taken place, took the view that further liberalization of the economy would inevitably lead to more demands for a Western-style democracy. This book will argue that Deng's gambit has paid off only in the short term and that while China has changed in many important ways it is, if anything, less stable than it was in the buildup to the unrest of 1989.

China's history since the early nineteenth century has been one of periodic upheavals in which the country has struggled to find a modern identity and come to grips with the outside world. The antigovernment protests of 1989 were one such convulsion. They arose out of a conflict between the fast-growing aspirations of the urban population and the conservatism of an inward-looking leadership, which in many respects still operates like the imperial court of old. The demonstrators in Tiananmen Square wanted an end to corruption, a press that was free to report on real problems, and a government that listened and responded to concerns about everything from inflation to political representation. Deng's economic boom has done little to address these concerns.

In the mid-1990s few rules govern China's transition to a market economy. Officials double as businesspeople, local governments specu-late in real estate. Tens of millions of peasants are moving into the cities in search of work. Millions of employees of loss-making state enterprises face unemployment. The basic services they could once rely on such as free health care and education are crumbling in the onslaught of Dicken-sian capitalism. Crime is soaring and strikes, demonstrations, go-slows, petitions, and other forms of protest are becoming more common. The foreign investor is finding China an increasingly complex and risky place to do business as central government control weakens, workers become more militant and corruption more rampant, and regulations are bla-tantly ignored.

Deng Xiaoping himself has said that if any problems do occur in China they will begin inside the Communist Party.[3] Those problems are already apparent. The party defied widespread predictions that it would collapse along with its counterparts in Eastern Europe and the former Soviet Union. The main reason for the Communist Party's continued hold on power is that the leadership in 1989 experienced at first hand the dan-gers of mass revolt and redoubled its efforts to prevent a recurrence. But factional rivalries, ideological rifts, and personal enmities have been exacerbated not only by Tiananmen but by the fall of communism in the place of its birth.

Among the general public, contempt for the party and cynicism about its policies are all-pervasive. There may be far more day-to-day interest now in making money than in politics, but tolerance of the status quo should not be mistaken for approval.

When communism collapsed in Europe, none of the populations affected had experienced repression on the scale of the Cultural Revolu-tion and the 1989 Tiananmen crackdown as recently as had the Chinese people. Prosperity may have increased in China but not enough to wipe out memories of decades of ruthless political campaigns. Nor has it boosted the morale of those who are on the losing side in the race to establish a market economy.

Some Chinese city dwellers describe their country as being in a state of *xiaoluan* or "little chaos." Fear of chaos—*luan* in Chinese—is a national characteristic, inspired to a great extent by not-so-distant mem-ories of the Cultural Revolution and the civil war. The word *luan* has far greater resonance in Chinese than in its English translation. In a country as large and populous as China, order is all-important. *Luan* at its worst means catastrophe on a colossal scale. The Cultural Revolution unleashed by Mao Zedong in 1966 was *luan*. So too was the civil war that preceded the communist takeover and the warlord fighting of the 1920s and 30s in which millions died. As the following chapters explain, even in the booming 1990s this fear of chaos is not irrational. Among many Chinese, the seemingly uncontrolled and uncontrollable economic explosion now under way reinforces their fear that chaos in the form of large-scale unrest is but a short step away.

Yet when I left China in 1994 foreign governments dealing with Beijing had all but forgotten the army's bloody suppression of the Tiananmen Square protests in 1989. Of the major Western powers, only the United States had yet to send its head of government to China to restore normal contacts with those who had ordered the crackdown. But even Washington had changed its position dramatically. Within two years of taking office, President Clinton had completely reversed his once militant stand against China's "dictators." Having pledged during his campaign to impose trade sanctions on China if it failed to make progress on human rights he had come to the conclusion that access to the vast Chinese market was more important to America than persisting with seemingly futile efforts to force Chinese leaders to change the way they run the country. Market economics, Washington hoped, would bring about political change far more effectively than brandishing sticks.

China was a country America literally could not afford to shun. It represented potential salvation for key American industries in decline. The Big Three auto companies—Chrysler, Ford, and General Motors—battered at China's still protectionist doors, mesmerized by the explosive growth of its car market. Boeing saw the People's Republic as one of the few bright prospects in an otherwise depressed global market for jetliners. China boasted a 30 percent increase in air traffic volume a year and was buying 80 percent of its passenger jets from Boeing. On the other side of the coin, the United States was being deluged with Chinese consumer goods churned out by the factories that were mushrooming in the myriad boomtowns and the paddy-fields-turned-industrial-estates along China's coast. In 1994, the U.S. trade deficit with China was, according to U.S. figures, $29 billion—second only to that with Japan, which stood at $69 billion, and catching up fast. Well over a third of China's exports were destined for the United States. Bilateral U.S.-China trade had ballooned from roughly $2 billion at the start of China's economic reform era in 1979 to $40 billion in 1994. Look at the label on almost any product, from toys to computers, in a U.S. or European store, and the chances are that it is made in China.

In 1992, Deng was named Man of the Year by London's *Financial*

Times, albeit in an article tinged with caution about the lack of political change.[4] In its amazement at China's rapid economic transformation, however, the world is in danger of forgetting the lessons of Tiananmen. We should not be blinded by the mood swings that have long affected the West's understanding of China. If it was fashionable after Tiananmen to predict the rapid demise of communist rule in China, it is equally so now to predict the emergence of China within a generation or so as a new economic superpower with sufficient internal political cohesion to enable it to project its power with increasing confidence internationally.

In this book I look at the factors contributing to instability in China, keeping the lessons of Tiananmen firmly in mind. I describe the political and social tensions underlying and engendered by China's economic boom. Although I concentrate largely on domestic issues, Beijing's efforts to resolve these internal tensions will have a crucial bearing on the country's future and its relations with the outside world.

The chapters that follow are based mostly on my own interviews, information provided by Chinese sources, and analysis of the Chinese media and speeches made by officials. I regularly use phrases like "I believe" or "apparently" or "it seems that." Terms like these, which should normally be used only sparingly by journalists, are inevitable in China-watching because of the way information is controlled. The country has an extraordinary capacity to appear differently to different people. A large part of China-watching still consists of the sort of Kremlinology that those who studied the Soviet Union practiced. This art often boils down to educated guesswork.

The Chinese authorities do not directly censor news reports, but they do attempt to exercise tight control over access to people, places, and information. All foreign correspondents need to be approved by the Foreign Ministry before they can work in China. If the Foreign Ministry considers a journalist or his or her organization to be particularly hostile, it will often turn down the application.[5] In theory, a foreign journalist may not interview a single man, woman, or child without prior approval, even in Beijing. In times of increased political tension, reporters are often followed by secret police.[6] Foreign journalists have to apply to the authorities to go on working trips to the provinces. Most provinces require one or two weeks' notice and often refuse journalists' requests to visit altogether for no clear reason. Even when permission is obtained to visit the provinces the regulations forbid reporters to approach interviewees directly. Instead, a provincial government official must arrange all meetings. Frequently, these officials require journalists to submit lists of questions in advance. Western correspondents have no choice but to break the rules. They often make unauthorized trips and almost constantly conduct unauthorized interviews.

During my eight years in China, I never once got official permission to visit either Tibet or Xinjiang (which between them account for nearly half of China's land mass, though less than 2 percent of its population). I finally managed to visit Tibet in 1994 in the guise of a tourist. In 1991, when I tried to do the same thing in Xinjiang I was followed by up to half a dozen plainclothes police from the moment I arrived in the city of Kashgar, near which anti-Chinese rioting had recently occurred. I tried to keep a low profile, but when I reached the regional capital Urumqi I was summoned to a meeting with provincial government officials who interrogated me about my trip, listened to my tapes, read my notebooks, and ordered me to write a detailed account of my activities and an apology.

Perhaps most importantly, there are huge areas of the Chinese countryside that are out of bounds to foreigners altogether. As of May 1995 foreigners (not including ethnic Chinese visitors from Hong Kong, Macao, and Taiwan, who are subject to fewer travel restrictions) were allowed to visit about 1,100 cities and counties without special permits, considerably more than a decade earlier but still fewer than half of the total number in the country.[7] Such restrictions, of course, are a major impediment to understanding a country run by a Communist Party that came to power on the back of a peasant rebellion and 70 to 80 percent of whose population lives in the countryside. Most members of the 3-million-strong armed forces are peasants too. Like other journalists I talked to peasants in the environs of Beijing and those who had migrated to the cities. I made forays into the countryside both in the company of government officials and without their knowledge. But these brief, sometimes clandestine, visits were by no means an ideal way to understand the problems of a widely scattered population of 800 million people—more than three times the population of the United States.

In recent years, one of the few significant improvements in our access to information about China has, however, been offered by an unlikely source, namely, the state-controlled media. Although the Chinese press rarely gives much away about what is happening politically, there has been a marked improvement in its coverage of social and economic trends, ranging from crime to the problems of economic reform to the increasing dissatisfaction of peasants. Some newspapers, particularly local ones, now dare tackle hitherto taboo subjects such as homosexuality in a relatively objective fashion. The quality of reporting in the official press took a turn for the better after Deng launched his new campaign for faster reform in 1992. Newspapers, although still owned and controlled by the party or local governments, found themselves being forced into the marketplace. To make up for cuts in their subsidies, they were forced to rely more heavily on advertising. Advertisers in turn wanted to see good circulation figures. The result has been more lively and interesting coverage. Newspapers like the *Beijing Youth News,* the *China Business Times,* and *Southern Weekend* have become, at least on occasion, a pleasure to read. In the following chapters I quote extensively from such newspapers because I believe that nowadays they can fill vital gaps in our understanding of Chinese society.

I also frequently refer to classified material that is not intended for foreigners' eyes but is circulated widely among officials and even ordinary members of the public. The lowest level of classification, "internal" (*neibu*), is so common that some books on sale in public bookshops are marked as such. This means that in theory foreigners may not buy them, but bookshops increasingly ignore this restriction in their eagerness to make money. Documents marked "secret" (*mimi* or *jimi*) are often obtained by low-ranking party members who in turn sometimes make their contents known to foreign journalists.[8] The kind of information classified as "internal" or "secret" in China would usually be publicly available in most other countries, and many Chinese themselves think nothing of handling such material—hence the frequent leaks. But these low-level classified documents do contain analyses of events in China and abroad that shed more light on government thinking than the official press and sometimes reveal policy decisions that have not been made public.

The Hong Kong press often contains highly plausible accounts of political developments on the mainland, but there is usually no way of independently verifying them. Thus the only Hong Kong newspapers to which I frequently refer are those controlled by Beijing and which therefore reflect at least one strand of official thinking on the mainland.

While this book focuses on factors for instability created by Tiananmen and by Deng's response to Tiananmen it does not attempt to cover every aspect of China. Population control and unrest in Tibet, for instance, are among the issues that I only touch upon. This is because I do not see them as possible flash points for nationwide upheaval, although the growth of the population plays into such problems as unemployment, social welfare, and migration from the countryside.

As China prepares to take over Hong Kong, political and social stability on the Chinese mainland is becoming a subject of urgent importance, not only to residents of the colony but also to policy makers in London and Washington. How would Britain respond if, on the eve of Hong Kong's handover on July 1st, 1997, China were in a state of political turmoil similar to that which existed around the time of Tiananmen? At the height of that crisis, it was even unclear who was in command of the world's largest nation. Handing over Hong Kong to a country in such a state of confusion would be a difficult decision to sell to the British electorate. Not to do so would risk major, possibly bloody, confrontation with Beijing. In either case, the territory itself would be thrown into turmoil. While it may be unlikely that China's resumption of sovereignty over Hong Kong would coincide with another Tiananmen, an upheaval of that magnitude any time in the future would send shock waves not only through Hong Kong but through the capitals of some of the world's most successful economies, which are perched on China's rim.

China is now facing the most uncertain period of its political life since the communists came to power. The death of Deng will mark the end of a leadership system dominated by veteran revolutionaries whose authority rests on careers dating from well before the communist takeover in 1949. Those fighting for power after Deng's death will be younger men in the main who played little if any role in the civil war that brought the communists to power. Deng's strength, like Mao Zedong's, has depended to a considerable extent on his credibility within the military, built up during his years as a guerrilla commander. Mao and Deng were able to control a country as large and diverse as China not least because there was mutual respect and understanding between themselves and professional soldiers. Deng's designated civilian successors have no combat experience.

It was lucky for the party and its leaders that Deng eventually managed to override the paralyzing factional disputes during Tiananmen. Without him, the crisis might have ended very differently. Deng himself has often warned that civil war might break out and millions of refugees pour across the country's borders if communist authority collapses. While such apocalyptic statements are, of course, aimed at frightening radical reformers into silence, they are not to be dismissed as mere propaganda. Many Chinese, including many firebrand dissidents, see his point, as do many of China's neighbors.

When cracks begin to appear more openly in the political structure, as I believe they eventually will, the Pandora's box of rivalry, hatred, vengefulness, and a myriad other destructive emotions will spill open just as they did in some of the former communist countries of Eastern Europe and parts of the former Soviet Union. There are those who might argue that China has been through chaos before, during the Cultural Revolution and in 1989, for example, and has managed not only to reorganize but, in the end, to achieve astonishing growth. This, however, was achieved under the direction of powerful personalities such as Mao Zedong and Deng Xiaoping, who may have been responsible for creating the chaos in the first place but nonetheless had the strength to curb it when it threatened to spin out of control. What would happen if, as seems likely in the not-too-distant future, there is no one in the leadership with the political authority of Mao or Deng? Hong Kong and Taiwan—the latter being home to the only armed political opposition to the Communist Party—might find themselves sucked into the maelstrom. But the consequences of chaos would be felt all over the world.

The Chinese revolution that began in the twilight years of the Qing dynasty more than a century ago is still far from reaching its conclusion. For all its seeming familiarity with the modern ways of the capitalist West, China is a country saddled with enormous baggage from its past. The rapid economic growth of the last few years is by no means a guarantee that China has at last found the secret of cohesion, nor do Deng's hard-line critics offer any viable alternatives.

Rivers of Blood

If some so-called democratic fighters seize power, they'll start fighting among themselves. As soon as civil war breaks out there'll be rivers of blood. What would be the point then of talking about 'human rights'?
—Deng Xiaoping to Pierre Elliott Trudeau, 1990

The visitor to China could be forgiven for thinking that Tiananmen is forgotten. China has a remarkable ability to cover up its wounds. The physical reminders of Tiananmen were quickly erased after the event. Within a few weeks of the bloodshed most of the scars left by bullets on the facades of buildings had been patched up. Flagstones charred by fires and chipped by armored vehicles had been replaced on the square itself. By mid-1994 when I left China, the only tangible evidence of the military action was the barely visible imprints of tank tracks on the tarmac of Changan Boulevard near where it intersects Tiananmen. You had to listen carefully for the faint, eerie hum produced by the tires of your vehicle as they passed over the indentations. The unknowing visitor might see Beijing's lavish new department stores, its open-air restaurants, and its busy, well-stocked markets and believe that everything was back to normal.

Some observers argue that China's fast-growing prosperity since Tiananmen has helped to blot out memories of the bloodshed and ensure social stability. Suppressing memories is one thing but erasing them is quite another. I believe that anyone directly involved in the upheaval of 1989—and there are tens of millions of such people in Beijing and other cities around the country—remains profoundly affected by the experience. Those tumultuous seven weeks generated more heartfelt, sustained emotion in China than any other event since the Cultural Revolution. These feelings will take a very long time to dissipate. No matter how successful the economy, no matter how affluent they may become, many

Chinese will long continue to want revenge or at least a public acknowledgment by the leadership that what the demonstrators did in 1989 was right.

The economic boom since Tiananmen may have blunted the demands of some for radical political change. But the very boom itself has caused such social and political dislocation that, I believe, the potential for large-scale unrest has increased. Tension between the old order and the new economic structures and interest groups emerging from it shows no sign of diminishing as China's rapid transformation continues. By the mid-1990s many Chinese observers were both in private and, to an increasing extent, in open publications expressing the same opinion.

Tiananmen was a watershed in Chinese history. It has had an enormous impact on China's foreign and domestic policy and continues to do so. It was with Tiananmen and the collapse of communism in Europe in mind that Deng Xiaoping launched the new economic reform campaign of 1992, which caused a surge of economic growth and triggered an explosion of entrepreneurial activity. He gambled that giving people more opportunity to make money would make them less inclined to take to the streets demanding democracy as they had done in 1989. It was because of Tiananmen and the diplomatic isolation it suffered as a consequence that China decided to seek a new accommodation with the West. Beijing abandoned its policy of refusing to discuss human rights. It decided to avoid confrontation with fellow permanent members of the United Nations Security Council and tacitly to accept Washington's preeminence in the post–Cold War order. This was in spite of its continuing disputes with the United States over a host of issues, including human rights, bilateral trade, and dealings with Taiwan.

The "counterrevolutionary rebellion," as China describes the largely peaceful resistance to the imposition of martial law in Beijing, is now hardly ever mentioned in the mainstream official media. By the second anniversary of the bloodshed the leadership had decided that dwelling on what had happened would only serve to keep the issue alive. Now only dissidents and Deng's extreme hard-line critics—whose voices are heard in the pages of a few theoretical journals under their control in Beijing—still try to remind the public of Tiananmen.[1] Their views reach only a limited audience. The leadership's silence, however, is misleading. Tiananmen remains the most divisive political issue in China. The question of whether a spontaneous uprising involving so many people—clearly not just a small group of "hostile forces"—should be termed revolutionary or counterrevolutionary is an issue involving the basic tenets of Chinese communism. If it was not counterrevolutionary, then the use of the People's Liberation Army to crush the demonstrations was an unforgivable violation of party principles.

In 1989 the party was deeply split over this question, and my own conversations with many party members since then suggest that it remains so. Deng Xiaoping has been the main force stopping these differences from being aired more openly. It was Deng who ordered the army into Tiananmen Square, and few would dare challenge the country's most powerful man while he remains alive. But there is undoubtedly enormous support inside and outside the party for a formal reevaluation of Tiananmen involving at the very least the removal of the "counterrevolutionary" tag and the affixing of a more positive label—"patriotic democratic movement" perhaps, as the demonstrators once demanded. But the process is unlikely to be as straightforward as simply changing the official description. A reevaluation would inevitably involve a search for scapegoats. After Deng's death it would be easy to pin the blame on him. But there are many other leaders who played prominent roles in quelling the unrest. The witch-hunt could prove fatally damaging to the party's fragile unity.[2]

Why should the killing of demonstrators be an issue of such paramount political importance? Many governments frequently use bullets to quell unrest without unleashing the same degree of soul-searching as has occurred in China over Tiananmen. In the Indian subcontinent, for example, where I was based as a correspondent before arriving in China, shooting at demonstrators is so routine that foreign journalists often pay little attention unless the death toll is unusually high. Many Indians pay even less attention to the terse reports of police shooting at protesters that regularly appear in the Indian press. But under communist rule the Chinese are used to different methods of social control, such as preemptive arrests and intimidation in the workplace, rather than tear gas and rifles. Before Tiananmen, the use of bullets to stop antigovernment unrest in Chinese cities had been almost unheard of since 1949, except in Tibet. Even though every Chinese knows that the government is capable of enormous brutality, few city dwellers before 1989 had seen it in the raw.

Hardly anyone I met during the Tiananmen Square protests believed the army—which prided itself on being a "people's army" that "never takes a needle or thread from the masses"—would actually open fire on demonstrators and crush them with tanks in the nation's hallowed capital. Even many soldiers, "the sons and brothers of the people" as they are often referred to in official texts, thought the use of force was unlikely.

An officer cadet I met in Beijing four days before the bloodshed said "at least 90 percent" of his colleagues supported the demonstrators. "Most of the soldiers support the students; they would not point their guns at students," he said. "Some would obey orders, but most would disobey. . . . The army has done many good things for the people during the war of liberation against the Japanese and against the Kuomintang (KMT).[3] The army serves the people, and the people like the army. Now the party is using the army. The army is not on the government's side."

The cadet's remarks reflected a widespread, if naive, belief at the time in the sanctity of the Chinese army. Even though it could be argued that the military crackdown restored stability and thereby paved the way for China's subsequent economic takeoff, I would still be surprised if the majority of party and military cadres believe that what the leadership ordered the army to do in June 1989 was morally and ideologically correct.

Talk to a Beijing resident for any length of time and the subject of Tiananmen is likely to be raised. "Where were you on June 4th?" they often asked me on learning that my residency in Beijing spanned the unrest. After telling them where I was, they would recount their own experiences that night with the passion of someone divulging a long suppressed secret. I left China more than five years after Tiananmen, but residents would still on occasion, without my asking, tell me what they saw and did on the night of the bloodshed with almost the same intensity and sense of horror as if it had just happened. The sullenness and rage that so obviously characterized the mood of many Beijing residents in late 1989 was no longer evident, but the issue of Tiananmen still stirred deep-seated emotions among many citizens when the subject arose in conversation.

Violence on that scale leaves deep scars and changes people's lives. Let us say, very conservatively, that 5,000 civilians were killed or injured that night.[4] If that figure is then multiplied by the number of close relatives and friends, the population profoundly affected by what happened is already substantial. Add the hundreds of people arrested in Beijing and their friends and relatives as well as the tens of thousands of people not already included in these calculations who were out on the streets trying to stop the troops coming in, and the figure is huge. Those affected do not necessarily go around looking gloomy. Most continue living normally, but the memories undoubtedly still haunt them.

Tiananmen's importance to many city residents is not just as a mass protest that ended in terrible bloodshed or as a rude awakening to the ruthlessness of the powers that be. Also of crucial significance is that Tiananmen belonged to a hallowed tradition of student-led activism against unpopular governments. Students have long been at the forefront of revolution in China. Under Chairman Mao intellectuals may have been officially reviled as the lowest of the low, but it was college and high school students who formed the core of the violent Red Guard movement against Mao's alleged enemies in the party bureaucracy.

Many urban Chinese feel a deep-rooted reverence for the educated elite. When the student demonstrators in 1989 began their hunger strike on Tiananmen Square any sector of society that had hitherto refrained from joining the protests was suddenly out on the streets. Factory workers, policemen, Foreign Ministry officials, and journalists in the state-controlled media were among those who carried banners and shouted slogans proclaiming that the students were precious children who had to be saved. Befitting their image, the students stayed aloof from other demonstrators, reserving for themselves the space around the Monument to the People's Heroes in the center of Tiananmen Square and forcing a group of worker activists to occupy a distant corner of the plaza. When the troops had finished clearing the square, the first precise figure the government gave of casualties was of the number of students killed, even though this figure turned out to be tiny in proportion to the total number of dead.[5] The government knew that the student death toll was a key concern of the public. The aim was to show that not nearly as many students died as people first thought. But to many Beijing residents, the fact that students died at all was unforgivable.

The modern history of China is dotted with student-led movements that have assumed enormous significance in the popular imagination and political mythology of the nation. The May 4th Movement of 1919 set the trend. On that date more than 3,000 students marched on Tiananmen Square to protest against the decision by the victorious powers of the First World War to acknowledge Japanese control over part of eastern China. The demonstrations snowballed to involve several hundred thousand students as well as tens of thousands of workers in more than a hundred cities. Deng Xiaoping, then 14 years old, was among the demonstrators. The May 4th Movement lasted only a few weeks, yet it acted as a catalyst for the intellectual revolution in China that gave birth to Chinese communism and paved the way for the communist victory thirty years later. May 4th is officially celebrated now as Youth Day. Many students, however, regard the May 4th Movement as the start of an unfinished struggle for democracy, and the authorities are hence careful to maintain tight security around campuses on Youth Day to prevent any efforts to revive the 1919 campaign.

The Chinese Communist Party still commemorates the May 30th Movement of 1925, when British security forces killed 13 students and workers in Shanghai who were protesting against the extraterritorial powers of foreigners in China. The bloodshed sparked protests across the country involving millions of people. A year after Tiananmen, on the 65th anniversary of the killings, the Shanghai authorities unveiled a monument in the city's main park dedicated to the "nationwide anti-imperialist protest against the massacre of Chinese people by British police."[6]

During the December 9th Movement of 1935, KMT security forces used water hoses, leather belts, clubs, and rifle butts to break up an anti-Japanese demonstration involving 3,000 students near Tiananmen Square. About 40 students were injured in the clash, which sparked nationwide workers' strikes and student demonstrations. Among the participants was the woman who was later to become Deng's third wife, Zhuo Lin—then a 19-year-old high school student in Beijing. The movement played an important role in eventually forcing the KMT to forge an alliance with the communists against the Japanese. In 1990, the party staged a large commemorative gathering in the Great Hall of the People to mark the 55th anniversary of the protests, at which, ironically, the hard-line Politburo member Song Ping called on students—still reeling from the Tiananmen crackdown—to "inherit and carry forward the glorious revolutionary traditions of the December 9th Movement."[7]

Under communist rule, university campuses continued to turn periodically into hotbeds of political activism. During the short-lived Hundred Flowers Movement of 1957, when Mao encouraged citizens to air their criticisms of the government, students at Beijing University responded by covering walls with handwritten posters calling for greater political and intellectual freedom. The movement was crushed later that year, but campuses erupted in ferment again in the late 1960s during the Cultural Revolution when, at Mao's urging, Red Guard factions fought the bureaucracy and each other, sometimes with guns and bombs. Under Deng's rule, student activism flared again during local congress elections in 1980 when candidates at some universities staged unprecedented Western-style campaigns. In late 1986, shortly after my arrival in China, the anniversary of the December 9th Movement triggered demonstrations involving tens of thousands of students in more than 20 cities, including Beijing and Shanghai. The students' main demands were for greater freedom and democracy. The protests died down almost as soon as the government made threatening noises, but the political repercussions were enormous. A few days after the demonstrations the reform-minded party leader Hu Yaobang was forced to resign and several prominent intellectuals were expelled from the party because of their advocacy of "bourgeois liberalization," the party's catchphrase for Western political ideas.

The June 4th Movement of 1989, however, eclipsed every other student-led mass campaign of this century. By any reckoning, many times more people were killed than in any previous movement. Tens if not hundreds of thousands of troops were deployed to quell the unrest. Tens of millions of people around the country took part in the demonstrations. The numbers alone guaranteed its place in history.

A few weeks after the bloodshed, the authorities staged an exhibition of memorabilia from the antigovernment protests at Beijing's Military History Museum, including a striking collection of burned-out armored vehicles assembled in the forecourt. One of the most interesting exhibits was a map showing where demonstrations had occurred. More than 80 cities were marked—a far greater number than previous reports had documented. That was the official count. The actual number of cities affected was probably higher still. Even on the tiny island of Gulangyu off the port of Xiamen in the Taiwan Straits, protesters took to the narrow streets in support of the students in Beijing.

The Communist Party leader Jiang Zemin once described the West's response to Tiananmen as "much ado about nothing."[8] The prime minister, Li Peng, said dismissively less than a year after Tiananmen that the event was no longer "news."[9] Few other Chinese officials, however, have dared be so dismissive about the importance of what took place.

For foreign journalists and other observers standing on the sidelines, Tiananmen provided a glimpse of the madness, chaos, and senseless violence that could again be unleashed if the government loses its grip and tries desperately to regain it. At two o'clock on the morning of June 4th, 1989, I arrived at an intersection about three miles west of Tiananmen Square. The night sky was lit by flames leaping from buses set on fire by residents in a futile attempt to keep out the army. Armored vehicles had bulldozed the roadblocks aside, and in the smoke and glare truckload after truckload of soldiers roared toward Tiananmen. The air was filled with the sound of wailing sirens as ambulances raced up to carry away the dead and wounded. Periodic bursts of automatic gunfire crackled in the distance. Hundreds of people milled around or scattered and crouched when they heard shots. Some of them came up to me almost in tears and begged me to tell the world what was happening.

For the next three or four days Beijing looked like a city at war. Groups of frightened, angry residents gathered here and there in otherwise near deserted streets. Tanks and trucks crammed with troops rumbled and thundered through the city, past the burned-out or still smoldering wreckage of buses, trucks, and military vehicles. Sometimes the troops would fire volleys of blank and live rounds into the air or take potshots at bystanders who scattered in their wake. Plumes of smoke could be seen rising above the city as residents vented their anger by starting new fires amid the scattered remains of their ineffective barricades. A few bolder citizens placed flowers at the spots where demonstrators had been killed or erected defiant banners on the streets calling on residents to avenge the bloodshed.

In other cities students and residents poured out onto the streets to protest against the bloodshed in Beijing. In Shanghai, thousands of students set up dozens of roadblocks on major thoroughfares, shouting slogans such as "pay the debt of blood" and "down with tyranny." During the small hours of June 7th protesters set fire to a train after it had ploughed into a crowd of demonstrators blocking the tracks, killing at least six of them. Thousands battled with police who were dispatched to the scene. In Chengdu, the capital of the southwestern province of Sichuan, demonstrators set fire to a huge indoor marketplace, torched firefighting vehicles, threw stones and bottles at the municipal government headquarters, and ransacked the foyers of the city's two top hotels for foreigners.[10] In the central city of Wuhan, thousands of students blocked China's main north-south railway line where it crosses the Yangtze River, stopping all rail traffic for several hours. In Zhengzhou, the capital of the central province of Henan, thousands of students marched through the streets, shouting slogans such as "seize weapons and smash the reactionary government," "repay blood with blood," and "hang Li Peng."[11] Similar scenes were played out in city after city across the nation—evidence that, when pushed, a people so often described by foreigners and Chinese alike as politically passive and easily intimidated by authority can be fiercely defiant.

Even during the most tumultuous phases of the Cultural Revolution of the 1960s and 1970s, Beijing itself had never witnessed such violence nor such a total breakdown of order. One of my most vivid memories is of standing on a flyover due east of Tiananmen Square the day after the army moved in. The normally busy thoroughfare leading toward the square was a maze of burning barricades. I was surrounded by a group of about a dozen people who vied with each other to tell me their stories of what had happened. One man gestured toward the smoking debris. "What have they done to our capital?" he asked, his voice choking with emotion. "They said it was chaos before, but this is chaos; they've turned it into chaos."

Those were nightmarish days, made all the more so in my memory by the exhaustion of covering the story round the clock for the BBC with occasional catnaps replacing proper sleep for days on end. Foreigners rushed to leave the country, scrambling amid crowds of fellow refugees at the airport to buy standby tickets. For a long time after the troops moved in Beijing had almost no visible government except for the soldiers. Ministries stopped work. The Foreign Ministry did not answer journalists' phone calls. It was not until three days after the bloodshed began that a senior Chinese official, the government's chief spokesperson, Yuan Mu, appeared in person to comment on the crackdown. "The current struggle to put down the rebellion is one of life and death for the party and the state," Yuan said at a news conference that was broadcast later the same day on Chinese television.[12]

It was indeed a life-or-death struggle. It was a struggle not just between the demonstrators and the government but within the party itself. Yuan Mu's appearance was significant not just as the first by a top Chinese official since the bloodshed but the first for some days before then. On May 27th, Li Xiannian, the chairman of the legislature's advisory body, the Chinese People's Political Consultative Conference, said on television that "a few individuals within the leading strata" of the party were an important cause of the unrest and promised that "no punishment will be meted out to students for some of their radical remarks and radical deeds."[13] On June 1st, the mayor, Chen Xitong, was quoted by Xinhua News Agency as saying at a celebration of Children's Day attended by some 20,000 youngsters in Beijing that "Tiananmen Square belongs to all Young Pioneers in China and to the people of the whole country. I think that you will soon be able to pay tribute to the revolutionary martyrs at the Monument to the People's Heroes."[14] But for days before and after the bloodshed there was no public attempt by a top party leader to rally the nation.

This prolonged lack of visible leadership at a time of acute crisis was a sign of how terrified the government was. For all the outside world really knows to this day the party could have been teetering on the brink of collapse in the same way that East European and Soviet communist parties crumbled in the face of popular opposition.[15] To observers, China seemed a country no longer ruled by a government but by a small quarrelsome group of people who did not dare show their faces.

It was not until June 7th that the Foreign Ministry issued its first formal statement since the clearing of the square. To me it was a memorable and startling moment. Here was an actual government representative on the other end of the telephone. Here was evidence that the machinery of government was beginning to work again. It was a young man, a fluent English-speaker, and he sounded eager when I suggested recording his statement for broadcast to the world. With my tape machine rolling, the official said in a confident voice that the Chinese government was stable and fully capable of putting down what he called "the rebellion in Beijing." The Foreign Ministry statement was less than convincing. American officials said Washington had made contact with middle-ranking counterparts in the Chinese government but could not get in touch with the leadership. The White House press secretary said there had been "speculation the top leadership may have dispersed" to other parts of the country.[16] Chinese leaders have yet to reveal where they were or what they were doing on the night of the carnage in Beijing.

Three months later, Deng Xiaoping described his feelings at the time of Tiananmen during a meeting with the physicist Tsung-Dao Lee of Columbia University, an American of Chinese ancestry. "In putting down the counterrevolutionary rebellion, the People's Liberation Army made sacrifices," Deng said. "That was no easy thing, I can tell you. If the rebels had had their way, there would have been a civil war. If there had been a civil war, we would have won, but how many people would have died, and how many more would have grieved for them? That would have been a real disaster. . . . If we had not taken resolute measures to put it down, the consequences would have been unimaginable."[17] Deng also emphasized his role in curbing the unrest. "Fortunately I was still around, and it was not difficult to deal with the matter," Deng said, adding modestly, "Of course, I was not the only one to play a role."

A year after Tiananmen, Deng elaborated on his fears of civil war during a meeting with the former Canadian prime minister Pierre Trudeau. "You can imagine," Deng said, "what China in turmoil would be like. If turmoil erupts in China, it wouldn't just be a Cultural Revolution-type problem. At that time [during the Cultural Revolution] you still had the prestige of the elder generation of leaders such as Mao Zedong and Zhou Enlai. Even though it was described as 'all-out civil war,' actually there wasn't any major fighting. It wasn't a proper civil war."

"Now it's not at all the same. If turmoil erupts again, to the extent that the party is no longer effective and state power is no longer effective, and one faction grabs one part of the army and another faction grabs another part of the army—that would be civil war. If some so-called democratic fighters seize power, they'll start fighting among themselves. As soon as civil war breaks out there'll be rivers of blood. What would be the point then of talking about 'human rights'? As soon as civil war breaks out, local warlords will spring up everywhere, production will plummet, communications will be severed, and it won't be a matter of a few million or even tens of millions of refugees—there'd be well over a hundred million people fleeing the country. First to be affected would be Asia—now the most promising part of the world. It would be a global disaster."[18]

Deng was in effect saying that China might not be such a stable place when the old guard, including himself, is no longer alive. He had already hinted at this shortly after Tiananmen when he said it was fortunate that the unrest had happened when it did because "we still have a large group of veterans who have experienced many storms and have a thorough understanding of things."[19] In 1992, Deng made the point even more explicitly. "Hostile forces realize that so long as we of the older generation are still alive and carry weight, no change is possible," he said. "But after we are dead and gone, who will ensure that there is no peaceful evolution?"[20] The party leader Jiang Zemin implied in 1989 that he felt a similar concern when he said that "the health and longevity of Comrade Xiaoping is of great significance to the smooth progress of the work of our party and government."[21]

Deng has devoted much of his energy since becoming China's paramount leader in the late 1970s to reorganizing the armed forces in such a way as to prevent local military commanders from gaining too much power. But the point of his remarks about civil war is that if the party collapses the military will collapse with it, with devastating consequences. The dynamics of the Chinese military being an even greater enigma to foreign observers than those of the political structure, it is difficult to produce evidence to refute Deng's analysis of the dangers of civil war beyond simply arguing that Deng has good reasons for exaggerating the dangers.

As we consider China's prospects in the post-Deng era it is sobering to speculate that without Deng in charge in 1989 civil war might indeed have broken out. It was clear to foreign observers in Beijing that some units under the martial law command were less enthusiastic than others about shooting at protesters. At the Jianguomenwai flyover, about three miles east of Tiananmen and next to a compound of high-rise apartment blocks housing mostly foreign diplomats and journalists, some 50 truck-loads of Chinese soldiers remained camped on June 5th at the same spot where they had been since before the violence began. There were no reports of this detachment having fired once at protesters, even when other passing convoys of troops—apparently from different units—had done so in front of them. Many foreign journalists speculated at the time that forces opposed to the violence were preparing to go to war with its perpetrators.

The speculation was fueled by an unusual new deployment at the Jianguomenwai flyover on the evening of June 5th. Several dozen tanks took up positions on and around the overpass, their guns pointing in every direction except back toward the city center to the west. Some Western diplomats told journalists that this indicated that the tanks were expecting an attack from the east by a rival unit from outside the city. The Jianguomenwai flyover would be a natural spot to defend, they thought, since it has a commanding view both of Beijing's main east-west thoroughfare and the ring road that follows the line of what used to be the city wall.

As dusk fell on June 5th, my imagination—like those of most of my colleagues in the foreign press corps—was running riot. "As the night wore on," I wrote in a dispatch for the BBC, "the tension in Peking mounted. There's a widespread fear now that a new phase of violence could be about to begin—not this time between soldiers and civilians, but between the soldiers themselves. The capital seems to be occupied by two distinct forces—one that's loyal to the Chinese president Yang Shangkun,[22] a veteran communist who's known for his hard-line views.[23] Another force, of unknown loyalty, has so far shunned the violence. It's thought now that the two forces could be on the verge of war. . . . It seems now that only such a conflict—bloody though it may be—could end the horror in Peking."

Newspaper headlines around the world sounded a similar note of alarm. "Crackdown in Beijing; Civil War for Army?" asked the *New York Times*. "Chinese Army Units Seen Near Conflict; Military Maneu-vers in Beijing Raise Prospect of Civil War," declared the *Washington Post*. "Civil War Threat as Troops Clash; 'The Army Is Preparing to Fight the Army in Peking,'" said the *Daily Telegraph* in London.

It proved to be a false alarm. No attack occurred, and within a day or so Western military attachés and foreign correspondents—wiser in ret-rospect—put forward a new theory that the tanks were stationed on the flyover simply to intimidate the local population. Western diplomats now believe that none of the hundreds of tanks deployed during the Tiananmen operation were carrying ammunition for their main guns. That there was no intentional fighting among the units involved in the crackdown was testimony to Deng's clout as chairman of the Central Military Commission, the party body that exercises ultimate control over the armed forces. Nonetheless there were signs of dissent within the military and among retired senior officers over the use of force. In late May 1989, soon after the imposition of martial law, copies of a letter circulated widely among protesters purporting to be from seven retired generals, including a former defense minister and former chief of staff. The letter, addressed to the martial law command, said, "The people's army belongs to the people. It must never oppose the people, let alone suppress them. They must never shoot at the people, or create any incidents of bloodshed. To prevent the situation worsening, troops must not enter the city."[24] The state-sponsored China News Service reported on the contents of the letter, which Chinese sources told foreign journalists had been sent originally to the *People's Daily.* The newspaper reportedly refused to publish it.[25]

Credible accounts say that the commander of the 38th Army, General Xu Qinxian, was arrested for refusing to carry out martial law duties. General Xu was reportedly released in 1990 but remained in disgrace.[26] The authorities, of course, denied there were any problems. The chief of staff, General Chi Haotian, said that during the unrest "all military officers and soldiers maintained a high degree of consensus with Chairman Deng Xiaoping and the Central Military Commission he led. . . . Their unity can be described as firm as a rock without a crack."[27] But the army's mouthpiece, the *Liberation Army Daily,* hinted a few months later that maintaining such unity was not an easy task. "In the international arena there are some bourgeois politicians and instigators of unrest . . . who believe that a major factor in the failure of last year's turmoil was that they did not gain hold of the military," the newspaper said. "Determining whose hands will hold power over the army will be a focus of our long-term struggle with the supporters of bourgeois liberalism."[28] Given how little the outside world actually knows about the Chinese armed forces, Deng's fears of civil war certainly cannot be dismissed.

For a crucial few days in 1989 even Deng seemed to be paralyzed with uncertainty over how to deal with the unrest. His reformist protégé, the then party general secretary Zhao Ziyang, must have sensed this indecision when, in early May, he publicly took a much softer line on the demonstrations than that expressed by Deng a few days earlier. The long gap between the imposition of martial law on May 20th and the military action on the night of June 3rd and the morning of June 4th also suggested that Deng was unsure how to proceed.

To the outside world it looked for a while as if Deng might have been sidelined. Deng's last public appearance before the clearing of Tiananmen Square was on May 16th when he met the Soviet leader Mikhail Gorbachev in the Great Hall of the People, a stone's throw from where huge crowds of protesters were calling for his resignation, saying he was too old and too conservative to run the country. Deng's appearance was in startling contrast to that of the relatively young and vigorous Gorbachev. His words sounded badly slurred, and during a luncheon in Gorbachev's honor he had difficulty handling his chopsticks. When Deng finally did reappear, five days after the military action, he looked, as usual, physically feeble but still mentally alert. In his speech, he strongly implied that it had been a struggle even for him to win the party's cooperation. "I believe," he said, "that if we work at it, we can win the support of the overwhelming majority of party comrades for our assessment of the nature of the incident and for the measures we have taken to cope with it."[29]

The occasion of Deng's June 9th reappearance was a meeting with the martial law command. The televised gathering was meant to show that he was still in command and that the leadership was united. But while it certainly did dispel rumors that he had been ousted, it failed to convince anyone that the party had healed its wounds. Perhaps Deng could have tried after Tiananmen to calm tempers in the party by letting bygones be bygones. In 1987, after the previous bout of student demonstrations, Deng tried to stop zealous hard-liners from getting carried away with the purge. The reformist party leader Hu Yaobang was removed from his post but allowed to remain in the Politburo. His successor, Zhao Ziyang, announced that the campaign against "bourgeois liberalization" would only be conducted inside the party and would not affect the economic sphere. "In enterprises and institutions, there will only be education by positive example and no attempt will be made to ferret out exponents of bourgeois liberalization," Zhao said.[30] In the end the only victims apart from Hu Yaobang were a handful of radical intellectuals in the party whose ideas Deng believed had encouraged the students to rebel. These intellectuals were criticized publicly and expelled from the party, but none of them was arrested.

In 1989, the purge was considerably more far-reaching. Deng set no limits except to say that his economic reform program should not be affected. His failure to lay down stricter parameters resulted in sweeping attacks against liberals inside and outside the party who had supported the demonstrations and a deepening of the political crisis. Zhao was the first prominent victim, losing all his party posts for his alleged role in the unrest. The leadership abandoned the scrupulous efforts it had made in 1987 in the case of Hu Yaobang to convince the outside world that the days of Maoist-style disappearances were over. Whereas Hu was back in public circulation less than four months after his forced resignation, Zhao became a nonperson. More than six years after Tiananmen, the man once regarded by Deng as his successor had yet to attend a single public event and was still not free to travel around the country as he pleased.

Never during the reform era had the party mounted such a sweeping purge of liberals in its ranks as it did after Tiananmen. In the mid-1980s it had tried to weed out "leftists" responsible for the worst excesses of the Cultural Revolution as well as those considered corrupt. More than 120,000 people lost their party membership during the campaign, which, though widely resisted within the party ranks, was supported by the general population.[31] The post-Tiananmen *qingcha* (ferreting out) movement was bitterly resented by party members and nonmembers alike. To many intellectuals it was frighteningly reminiscent of the Anti-Rightist campaign ordered by Chairman Mao in 1957, when more than 500,000 people were dismissed from their jobs or sent to work in the countryside because of their criticisms of the Communist Party during the Hundred Flowers Movement. The Anti-Rightist Campaign inflicted deep wounds on the party that only began to heal in the 1980s. The purge after Tiananmen reopened them.

To ease public fears of another Anti-Rightist Campaign the party tried to say as little as possible in public about the mechanics of the purge. But in its secret Document Number 10, the party specified the target areas as central government and party organizations, universities and colleges, the media, scientific research institutes, and official institutions engaged in literary or other artistic pursuits—in other words, those bodies considered most supportive of the demonstrations.[32] Other confidential documents said that at least 4 million party members in these organizations—nearly a tenth of the party's total membership—would be investigated to find out what role they had played in the unrest.[33]

The aim of the purge was stated to be "resolutely getting rid of hostile elements, antiparty elements, and corrupt elements" as well as "dealing strictly with those inside the party with serious tendencies toward bourgeois liberalization."[34] The leadership decreed that party members in the target institutions must reapply for membership. In order to qualify for readmittance, members had to show that they supported the use of troops against the demonstrators and that they had not played an active role in the unrest after the declaration of martial law on May 20th, 1989. If they had joined demonstrations before martial law, they had to show they were fully repentant. To do this, members had to write out detailed accounts, often several thousand words long, of their thoughts and actions during the main stages of the unrest. Their party cells would then decide whether these accounts conformed with police records and whether they were sufficiently sincere. If not, then the member would be expelled or kept under observation for a certain period to assess his or her true attitude. Any member who had expressed the desire to resign from the party in protest against the crackdown would be expelled rather than allowed to bow out.[35]

Loss of party membership may not have been as big a deal in 1989 as it had been a few years earlier, but it still meant a black mark in one's file. Every urban resident has a file (*dang'an*) containing records of that person's political outlook, any criminal activities, and their history of employment. Any negative comment could be grounds for denying someone a job. A black mark stays with a person forever, and because the contents of the file are kept secret they are impossible to challenge.

The senior Politburo member who supervised the purge was Song Ping, a hard-line party veteran. In a classified speech, Song said getting party members to reapply for membership would give them a chance "to think carefully and make a serious choice" as to whether they wanted to remain in the party. "After this, even though our 48-million-member party might be somewhat smaller, all our party members will be communists in reality as well as in name. They'll be people who really want to struggle for communism to the end. The party's fighting ability will be enormously enhanced."[36]

But the purge served only to prove how deeply divided the party was over Tiananmen. The campaign lasted for one and a half years, during which time internal documents hinted at significant resistance among party members. "Some comrades are resentful, and some are just going through the motions. When they organize [the re-registration of party members], some even lay down the line, saying that in our unit all party members can get their [new] registration," a party circular said in April 1990.[37]

A friend of mine who is a low-ranking party official in a Beijing-based news organization reacted to the campaign with the kind of disdain that was widespread among party members at that time. Although he had joined the demonstrations and strongly opposed the military action, he, like most other Chinese, dutifully wrote in a 10,000-word report what his superiors wanted to hear. His unit happened to have photographs of him taking part in the protests, so he had to come clean. He said in his statement that he took part in the demonstrations only because he supported the students' demands for an end to corruption and an increase in the education budget—demands that the government itself had agreed should be met. My friend said his account was carefully worded so that if the party ever changed its mind about Tiananmen it could be interpreted as a statement of opposition to the party's suppression of the unrest. But it also contained a sufficient hint of contrition to satisfy his investigators at the time.

Schooled in the art of lying through decades of political movements, most Chinese feel no shame in keeping their heads down when necessary. My friend's testimony impressed his inquisitors so much that he was allowed to stay on in the party. In reality he had no faith whatsoever in the party or communism, but he knew that to be kicked out would damage his career by giving him a black mark and depriving him of good contacts and inside knowledge. It would also increase the risk that he might be arrested.

The re-registration campaign at the Ministry of Communications ran into particular difficulties. The ministry overlooks Fuxing Road, the western extension of Changan Boulevard, the main route of the army's advance into Tiananmen Square. Staff were on duty throughout the military action, so many of them witnessed the random violence. On June 5th, a bullet even pierced the window of a senior official at the ministry, narrowly missing him. A Chinese source told me that staff at the ministry were highly reluctant to write statements endorsing the government line.

A confidential memorandum, circulated among party officials in August 1990, complained that in some work units, party members who had confessed that they had taken part in illegal demonstrations were being assessed as "having a clear-cut stand—capable of keeping line with the party center politically, ideologically, and in action."[38] The memorandum noted that "this is clearly wrong." The number of members expelled as a result of the drive was never publicly revealed, but it certainly was not as many as the leadership had hoped. The party remained nearly as full of dissenters as it had been before the purge began.

The ferreting-out campaign was only one part of the leadership's ham-fisted efforts to settle scores after Tiananmen. At the same time, it launched an investigation of officials from the rank of county chief upward to assess their political reliability. More than 30,000 officials were deployed to carry out the task. Their targets were more than 1 million party and government cadres across the country. As the head of the party's Organization Department Lu Feng said in a confidential speech circulated among party members, "In terms of the gravity, scale, and scope of the task, this [kind of campaign] has rarely been conducted since the founding of the [communist] nation."[39] Investigating teams were ordered to look into not only how officials behaved during the unrest but their political tendencies over the years. Those who disagreed with the government's measures to control the unrest were to be dismissed, and those who supported the military crackdown were to be promoted.

The party had to admit that this campaign also failed to achieve its goals. Lu said in his classified report that in some places it was going well, but in others only half of the officials who should have been targeted actually had been or were being investigated. As with the re-registration campaign many people tried to protect each other from punishment.

In Beijing, the witch-hunts extended well beyond party members and officials. Everyone working for a state-run enterprise or institution had to write an account of what they did and thought during the "turmoil and counterrevolutionary rebellion" between April 15th and June 4th. Chinese sources told me, however, that only about 50,000 workers in state-run enterprises in Beijing confessed to having taken part in demonstrations, whereas the actual number involved was obviously many times that figure.

For days after the army moved into Tiananmen, Chinese television news carried endless reports of "rioters" being rounded up, showing them surrounded by armed and helmeted police or soldiers, sometimes with their heads forced down or with their faces obviously scarred and bruised by beatings. Rumors abounded of citizens wreaking revenge by taking potshots at the martial law troops who manned checkpoints around the city. There were unconfirmed reports of the bodies of soldiers being found floating in canals. A tank driver who had taken part in the crackdown told me five years later that there were rumors in the army that a soldier wearing an official watch commemorating the clearing of Tiananmen had had his hand severed by an angry citizen. Beijing residents eagerly swapped such tales. A Chinese academic told me that mothers sometimes warned their children to behave "otherwise I'll send you to martial law headquarters."

It is difficult to overestimate the contempt for the government engendered among officials, ordinary party members, and the general public alike as result of these arrests and purges. In private, some party members expressed nearly as much anger about the re-registration campaign as they did about the bloodshed itself. They complained that support for the Tiananmen crackdown had become the official benchmark of loyalty to the party—not adherence to any lofty Marxist or Maoist beliefs. By the mid-1990s tempers may have outwardly cooled, but there were undoubtedly still large numbers of party members who continued to feel they had been badly wronged and that the party had betrayed its principles.

Those who accuse the Western media of dwelling too much on Tiananmen underestimate the scale of the suffering involved, not just on the night of the bloodshed but in the weeks and months that followed. Millions of people who had joined the protests, not to mention those who had played a leading role, lived in terror. The authorities arrested tens if not hundreds of thousands of people across the country. Many were jailed or sent to labor camps without being tried and often denied any access to their families. Some were seized in broad daylight as they walked along the streets. Others were taken from their homes at night. The vast majority of detained workers, students, and intellectuals were treated as common criminals. Several described to me how they were thrown into cells so crowded that there was not enough space for everyone to sleep lying down at the same time. Dissidents were kept in the same cells as rapists and murderers. They were tortured by jailers and cellmates alike. The names of most of them are unknown to the Western media, so their individual sufferings received little attention outside China. Even in the mid-1990s, cases of people imprisoned in connection with Tiananmen were still frequently coming to light for the first time.

There was no consistent logic to the way the government handled its huge new population of political prisoners. Some dissidents, usually the better-known ones, were treated relatively well by the brutal standards of China's prison system. But some equally well known ones were subjected to abominable suffering. The newspaper editor Wang Juntao, who was sentenced to 13 years in prison for his role in the Tiananmen Square protests, was kept in solitary confinement in a tiny, dimly lit, poorly ventilated, and foul-smelling cell in Beijing's Number 2 Prison. Although Wang was suffering from hepatitis B, a serious liver condition, the authorities refused to give him proper treatment until he was eventually moved to a civilian hospital in March 1993. Wang went on hunger strike 21 times to demand better care. Prison officers responded by force-feeding him through tubes inserted into his nose. Wang's associate, Chen Ziming, who was also sentenced to 13 years in prison, was similarly denied treatment for a serious skin ailment, heart trouble, and high blood pressure. Fortunately for both Wang and Chen, American pressure secured their early release in 1994. Wang was sent abroad, but Chen, still suffering from heart disease and hepatitis B, was reimprisoned in June 1995. One of their colleagues, Liu Gang, was released that month after serving a six-year sentence for his role in the 1989 unrest. He described his jail conditions as "worse than a concentration camp," with guards frequently subjecting him to powerful electric shocks and the "tiger bench" torture, which involved sitting on a plank for many hours on end until his legs swelled up in excruciating pain.[40]

Even Bao Tong, a former top adviser to Zhao Ziyang and the most senior official detained in connection with Tiananmen, has hardly been given VIP treatment. His relatives complain that he too has been given inadequate medical care for a variety of ailments. Ironically, Bao is being held in Qincheng Prison, the same facility north of Beijing where Mao Zedong's late wife Jiang Qing, undoubtedly the most widely hated politician of Chinese communist rule, was imprisoned for her role in the Cultural Revolution. Jiang, however, was freed on medical parole a mere three years after she was given a suspended death sentence for allegedly causing the deaths of hundreds of thousands of people.[41] Bao, who is serving only a seven-year prison term for the "crime" of telling the demonstrators in Tiananmen that martial law was about to be imposed, has been denied medical parole.[42]

A few of the students and intellectuals who were jailed, however, told reporters after their release that some of their guards showed signs of sympathy, apparently out of fear that they might be held responsible for any excesses should there be any sudden change in the political mood. Many Chinese are mindful of how quickly the government changed its stance on the Tiananmen Square protests of April 1976, which erupted when the authorities cleared away thousands of wreaths laid by residents at the Monument to the People's Heroes in honor of the late Zhou Enlai. Thousands of police and militia members armed with clubs and leather belts cleared the square after a day of rioting by angry crowds, injuring dozens of people in the process.[43] Two days later, the leadership announced the dismissal of the deputy prime minister Deng Xiaoping from all his posts, a move echoed in 1989 by the dismissal of Zhao Ziyang. But the sands of Chinese politics shifted quickly. In September 1976 Mao died, and within a year Deng was rehabilitated. In November 1978, the party announced a reversal of its verdict on the Tiananmen protests, praising them as "a wholly revolutionary action." Many Beijing residents believe that history will repeat itself after Deng's death, and that the party will eventually adopt a very different view of the 1989 demonstrations.

In spite of the purges and persecutions that began in June 1989, the party has managed to maintain a semblance of unity since Tiananmen. Just two weeks after Deng's June 9th meeting with the martial law troops—the first signal to the nation after Tiananmen that he was still in charge—the party's Central Committee held a plenary session in Beijing. All but 5 of the body's 175 full members turned up—an achievement in itself given that many of them must have sympathized with the demonstrators. Not a word of the deliberations was leaked to the outside world until the publication of a communiqué several hours after the two-day meeting was over. The document announced Zhao's dismissal, giving no hint of any opposition to the decision, even though the Central Committee had been appointed in 1987 when Zhao's political fortune was at its zenith. Not a single one of the 276 full and alternate members who attended the gathering has ever openly challenged the verdict that Zhao made "serious mistakes," including those of "splitting the party" and "supporting the turmoil." What has held the party together is the brute force displayed during Tiananmen, fear of chaotic collapse, and loyalty to Deng.

Beneath the surface, however, divisions within the party over ideology, personality, and policy were far more serious than the Central Committee's bland communiqué suggested. Far from reuniting the party after weeks of upheaval, the meeting merely provided a smoke screen for an escalating struggle between rival factions.

Years of pent-up animosity between different personalities in the leadership began in the subsequent months to emerge in the open. The chaos on the streets may have ended, but the party itself was in turmoil. The main conflict was not between radical pro-reform supporters of Zhao Ziyang and the party's mainstream led by Deng. Zhao's supporters—senior officials who had once advised him on economic and political reforms, provincial officials who had profited from his advocacy of decentralization, and liberal intellectuals—had been largely silenced by the vehemence of the crackdown. The more serious rift was between

Deng's camp and ultrahard-liners who believed the entire reform process was to blame for what had happened.

Tension between these two groups had been one of the main themes of Chinese politics throughout the 1980s. Since the party's 13th Congress in 1987, however, many foreign observers had tended to understate the power of the extreme hard-liners. At the congress, Zhao outlined a new vision of economic and cautious political reform, many veteran leaders were retired to make way for younger ones, and, in an unprecedented display of inner-party democracy, delegates voted to exclude the prominent hard-liner Deng Liqun from the Central Committee. The post-Tiananmen power struggle showed, however, that while the 13th party congress may have marked a victory for Deng Xiaoping and his supporters, it was by no means a final one.

After Tiananmen, the extreme hard-liners used the dismissal of Zhao Ziyang as a way to get their own back. Deng himself accused Zhao publicly of being too soft on "bourgeois liberalization." But Deng clearly wanted to avoid dwelling on this subject because Zhao after all had been put in place by him and had carried out Deng's own policies. Deng had made it clear in his speech on June 9th that he intended the economic reforms he launched in 1978 to continue. "If anything can be said to be insufficient," said Deng, "it is that we have not yet done enough reform and opening." Although Deng was generally acclaimed in China as the "chief architect" of those reforms, Zhao had always been thought of, both inside the party and among the public, as the chief administrator of the reform process. The Central Committee therefore refrained from openly attacking the way Zhao had handled the economy as prime minister and later as general secretary.

But the extreme hard-liners saw things differently. In their view, Zhao had committed mistakes not just in ideology but in almost every sphere of decision making. The turmoil of April to June was not just a result of Zhao's failure to take a tough stand on "bourgeois liberalization." It was, in their view, the product of economic mismanagement, the blind worship of things foreign, and the decay of party discipline. Through the pages of the official media, including the Communist Party's own mouthpiece the *People's Daily,* the extreme hard-liners fulminated.

In a classified speech circulated among party members at the end of 1990, a provincial Communist Party leader commented, "Do we continue with reform and opening to the outside world, or do we seal ourselves off and stick to the old ways? . . . On this question, there is far from being a consensus."[44]

Rarely in the Deng era had the country witnessed such obvious differences over policy and ideology. It was a sign that although still in overall command, Deng was losing his grip. His declining health probably had a lot to do with it. The damage he had suffered to his prestige both inside and outside the party during the Tiananmen Square protests was also a major factor. His enemies saw a chance to strike, and they did so with a vengeance, quickly establishing almost complete control over the official media.

There were a few isolated exceptions. The *Beijing Youth News,* a newspaper known for its relatively liberal tone, carried an unusual article on June 27th, 1989, about the problem of phone tapping—not an issue the authorities usually like to discuss. The article, of course, faithfully reported the government line that no such eavesdropping occurs in China. But it revealed in the course of saying so that many people in Beijing had recently become rather worried about the possibility that their phones might be tapped. In other words, it implied, a lot of telephone owners in Beijing did not support the military crackdown, otherwise why would they have cause to worry?

"In recent days, people in Beijing who love to make phone calls have suddenly become cautious. Many of them now say on the phone, 'Let's write or talk about this next time we meet to avoid trouble,'" the newspaper said. "People feel like this because of rumors that every telephone has been installed with a tapping device. . . . There are also astonishing rumors that advanced scanning equipment is being used . . . so that if when you make a call you say something inappropriate, you'll get in trouble. If indeed such were the case, how could the people of Beijing not be thrown into panic?" This rather bold admission of the concerns of Beijing residents was followed by a lame response by a Beijing telephone official, who told the *Beijing Youth News* correspondent that "tapping, like opening others' letters, is illegal, because freedom of communication is a right granted by the constitution."

The journalist concluded the article with a clearly ironic comment that the Beijing Telephone Bureau's spokesperson "looked like a very kind person, and his words should therefore be reliable." In other words, the newspaper implied, being an official spokesperson did not in itself bestow credibility.

But such articles were rare indeed. As communist governments began to collapse in Eastern Europe, critics of Deng's reforms further tightened their control over the press. Although they still dared not attack Deng openly, they used what was happening in the Soviet bloc to illustrate their concerns about the effects of Deng's policies. In their view, Gorbachev's reforms and ideological infiltration by the West were the main causes of the collapse of these governments. Deng's view was quite different, namely, that it was Moscow's failure to carry out effective economic reform that caused communism's collapse. This argument clearly did not hold up when applied to some other communist countries that had indeed been implementing Chinese-style economic reform programs. In these cases, however, the pro-Deng camp argued that communism crumbled because of nationalistic resentment of Soviet domination.

The struggle between Deng and his extreme hard-line critics reached a crescendo in early 1992, when Deng emerged from retirement to make a dramatic plea for faster and bolder reforms. Deng's appeal, made during a trip to southern China, proved to be a turning point in China's development after Tiananmen.[45] His words triggered a tremendous upsurge in economic activity and almost completely banished the views of his critics from the pages of the mainstream press. The economic boom astonished the world, convincing many foreign observers that the Chinese communist party had indeed found a formula for survival that had eluded its counterparts in Eastern Europe and the former Soviet Union.

In reality, however, the surge of economic energy unleashed by Deng wrenched further at the fraying fabric of Chinese society. The rapidly widening gap between rich and poor and between town and countryside; the spread of corruption, inflation, unemployment, and crime; the breakdown of the health service and education system—all were becoming increasingly explosive issues by the mid-1990s. Reports of protests in the countryside and industrial action in the cities were becoming more frequent.

Popular discontent would almost certainly have triggered larger-scale disorder had not the government emphasized the crucial importance of nipping any unrest in the bud.[46] *Wending yadao yiqie*—"stability is the overriding priority"—became one of the leadership's favorite slogans after Tiananmen and remained in common use in the mid-1990s.

Deng's trip to southern China undoubtedly helped him to regain some of the popularity he lost because of Tiananmen. But the standing he enjoyed in the late 1970s and early 1980s was lost forever. Indeed, it would have taken a miracle to regain it, given that even before the army moved in to crush the demonstrations Deng was vilified by the protesters to a degree that few other Chinese leaders have ever been before while still in office. Chairman Mao, though responsible for some of the most brutal policies ever masterminded by a national leader in this century, was never publicly attacked to the same extent. Ironically, some demonstrators in 1989 carried huge portraits of Chairman Mao and the late prime minister Zhou Enlai as a way of showing their contempt for Deng and his colleagues.

If Deng was unpopular before the bloodshed, he was considerably more so after it. In the minds of many ordinary Chinese, particularly in the cities, Deng was inextricably linked with Tiananmen despite his low profile during most of the unrest. A university professor who happened to be hospitalized when the army moved in said he saw a man cycling out of the hospital compound whose close relative had been killed by the troops. As he went along, the man cursed "Deng Xiaoping should be cut into a thousand pieces." Everyone knew that it must have been Deng, the head of the armed forces, who gave the order to open fire, even though Chinese leaders have never said in public who was responsible.

Deng's economic reform campaign of 1992 was a godsend to many Chinese, to whom it gave unprecedented opportunities to get rich. The main point of Deng's rallying speeches early that year was that almost any kind of moneymaking venture was acceptable as long as it helped to make the country prosper. Whether it was socialism or capitalism was irrelevant. Undoubtedly a large number of city dwellers began to change their views of Deng as a result of his words, grateful that he had smashed the remaining shackles of the old centrally planned economic system. But not everyone had the wherewithal to benefit from the changes. Many workers, used to the old system of guaranteed jobs for life, found themselves threatened with unemployment and unable to afford simple health care and education for their children. Retired old people found their meager pensions being eaten away by inflation. To these people, Deng was more than ever a villain. Many privately cursed him.

As Western memories of Tiananmen receded, politicians in the West began to argue that it was both hypocritical and meaningless to focus on Tiananmen when dealing with China. Their arguments made a lot of sense. The West had been maintaining close ties with many other governments whose human rights records were little, if at all, better than China's. Besides, the West badly needed China's cooperation in resolving numerous international problems, from weapons proliferation to the Gulf War. Many ordinary Chinese were indifferent at best to the idea of punishing the Chinese leadership with sanctions. They wanted more opportunities to make money, and the West was a vital source of funds.

But public support for an end to sanctions and a resumption of normal ties with the West certainly did not mean that in domestic political and psychological terms Tiananmen was losing its relevance.

Behind the high red walls of Zhongnanhai, the Communist Party's headquarters in a former imperial palace a few hundred yards down the road from Tiananmen Square, the bloodshed continues to haunt the leadership. The official media may have been long since ordered not to mention the subject, but even in the mid-1990s a handful of journals still controlled by extreme hard-liners were ignoring the directive and raising it in almost every issue.

Deng's death is likely to lift the lid from this cauldron of discontent, slowly perhaps at first, but sooner or later everything will pour out—Tiananmen, worries about reform and its side effects, and decades of resentment against the party's heavy-handed rule. Every official knows that the history of almost every mass political movement since the communists came to power has been rewritten to suit changes in the political mood. The Cultural Revolution, which at one time Chinese propaganda used to declare would last forever, is now officially regarded as a "great disaster." The official verdict on the Tiananmen Square protests of 1976 did an equally dramatic somersault. Deng ordered the reassessment of the 1976 protests when he took over power two years after the event, knowing that doing so would considerably strengthen public support for his leadership. Similarly, any future leader might feel the desire to win over the masses by giving the 1989 "counterrevolutionary rebellion" a new, more positive label.

Labels, in Chinese, are all-important. To the outsider, the phrase "counterrevolutionary rebellion" might not seem that offensive. After all, what happened between April and June 1989 was in essence a rebellion against communist rule. But "counterrevolutionary" is not necessarily a badge worn with pride by Chinese dissidents. Paradoxically, there is a strong desire for acceptance even by the government they hate.

Hou Xiaotian, the wife of Wang Juntao, one of the key dissidents involved in the Tiananmen Square protests, recalled her anger when the word "counterrevolutionary" was used by the judge to describe her husband's behavior both during Tiananmen and in the years beforehand. "I really wanted to stand up and ask him [the judge], how much do you understand of Wang Juntao's history?" Hou wrote.[47] She described how Wang had been imprisoned in the 1970s for his role in the April 5th demonstrations of 1976 but had later been hailed by the authorities as a hero and had risen to a prominent position in the Communist Youth

League. She argued that Wang Juntao's career showed simply that his thinking was ahead of his time.

The pressures for change after Deng's death will be enormous. They will not necessarily be constructive. Some will want greater democracy; others will want a new dictatorship. Some will want more capitalism, others more socialism. Most, however, will want an official reevaluation of Tiananmen. Victims will want their names cleared, dissidents will want to be declared heroes, and extreme hard-liners will want Deng discredited. What is more in doubt is whether any Chinese leader after Deng will have the ability to juggle these demands and preserve China's political coherence.

2

The Smokeless War

The West really wants unrest in China. It wants turmoil not only in China but also in the Soviet Union and Eastern Europe. The United States and some other Western countries are trying to bring about a peaceful evolution toward capitalism in socialist countries. The United States has coined an expression: waging a world war without gunsmoke. We should be on our guard against this.
— Deng Xiaoping, September 1989

On the same day that Chinese troops were shooting demonstrators in Beijing, history was also being made on the other side of the communist world. Chinese leaders may have been too preoccupied with events in their own capital to worry that day about the fate of fellow communists in Poland, but their alarm at the victory of Solidarity in the elections of June 4, 1989, became apparent soon enough. The Polish elections were only partly free. The ruling communist party reserved a majority of seats for its supporters in the main house of parliament. But competition for seats in the less powerful senate was completely open. Even as residents of Beijing were reaching the conclusion that fighting the party was futile, Polish voters were returning the first democratically elected parliamentary institution in Communist-ruled Eastern Europe since the end of the Second World War.

If Tiananmen was a body blow to the Chinese communist structure, the elections in Poland and the rapid collapse of communism across the European continent in the months that followed were a series of debilitating follow-up punches. The Chinese party continued to function but with its morale severely sapped and with many members deeply uncertain about how long the organization would survive. Many adult Chinese know the phrase "the Soviet Union's today is our tomorrow." This was an official party slogan in the 1950s when Beijing's relations with Moscow were at their most intimate. By the end of 1991, the same slogan had become a favorite joke among Beijing intellectuals, who saw events across the border as a precursor of similar collapse in China itself. Within the leadership, the demise of communism elsewhere exacerbated divisions. Among the party rank and file it created a profound crisis of faith and thoroughgoing cynicism. As ideological blows began to rain down on China thick and fast from June 1989 onward, the leadership responded with what I would describe as barely controlled terror.

Poland had long been a worry to China. The emergence of the independent trade union Solidarity in 1980—the first of its kind in the communist world—horrified the Chinese leadership just as did the Hungarian uprising of 1956 or the Prague Spring of 1968. At the time of Solidarity's formation Deng Xiaoping was trying to suppress the Democracy Wall movement and curb growing prodemocracy activities on campuses. Events in Poland convinced him all the more that dissent had to be firmly suppressed. Although China at the time was still at ideological war with the Soviet Union, and by extension with Poland, it was quietly pleased when the Polish leader General Wojciech Jaruzelski imposed martial law the following year. As relations with Poland improved in the mid-1980s, China began to express public approval of Jaruzelski's measures, even though the Polish leader was being roundly condemned in the West. On May 20th, 1989, China used Jaruzelski's own tactic—the imposition of martial law—to suppress the Tiananmen Square protests. It was the second time it had done so in less than three months. In early March, martial law had been declared in the Tibetan capital Lhasa following one of the most serious outbreaks of nationalist unrest there in 30 years.

The Chinese leadership was, of course, unwilling to make any public comparisons between events in China and Poland. But the similarities were not lost on the Chinese public. The *Ta Kung Pao,* a Hong Kong newspaper that is normally under Beijing's control but which sided with the students during Tiananmen, reminded the Chinese leadership of the Polish example in a blistering commentary published on the day of the June 4th bloodshed. "Blind faith in force and the barrels of guns are no longer suitable to today's conditions," the newspaper said.[1] "The strong current of the world today as well as the current of reform in East European socialist countries have all demonstrated that only by following the popular will to conduct democratic political structural reform will there be a way out, while the order to impose martial law, witch-hunts, and massacres can only rouse more people to oppose the powers that be. The example of Poland has illustrated that point. The suppression of students, workers, and citizens and the arbitrary apprehension of political offenders under martial law would only end in acknowledging the people's strengths and conducting dialogues with the people."

As the threat of mass unrest in China subsided the leadership became increasingly preoccupied with the quickening pace of events in Eastern Europe. So too did ordinary Chinese, many of whom privately gloated as one communist government after another caved in to popular demands for democracy.

First it was Poland, then came the mass exodus from Germany. At the end of September and early October, tens of thousands of East Germans sought political asylum in Western embassies or traveled illegally to West Germany through third countries. Anticommunist demonstrations swept the country, leading to the tearing down of the Berlin Wall on November 11th, 1989.

During those tumultuous autumn and winter months, Hungary too announced it would hold multiparty elections the following year. The security forces in Czechoslovakia tried to suppress student demonstrations but succeeded only in fueling widespread protests that forced the government in November to revoke the Communist Party's monopoly of political power. In December Bulgaria, once among the most orthodox of communist states in Eastern Europe, said it too would establish a multiparty democracy. The Soviet newspaper *Pravda* published a front-page article suggesting the Soviet Communist Party might even follow suit.

The official Chinese media kept as quiet as they could about these dramatic events. Although Chinese leaders kept saying that China was now stable after the upheaval earlier in the year, they were clearly in a jittery mood. The last thing they wanted was to encourage domestic dissent by publicizing the collapse of communist governments elsewhere. Rarely in the era of Deng Xiaoping had international news carried by the official media been so persistently at variance with reality.

It was not until June 10th, six days after Poland's historic election, that the Chinese Communist Party's official mouthpiece, the *People's Daily*, reported that it had even happened. The newspaper glossed over the humiliation of the ruling communist party and the overwhelming show of support for an opposition party that until a few months earlier had been outlawed. But it did name some of the government-sponsored candidates who had failed to get elected. Among them was the interior minister, General Czeslaw Kiszczak, the same man who had ordered the internment of Lech Walesa and many other Solidarity activists during martial law in Poland. It must have been unsettling to Chinese leaders, then engaged in a massive roundup of dissidents under martial law in Beijing, to consider what the Polish example might portend for their own country.

By the time Hungary's ruling party decided on October 7th to introduce a multiparty system, the *People's Daily* was marginally less hesitant. This time it waited only three days before telling its readers the news. The bald eight-paragraph item on page 3 was followed by one of similar length quoting exclusively the views of Hungarian communist hard-liners who were opposed to the ruling party's decision to vote itself out of existence.

In the intervening days between this historic development in Hungary and the *People's Daily*'s terse account, the official Chinese media had kept up a barrage of propaganda aimed at convincing a skeptical public that communism was doing all right. The *Beijing Daily*, a newspaper particularly noted for the virulence of its views on capitalism, argued one day after the demise of communism in Hungary that the ideology had enabled the Soviet Union to rank second only to the United States in gross national product (GNP) and had helped China surpass many Western countries in output of coal, steel, and oil. "Communism will gain certain victory," the newspaper said.[2]

One of the biggest shocks to the Chinese leadership in 1989 must have been the realization that communism was not so resilient after all. But it appeared to take a long time for this message to sink in. In October and November 1989, as anticommunist uprisings swept Eastern Europe, China tried hard to boost its ties with those states it believed would resist the tide—East Germany, Romania, and Bulgaria. Had they seen the writing on the wall, the Chinese might not have been as ready as they were to send their top leaders to those countries to express solidarity. Later, the Chinese leadership was to pin the blame on the information provided by Chinese embassies in Eastern Europe. Western diplomats said they believed this information was usually slanted in favor of the ruling communist parties—not surprising, perhaps, given that after Tiananmen Chinese diplomats would have been terrified of being accused of supporting opponents of communism.

The Chinese leadership was also blinded by its desperation to make friends abroad after Tiananmen. Chinese officials had become pariahs in the West. But rebuttals of Western criticisms of Tiananmen were not enough to fill the pages of the official press. The leadership wanted to show the Chinese public that it had supporters—even if those supporters were themselves international pariahs.

Such was the case with East Germany. During August and September, the exodus of thousands of refugees became an enormous embarrassment to the East German leadership. But China was clearly impressed by East Germany's uncompromising stance in the face of popular dissatisfaction. Unlike the Polish leadership, which had given in step by step to pressure from Solidarity, East Germany's Erich Honecker, then 77 years old, was a man more in the mold of China's gerontocracy.

Sensing trouble in East Germany, China could have ordered its media to say as little as possible about the country, either good or bad, until the situation became clearer. Instead, it instructed that while there should be minimal coverage of the refugees, praise should be heaped on the leadership. October 7th, 1989, marked the 40th anniversary of East German communism, and China—which until Honecker's groundbreaking trip to Beijing in 1986 had been at ideological war with East Germany for three decades—did not want to let such an event pass unremarked. After all, China too was celebrating 40 years of communist rule on October 1st, and the East Germans were giving Beijing face by sending their senior Politburo member Egon Krenz to take part. Krenz, who took over from the ailing Honecker less than three weeks after the Chinese festivities, was the most senior East European leader to visit Beijing for the anniversary. Western diplomats boycotted the occasion in protest at the bloodshed in Beijing earlier that year. China was in East Berlin's debt.

Chinese leaders must have thought that East Germany could weather the storm. They decided to send the deputy prime minister and Politburo member Yao Yilin—an influential hard-liner who died in December 1994—to East Berlin to take part in the anniversary celebrations. But if it was not clear to Yao before what was going on it must have become clear enough after his arrival. On the anniversary—the same day that Hungary renounced communism—the East German authorities deployed troops in East Berlin after thousands of people chanting "Gorby" and "Freedom" marched to the Palace of the Republic hoping to see the Soviet leader Mikhail Gorbachev, who was attending an anniversary reception inside. It is not known whether Yao was among the several guests who were seen peering out of the windows of the congress hall at the crowd.

East Germany had been convulsed by antigovernment demonstrations for several days by the time the celebrations were held. But on the day of the anniversary, the *People's Daily* in Beijing said not a word about this. Instead, it published a lengthy review of the "glorious 40 years" of communist rule in East Germany, concluding that "the East German people are now strengthening their unity under the leadership of the party and are struggling for the further promotion of economic and cultural construction, the consolidation and expansion of the achieve-ments of socialism, and the preservation of world peace." The following day, the *People's Daily* said Yao had watched a military parade in East Berlin and had listened to a speech by Honecker in which the East Ger-man leader described the abandonment of socialism as "a rotten idea." But the newspaper kept quiet about the unrest.

During talks with his Chinese guest, Honecker said there was "a fun-damental lesson to be learned from the counterrevolutionary revolt in Beijing and the present defamation campaign against [East Germany] and other socialist states." In Yao's view, and probably in Honecker's as well, that lesson was that ruthlessness was the only way to solve the problem. But in the end East Germany shrank from going as far as China had, and less than two months later the authorities placed Honecker under house arrest.

When the Berlin Wall was breached the following month, China must have realized that its decision to promote East Germany as the model of East European communism had been a big mistake. But the leadership still remained determined to show solidarity with Eastern Europe's remaining communist leaders. During a visit to Pakistan in mid-November, Prime Minister Li Peng expressed concern about develop-ments in Eastern Europe, but he said it was still necessary to wait and see whether the changes were positive or negative. Later during his South Asia tour, Li told reporters the world "should not rejoice too soon" over the situation in Eastern Europe. His meaning was clearly that commu-nism might yet revive.

The Romanian leader Nicolae Ceauşescu was a particularly good friend of China's. When Moscow and Beijing began quarreling openly in the 1960s, Romania—led by Ceauşescu after 1965—refused to side with the Soviets. During a visit to Beijing in 1985, Ceauşescu draped a red sash and pinned the golden star of the Socialist Republic of Romania (First Class), the country's highest honor, on Deng Xiaoping. A photograph of a smiling Deng shaking Ceauşescu's hand after receiving the award takes up a full page in an official picture album of Deng's career published three years later.[3] Ceauşescu was, in the words of Chinese officials, "an esteemed old friend of the Chinese people."[4] In a highly unusual mark of respect for a foreign leader, the Chinese arranged for Ceauşescu to address mass rallies during his trips to China in 1982 and 1985.

Three months after the crushing of the Tiananmen Square protests, China sent one of its top government officials, the state councillor Zou Jiahua, on an official visit to Romania. There Ceauşescu told him that "the party and government of a socialist country must take measures to suppress counterrevolutionary rebellion in order to allow the country to continue progressing. . . . Romania in the past and still now believes that the Chinese party and government should adopt any kind of measure to protect socialism, the country's independence, and the welfare of the people."[5] The *People's Daily* said that in response Zou thanked Ceauşescu for "the support he had given" to China's crackdown.

By November, Ceauşescu's support was becoming increasingly precious to China as other East European countries conspicuously excluded violence as a possible measure for coping with their rebellions. The Romanian Communist Party was to hold its 14th Congress in Bucharest at the end of November, and China decided to send no less a figure than Qiao Shi, a member of the Politburo's Standing Committee, to attend. A few days before Qiao's departure, the *People's Daily* published a lengthy interview with Ceauşescu in which the Romanian leader appealed for socialist solidarity in the face of the anticommunist tide. It was a sign of China's growing confusion and desperation that this part of the interview was published at all. Chinese newspapers are normally careful to omit any remarks that deviate from official Chinese policy or to add a note of criticism if they must be included. In this case, China's policy had always been to resist becoming part of an international socialist alliance. Ceauşescu, however, appeared to suggest in the interview that the remaining orthodox communist states form just such an alliance in order to resist political change.

"There are many problems in the world today and the international situation is very complicated," said Ceauşescu, using the veiled language often adopted by Chinese officials as well when referring to the recent collapse of communist governments. "This means cooperation between communist parties and socialist countries should be made stronger than it has ever been before. . . . In the face of the grim international situation, [China and Romania] should take measures to resolve the complex problems of our times, in order to benefit the socialist development of our two countries and of other countries as well."[6]

China never commented in public on Ceauşescu's appeal. But its appearance in the *People's Daily* signaled that at least some officials supported it and therefore that debates were raging behind closed doors over how Beijing should respond to events in Eastern Europe—whether to express solidarity with beleaguered communist governments or keep quiet about what was going on.

Chinese officials, however, were kept fully abreast of how the Western media were reporting events in Eastern Europe. While state-controlled newspapers said virtually nothing about the changes, classified bulletins circulated among officials provided full translations of foreign news agency reports on the situation. Every day, the 96-page bulletin *Reference Materials,* published by Xinhua News Agency, contained special sections on Eastern Europe and the Soviet Union.[7] On November 20th, 1989, the day that Romania's 14th Congress opened in Bucharest, *Reference Materials* published a translation of a Reuters report that described Ceauşescu as ruling Romania with an "iron fist." An Agence France Presse report underneath it said Romanian party dissidents had smuggled a letter out of the country calling on Ceauşescu to step down. Other foreign news agency reports mentioned attacks on Ceauşescu in the Soviet media, the Romanian leader's growing isolation, his abuse of human rights, and his "brutal" methods. A dispatch from Bucharest by Xinhua itself, for *Reference Materials* subscribers only, said Hungary was boycotting the congress for the first time ever, as were several Western communist parties and Western diplomats based in Romania. The bluntness of these reports suggested that at last the Chinese leadership was beginning to suspect that Ceauşescu might not see out the additional five-year term of office he was later to be unanimously elected to by the congress and wanted to prepare officials in China for the eventual political demise of their old friend.

Traveling on to Bulgaria, Qiao Shi found a country in the process of rapid transformation. Just two weeks before his arrival, Bulgaria's 78-year-old Stalinist leader, Todor Zhivkov, who had ruled the country for 35 years, was ousted by members of his own Politburo. He was replaced by a 53-year-old reformist, Petar Mladenov, who proceeded quickly to expel hard-liners from the leadership, grant amnesty to political prisoners, and express support for free elections. Just as alarming for China as the street protests that had toppled communism elsewhere, Bulgaria's metamorphosis had occurred not as a result of any mass uprising. Reformist forces within the party itself had transformed it overnight.

Less than halfway into Qiao Shi's five-day visit to Bulgaria came yet another blow. Czechoslovakia's parliament voted to end the Communist Party's guaranteed monopoly of power. Qiao reminded his Bulgarian hosts that China would do no such thing. "Maintaining socialism under the leadership of the Communist Party is the only way for China to develop," he was quoted by Xinhua as telling a member of the Bulgarian Politburo.[8] But the now reform-minded Bulgarians clearly did not share Qiao's political outlook. At the end of the visit, there was no talk of strengthening communist ties of friendship. Xinhua was only able to note that the two sides agreed "to stress political stability and unity to guarantee the success of reform."[9]

The authorities' efforts to prevent the general public from learning the true story of Eastern Europe proved futile. In Beijing and other cities, many people simply tuned in to the shortwave broadcasts of foreign radio stations. The government had been jamming the Chinese language broadcasts of the BBC and the Voice of America since the imposition of martial law in May, but strangely the jamming did not affect all of the frequencies at the same time. The determined listener could still get Chinese news from both stations by trying several frequencies.[10]

News of Eastern Europe, therefore, proved irrepressible. But while the leadership was obviously confused and fearful of a possible domino effect, and while many city dwellers were clearly excited, there was little visible sign of unrest. Memories of the bloodshed were still strong, and martial law troops were still guarding Tiananmen Square itself as well as key intersections and buildings around Beijing. But in the expectant atmosphere generated by events elsewhere in the communist world, rumors of imminent ferment abounded. As China prepared for its 40th anniversary celebrations on October 1st, many Beijing citizens swapped tales that antigovernment terrorists were preparing to sabotage the festivities. A Foreign Ministry official privately warned me to stay away from public areas on the anniversary for my own safety. Such fears were not without basis. The Public Security Minister, Wang Fang, had said in early September that there had been an increasing number of "reactionary slogans," notices, threatening letters, explosions, and acts of sabotage.[11] Security was visibly tightened in the buildup to the anniversary, particularly at night, with cars and pedestrians being stopped more frequently than usual by soldiers or police to check identity papers. In the end, however, no untoward incident was reported.

In early December, seven students staged the only public act of protest reported in Beijing that year after the suppression of the Tiananmen Square protests. The students gathered in front of the closely guarded Soviet-style building in western Beijing that houses the Ministry of Radio, Film, and Television. A witness, quoted by the *Washington Post,* said the students carried two protest banners, one reading "Why Is China So Poor?"[12] According to this source, one of the demonstrators told a crowd of about 200 nervous onlookers, "There is change going on all over the world, except in China. China is stagnating. We can only become richer through economic and political change."

The students ignored warnings by sympathetic members of the crowd that they should quickly disperse to avoid being arrested. Within half an hour, about two dozen policemen arrived and dragged the students into the ministry compound. The witness said many onlookers wept as they watched the demonstrators being hauled away. No one dared to intervene.

Later that month, events in Romania came closer to disturbing Beijing's uneasy calm than any other upheaval in Eastern Europe in 1989. Of all the anticommunist uprisings, that in Romania most closely mirrored China's own experience. Ceauşescu was the only East European leader to order the security forces to open fire on demonstrators. When dozens of protesters were slaughtered by the Romanian Securitate secret police in the city of Timisoara, the Chinese media maintained an embarrassed silence. It was not until four days later that the *People's Daily* mentioned Romania and then only to say that Ceauşescu was paying a visit to Iran.[13] There was no mention of the bloodshed. Unlike Ceauşescu after Tiananmen, Deng Xiaoping and other Chinese leaders did not express support for Romania's actions. For one thing, it was not their style to comment directly on events in other countries. For another, they were afraid that drawing public attention to Romania would reopen the still festering wounds of Tiananmen.

The failure of the bloodshed in Timişoara to curb the antigovernment protests in Romania was both an encouragement and an embarrassment to ordinary Chinese. To the leadership, it must have been a terrifying reminder that brutal methods do not invariably succeed. Five days after the first killings in Timişoara, the *People's Daily* gave its first hint of what was going on, but it still did not mention the fact that protesters had died. The newspaper simply said that after his return from Iran Ceauşescu had declared a state of emergency in western Romania and called on the country to remain united and protect socialism. It quoted him as describing the demonstrations in Timişoara as "terrorist activities" carried out by "a few gangs of hooligans." The military, he said, had acted with great restraint and had carried out its duty to protect the people and the achievements of socialism.[14] His description was uncannily reminiscent of the language used by Chinese leaders after Tiananmen. What the newspaper failed to say was that Ceauşescu's tactics were not working. The extraordinary act of defiance by the crowd in Bucharest who shouted Ceauşescu down while he was making a public speech was never mentioned.

Not until December 24th, two days after the outbreak of widespread violence in Bucharest, did the Chinese authorities allow the media to begin suggesting the scale of events in Romania. The press admitted for the first time that fierce gun battles were raging in Bucharest between the pro-Ceauşescu Securitate and rebel army troops. Xinhua News Agency even introduced a rare snippet of originality into its reporting instead of slavishly adhering to Ceauşescu's line. Given that the Ceauşescu government had effectively ceased functioning and Romania was in anarchy, it had little choice. "[The shooting] rattled the windows of the Chinese embassy and the Xinhua office, which are about six kilometers from the city center," the news agency said. "Some of the windows were shattered by bullets."[15]

On December 27th, a day late, the *People's Daily* printed what to the Chinese leadership must have been the most horrific news of the year. The dispatch took up no more than four lines three-quarters of the way down page 4 of the newspaper. It consisted of just one sentence: "Romanian television announced on December 25th at 8:30 P.M. (2:30 A.M. Beijing time) that the Romanian Special Military Court had condemned N. Ceauşescu and Elena Ceauşescu to death and had carried out the sentence."[16]

Western governments may have reacted with some distaste to the hasty execution of the Ceauşescus, but for many ordinary Chinese in Beijing this was precisely the outcome they had dreamed of, not only for Romania's revolution, but for their own. In Romania, the debt of blood had been repaid with blood. They wished it could have been the same in China. The atmosphere on university campuses turned electric. Several posters were furtively put up by students hailing the downfall of the Ceauşescus. The Romanian Embassy in Beijing was flooded with telephone calls from Chinese asking about events in Romania.[17] One resident told me he had seen a person let off fireworks to celebrate Ceauşescu's arrest. After rumors had circulated a few days earlier that Ceauşescu was fleeing to China, a handwritten poster was seen at Beijing University describing the Romanian leader as a dog trying to join fellow dogs in China, a reference to the Chinese leadership. Many Beijing residents spoke with sadness, pointing out that had it not been for the Chinese army's support for the leadership China's own democracy movement might have produced similar results.

Chinese sources told me that the authorities responded by sending extra plainclothes police to patrol campuses and by posting additional uniformed guards at key installations. Workplaces were secretly ordered to look out for potential troublemakers. The Communist Party hurriedly circulated a classified analysis of the East European situation among senior and middle-ranking officials. Chinese sources said the document was aimed at dampening speculation that China might be the next domino to fall. In an obvious warning to dissidents who might be tempted to take to the streets again, the prime minister, Li Peng, said events at home and abroad showed that the Chinese leadership had been "completely correct" in its decision to use "resolute methods" to suppress the "counterrevolutionary rebellion" in Beijing in June. The crackdown, he said, had been in defense of the party's supremacy, the socialist system, and the country itself.[18]

Foreign journalists attempted in vain, however, to get government officials to comment directly on what was going on in Eastern Europe. At the Foreign Ministry's regular weekly briefing for correspondents on December 28th, 1989, the spokesperson Jin Guihua would say only that "both external and internal forces" had undermined European communism. "In history, there has never been a single social system that has not had twists and turns," Jin said. "We have full confidence in socialism."

As if to prove that China was not afraid, the authorities announced the lifting of martial law in Beijing on January 10th, 1990. They said martial law was no longer necessary because the situation in Beijing and the rest of the country was stable, and social order had returned to normal. Most martial law troops had been withdrawn from the streets in early November. But security had remained tight, with large numbers of troops remaining on standby in the vicinity of Beijing in case of unrest, and access to Tiananmen Square restricted. It was not until the lifting of martial law that citizens were allowed onto the square for the first time since the bloodshed without special permits. But they still could not approach the Monument to the People's Heroes, the granite obelisk in the center of the square, which was roped off and guarded by armed police.

The lifting of martial law was only a cosmetic measure of minimal risk to the authorities. Huge numbers of plainclothes police deployed around the square ensured that any public display of dissent could be quickly suppressed. On January 11th, the first morning after the lifting of martial law, a student arrived at Tiananmen carrying wall posters, which he told foreign reporters he planned to paste up. The police, however, intervened before he could do so and warned him not to try it. Astonishingly, they did not arrest him—at least not in the presence of reporters. The student went off, saying that persisting would be "like sacrificing myself for nothing."

It was a classic demonstration of what the Chinese call *waisong nei-jin,* which can be translated as "relaxed on the surface but tense inside." Most Chinese leaders wanted desperately to avoid public polemics against the Soviet Union and the noncommunist governments of Eastern Europe, not least because they feared that attacking the internal politics of other countries would justify similar criticism by the outside world of China itself. They also wanted to convince the outside world that calm and stability had been restored after Tiananmen. Hysterical outcries over the collapse of communism in Eastern Europe would not help to project the desired image.

In September 1989, Deng told party leaders how they should respond to the East European crisis. He said China's appropriate reaction could be summarized in three sentences. "First, we should observe the situation coolly. Second, we should hold our ground. Third, we should act calmly. Don't be impatient; it is no good to be impatient. We must be calm, calm, and again calm, and quietly immerse ourselves in practical work to accomplish something, something for China."[19] They sounded like words addressed to a very jittery audience.

Deng knew that events in Eastern Europe and the Soviet Union, not to mention Tiananmen, were raising questions within the party about the wisdom of his reforms, particularly among extreme hard-liners who believed his policies were the root cause of instability in China. One of the main points of Deng's September speech was to emphasize that in spite of what was going on elsewhere in the communist world, the reforms must continue.

"The problem now is not whether the banner of the Soviet Union will fall—there is bound to be unrest there—but whether the banner of China will fall. Therefore, the most important thing is that there should be no unrest in China and that we should continue to carry on genuine reform and to open wider to the outside. Without those policies, China would have no future. How did we achieve what we did over the past 10 years? Through reform and opening to the outside. As long as we pursue those policies, and as long as our socialist banner stands firmly planted, China will have tremendous influence."

Deng also implied that he did not want any public attacks against individual leaders or countries in the crumbling communist world, saying "we should not criticize or condemn other countries without good reason or go to extremes in our words and deeds." He warned that the West would become even more wary of China now that communism was collapsing elsewhere but that China should still try to make friends.

"No one will be able to overwhelm us. As long as China doesn't collapse, one-fifth of the world's population will be upholding socialism," Deng said, adding, in a phrase that became the refrain of Chinese officials, "We are full of confidence that socialism has a bright future."

On the surface at least, Deng's words appeared effective. Chinese leaders refrained in public from attacking the Soviet Union and Gorbachev. But Deng was incapable of stopping the furious debate that raged behind closed doors over who and what was really responsible for the collapse of communism.

A secret party document that was leaked to the Hong Kong press in mid-December 1989 reflected the view of the Deng camp in the debate.[20] It said that the communist parties of Eastern Europe had contributed to their own collapse by resisting reform for several decades. It said the bureaucracies of these countries had become corrupt and had lost touch with the masses. China, it said, was able to suppress the Tiananmen Square protests because people had seen the benefits of reform and still generally sided with the party. In Eastern Europe, however, when reforms were eventually introduced they were carried out too quickly. According to the document this led to a loss of political and economic control. It said another reason for the weakness of East European parties was that they did not seize power as a result of indigenous revolutions, unlike the Chinese communists.

The document's basic message was that Chinese-style reform was the best guarantee for the survival of communism. The flaws in the argument were abundantly obvious, however, not only to the disinterested Western reader but also to Deng's critics. The analysis ignored the public outcry against corruption that was one of the major forces behind the Tiananmen Square protests. It also ignored the fact that Tiananmen occurred in spite of 10 years of reform and rapid economic growth. Why then should continuing reform along the same lines be any guarantee of future stability?

Just as Chinese politics were thrown into turmoil by . Nikita Khrushchev's speech attacking Stalin in 1956 and the Hungarian Uprising of later that year, so too were they roiled by the crises in the Soviet bloc in 1989. When Li Peng admitted in November 1989 that "it would be impossible to say the dramatic changes have had no effect at all on China"[21]—a phrase that Chinese officials often parroted but never explained—he was understating the gravity of the situation. Chairman Mao's fear of a Hungarian-style uprising in China was one of the main reasons why, after critics of the party became increasingly outspoken during the Hundred Flowers Movement, he launched the ruthless Anti-Rightist Campaign of 1957. His fear of posthumous denunciation similar to that of Stalin by Khrushchev was one of the catalysts of the Sino-Soviet split of the early 1960s and of the Cultural Revolution of 1966–76, during which Mao unleashed the Red Guards against any party leader who he feared might become another Khrushchev. Chinese politics had changed a lot by 1989, but the old guard, including Deng, who continued to rule the country from behind the scenes were people long used to comparing their experiences with those of Moscow and its allies and using what they found as ammunition in their battles back home.

Deng had emerged from Tiananmen severely bruised politically. Although he undoubtedly remained the single most powerful man in China, his extreme hard-line opponents had gained considerable ground as a result of the unrest. Many members of the old guard whose support he had enlisted during Tiananmen were in fact among his harshest critics. Although it did not appear that they harbored ambitions to replace Deng as paramount leader, they disapproved of some of his policies and proved themselves capable of disrupting their implementation. Deng normally maintained a balance in top leadership posts between liberals and hard-liners in an effort, it seems, to contain Chinese politics within the middle range of the ideological spectrum. In a crisis he would lean toward the hard-liners because of their unquestioning support of the Communist Party's dictatorship. But after Tiananmen, by allowing such vehement attacks against the party's liberal wing, Deng upset the delicate balance of power that had prevailed for much of the reform era. After several years in the margins, the extreme hard-liners thus found themselves back in the center stage of political life.

Foremost among Deng's critics was the veteran leader Chen Yun who died on April 10th, 1995. Although his name is little known outside China, his influence in Chinese politics during the 1980s and early 1990s was second only to Deng's. Some foreign observers of China tended to disregard Chen (who was only a few months younger than Deng) as a senile political has-been, but in spite of his low public profile during the last few years of his life and his obvious infirmity, I believe he remained a key figure until his death. When Deng rose to power in the late 1970s, Chen—a fellow victim of the Cultural Revolution—was a strong backer of his moves to end Maoist stagnation. But as the reforms got under way Chen and Deng appeared increasingly to differ over their pace, scope, and emphasis. From 1987 until his retirement five years later, Chen was chairman of the Central Advisory Commission, a Communist Party body consisting of retired senior officials. Deng set up the commission in 1982 and made himself its first chairman in order to provide a forum for retired party veterans that would give them a voice but keep them out of day-to-day decision making. But under Chen's chairmanship the commission turned into a bastion of Deng's critics.

Because of his frail health, Chen stayed out of public view. But on May 26th, 1989, six days after the imposition of martial law, he made a dramatic reappearance—only his second since his appointment as chairman of the Central Advisory Commission. The occasion was a meeting of the commission's standing committee. Deng himself had not appeared in public since his meeting with Gorbachev on May 16th. Chen was thus the most senior party veteran to speak out since the declaration of martial law, and he sounded impatient for action. "We are all veteran comrades who have struggled for several decades for the founding and construction of the Republic,"[22] he said, clad in a blue Mao suit. "If the turmoil created by a very, very few people is not resolutely put down, then there will be no peace in the party and the country. Not only is there the danger of losing the achievements of 10 years of reform, but there is also the danger of losing all the fruits of revolution, which were won with blood, and all the achievements of socialist construction," he told his audience of 22 veterans.

"Therefore in such a critical moment," Chen continued, "we the veteran comrades must step forward boldly and, together with comrades of the whole party, resolutely expose the schemes and intrigues of the very, very few people who have created the turmoil and resolutely wage a struggle against them. We must never make concessions. There should be not the slightest amount of vagueness."

Chen was on Deng's side for once. Both men wanted to save the party from destruction. But after Tiananmen was over and communism began to crumble in Eastern Europe, those who regarded Chen as their figurehead turned their anger against Deng himself. They now saw that what was going on in Europe was as great a threat as the presence of millions of demonstrators on the streets of Chinese cities, and they disagreed strongly with Deng over how to deal with it.

Deng, meanwhile, was becoming increasingly aware of his own mortality. The state of Deng's health is one of the most closely guarded secrets in China. Until his daughter Deng Rong revealed in early 1995 that his health was declining "day by day,"[23] Chinese officials refused to admit that anything was wrong with him, not even a cold. Even Deng's daughter tried to back away from her admission when it became clear it had caused considerable consternation in China and abroad. The Foreign Ministry's standard response when asked by foreign correspondents about Deng's health was that "he is very well," a formula that was eventually replaced by "well for a man of his age." Deng did indeed appear to be fitter than Chen Yun, to judge from their rare and fleeting public appearances. But by 1989, at the age of 85, he was nonetheless showing signs of his age. His movements were slow, and his speech—never that clear to many Chinese and foreigners because of his thick Sichuan accent—was becoming almost incomprehensible.

On September 16th, 1989, Deng made his first public appearance since his meeting with the martial law command shortly after the bloodshed. This time it was to see Tsung-Dao Lee, a physics professor from Columbia University in New York. Deng was shown on state-run television walking slowly forward to greet his guest in the Great Hall of the People. He grinned broadly and grasped the visitor's hands as the two moved toward their seats. As usual, Deng spoke slowly and his hands trembled, but he appeared in good spirits. Xinhua News Agency said Lee expressed delight at seeing Deng in "such good health."[24]

Deng told his guest "I'm still in good health and have a clear mind and a good memory."[25] But he also revealed that it was time for him to retire. In fact, Deng had sent a letter to the party Central Committee 12 days earlier formally asking permission to step down, but this was still a secret. "I have never believed in exaggerating the role of any one individual because that is dangerous and makes it difficult for others to carry on," Deng told Lee. "The stability of a country and a party cannot be based merely on the prestige of one or two persons. That tends to create problems. . . . Recently the story circulated in Hong Kong that I had been assassinated or that I was seriously ill, and that rumor caused fluctuations in the stock market there. This shows that it would be better for me to retire soon. I hope to do so in the near future."

Deng's remarks were an admission that in spite of Jiang Zemin's appointment as party leader in place of Zhao Ziyang, the succession issue that had plagued him for so much of the previous decade was still unresolved and that as long as it remained so China's stability was in jeopardy. In 1995, when Deng's daughter admitted her father's health was declining, many observers believed that the question of who, if anyone, would become the country's paramount leader after his death was still very much in doubt.

Deng thought that the best way to establish a strong successor was to name a person well before his death and then sit back and see how he performed. On November 9th, 1989, the Central Committee announced at the end of a plenum in Beijing that it had accepted Deng's resignation from the post of chairman of the party's Military Commission.[26] It named the party leader Jiang Zemin as his successor. This meant that Deng had surrendered his most important title. He still remained chairman of the state's Military Commission, but since this body was effectively the same as the party's Military Commission the title was meaningless. In order for Deng to resign from the state post as well he needed formal approval from the National People's Congress, China's rubber-stamp parliament. This was duly given in March of the following year when the legislature held its annual meeting.

In his letter asking for permission to step down, Deng said he wanted to do so while he was still healthy. He did not want a repeat of the succession crisis that followed the death of Mao Zedong. Mao had remained chairman of the Central Committee and of the party's Military Commission until his death at the age of 82. His successor, Hua Guofeng, was a virtual unknown who was ousted within two years by Deng and his followers. Deng wanted to make sure that the same fate would not befall his designated successor, Jiang Zemin. In 1989, Jiang had less than two years' experience at the Politburo level compared with Hua's three years when he took over from Mao. During his meeting with the American physicist, Deng made it clear that he did not entirely trust Jiang to assume full command. "If there are disturbances, I shall have to intervene," he said.

Deng apparently saw Jiang as a man he could manipulate. Jiang's elevation from party secretary of Shanghai to the post of general secretary in June 1989 had come as a shock to many observers. Jiang had little experience in the central leadership, no military credentials, and no support to speak of among the general public. Unlike Zhao Ziyang and Hu Yaobang, he did not appear to be someone who would ever get too big for his own boots. He would remain fiercely loyal to the man who promoted him. To make sure his strategy worked, Deng had one other item of business to conclude.

On September 4th, 1989, Deng addressed a small gathering of top leaders, including Jiang, to explain his decision to retire.[27] He told them that the Central Advisory Commission headed by Chen Yun would be abolished at the party's 14th Congress, which was due to be held in 1992. As head of the Central Military Commission, Deng in fact had no right to dictate what should happen to Chen Yun's post. That should have been up to Jiang Zemin and the Politburo to decide and for the congress to approve. But Deng clearly wanted to make sure that Chen's commission was disbanded while he was still alive so that he could be sure that Chen would not use his position to control Jiang after Deng's death—although, as it turned out, Chen was the first to die. In 1982, when the commission was established, Deng said it would be only a "transitional" body aimed at smoothing the transfer of power from the old generation to the young.[28] He said it should be abolished in 1992 or at the latest in 1997. Now the first of Deng's suggested dates was approaching, and he appeared anxious to disband the commission without delay in order to keep Chen and his cohorts away from the center of decision making.

Deng's decision to retire when he did, rather than wait until after the 14th Congress when he could be sure that other more conservative members of the old guard would be safely out of the way as well, was a gamble. But as Deng told the gathering on September 4th, "If I wanted to wait for the best possible time to retire, the time would never come. There'd always be some reason for saying I couldn't retire."[29] Perhaps his health was failing faster than he was prepared to reveal. At a meeting with the former U.S. Secretary of State Henry Kissinger the day after his resignation was approved, Deng said he was "quite healthy" but warned Kissinger enigmatically of "false appearances."[30] Perhaps Deng also felt that by retiring then he would help diminish some of the resentment harbored toward him by the public because of his role in the Tiananmen Square protests. After all, his complete retirement had been one of the demonstrators' main demands. Whatever Deng's motives, his retirement achieved little. Jiang proved not to be an ardent Deng loyalist but a political opportunist who realized that contrary to Deng's wishes Chen Yun's star was on the ascendancy. In the months that followed, Jiang often appeared closer to Deng's chief rival than he did to his own patron.

In early 1990, as anticommunists or former communists who had renounced their ideology were swept to power in a series of multiparty elections in Eastern Europe, the inner-party debate in China over the import of these changes intensified. The Soviet Union itself was disintegrating, with the Baltic republics declaring independence and voting communists out of office. In early February, the Soviet Communist Party committed what was in China's eyes the gravest sin of all by agreeing to give up its guaranteed monopoly of power. While the Soviet party was convening a plenum in Moscow to deliberate this historic decision, the

Chinese authorities maintained a news blackout. On the day the meeting ended, the *People's Daily* published an editorial that, without mentioning the Soviet Union, delivered Beijing's clear response.

"In China, without the strong leadership of the Chinese Communist Party, new turmoil and wars would surely arise, the nation would be split, and the people, not to mention state construction, would suffer," the newspaper said.[31] The following day, the official media finally broke their silence about the news from Moscow, reporting what had happened tersely and without comment. Many ordinary Chinese had already heard the news anyway by tuning into foreign radio broadcasts. So excited were some Beijing residents that when one of the BBC's news bulletins went off the air for a few minutes during the Moscow plenum because of a technical problem, several anxious listeners called my office to ask what was going on.

Developments in the Soviet Union did not stop the prime minister, Li Peng, from paying a long scheduled visit to Moscow in April 1990. Li was the highest-ranking Chinese visitor to the Soviet bloc since the upheavals began. Despite a few small-scale protests in Moscow against the Tiananmen crackdown, he remained calm, faithfully following Deng's instructions not to engage in polemics. It must have been a poignant moment for him as he attended the ritual wreath-laying ceremony at Lenin's Tomb on Red Square—the first top Chinese leader to do so in more than 30 years. From where I stood about 20 yards away, Li looked a little embarrassed and unsure of himself. He asked the officials with him how he should proceed, then fingered the ribbons of a wreath propped against the wall. As he stepped into the red granite vault and looked at the body of Lenin in its glass sarcophagus, the irony of the occasion might well have flashed across his mind—that China was the last major country where the sanctity of this long deceased Russian was still officially beyond doubt.

At a news conference at the end of his trip, Li showed remarkable politeness to his hosts. He even went as far as saying that Soviet reforms were socialist in nature. He noted that Gorbachev had recently pledged to uphold the principles of Leninism. His own understanding of reform was therefore, he said with considerable irony, similar to Gorbachev's. Relaxed on the surface but tense inside—Li embodied the Chinese principle. In reality, secret Chinese documents being circulated among officials at the time were accusing Gorbachev of conniving at the collapse of communism in Europe.[32] One circular described Gorbachev's call for a humane, democratic socialism as a violation of the basic principles of

Marxism. It said Soviet reforms were not aimed at perfecting socialism but at changing it into capitalism. Changes in the Soviet Union, it said, would have an even greater impact on China than developments elsewhere in Eastern Europe, and it called for the suppression in China of anything that could lead to unrest.

Deng had spelled out his strategy for dealing with the Soviets at a meeting with senior officials in early March. He told them that no matter what happened in Moscow, China should continue to develop political ties.[33] "Things," he said, "are not so bad as they seem." Deng had strategic reasons for maintaining and developing relations with the Soviets, namely, his desire to keep a balance between Moscow, Beijing, and Washington, particularly at a time when the United States was perceived as stepping up its efforts to undermine communism in China. A confidential document circulated within the party in response to the Soviet party's abandonment of its right to rule said China should avoid isolation.[34] In spite of recent setbacks in China's ties with the United States and the improvement in relations between Washington and Moscow, it said, the overall world situation remained much the same. It said there were still "serious contradictions" between the United States and the Soviet Union and that China should maintain its usual position in the "big triangle" of the three powers.

For Deng, however, the main point of the meeting that March—details of which were published for the first time three years later—appeared to be to protect his reforms from the party's increasingly vocal extreme hard-line wing. In previous speeches, Deng had pinned much of the blame for the collapse of communism in Eastern Europe and the Soviet Union on the West. During his meeting with the Chinese-American professor on September 16th, 1989, he accused Western countries of waging a "smokeless war" against communism by trying to bring about the "peaceful evolution" of socialist nations toward capitalism.[35] In November of that year Deng said the West had begun a new Cold War against the socialist world.[36] In his speech of March 1990, however, after what in theory should have been the biggest shock of all, namely, the Soviet Communist Party's decision to give up its monopoly of power, Deng's main concern was not "peaceful evolution" nor was it to attack Gorbachev's heretical political views. It was to speed up economic growth in China. He was drawing up the battle lines not with renegade socialists in Moscow but with his critics at home who were worried that he was neglecting ideology in his drive to build up the economy. "Considering the overall situation," Deng said in an apparent rebuttal of his opponents' views, "no matter what changes may take place over the next 10 years, we should do solid work to develop the economy without delay."

Deng said he was worried about the sudden slowdown in economic growth. The government had launched an economic austerity campaign in 1988 in order to curb an unusually severe bout of inflation in the summer of that year that had caused panic buying and a run on banks. Since Tiananmen, the campaign had gained in intensity, partly because provincial leaders who had resisted Beijing's austerity measures before Tiananmen were now toeing the line and partly because extreme hard-liners were taking control of the campaign in an effort to slow down Deng's reforms. The austerity measures included extremely tight controls on bank lending as well as spending by government institutions. As a result, the country's GNP growth rate plunged from 11.2 percent in 1988 to 3.9 percent in 1989. To avoid political unrest, the government made sure that employees of state enterprises in the big cities kept their jobs and wages. But in smaller towns and villages, nearly 20 million industrial workers lost their jobs in 1989 and 1990.[37]

"Some countries have problems basically because they have failed to push their economy forward," said Deng in his speech of March 1990, referring to the Soviet Union and the countries of Eastern Europe. "In those countries people don't have enough food or clothing, their wage increases are wiped out by inflation, their living standards keep dropping, and for a long time they have had to tighten their belts. If our economy continues to grow at a slow rate, it will be hard to raise living standards. Why do the people support us? Because over the last 10 years our economy has been developing and developing visibly."

Deng said that if the growth rate persisted at around 4 or 5 percent it would not just be an economic problem, it would be a political problem too. He told the gathering that the issues that "will keep us awake at night" in the coming decade would be those of how to avoid an economic downturn and how to achieve China's goal of quadrupling the country's 1980 GNP by the year 2000. "If China is to resist hegemonism and the pressure of strong-arm politics and maintain its socialist system, what really matters is whether we can achieve a relatively fast growth rate and achieve our development goals," Deng said.

If the economy rather than ideological subversion was indeed the main thing keeping Deng awake at night, no indication of this was given at a four-day Central Committee meeting that began less than a week after he spoke.[38] On the day after the meeting ended, the People's Daily marked the event with an editorial stressing "the extreme importance of upholding the four cardinal principles, opposing bourgeois liberalization and foiling peaceful evolution activities by anticommunist, antisocialist forces at home and abroad."[39] It mentioned the economy only in passing. Deng did not seem to be getting his message across very effectively. Perhaps he should have established his priorities before retiring. At the end of March, the National People's Congress agreed to Deng's retirement from his last official post as chairman of the State Military Commission. During the Tiananmen Square protests, Zhao Ziyang told Gorbachev that the party had agreed in November 1987 that, although he had retired from some of his posts, "Deng Xiaoping's helmsmanship is still needed for the most important issues." There had been no public announcement of any change in the party's position, and most Chinese assumed Deng would remain enormously powerful behind the scenes. But Deng's critics knew too that without a government or party title, he was, in theory, just another veteran revolutionary whose views were merely his own.

Deng's inability to lay down the line was abundantly clear. Rarely since he had become China's paramount leader a decade earlier had leading official newspapers kept publishing such a steady stream of articles containing views so out of line with his policies—except, of course, during the heady days of the Tiananmen Square protests when the press briefly cast off its party shackles.

In a typical article published by the *People's Daily* in November 1989, the president of Beijing University, Wu Shuqing, said China had been deviating from socialism for several years.[40] He obliquely attacked moves toward reducing state control over the economy, saying corruption was a product of the "system of private ownership." Although Deng had said it was fine for some Chinese to get rich before others, Wu said "the emergence and development of widely divergent and unfair disparity in income is also inseparable from our deviation from the socialist orientation and the various irrational and 'lopsided' policies we have implemented in the course of our reform and opening up to the outside world over the past few years." He said critics of the economic austerity campaign "do not really care for the development of China's reform along the socialist orientation but are trying to lead the young people, who are enthusiastic in reform but lack sufficient social experience, onto a wrong road under the signboard of 'reform.'" In Chinese political terms, these were harsh words.

In mid-February 1990, several Beijing news organizations published or broadcast an article by the extreme hard-line chief of the party's Propaganda Department, Wang Renzhi.[41] Wang hinted that economic reforms were providing a basis for the spread of anticommunist beliefs in China.

"Those who advocate bourgeois liberalization . . . have become a political force waging an overt and covert political struggle against us," said Wang. "Is there an economic basis for waging such a class struggle in the ideological and political realms, or is there an economic force that supports them and serves as their foundation? This is a question to be studied. For them, the concept is clear. They pin their hopes on the formation of a mighty middle class, that is, the bourgeoisie, in China."

Deng's hard-line critics had an easy way of getting at Deng without criticizing him by name. This was to attack the policies of Zhao Ziyang, the party leader who had been ousted for allegedly supporting the Tiananmen Square protests. Until he tried to resist Deng's efforts to put a forceful end to the demonstrations, Zhao had been Deng's protégé. Throughout the 1980s—as prime minister from 1980 and as party general secretary from 1987—he had been the man most closely associated with implementing Deng's reforms. Although Deng had only spoken after Tiananmen of Zhao's failure to take a tough stand on "bourgeois liberalization" and not of any economic mistakes, Deng's critics saw the disgrace of Zhao as an opportunity to attack his—and by association Deng's—economic strategy as well.

In November 1989, the *Economic Daily,* one of Beijing's leading newspapers, published an interview with Xu Yi, a former senior official in the Ministry of Finance.[42] Xu accused Zhao of "ignoring suggestions from many comrades in financial circles" and of adopting Keynesian fiscal policy "unsuited for China's economy." The only high-ranking official to defend Zhao's economic program strongly in public was Xiao Yang, then the Communist Party secretary of Chongqing in the southwestern province of Sichuan. In February 1993 he was promoted to provincial governor, becoming one of the most outspoken reformists in the top echelons of the Chinese leadership. In October 1989, Xiao gave an astonishingly bold interview to a Beijing-controlled newspaper in Hong Kong, the *Wen Wei Po.*[43] The outspoken, plain-talking Xiao said Zhao had scored "quite great achievements" and admitted that criticism of Zhao had had a negative impact on reforms in Chongqing.

Xiao warned against "indiscriminate criticism" of the former party leader, saying this would mean "things that had been successful in the course of reform would likely be negated," including the development of private enterprise. His fears were well founded. After Tiananmen, extreme hard-liners mounted an ideological campaign against the fast-growing class of private entrepreneurs, many of whom were acquiring enormous wealth thanks to Deng's reforms. Deng's critics did not dare openly question the party's decision 10 years earlier to lift its long-standing ban on private enterprise, but they did make it clear that they had strong reservations about allowing private enterprise to flourish in a communist society. Xu Jiatun, the former top Chinese official in Hong Kong who, in 1990, moved to California fearing possible arrest by hard-liners, said in his memoirs that Jiang Zemin and Li Peng were the chief advocates of a clampdown on private enterprise in the cities and countryside. "They raised the great banner of 'putting in order and rectifying' [the economy] to block reforms and opening to the outside world," he wrote.[44]

In late 1989, the party decreed that private entrepreneurs would not be allowed to become party members. The order, which the leadership tried to keep secret in order not to give the impression that it was waging a campaign against private enterprise itself, provoked widespread alarm within the party rank and file.[45] Members feared that it heralded a reversal of one of the fundamental tenets of Deng's reform program, namely, that private business could coexist alongside the state sector as long as public ownership remained predominant. The Organization Department—one of the extreme hard-liners' strongholds—tried vigorously to defend the new policy in confidential circulars. One issued in March 1990 said private entrepreneurs did not qualify to join because they engaged in "exploitation," an evil the party was pledged to wipe out.[46] "If we keep failing to make clear rules about this, the nature of the party will become blurred," it said. The following month, the department issued another circular admitting that many parts of the country were failing to implement the new rules and that party cadres were in some cases failing even to tell their subordinates about the regulations.[47] "This has caused some misunderstandings and ideological confusion," it said. But the hard-liners were not deterred by the show of resistance. The document went on to say that the ban on private entrepreneurs joining the party was part of important measures aimed at "thoroughly correcting Comrade Zhao Ziyang's serious neglect of party construction and his weakening of the party's leadership." These measures, it said, should be implemented "in their entirety and absolutely to the letter."

Although few of the 20 million people registered at that time as private entrepreneurs would have been keen to join the party, the decision to bar them was a clear signal of a change of mood. Before Tiananmen, many official newspapers had published views in support of private entrepreneurs gaining party membership. Now it was back to the Maoist idea of class struggle. Private businesses were not closed down as they were during Mao's reign, but private entrepreneurs did find that in the new conservative atmosphere dealing with officialdom became all the more difficult. The Chinese media began to portray them as tax-evading exploiters—in many cases a reasonable description perhaps, but not one that exactly encouraged officials to grant new business licenses or to offer incentives to the private sector such as tax breaks. Indeed, many officials saw the more hostile mood toward private business as a good pretext to step up their extortion of bribes and other kickbacks from entrepreneurs.

In March 1990, the mayor of Beijing, Chen Xitong—a prominent hard-liner who was forced to relinquish his posts five years later because of alleged corruption—attacked the "unfair distribution" of wealth in China.[48] In a long, passionate reply to reporters at a news conference, Chen said some private businesspeople earned several times more than ordinary people, and warned that if polarization reappeared in the country, it might topple the Communist Party. Later that year another extreme hard-liner, Vice President Wang Zhen, made the views of his camp even clearer. "That we encourage some people to get rich first means we encourage getting rich through labor and honesty," he said.[49] "Our goal is to make all the people rich. We must not allow the birth of capitalist millionaires or billionaires in China. The birth of a tiny minority of upstarts will surely mean poverty of the overwhelming majority of the people. Should that happen China will never be in peace and will never get prosperous."

As the split widened between Deng and his hard-line critics, so too did that between radical reformers and the rest of the party. Liberal officials and academics in the party who had once been enthusiastic supporters of and participants in the reform process under Zhao Ziyang found themselves being treated with suspicion by some of their colleagues and superiors who feared they might be closet opponents of the party waiting for an opportunity to replicate the revolutions of Eastern Europe. The obvious failure of Eastern Europe's and the Soviet Union's new political forces to revive their countries' economies and maintain social stability gave ammunition both to Deng and to extreme hard-liners in their efforts to silence potential opponents inside and outside the party. They were able to point to the chaos in the former communist countries as evidence that China's decision to take a tough line on dissent was correct. As the glow of optimism surrounding the revolutions in Eastern Europe gave way to increasing despair, both in the countries concerned and in the West, the Chinese media began reporting on events in the former communist world with far greater relish.

In 1991, the party circulated classified analyses of the East European situation among its members, highlighting the sufferings of fellow communists elsewhere. The aim was clearly to warn Chinese party members that they could face similar persecution if they pushed for radical change. One such document, entitled *The Reasons for the Changes in Eastern Europe and Their Lessons,* was issued in the summer of 1991.[50] "Reactionary forces are getting more and more arrogant, and party members are undergoing all kinds of discrimination and persecution" in Eastern Europe, it said. "The landlords and capitalists are beginning to settle accounts and take revenge." The document described how former communist leaders such as Honecker and Zhivkov were being investigated or had been imprisoned. "Czechoslovakia, Hungary, and Poland have all set up investigative committees. Any party members who worked in important ministries such as defense, foreign affairs, or the interior have been fired. . . . According to official Polish figures, by September 1990 party members accounted for the majority of the unemployed. . . . A former professor at the Marxist school now sells tickets in the subway, former well-known journalists and commentators are selling cigarettes, and former ambassadors are selling newspapers in newsstands or waiting for work. Even their sons and daughters at school and work have also been discriminated against and insulted. . . . The oppressing class that had been overthrown is now up to its old tricks again."

The official media refrained from commenting so directly, keeping their descriptions of events in Eastern Europe as neutral-sounding as possible in order not to give the impression to the outside world that China was engaging in polemics. But for internal consumption, the party was far less inhibited. The alarmist invective of the party's classified documents—and indeed the almost unremittingly gloomy reports about Eastern Europe published by the Western media—played an important role in helping the party to prevent renewed unrest in the wake of Tiananmen and the collapse of communism in Europe.

But even if economic decline and violent upheaval in Europe made many ordinary Chinese increasingly willing to put up with the status quo, few people went so far as to become positively grateful for the way the Chinese Communist Party had handled Tiananmen. In 1990, the alienation of ordinary city dwellers from their government if anything only intensified, thanks in part to the authorities' continuing ham-fisted efforts to keep the populace in line. This was clearly demonstrated in the buildup to the Asian Games, which were held in Beijing in September 1990—the biggest international sporting event ever staged in China. The games are a mini-Olympics for the region held every four years. Beijing was chosen as the site for the 1990 Asiad well before the Tiananmen Square protests, and the Chinese leadership was naturally delighted that no Asian country, including Taiwan and Hong Kong, where feelings about the bloodshed had run particularly high, decided to boycott the games in protest against the crackdown. Officials hoped the razzamatazz of such a big occasion would help erase memories of Tiananmen and the problems faced by communism elsewhere.

Officials pulled out all the stops to make the games a success. In the month beforehand, they mobilized more than 100 million people to take part in a nationwide torch relay of the Asian Games flame. Thousands of students on university campuses, which a year earlier had been hotbeds of unrest, trained for mass calisthenics displays at the opening and closing ceremonies. To beautify Beijing, the authorities arranged the display of more than 2 million potted plants on the city's pavements. They put up a huge statue of the Asian Games' cuddly mascot, Pan Pan the Panda, on Tiananmen Square and similar images on street corners around Beijing. Pan Pan was the centerpiece of the government's efforts to create an image of normality in Beijing. On street corners where once had stood martial law troops on guard against counterrevolutionaries, now stood images of Pan Pan. The name Pan Pan itself meant "Looking forward with longing"—an expression of the government's optimism about the future. The normally drab city was transformed into an astonishing blaze of color with Asian Games flags, banners, and slogans draped from almost every building and lamppost.

But the response from Beijing citizens was far from enthusiastic. As the Asian Games torches were carried back into the city at the end of their nationwide relay, hundreds of residents lined the streets to watch, but hardly anyone clapped or cheered. Officials said unspecified "hostile forces" were determined to disrupt the games. Rumors swirled around the city that the Chinese designer of the official 14th Asian Games logo had deliberately shaped it to look like an Arabic numeral 6 next to a Roman numeral IV—"6-4" being the Chinese way of referring to the date of the Beijing bloodshed: June 4th, 1989. The cryptic protest was supposedly made complete by a red star on the top left-hand corner of the motif. This, some residents believed, represented a drop of blood. The rumored hidden message behind the logo was probably sheer fantasy, but the way many Beijing residents gleefully swapped tales of it suggested that they were not as keen as the government was to make the games a great success. Western diplomats said they believed thousands of extra soldiers were drafted into the Beijing region in case of any antigovernment demonstrations during the event.

Residents knew that open protest was unlikely given the political climate, but many grumbled among themselves—particularly about the coercive methods used by the government to raise money for the games. In many workplaces, officials told employees to make "voluntary" donations. The names of every contributor would be recorded and in many cases publicly displayed—thus putting enormous psychological pressure on workers to give money. Those who did not do so feared being branded as malcontents. In some parts of the city residents complained they had to contribute funds for the construction of new walls or a coat of whitewash to obscure shabby housing. Even children were told by their teachers to make donations—money that, of course, came from their parents' pockets.

The authorities' efforts to improve public behavior during the games also caused considerable bitterness. Some taxi drivers refused to pick up passengers for short journeys because the police began imposing heavy fines for traffic violations. The government also increased by tenfold the fine for the common Beijing habit of spitting—making it the equivalent of half a day's wages for the average factory worker. Stern reminders of this were broadcast from loudspeakers in busy shopping areas. Officials stepped up their efforts to enforce the widely ignored ban on pet dogs in the city, telling residents to bludgeon any unregistered dogs to death. Official dogcatchers patrolled the streets to perform the task on animals they found.

In the end, the games were held without any obvious hitch. The authorities were visibly relieved. A front-page commentary in the *People's Daily* said it would have been impossible to stage "this magnificent gathering" if China had been in a state of turmoil.[51] The *Beijing Daily* said the games could be described as a "big school for the study of communism."[52] It said some foreigners had remarked that only in a socialist country like China could the games be held so successfully with what it described as "so little time for preparation." The games did indeed help to reinforce the growing impression abroad that China was capable of weathering the storm of upheaval in Eastern Europe. But it was capable of doing so not because of public support for party policy but because of intense security and public reluctance to risk another bloody confrontation with the government.

Early the following year, the party's failure to rally the public behind it became apparent again when the United States sent troops to expel Iraq from Kuwait. The Communist Party instructed its members to regard the war as a struggle between the "big hegemonism" of the United States and the "small hegemonism" of Iraq.[53] But it was clear during the Gulf War that public opinion in China was strongly behind the United States. One Chinese journalist told me in 1991 that the reason why Beijing residents appeared so enthusiastic about the Gulf War was that they were desperate for ways to relieve their antigovernment frustrations after the June 4th bloodshed. "The execution of Ceauşescu provided one such release," he said. "Now they have the Gulf crisis."

Worried about the pro-American stance of many Beijing residents, the government ordered state television not to give too much prominence to news about the war. The *People's Daily* said the conflict exposed U.S. discrimination against blacks because blacks had to shoulder an unfairly heavy burden of the fighting.[54] But the swift victory of the United States and its allies in February 1991 was greeted with delight by ordinary Chinese. Several telephoned my office to express their support for Washington and ask for the latest news. Not since Tiananmen had I received so many calls from members of the public.

The authorities had reason to worry not only about the mood of Beijing citizens but also about growing restlessness in more remote parts of the country populated by ethnic minorities who were drawing inspiration from separatist struggles in the Soviet Union. In April 1990, shortly before Li Peng's trip to Moscow, major antigovernment riots erupted among Muslim Uighurs near the city of Kashgar in the far western province of Xinjiang, about 150 miles from the Soviet border. Chinese paramilitary troops crushed the uprising, killing dozens of people. In Tibet, tensions remained consistently high after the eruption of the first of a series of anti-Chinese protests in 1987. In Inner Mongolia, some ethnic Mongols took note of the sweeping political changes across the border in Mongolia, which in 1990 held its first free elections after decades of Soviet domination. The Chinese authorities confirmed in early June 1991 that they had arrested two members of an illegal Mongolian nationalist organization, the first of its kind reported on the Chinese side of the border in many years. China's minorities make up less than 10 percent of its population and therefore pose far less of a threat to the unity of China than did minority nationalities in the Soviet Union, where some 50 percent of the population were non-Russians. But minorities in China occupy half of the country's total area and, in the case of the Tibetans at least, are a headache for the leadership because of the international attention they receive.

For all their ideological contempt of Gorbachev, the Chinese leadership saw him as one of the few Soviet leaders who stood some chance of keeping the Soviet Union united. In May 1991, Jiang Zemin traveled to Moscow to meet him, his first trip to a major foreign capital since his appointment as party leader nearly two years earlier. In a speech given around that time, Jiang went so far as to express the belief that the future of communism looked rosier than ever. "Historical experience has repeatedly shown that a low ebb precedes a high tide," he said. "As a consequence, the present upheavals in the international communist movement mean a new development of Marxism as well as a new and victorious stage in the socialist cause."[55]

But the low ebb in the Soviet Union was not to be followed by a high tide. Three months after Jiang's visit, Soviet hard-liners staged an abortive coup against Gorbachev, sounding the death knell both of his political career and of Soviet communism.

The August 19th coup in Moscow made clearer than ever the deep divisions in the Chinese leadership over how to respond to the collapse of the communist world. Deng's advice that party leaders should be "calm, calm, and again calm" was ignored by his jubilant hard-line rivals who thought at first that the coup was sure to succeed. Xinhua, which had responded sluggishly at best to the rapid developments in the Soviet Union and Eastern Europe over the previous few months, reported on Gorbachev's replacement by Vice President Gennadi Yanayev and the declaration of a state of emergency within minutes of the first announcement by Tass.[56] Chinese sources said the Politburo convened an emergency meeting that day at which Jiang Zemin hailed the overthrow of Gorbachev. The spirit of Jiang's remarks was immediately relayed to top-ranking officials in a secret document entitled *The Victory of the Soviet People Is a Victory for the Chinese People*. There indeed appeared much for the hard-liners to celebrate. China's official media reflected the leadership's jubilant mood by giving considerable prominence to the declarations of the Soviet coup leaders and almost totally ignoring Yeltsin's resistance.

On the day after the Politburo meeting, while the hard-liners in Moscow were still clinging to power in spite of opposition, Deng addressed a small gathering of top leaders. Part of his speech was published two years later in the third volume of his selected works.[57] Although the full context of the published extract is not known, it sounded far more sober than Jiang's exultant address to the Politburo on the previous day. In the extract, Deng did not mention the events in Moscow, but he was clearly criticizing the Politburo for ignoring his calls for reform and devoting too much attention to cracking down on dissent. "It is right to stress stability," he said, "but if we overdo it, we may let opportunities slip by." Deng obviously did not want events in Moscow to lead to an intensification of the campaign against liberals in China. "The future of China hinges on our adhering to those policies [of reform and opening to the outside world]," Deng said, "and we should explain that fully to the people."

The hours following the attempted Soviet coup must have been tense ones among members of the Chinese Politburo. When the leadership realized that the coup was failing, it hurriedly withdrew its jubilant document. But the damage had already been done. The party had been plunged into even greater confusion and division. Gorbachev's resignation as party leader, Yeltsin's ban on Communist Party activities, and the final dissolution of the Soviet Union on December 25th, 1991, inflicted yet more grievous wounds on an already traumatized party.

"People inside and outside the party are baffled by the setbacks suffered by socialism," said an article published in the extreme hard-line journal Contemporary Trends of Thought around the time of the Soviet coup. "They're confused and unsure about the future of socialism. Some intellectuals and young people don't even have any feeling of opposition to peaceful evolution. Some are just waiting for it to happen. All this is a clear indication that contemporary socialism is facing a life-and-death struggle, that the situation faced by Chinese communists is grim and that the task in hand is formidable."[58]

In a series of classified documents, the party struggled to explain events to its members. One such circular, dated September 23rd, 1991, admitted that the collapse of the Soviet Communist Party had had "a serious impact" on the international communist movement.[59] It accused Western nations led by the United States of "interfering" in the coup attempt by backing Gorbachev and Yeltsin. The document did not bear the imprints of Deng's thinking. Its analysis of the causes of communism's collapse in the Soviet Union dwelt far more on politics and ideology than on the economy. The factors it listed ranged from the criticism of Stalin and Lenin and the easing of government controls over art and literature to "religious fever." It said Christian and other religious groups in the Soviet Union "all have a very anticommunist tint." The document traced the roots of the crisis back to the 1950s when Khrushchev took over and "repudiated Stalin's dictatorship and created great ideological confusion." It accused Gorbachev of implementing "completely erroneous policies" that caused "deep discontent inside and outside the party." Gorbachev and Yeltsin, it said, had been leading "antisocialist and anticommunist forces" in a "mad counterattack against progressive forces that support socialism and national unity." Their actions, said the document, "are in essence an anticommunist coup." It accused Yeltsin and "the plotter and opportunist" Gorbachev of orchestrating "white terror" in the Soviet Union. Party members, it said "must take the Soviet changes as a living negative example, earnestly take in the lesson and increase their consciousness in order to prevent peaceful evolution."

The September 23rd document also tried to convince party officials that China would not experience similar upheaval. "The huge changes in the Soviet Union could perhaps create an unfavorable international environment for us, and Western hostile forces might aim their spear at our country and put even more pressure on us," it said. "The small minority of people who are taking the bourgeois liberal stance in this country might also take this opportunity to make trouble. At the same time, within the party and among the masses, some comrades will feel worried or doubtful and even have erroneous thoughts. . . . There are some comrades who wonder if the Soviet Union changes, will China change too? Can China hold out?"

The answer, said the document, is that China is a very different country. For one thing, it has never been controlled by Moscow. "Socialism in China is deeply rooted among the billion people here," it said. "The changes in the Soviet Union and Eastern Europe have made the broad masses of the people value the socialist road even more highly." The document cited the Chinese Communist Party's efforts to bring relief to victims of widespread flooding during the summer of 1991 that left more than 2,000 people dead and tens of millions homeless. The party's response to the disaster had been widely touted in the official media as evidence of the leadership's ability to respond swiftly and effectively to the people's needs. In Beijing, however, many residents saw the exercise as cheap propaganda and resented being ordered by officials at their workplaces to make cash contributions to the relief work.

But, in words echoing Deng's address to the martial law command on June 9th, 1989, the document hinted at the leadership's worries about the party's ability to survive after veteran revolutionaries pass from the scene. "We have a big group of old comrades who have experienced the test of long revolutionary struggle, who have a rich experience of running the party, the country, and the army, and this is the reason why we can deal with this very complicated situation and can persist along the socialist road," it said. "Because of all these people, we can withstand the test of any political storm."

The circular said the party could depend on the armed forces for support. "Under the leadership of the Communist Party, we have an army of 3 million people. They have all kinds of experience, especially in suppressing counterrevolutionary turmoil. They can cope with invasion and subversion. The party and the people can completely rely on them." It was a bleak statement of the state of the party—dependent on octogenarians and brute force for its survival.

"Changes in Eastern Europe and the Soviet Union now mean that the whole world is looking at China," the document said. The party's problem was that the octogenarians in control of it disagreed bitterly over what China should do next.

3

The Deng Whirlwind

In the spring of 1992, a crucial historical moment, Deng Xiaoping journeyed to south China on an inspection tour. The ensuing publication of his important remarks, much like a southerly spring breeze instantly replacing the chilling air in the late days of winter, injected fresh impetus and vigor into China's reform and opening cause. Deng's south China talks marked the turning point. . . . People throughout the world marveled as to how Deng's south China remarks have created a so-called Deng whirlwind, a whirlwind which thus far has not subsided.
—Beijing Review, *February 1994*

For more than two and a half years after Tiananmen, Deng had to battle to make himself heard. His political influence was at its lowest ebb since coming to power. Not only had the protests and the bloodshed dented his pride and prestige, but his hard-line critics were on the rampage. Any sensitive reader of the official Chinese press could see that Deng's economic reforms were under fierce attack and that Deng himself was no longer the unassailable strongman of Chinese politics.

In spite of endless protestations by Chinese officials that political stability had been fully restored after Tiananmen and that the party was united around Deng's chosen successor Jiang Zemin, nothing could have been further from the truth. Factional warfare in the party leadership was raging, made evident by the sharply divergent tone of speeches by leaders and commentaries in the official press. To many ordinary Chinese in the capital, the struggles seemed remote and irrelevant, but Chinese intellectuals as well as the foreign media and diplomats avidly monitored the outward signs of conflict as well as the rumor mill of political intrigue.

As the former editor of a major Beijing daily newspaper put it to me, in 1989 every Chinese leader was too preoccupied with the need to maintain stability after Tiananmen to engage in serious political combat. He described 1990 as a "preparatory year" for the extreme hard-liners. In the following year they launched their offensive. It was, he said, "the most reactionary year" with Deng's conservative critics appearing at their most aggressive since Tiananmen though still not yet strong enough to bring about any significant changes in his policies. "The leftists [extreme hard-liners] wanted to create the right ideological climate for reversing Deng's policies before making any actual changes," the journalist said. Deng's critics, who saw as their guru the reclusive Chen Yun, began instead by tightening control over the media and attacking the theoretical underpinnings of Deng's reforms.

The hard-line camp included the Politburo Standing Committee members Song Ping, Li Peng, and Yao Yilin (who died in 1994); the Beijing party secretary and Politburo member Li Ximing; veterans in the Central Advisory Commission such as the former propaganda chief Deng Liqun as well as top officials in the media, the party's Organization Department and Propaganda Department, and the Ministry of Culture. Helping them were numerous essay writers and theorists who churned out articles for publication in the official press. These were not people who relished contacts with the foreign media, so what we know about them comes mainly from their critics. A book in support of the opposing liberal camp published in 1993 disparaged these hard-line scribes as people motivated purely by the desire for power and influence.[1] Some, it said, were leading essayists during the Cultural Revolution who had enthusiastically supported the purging of Deng, and some were supporters of Mao's immediate successor, the conservative Hua Guofeng. The book said the leftists included officials who had managed to avoid being purged during Deng's efforts to rid the party of Cultural Revolution extremists in the mid-1980s. Although Chen Yun and other top officials associated with the hard-line camp were victims of the Cultural Revolution rather than its perpetrators, it appeared that those who rallied under them included a broad range of malcontents united by their suspicion of or downright hostility toward Deng as well as their opposition to liberal dissent.

For Deng, the escalating hard-line criticism of his policies came at a particularly bad time. By 1991, Chinese leaders were already making plans for the party's 14th Congress, which was due to be held late the following year. Congresses are all-important in Chinese political life. Some 2,000 to 3,000 delegates take part, ranging from grassroots party members to top leaders. They "elect" a new Central Committee, which stays in office for five years, and establish party policy. Each of the party's previous congresses in recent years had marked watersheds in China's political development. The 12th Congress in September 1982 set the goal of establishing "socialism with Chinese characteristics"—a catchphrase that gave Deng considerable leeway to deviate from traditional Marxist principles. It also established the target of quadrupling China's 1980 GNP by the year 2000, which was aimed at making the Chinese people "comparatively well off." The new Central Committee elected by the 12th Congress appointed Hu Yaobang, a reformist protégé of Deng's, as party chief. The 13th Congress in 1987 marked a major push toward handing over power by the old guard to a younger generation of professionals and technocrats. Deng himself gave up his membership of the Central Committee, as did many other veterans of the Long March of 1934–1935—the name given to the historic trek of some 6,000 miles by beleaguered communist forces to a new base in northern China. The congress formally agreed that China was only in "the initial stages of socialism," which gave it even more leeway to experiment with unorthodox policies. It pronounced "leftism"—or hard-line conservatism—to be the greatest danger to China's modernization. The 13th Congress was widely hailed at home and abroad as a major political victory for Deng. The new Central Committee immediately met and voted secretly to keep him as the party's chief decision maker on important issues. The main conclusions of a congress are determined in advance by the leadership. Hence precongress jockeying behind the scenes among top leaders and retired party veterans is far more important than any deliberations during the conclave itself. Deng probably believed that the approaching 14th Congress would be the last such event of his lifetime, making it all the more important that it endorse his vision of China's future. If he wanted it to do so, he would have to lay the groundwork well in advance.

Deng began his first major push to set the agenda for the congress in early 1991 with a visit to Shanghai around the time of the most important holiday for Chinese, the Lunar New Year, which normally falls in January or February in the solar calendar. Deng had spent every New Year Festival in Shanghai since 1988, staying in a closely guarded state guest house in the suburbs close to the airport. Though cold and damp at that time of the year, Shanghai enjoys a better climate in the winter than Beijing, which turns bitterly cold and chokes with the dust of coal fires and dust storms blowing in from the Gobi Desert to the north. Deng was joined on his 1991 visit to the city by his old comrade in arms, the 85-year-old President Yang Shangkun as well as by the former President Li Xiannian, aged 83—a man known to have reservations about Deng's reforms. On February 14th, the eve of the Year of the Sheep, the three veterans were shown on Chinese television meeting Shanghai officials at a New Year reception earlier in the day. The reformist mayor and party leader of Shanghai, Zhu Rongji, was also in view, loudly wishing Deng good health and long life. Deng walked unaided, though one of his daughters stood by his side to repeat what was said to him in a voice his poor hearing could make out. All that television viewers were able to hear of Deng himself was one sentence: "Let me take this opportunity to extend warm regards and happy festival wishes to the heroic people of Shanghai."

Apart from the brief report on Deng's appearance the media kept their usual silence about his activities in Shanghai. This was in line with Deng's own stated wish at the time of his retirement that the press should henceforth avoid covering his activities.[2] But Deng was doubtless very anxious that his opinions, at least, be publicized, even if they were not directly attributed to him. When the third volume of the *Selected Works of Deng Xiaoping* was published more than two years later, it contained a speech made by Deng to local leaders during his stay in Shanghai. In it, Deng stressed the main point that he was trying to impress upon his conservative critics: "Don't think that any planned economy is socialist and any market economy is capitalist," Deng said. "That's not the way things are. In fact, planning and regulation by the market are both means of controlling economic activity, and the market can also serve socialism."

In March and April, Shanghai's *Liberation Daily* newspaper published three signed commentaries prominently on its front page, which many Chinese sources say were based on remarks made by Deng to officials in the city.[3] Mao Zedong had used just such a technique in 1965 in the buildup to the Cultural Revolution, when he found himself under increasing attack in the Beijing media because of his disastrous social and economic experiments. The three *Liberation Daily* commentaries of 1991 were strikingly out of keeping with the vitriolic diatribes against capitalism and dissent that were the main output of commentary writers acting under the orders of extreme hard-liners in Beijing.

Like Deng in 1991, Mao in 1965 had used the media in Shanghai as a springboard for his counterattack. Instructed by Mao and his wife Jiang Qing, the Shanghai newspaper *Wenhui Bao* published an article criticizing a play written by the deputy mayor of Beijing, Wu Han. The historical drama contained allusions to Mao's autocratic style of rule. The *Wenhui Bao* article was the first salvo of what developed later the following year into the Cultural Revolution. Mao's critics tried at first to ignore the attack from Shanghai, but within three weeks they were forced by the prime minister, Zhou Enlai, to instruct national newspapers in Beijing to reprint the article. Many Chinese paid little attention, believing it all to be part of an abstruse academic battle. But it soon became clear that China was in the grips of a major political struggle.

Deng's struggle with his critics appeared no less abstruse. To the casual reader, it was not at all obvious that Deng was behind the *Liberation Daily* pieces. The author's name was given as Huangfu Ping, which was not a name anyone had heard of before. This in itself would not have raised eyebrows. Chinese journalists frequently use pen names, sometimes several different ones. Since the *Liberation Daily* is under the direct control of the Shanghai Communist Party committee, the reader would have assumed that the commentaries reflected the views of the Shanghai leadership.

Unknown though the author was, what he wrote was sensational given the political climate of the time. Huangfu Ping's first commentary, published on March 2nd, was provocatively titled, "Reform and Opening Up Requires a New Way of Thinking."[4] It quoted the Shanghai mayor, Zhu Rongji, as saying that "the liberation of ideas must enter new realms, reform and opening up must explore new ways of thinking, and economic construction must make a breakthrough." The article said the Shanghai party committee had already "come up with many new ways of thinking" in order to invigorate the city's economy in the 1990s. "Some of these new ways of thinking take us into new realms that have not been explored in the last 10 years," the commentary said. "We must adopt new ways of thinking. Coming up with new tricks will not do. Simply copying the practices adopted during the reforms of the 1980s will not do."

Huangfu Ping's commentary tackled some of the arguments of the extreme hard-liners head on. For example, three months earlier, the *People's Daily* had published an article that argued "a market economy means getting rid of public ownership, which means negating the leadership of the Communist Party, negating the socialist system, and practicing capitalism."[5] Huangfu Ping attacked this notion saying, "Some comrades are always in the habit of equating the planned economy with a socialist economy, a market economy with capitalism. They believe the ghost of capitalism must be lurking behind market regulation. Along with deepening of the reforms, however, more and more comrades have begun to understand that planning and the market are simply two different means of deploying resources and are not the hallmarks of either socialism or capitalism." Huangfu Ping warned against sliding into "a kind of new ideological stagnation." In an obvious allusion to hard-line critics of Deng's reforms, the commentary said the principle of "self-reliance"—one of the favorite slogans of the hard-liners—should not be used as an argument against attracting foreign investment. Nor, it said, should the austerity campaign be used as a weapon against economic reforms.

It was not until nearly a year later that it became clear that many of these phrases were, almost word for word, the ideas of Deng Xiaoping and that this was the first major public salvo of a counterattack by Deng's forces against the hard-liners. At the time the significance of Huangfu Ping's first article went almost unnoticed, either by ordinary Chinese or indeed the foreign media. This was not surprising, given that no other newspaper in the country echoed the *Liberation Daily*'s views. It looked more like a stray shot in the dark than the start of a bombardment.

Nearly three weeks later, Huangfu Ping lashed out again. This time it was in a commentary entitled "We Must Have a Better Understanding of Opening Up."[6] The article argued that the opening up of Shanghai to foreign business had become a matter of greater urgency than ever before. "To gain a better understanding of opening up, we must further liberate our thinking, reject any conservative, ossified or inward-looking ideas, and create an open environment compatible with an advanced international city." The commentary said Shanghai had opened to the outside world too slowly in the 1980s. "This is directly related to the fact that the ideas of some comrades are not sufficiently liberated," it said.

The commentary described how conservative thinking became manifest soon after the reforms began in the late 1970s when officials worried about allowing a neon advertisement for a foreign company to be placed on the roof of the Park Hotel, an 18-story, 1930s art deco edifice on Shanghai's main commercial thoroughfare. It also cited opposition to leasing land to foreigners in Shanghai's Hongqiao Development Zone—a breakthrough that was finally achieved in 1988 in defiance of conservatives who feared the move was redolent of the way Shanghai was carved up by foreign powers in precommunist days. "All these [examples of conservative thinking] indicate that on the question of opening up we need to liberate our thinking anew. In the 1990s Shanghai must take great strides in opening up, it must have a completely new way of thinking, it must dare to take risks and do things that have never been done before."

Huangfu Ping returned again to the theme of what defines socialism and capitalism. "If we remain bogged down by the question of whether something is 'surnamed socialist or surnamed capitalist,' we will let a golden opportunity pass us by," the commentary said. Deng himself had tried to make a similar point in December 1990, just before a meeting of the Central Committee.[7] Although he had said at the time of his retirement in 1989 that "I'm not going to concern myself with the work of the Central Committee, except for extremely serious problems,"[8] he clearly considered the debate over the nature of socialism and capitalism to be one such problem. On the day before the Central Committee meeting, Deng summoned a group of top party leaders and told them, "We must understand theoretically that the difference between capitalism and socialism is not a market economy as opposed to a planned economy. Socialism has regulation by market forces, and capitalism has control through planning."[9]

These remarks, which were not published until nearly four years later, were aimed directly at Deng's hard-line critics. At the time, however, they were relayed little further than the Soviet-style, military-run Jingxi Guest House in western Beijing where the typically secretive Central Committee meeting was held. An official communiqué issued by the plenum paid tribute to Deng's reforms but also contained an equal measure of phraseology favored by the hard-liners. To Deng's critics, the question of whether his reforms were "surnamed socialist or surnamed capitalist" remained a key bone of contention.

Another month passed before the final Huangfu Ping commentary appeared in the *Liberation Daily*. In the interim, the National People's Congress held its annual plenary session in Beijing. The meeting—which as usual merely rubber-stamped decisions made in secret beforehand by party leaders—gave something of a boost to the proreform camp. Zhu Rongji, Deng's liberal protégé from Shanghai, was appointed deputy prime minister. This was not necessarily a position of great authority but one from which the Deng faction clearly hoped he would climb to greater heights in the future. Zhu's appointment was a sign that Deng was still capable of wielding considerable influence. At the same time, however, the congress promoted the more conservative Zou Jiahua to the same rank, and the cautious keynote speech by the prime minister, Li Peng, hardly smacked of the "completely new way of thinking" Huangfu Ping had called for.

Huangfu Ping's final commentary did not refer to Li Peng's address. But it expressed jubilation over the appointment of the two new deputy prime ministers. It refrained, of course, from expressing explicit preference for either one but described it as a "spectacular decision of strategic

importance."[10] The commentary went on to advocate criteria for selecting officials, implicitly rejecting the hard-liners' repeated insistence that
the primary consideration should be loyalty to Marxism. "In efficiently
selecting and using a large number of cadres with both morals and talent,
we should, first of all be bold. . . . The practice in the past decade and
more shows that there should not be excessive misgivings and innumer-
able rules and regulations in selecting and promoting young and middle-
aged cadres. We should be bold in reform and opening, as well as in
appointing cadres." Huangfu Ping seemed to be hinting that China
should have more senior officials like Zhu Rongji, a troubleshooting
technocrat of sharp intellect who had made it to the top in spite of having been a victim of the Anti-Rightist Campaign of 1957.

Few China-watchers had expected that in 1991, 15 years after Mao's
death and 13 years after the launch of Deng's reforms, the country would
again witness a political struggle waged in much the same manner as that
which had once plunged the country into near anarchy. Deng, of course,
had no intention of launching a Cultural Revolution–style upheaval. But
even his less grandiose scheme, that of getting his reforms moving forward swiftly again, proved more difficult to get off the ground than did
Mao's campaign in 1965. In 1991, the hard-liners in the north fought
tooth and nail against the offensive from Shanghai.

After the second Huangfu Ping commentary appeared, with its sting-
ing "surnamed socialist or surnamed capitalist" line, extreme hard-liners
in Beijing launched an investigation into the author's background.[11] The
name turned out to represent a group of writers. The main author was
the Communist Party secretary of the *Liberation Daily,* Zhou Ruijin. The
others were the head of the newspaper's commentary department and a
cadre in the municipal party committee's research office. The investigators from the party's hard-line-controlled Propaganda Department discovered that the articles the three men had written were based on
remarks made by Deng and had been endorsed by Zhu Rongji. Before
1989, such high-level backing would have been enough to ensure that the
national media reprinted the articles. But in this case the hard-liners, who
controlled the major dailies, not only decided to stop the reprinting of the
Huangfu Ping essays but also arranged for the publication of articles
obliquely attacking them. From April onward, journals and newspapers
under hard-line control, including the *People's Daily* and the *Guangming
Daily,* carried a series of essays and commentaries stressing the need to
"ask whether something is surnamed socialist or surnamed capitalist"
when carrying out reforms. "Not asking whether something is surnamed

socialist or surnamed capitalist will inevitably lead the reforms and open-door policy along the capitalist road and destroy the socialist cause," said one of the diatribes.[12]

The hard-liners were apparently furious that the Huangfu Ping articles had failed to repeat the ritual attacks against "bourgeois liberalization" included in almost every theoretical article in the Beijing press. On April 22nd, the *People's Daily* published an almost hysterical commentary about the dangers of liberal trends. "We must raise the banner of opposing bourgeois liberalization," the article said, "otherwise there will be extreme ideological confusion within the party and among the masses that would have serious repercussions." Eventually, however, the *People's Daily* provided Deng's camp with an opportunity for revenge. On September 1st, the newspaper released in advance a copy of an editorial on reform that was due to be published the following day. The advance text was distributed by Xinhua News Agency and broadcast on national radio.[13] Although the title was innocuous enough—"Going a Step Further in Carrying Out Reform and Opening to the Outside World"—the article sounded like a typical blast from the hard-line camp. "It is imperative to keep to the correct orientation in carrying out reforms," it said. "We should never allow them to go along the bourgeois liberalization or capitalist line. . . . We should ask whether something is surnamed capitalist or surnamed socialist. . . . The reason why we ask whether something is surnamed capitalist or surnamed socialist is in order to keep public ownership as the mainstay."

Given the furious rhetoric over the socialist/capitalist issue in the preceding months, most readers would not have found the contents of this editorial particularly surprising. But this was no ordinary commentary. A *People's Daily* editorial is supposed to reflect the consensus of the Politburo. Normally, it would have to be approved in advance by the top party leadership, probably including the party chief himself. On this occasion, however, the *People's Daily* had clearly ignored the usual protocol because later, on the eve of publication, Xinhua News Agency issued a different version, this time omitting the reference to the "surnamed capitalist, surnamed socialist" controversy. Clearly someone powerful in the Politburo had decided not to side with the hard-liners. The abrupt correction was an embarrassment for Deng's critics but was equally an embarrassment for the leadership as a whole. Changing a *People's Daily* editorial is a major political act. Much of the Tiananmen Square uprising had been fought, after all, over the protesters' demand that a *People's Daily* editorial of April 26th, 1989, describing the peaceful demonstrations as "turmoil" be revised. The word "turmoil" was taken from a speech made by Deng, making it all the more difficult for the leadership to drop it without causing an unthinkable public loss of face for the senior leader. By dropping what appeared to be an important ideological point from the editorial of September 1992, the leadership was giving a clear signal to attentive members of the public that a fierce struggle was underway.

The *People's Daily*'s editor, Gao Di, was criticized by the leadership for his failure to get the editorial cleared in advance by the Politburo. But Gao, apparently aware that hard-line veterans were on his side, defended his views in the newspaper's classified in-house journal *Internal Situation*.[14] Two weeks after the editorial's publication, *Internal Situation* published a letter, purportedly written by "a few Communist Party members from central organs," that said "those who do not believe in asking whether something is surnamed socialist or surnamed capitalist when carrying out reform and opening up, are either politically confused or else simply yes-men for the likes of Gorbachev and Yeltsin." Gao Di added a note in his own name to this letter that said "we should be encouraged by these few Communist Party members to sacrifice all we have for the protection of Marxism-Leninism and Mao Zedong Thought."

Perhaps Gao Di had believed that Jiang Zemin would back his editorial. At the time, Jiang appeared to be on the side of the hard-liners. Though chosen by Deng, Jiang was clearly vacillating in his political loyalty as was apparent in a speech he made on July 1st, 1991, to mark the 70th anniversary of the founding of the Communist Party.[15] The anniversary was an important political event. Even at the best of times it would have received a lot of coverage in the official media. But this occasion was particularly significant because it coincided with the crumbling of communism in Eastern Europe and the Soviet Union. The outside world and many ordinary Chinese were waiting on tenterhooks to see whether China would be the next to collapse. Although Moscow had yet to make the final break with communism, China was the only major orthodox communist power left in the world. Its ideological allies could be counted on one hand and were all impoverished countries shunned by the West— North Korea, Cuba, Vietnam, and Laos. In his speech, Jiang used a hodgepodge of Dengisms and hard-line rhetoric to try to convince his audience that the Chinese party would survive. But the hard-liners in control of the media, apparently without any resistance by Jiang, decided to slant press coverage of the speech in favor of their cause. They launched an intense publicity campaign, publishing endless articles high-lighting Jiang's hard-line rhetoric and calling on the nation to study it. The newspapers devoted particular attention to Jiang's comments on the dangers of peaceful evolution and class struggle. "At present, the social-ist cause is encountering serious setbacks all over the world," thundered a *People's Daily* editorial on July 19th.[16] "Hostile forces at home and abroad are launching unbridled propaganda for their argument that 'socialism ends in complete failure' in an attempt to overwhelm commu-nists and destroy the socialist cause. It is an extremely grim struggle. Using both history and realities and both theory and practice, [Jiang Zemin's] speech proves, with incontrovertible facts, historical conclu-sions such as 'without the Communist Party, there would be no new China.' "

The final collapse of communism in the Soviet Union in August appeared to push Jiang more firmly into the hard-line camp. In a major public address on September 24th to commemorate the 110th birth anniversary of the famous left-wing Chinese writer, Lu Xun, Jiang Zemin lashed out against the West for "bullying" and "humiliating" China dur-ing the last century.[17] By praising Lu Xun's support for the communist cause at a time when it was under severe threat from the KMT in the 1930s, Jiang Zemin appeared to be criticizing party members who were losing their faith as a result of events in Moscow and Eastern Europe. "When the revolution was at a low ebb, while waging an uncompromis-ing struggle against the enemy, ready to sacrifice his life at all times, [Lu Xun] bitterly denounced renegades who betrayed the revolution and exposed parasites living on the body of lions, the opportunists who had sneaked into the revolutionary camps, as well as 'the revolutionaries who made an about-face change' because they became dejected . . . when the revolution suffered setbacks," Jiang said. Later in his speech he fumed that "international hostile forces have not, for a single day, stopped con-ducting peaceful evolution against us. Bourgeois liberalization is the inner power working with these forces in conducting peaceful evolution. These hostile activities have posed a real threat to our country's indepen-dence and sovereignty, as well as to our construction, reform, and open-ing efforts. . . . The Chinese Communist Party and the people of all nationalities in China will not allow this." Jiang's remarks on "bourgeois liberalization" were printed the following day in large bold type in a sep-arate box on the front page of the *People's Daily*'s overseas edition. Though Deng Xiaoping himself had on numerous occasions attacked "bourgeois liberalization" himself, his remarks in Shanghai in early 1991 suggested that he did not at that time regard it as a priority issue. To the hard-liners, however, combating the phenomenon was far more urgent a task than pressing ahead with economic reform.

It was not until October, some seven months after the first Huangfu Ping article appeared in the *Liberation Daily,* that a top leader from the pro-Deng faction publicly backed up the message that the commentaries had tried to convey. Since the Huangfu Ping essays, top reformist leaders had said nothing openly to defend their stance. It was the president, Yang Shangkun, who broke the silence. When he retired, Deng had not insisted that Yang, only two years his junior, step down with him. On the contrary, Yang not only had kept his job as president but had also been promoted to the number two position in the Central Military Commission under Jiang Zemin. Deng's apparent intention was that Yang would be the man who would keep the other leaders, Jiang in particular, on the right track. Yang, however, found that enforcing Deng's will was far from easy.

On October 9th, the day before the 80th anniversary of the 1911 Revolution that toppled China's last imperial dynasty, Yang and other top leaders—including key hard-liners—attended a mass rally at the Olympic Sports Center in northern Beijing to mark the occasion. With a large portrait of Sun Yat-sen, the leader of the 1911 Revolution, hanging on the wall behind him, Yang spoke for about 25 minutes, reading his speech from a script in a firm, loud voice. Ostensibly, it was about China's progress since 1911 and reunification with Taiwan, since October 10th is celebrated on the island as National Day. But Yang's speech had a more important subtext than the ritual call for an end to hostility between the Communist Party and the KMT.

After praising the achievements of Sun Yat-sen and his communist successors, Yang moved on to the present. "Our performance in the next one or two decades will have a great bearing on our country's future and fate," he said.[18] "We must be sober-minded and always grasp economic construction work. Unless we encounter a large-scale foreign invasion, we should firmly and unwaveringly continue our economic work. Work in other areas should be subject to or serve the central task of economic construction. We must never interfere with the central task. We should focus on the central task and never shift our attention."

Like Jiang Zemin's July 1st oration, Yang's speech—though much shorter than Jiang's—included overviews of the last few decades as well as an analysis of the present situation in China. Unlike Jiang, however, who made numerous references to peaceful evolution and bourgeois liberalization, Yang did not mention these issues once, even though he was speaking not long after the failed coup in Moscow and the collapse of the Soviet Communist Party—events that had given the extreme hard-liners all the more encouragement to lash out against unorthodox ideological trends. Many journalists and diplomats noted the unusual tone of Yang's speech. In a BBC dispatch, I echoed the general consensus of observers that "the president's speech marked a strong reaffirmation of China's commitment to economic reform following the collapse of orthodox communism in the Soviet Union."

But even the authority of Yang Shangkun proved insufficient to turn the tide in Deng's favor. In contrast with the nationwide campaign to study Jiang Zemin's July 1st speech, Yang's words received virtually no publicity at all. Hard-line rhetoric continued to dominate the media. The chief propagandist of the hard-line camp, Deng Liqun, declared in an essay published on November 20th that because of "changes in historical conditions abroad and at home," the struggle in China between supporters and opponents of Chinese communism's basic principles was "more conspicuous, fierce, and acute" than it had ever been since the founding of the People's Republic,[19] his implied point being that this and not the economy was what the party should be worrying about.

Chinese sources said Jiang—perhaps under pressure from Deng—began in the end to resent the way the media were presenting him as such a hard-liner. They said that sometime in early October, Jiang and Li Ruihuan, the liberal Politburo Standing Committee member responsible for ideology, separately wrote letters to Gao Di, complaining that the *People's Daily* was failing to give sufficient prominence to their views on the need for reform. The *People's Daily,* however, appeared simply to shrug off these criticisms.

At the end of November, the Central Committee met for the first time in almost a year, but there was no sign at the end of the secretive conclave, which focused mainly on agricultural issues, that the reformists had gained any ground.[20] The meeting decided that the party's 14th Congress would be held in the third quarter of 1992. Time was clearly running out for the Deng faction. Extraordinary measures were called for.

Having failed to get the media on his side, Deng decided to take his message directly to the people. It was an astonishing political gambit that, like the Huangfu Ping essays, was reminiscent of the tactics used by Mao. Chinese sources told me that Deng Xiaoping mapped out his strategy with the help of close friends, including Yang Shangkun and another veteran revolutionary Bo Yibo. This time Deng was determined to leave nothing to chance. The failure of the Huangfu Ping essays, which Deng had apparently hoped would prove effective without much direct guidance from himself, had shown the need for personal intervention. The plan was to travel 1,300 miles to the relatively prosperous south where he would make public appearances to reinforce his message. This would not be like the secretive discussions he had had with officials in Shanghai in early 1991. Deng this time wanted to be the focus of media attention.

Twenty-one years earlier, Mao had also journeyed to the south in a struggle against his opponents. According to official histories, Mao suspected that his designated successor, the defense minister Lin Biao, was plotting a coup d'état. So he decided to relay his concerns directly to provincial military commanders in order to rally their support in a showdown with Lin.[21] After Mao's return, Lin tried to flee the country but died when his plane crashed en route to the Soviet Union. In 1992, Chinese accounts of Deng's trip to the south used the same four-character phrase to describe the event as that used by official histories of Mao's trip in 1971: *nanxun jianghua,* meaning, "speeches made during a tour of the south." As one pro-Deng Chinese publication put it, "In modern China there have been two tours of the south made by leaders that have shaken the entire world. One was Mao Zedong's southern tour in 1971, and the other was Deng Xiaoping's southern tour in 1992. Mao Zedong's southern tour exposed and smashed Lin Biao's antiparty clique. Deng Xiaoping's southern tour halted at a critical moment the extreme leftist countercurrent that was seriously threatening the reforms."[22]

Around January 17th,[23] Deng left the frozen capital on board a special train. With him were his wife Zhuo Lin; his daughters Deng Nan, Deng Rong, and Deng Lin; and his wheelchair-bound son Deng Pufang—all of his children, in fact, apart from his second son, the businessman Deng Zhifang. The Deng family's first stop was in the city of Wuhan, the capital of Hubei Province in central China. Wuhan lies on the banks of the Yangtze River about halfway along the main north-south railway line. It was then a grim industrial city, conspicuously less prosperous than Beijing and the coastal regions. Official accounts say no more about Deng's activities in Wuhan than that he went there. A book about Deng's southern tour published in China later in the year, however, gave in addition to the official account some examples of "hearsay among the people" about Deng's trip.[24] This "hearsay" was probably a euphemism for facts that had not been authorized for official publication because of their sensitive nature. The book said that in Wuhan—which it referred to not by name but simply as "an area where the economy had not been invigorated or managed well"—Deng refused to get off the train, telling provincial leaders who were waiting on the platform, "I'll come back to see you when you've improved the economy." When I visited Wuhan nine months later, local officials were still unwilling to reveal anything beyond the fact that Deng had stopped in the city en route to the south.

Deng's main destination was the city of Shenzhen, on the border with Hong Kong. Shenzhen symbolized Deng's vision of China's future. He had launched the founding of the city 12 years earlier by designating what had once been a backward cluster of villages as a "Special Economic Zone" (SEZ) permitted to conduct bolder experiments with economic reforms than the rest of the country. The transformation of Shenzhen from a fishing and agricultural community of 20,000 people in 1980 into a boomtown metropolis of more than 2 million people a mere decade later is one of the most astonishing examples of urban growth anywhere in the world. In the late 1960s, local officials used to order Shenzhen residents near the border to sing revolutionary songs as they went to work so their Hong Kong neighbors would be impressed by socialism. By the end of the 1980s, Shenzhen had no need for songs to impress people. In spite of its communist leadership, it had become a powerhouse of raw capitalism. The city owed its economic success to billions of U.S. dollars in investment from neighboring Hong Kong, whose manufacturing industry was being shackled by soaring labor and real estate costs and was desperate to move into China with its abundant supply of cheap labor and land. By the end of the 1980s, most Hong Kong manufacturers had moved across the border, either to Shenzhen, or as Shenzhen prices began to rise, further into Guangdong Province. Investors from Japan, Taiwan, South Korea, and Western countries flocked to the region too. Two other SEZs in the province—Zhuhai on the border with Macao and the port city of Shantou in the east—also prospered, as did the port of Xiamen in neighboring Fujian Province as well as the zone occupying the whole of Hainan Island, which was created in 1988. But none of the other four zones was as spectacular as Shenzhen, a fenced-off jungle of skyscrapers, industrial zones, leisure resorts, and, inevitably, sleazy clubs and bars.

Deng loved Shenzhen, and indeed the rest of Guangdong Province to which it belongs, not just for its rapidly increasing prosperity. It was to him a showcase of how economic reins could be loosened without unleashing chaos. Deng did not make this point explicitly in public, but reformists did in books inspired by his southern tour that were published in China that year. "When students in the north were rising up and making trouble around June 4th, 1989, the SEZs in the south were quiet, and watched what was going on in Beijing dispassionately," one book quoted a Chinese journalist as saying.[25] "A peasant told some students who wanted to stir up trouble [in the south], 'If you want to create a disturbance on the streets, that's your business, but don't think you'll get us to follow you. When you demonstrate, make sure you shout slogans saying long life to Deng Xiaoping. Every time you shout such a slogan, I'll give you 100 yuan [about 10 days' wages for the average factory worker at the time]. I'll work out the total on a calculator, and then I'll pay you in full, there'll be absolutely no debts. Because we peasants here have benefited from Deng Xiaoping's policies of reform and opening to the outside world. We've all got rich.' "

This was not entirely propaganda. Countless times during my trips to the south after 1989 Guangdong residents told me they were uninterested in politics. This might seem odd, given that people in Guangdong have better access than most other Chinese to information about China's political workings thanks to Hong Kong television and radio and frequent contacts with visitors from the British colony. Guangdong residents probably saw more of the 1989 bloodshed close up on Hong Kong television than many Beijing residents did in real life. Yet the province is more than 1,000 miles from Beijing, and many of its residents feel detached from the mainstream of Chinese political life. Protests did occur in the province in 1989. Thousands of students and teachers from Shenzhen University took to the streets, as did tens of thousands of their colleagues in Canton, but the demonstrations never matched the scale and intensity of those in northern cities.

The Deng camp's explanation for the lack of political fervor in Shenzhen was that the city's economy, though still significantly less developed than Hong Kong's, gave its inhabitants unparalleled opportunities to get rich and therefore reduced their demand for political change. In spite of the city's exposure to "bourgeois liberal" influences from Hong Kong, there was no sign of it becoming a hotbed of dissent. In the minds of Chinese reformers, Shenzhen proved that ideological relaxation did not necessarily pose a threat to communism. The city authorities did not tolerate open dissent, but they were far less enthusiastic than their northern counterparts about pursuing ideological campaigns.

Deng probably felt that support for his reforms was strongest in the south and that mobilizing provincial leaders from wealthy, fast-developing provinces like Guangdong would prove a good way to counter the influence of hard-liners in Beijing. Deng's reforms had given unprecedented economic power to the provinces, allowing them to keep more of their revenues, do business with the outside world without reference to Beijing, and spend their money far more freely. The hard-liners wanted Beijing to reassert tighter control, fearing that runaway growth in the provinces could fuel inflation and undermine the political power of leaders in the capital. They were worried about the ideological impact of massive foreign investment in the south and along the coast and experiments in Shenzhen and Shanghai with traditionally capitalist economic practices such as share trading. Without the support of provincial leaders, however, any attempt by Chen Yun's camp to reverse or slow down such changes would prove futile.

It was an open secret that Chen Yun disliked Shenzhen and the whole concept of SEZs. Since the first four zones were established in 1980, he conspicuously failed to endorse them by paying a visit, an omission of powerful symbolism given Chen's political stature and his involvement in economic policy making for much of his working life. It was widely rumored that Chen believed the SEZs were practicing capitalism. In public, this was denied. In 1990, Chen's wife, Yu Ruomu, insisted that her husband had not visited Shenzhen "because he is advanced in age, and it would be unsuitable for him to go on a long journey."[26] But she also insisted that "rumors that Chen Yun is seriously ill and has become a vegetable are not true. . . . He pays close attention to state and world affairs." Chen certainly was capable of visiting his birthplace, Shanghai, which, though half the distance of Shenzhen, is still some 700 miles from Beijing. He may not have been an enthusiastic traveler during the last few years of his life, but given the importance of the SEZs to Deng's economic strategy and Deng's own great enthusiasm for them, Chen's apparent indifference was glaringly obvious.

In 1992, a few months after Deng's trip to Shenzhen, Chen wrote an article mourning the death of his fellow conservative Li Xiannian. In it he noted pointedly that both he and the late former president had never visited any SEZs. "We maintained that if we want special zones, we must keep summing up experiences and make every effort to ensure they are operated properly," Chen said with obvious disdain.[27]

Shenzhen was thus the best site for a head-on confrontation with Chen Yun and his hard-line followers. It was Deng's second visit to the zone. The first trip was in 1984 at a time when Shenzhen was similarly facing growing criticism from hard-liners who disliked the city's freewheeling ways. During his first visit, Deng rebuffed his critics by writing a now oft-quoted inscription saying, "The development and experience of the Shenzhen SEZ prove that our policy of establishing such zones is correct." The visit helped to keep the experiment on track and pave the way later that year for the designation of 14 other ports as "open cities" enjoying trade and investment privileges only marginally less attractive than those of the SEZs. The decision not to call them SEZs as well appeared to be a token concession to Chen Yun.[28]

Deng's second visit began at nine o'clock in the morning of January 19th, 1992, when his train pulled into Shenzhen Railway Station. Railway workers placed a red-carpeted stepladder at the doorway of his carriage. Grinning city and provincial leaders shook hands with the patriarch after he had descended onto the platform. Deng, wearing a gray jacket and black trousers, smiled as the officials extended their greetings. "We've missed you a lot," said the provincial party secretary Xie Fei. "The people of Shenzhen have been awaiting your arrival. They've been looking forward to it for the last eight years!" said Zheng Liangyu, the city's mayor.[29] It was a poignant scene—the leaders of a city of Shenzhen's dynamism and international standing paying their respects to a retired, doddery 87-year-old upon whom they still relied to a significant degree for protection. By making his high-profile trip to Shenzhen, Deng was sending a clear signal that he had little faith in Jiang Zemin's ability to fight off Shenzhen's critics. But as events of the previous months had shown, Deng himself was no longer quite the strongman he used to be.

It was not until two days later that the outside world learned of what was going on just over the border from Hong Kong. The first report appeared in the *Ming Pao,* a Chinese-language newspaper in the British colony that is often the first to break stories about developments on the mainland. *Ming Pao*'s sketchy report said Deng had a busy schedule but appeared in good health and high spirits and showed no sign of fatigue during the first two days of his trip.[30] The newspaper also revealed that President Yang Shangkun had arrived in Shenzhen the day after Deng. This was clearly more than just a family outing.

On January 23rd, one day after *Ming Pao*'s scoop, communist-controlled newspapers in Hong Kong began running the story. "An informed source has disclosed that soon after New Year's Day, and with the Spring Festival approaching, the aged Deng Xiaoping toured southward and arrived in Shenzhen, bringing a rich flavor of spring to this new city of reform and opening up," gushed the *Wen Wei Po.*[31] The mainland media remained completely silent. Deng, however, clearly wanted as much publicity as possible. If he had not, he would have avoided visiting public places in Shenzhen where he could easily be spotted by overseas visitors.

It is likely that Deng's strategy was to use the foreign media to convey uncensored news of his trip back to the audience at home. With so many people in China listening to foreign radio stations, or, in the case of those living near Hong Kong, watching Hong Kong television, any foreign news report about his activities would become instantly known to tens of millions of people. The technique of using the foreign media to influence public opinion at home is a well-tested one in Chinese politics. The Chinese call the practice *chukou zhuan neixiao*—"exporting for the domestic market." Deng must have hoped that, faced with a barrage of foreign news reports about his activities, Chinese leaders would realize it was a waste of time trying to stop reports appearing in the domestic press. And the news once widely known would put pressure on the hard-liners either to toe the line or be exposed to ordinary Chinese, many of whom were still ignorant of the true nature of the struggle going on, as being opponents of Deng. Fortunately for Deng, his faction still had control over the Beijing-controlled press in Hong Kong. He was thus able to ensure that the most detailed initial reports about his trip appeared in what were effectively official newspapers, thus making it more politically palatable for mainland publications to reprint them.

Another reason why Deng might have been eager for media attention was his irritation with the "Mao Zedong craze" that was then sweeping the country. Official accounts suggested that Deng was worried that hard-liners were trying to exploit this phenomenon to build up mass support for a return to the old ways of communism.[32] As he walked around Shenzhen, Deng might well have seen evidence of this craze. One of the most visible manifestations of it was the practice of hanging a plastic laminated photograph of Mao on the inside of car, bus, or truck windscreens. This fad began in southern China where rumor had it that someone displaying a Mao portrait in his car had survived what would normally have been a fatal traffic accident. Within months, almost every other vehicle across the country had one. Mao posters—once a required adornment of every Chinese household—also made a comeback. Between 1989 and 1992, bookshops and street stalls sold an estimated 30 million such posters.[33] Many of them were used by peasants to decorate their homes during the Spring Festival, when there is a tradition of putting up pictures and calligraphy designed to bring good luck for the coming year.

Old Maoist songs, usually with a disco beat added to suit modern tastes, suddenly could be heard everywhere too—in trains, in taxis, and in bars and restaurants. By the end of 1991, more than a dozen cassette tapes of such songs were on the market, of which more than 10 million copies had been sold.[34] Remarkably, most of these songs dated from the Cultural Revolution era. Even bad memories of those days were not enough to curb the new fad. Mao's works and books about his life and philosophy benefited from this extraordinary revival. Between 1989 and 1991, hundreds of new Mao-related titles were published. Chinese readers snapped up millions of copies. According to one Chinese account, probably somewhat exaggerated but nonetheless indicative of the mood, Mao books became more sought after than novels about love or kung fu.[35] Old Mao badges, once compulsory wear during Mao's lifetime, became hot items for collectors. A few Chinese even began wearing them again. The Mao craze was a reflection of various anxieties, tensions, and superstitions prevalent in China. For some Chinese, it was a chance to indulge in nostalgia for what they saw as the relatively corruption-free days of Maoist rule. For others it was simply a bit of fun. By 1993, the craze had spread to cuisine, with new Mao-theme restaurants decorated with Mao memorabilia filling tables with customers lured by the novelty or eager to meet up with friends from the old days. One such restaurant in the capital had a noticeboard on which hundreds of patrons pinned their name cards. On them they wrote details of the labor teams they were assigned to in the remote northeast during the Cultural Revolution in the hopes of contacting long lost comrades.

To the extreme hard-liners, the Mao craze provided timely ammunition in the war against Deng. They saw in the public fascination for Mao an opportunity to mock Deng for his relative lack of popularity. In late 1991, the hard-line ideologue Deng Liqun said young people were developing an "intense interest" in Mao because they felt that the late leader was a resolute opponent of corruption.[36] "If our party failed to check corruption, overhaul and consolidate party organizations, and prevent cadres from abusing power for personal gain—or even allowed it to spread unchecked, how could the people be satisfied, and how could we prevent the people from thinking of the past?" Deng Liqun asked, hinting that Deng Xiaoping was failing to do his job. In November, Deng Liqun said in the national newspaper *Guangming Daily* that Chinese officials "should try to gain enlightenment from the development of the Mao Zedong craze," which he described as "a healthy, progressive, and promising phenomenon."[37] Deng Liqun said Mao was the first to warn against the danger of "peaceful evolution" and was "the only Marxist strategist" who predicted what would happen in Eastern Europe and the Soviet Union. So much, he seemed to be saying, for Deng Xiaoping.

Analyzing the reasons for Deng's trip to the south, a Beijing-controlled journal in Hong Kong noted that "some people were using Mao Zedong to oppose Deng Xiaoping and raise the ghost of leftism."[38] Chinese journalists I spoke to speculated that Deng felt personally slighted by the publicity surrounding Mao and wanted to counter it with a mini personality cult of his own. He may always have been a strong critic of personality cults but probably better, he felt, that he be the object of one than Mao, who represented so much of what he was trying to change in China.

The first hint of Deng's trip in a national newspaper did not appear until February 3rd in the English-language *China Daily,* more than two weeks after Deng arrived in Shenzhen. *China Daily*'s coverage consisted merely of a photograph of a smiling, gray-haired Deng and Yang Shangkun in Shenzhen's botanical gardens, together with a brief caption that gave no indication of when the photograph was taken. On the evening of the same day, Chinese television broadcast an 80-second clip of Deng Xiaoping mingling among guests at a Lunar New Year party in Shanghai filmed just a few hours earlier. It was Deng's first televised appearance since his trip to Shanghai in 1991. But the television report did not even mention Deng's tour of Shenzhen. Nor did it quote any of Deng's remarks beyond saying that he had extended his Spring Festival greetings to the people of Shanghai. To many Chinese viewers who already knew of Deng's trip from foreign radio broadcasts it looked bizarre indeed.

Four days later a Canton newspaper carried a brief report on the Shenzhen visit based on an article published by the Beijing-controlled *Ta Kung Pao* in Hong Kong.[39] But the national press ignored it. The floodgates did not burst until late March, when first a Shenzhen newspaper and finally national newspapers and television carried detailed original accounts of what Deng had said and done three months earlier.

Deng spent five days in Shenzhen before taking a boat with his family and entourage to Zhuhai on the other side of the Pearl River estuary next to the Portuguese enclave of Macao. There he met Qiao Shi, one of the six members of the Politburo's Standing Committee and the man responsible for overseeing domestic security, who had been chairing a conference in Zhuhai on security issues. At the conference, Qiao had delivered a strong message of support for Deng, arguing that the SEZs "should also be pacesetters in political reform" and that "Marxism should not be regarded as a doctrine."[40] Also in Zhuhai was the 75-year-old General Liu Huaqing, a vice chairman of the Central Military Commission who had accompanied Deng in Shenzhen as well. Yang Shangkun, who had left Deng in Shenzhen to make a side trip to Canton, rejoined the group in Zhuhai. It was a gathering of the key men needed by Deng to wage his battle against the conservatives.

Deng spent a week in Zhuhai before boarding his train again for Shanghai. En route to Shanghai he stopped for less than an hour in Canton where he addressed dozens of provincial and city officials at the railway station, telling them, in his old catchphrase, to engage in "less empty talk."[41] On February 21st, after three weeks in Shanghai, Deng abandoned his train and flew back to Beijing.

"The Deng whirlwind," as the Chinese media later dubbed Deng's travels, proved to be a pivotal point in the history of the reform era. Deng's supporters hoped it would be the political act that he would be remembered for after his death rather than the decision to order troops to open fire in 1989. Shuffling slowly round Shenzhen and Zhuhai, supported by one of his daughters—whose duty was to repeat every word said to him in a loud voice—Deng bore no resemblance to a whirlwind. Although the Beijing-controlled media in Hong Kong kept stressing how healthy Deng looked and how good his memory seemed, their reports suggested that he was sometimes more of an absentminded professor than a fiery politician. "It is said that in Xianhu botanical garden, when the city party committee leader asked Deng Xiaoping to stay a few more days in Shenzhen, Deng did not answer directly," reported the *Wen Wei Po*. "When Deng was taking a walk in the guest house, the city leader again invited him to visit Shenzhen another time, he still did not reply and seemed lost in thought. After taking a few steps, he turned around and said 'You should speed up your pace.'"[42]

But slow of movement and hard of hearing though Deng clearly was, he kept up a punishing schedule, touring parks, receiving briefings, visiting factories, and expounding his views in off-the-cuff homilies to those around him. Most of his remarks must have been enormously encouraging to the officials he met, but not all of his advice was heeded. During a visit to the Xianke Laser Company, a leading manufacturer of laser video and compact discs, the near deaf Deng expressed delight with a karaoke performance put on by company managers. "Very good. I could hear clearly. The sound effects are also good," he said.[43] But Deng had clearly been briefed on Guangdong's notoriety as a center of pirate compact disc production. "What about the copyright?" he asked. The company director, Ye Huaming, the son of a famous communist general who died during the civil war, assured Deng that copyrights were bought from foreign film companies according to international regulations. "Yes, you should do so. We must abide by the international rules on intellectual property rights," Deng replied.

Three years later, in February 1995, the Chinese authorities reluctantly closed the plant down after the United States alleged that it was flooding the region with pirated discs. The move, which China resisted for months, helped to avert trade sanctions that had been threatened by Washington in response to widespread copyright violations in China.

As he toured around, Deng was greeted by rapturous crowds. On a tour of one factory in Zhuhai, Deng is said to have shaken hands with more than 100 managers and workers.[44] On another occasion, Deng had to be restrained by his security officers from going up to shake hands with members of a crowd of thousands who had gathered outside a building he had been visiting. Deng got to within a few feet of the applauding throng, some of whom jumped up and down shouting, "How are you, Deng Xiaoping!" and "We wish you the best of health," before he was persuaded by the bodyguards to return to his car.[45]

In Shenzhen too, while touring a park in an open-sided electric buggy to look at reproductions of Chinese ethnic minority dwellings, Deng was surrounded by delighted sightseers, including groups from Hong Kong and Indonesia. Scenes such as these would have been unremarkable in most other countries. In China, however, spontaneous contact between top leaders and the masses is rare indeed, and public walkabouts by Deng Xiaoping himself are almost unheard of. In Shenzhen and Zhuhai, Deng played to the crowd like a Western politician. It was reminiscent of the way he pandered to his audience during his visit to the United States in January and February 1979 when the then deputy prime minister Deng donned a cowboy hat at a rodeo in Texas and then waved it to a cheering crowd. There was a good deal more to Deng's tour, however, than public relations and symbolism. Deng spoke bluntly to those he met about what he thought of the hard-liners. He criticized some well-known conservatives by name, jerking his open hand in small karatelike chops to emphasize his points while one of his daughters picked up every word on a miniature tape recorder. Deng even hinted at his displeasure with Jiang Zemin and Li Peng. "When you turn on the television, it's always those two people, it's really annoying," a Chinese source quoted Deng as saying. Deng did not name Jiang and Li, but it was obvious who he was talking about. According to the same source, Deng also praised Zhao Ziyang, the disgraced former party chief, saying he had done a good job with the economy.

Even the remarks by Deng that were released to the public, either through the Beijing-controlled press in Hong Kong or later through the mainland media, were hard-hitting enough. In Shenzhen, Deng warned that "whoever is opposed to reform must leave office."[46] In a clear rebuttal of his critics, Deng said the SEZs were "surnamed socialist."[47] He encouraged further experiments with stock markets, the first two of which had opened in Shenzhen and Shanghai in late 1990, even though "some people say that stock transactions are a capitalist practice." Deng attacked people who believed that encouraging foreign investment meant introducing capitalism. "So long as we keep level-headed, there is no cause for alarm," said Deng, describing those who held such views as lacking "basic knowledge."

But Deng's most famous remarks during his tour concerned the problem of "leftism." According to official accounts, Deng said some theorists and politicians—a reference to the hard-line camp—were trying to intimidate people by pinning political labels on them. He spoke of the "dire consequences" leftist tendencies had had on the party's history. China, he was quoted as saying, "should maintain vigilance against the right but primarily against the left." This statement, though echoing remarks he had made before in the 1980s, signaled a dramatic shift in the ideological line that had prevailed in China since Tiananmen. Deng said leftists believed that economic reform was the main potential cause of "peaceful evolution" in China. His reply was that "if we did not adhere to socialism, implement the policies of reform and opening to the outside world, develop the economy, and raise living standards, we would find ourselves in a blind alley. We should adhere to the basic line for a hundred years, with no vacillation. . . . Had it not been for the achievements of the reform and open policy, we could not have weathered June 4th. And if we had failed that test, there would have been chaos and civil war. . . . Why was it that our country could remain stable after the June 4th Incident? It was precisely because we had carried out the reform and the open policy." Deng said China should be "bolder than before in conducting reform" and "have the courage to experiment." The country should not, he said, "act like women with bound feet."

Deng also stressed the need for faster economic growth, saying he feared that China would be left behind while other parts of Asia surged ahead. "The economies of some of our neighboring countries are developing faster than ours," he warned. "If our economy stagnates or develops only slowly, the people will make comparisons and ask why." Deng called on Guangdong to catch up with Asia's "four little dragons"—Singapore, Hong Kong, Taiwan, and South Korea—within 20 years, not only in economic development but also in social order and public conduct. This was a resounding vote of confidence in Guangdong's potential, given that by 1992 Hong Kong's per capita income was close to surpassing Britain's.[48] At $600, Guangdong's per capita income was less than one-twentieth that of Hong Kong. But Guangdong officials later said they were confident that with 13 percent annual growth for the next 20 years they could do it and that some cities in the province would reach little dragon status in a mere 15 years. In the first half of 1992, Guangdong's growth rate certainly looked well on target. Deng's call was reminiscent of Mao's appeal in 1958 at the start of the Great Leap Forward for China to surpass Britain's economy within 15 years. But unlike Mao's target, Deng's looked achievable, at least in terms of economic growth—barring, that is, political or social upheaval.[49]

Deng was determined that his remarks avoid the fate suffered by Huangfu Ping's articles a year earlier. According to a Chinese source, Deng decided that this time his speeches in southern China should be compiled in the form of an official party document that would be circulated among members and thereby become, in effect, law. Deng decided to appoint the senior government advisor Zheng Bijian to carry out the task of listening to what the source described as "a big box of tapes" of Deng's remarks and distill them into a single coherent text. Zheng was a deputy director of the Chinese Academy of Social Sciences who had served as personal secretary to Hu Yaobang, the liberal former party chief whose death on April 15th, 1989, triggered the Tiananmen Square protests.

Zheng interpreted the tapes liberally. According to the source, Deng never actually uttered the most famous remark that was later attributed to him from his southern tour, namely, that China "should maintain vigilance against the right but primarily against the left." This was simply Zheng's distillation of the various attacks against leftism made by Deng during the trip. He included in the document the names of some of the leftists Deng had mentioned. These were Deng Liqun, Hu Qiaomu (another prominent ideologue and fellow member of the Central Advisory Commission), the head of the party's Propaganda Department Wang Renzhi, the acting minister of culture He Jingzhi, and Gao Di, the editor of the *People's Daily*. To name names in this way meant serious business in a country where veiled attacks are the norm.

Presented with such a document from the man who installed him, Jiang Zemin had little choice but to agree to distribute it within the party.

Several days before Deng returned to Beijing, Zheng Bijian's text of his remarks was already being circulated as the Central Committee's "Document Number 2." In the normal fashion of party documents, it was not for the eyes of the masses. Less than three weeks after Deng's return, however, the 15-member Politburo publicly declared its loyalty to the Deng line after a two-day meeting in Beijing.[50] News of the meeting was released a day later. It was a sign of the change of political mood that it was released at all. Normally Politburo meetings and their verdicts are kept secret.

It looked like Deng was at last getting his way. Newspapers that for months had been trumpeting the views of Deng's critics carried banner headlines saying the Politburo had agreed the party's main task was to prevent leftism. The Politburo's communiqué made no mention of Deng's tour of the south, but it echoed almost word for word the main points Deng had made. The party clearly was not yet willing to admit that Deng was pulling the strings from behind the scenes, but thanks to the Hong Kong and Western media most readers would have known that he was the man behind the Politburo's sudden, extraordinary display of reformist zeal. They also knew that the communiqué represented a major political about-face, given that had there not been serious opposition to Deng's reforms, there would have been no need to take the highly unusual step of announcing a Politburo decision to support them.

After the stifling political atmosphere that had prevailed since Tiananmen, many ordinary Chinese felt renewed hope for change. The more liberal official newspapers could hardly contain their excitement. The *Shenzhen Special Zone News* celebrated the Politburo decision by filling one-and-a-half of its four pages with photographs of Deng, an intended signal that this was a personal victory for the elder statesman.[51] But in spite of the Politburo's verdict and the new spirit of reform permeating the official media, the hard-liners continued to put up a spirited struggle.

The version of Document Number 2 containing the names of leading leftists was circulated only at the very top level. Before passing the document on to the lower ranks, the leadership excised the names in line with the party's policy of trying to project an image of unity. But rumors quickly spread. Many Chinese intellectuals waited anxiously to see whether those they saw as their worst oppressors would indeed step down in line with Deng's warning that "whoever is opposed to reform must leave office."

No longer able to use the mainstream official press to air their views, the hard-liners were forced to rely on a clutch of journals with very small readerships that had always been under conservative control. One of these, the bimonthly magazine *Contemporary Trends of Thought (Dangdai Sichao)*, carried a fierce condemnation of Deng's political strategy in an edition published on the day before Deng's return to Beijing. "People who stubbornly cling to their liberal beliefs are using antileftism as a pretext to oppose the Communist Party leadership and the socialist system and to vilify and attack Marxism and upright people who adhere to Marxism," the article said. "Unless we fight back against this particular kind of antileftism in a timely and resolute manner with force and reason, the result of course would be a disastrous proliferation of all kinds of anticommunist ideas. It would damage the country and harm the people. It would increase ideological confusion among party members and the masses. It should be said that such confusion is precisely the basic means by which hostile forces at home and abroad wage their struggles."[52]

The article suggested that China's main political danger was not from the left but from the right. It hinted that rightism was the chief cause of the collapse of communism in Eastern Europe and the Soviet Union. "There is still a serious problem with bourgeois liberalization in China," it said, arguing that it was therefore "extremely important" that any campaign against political deviation be correctly focused. Campaigning against leftist or rightist political deviation was just like steering a ship, it said—leaning the wrong way could cause the ship to capsize. It was abundantly obvious to any reader that the article was a rebuttal of Deng's reported pronouncement that China should mainly concentrate on opposing leftism.

The *People's Daily*—whose editor had been attacked by Deng— defiantly showed its support for the magazine's views by printing a large advertisement for *Contemporary Trends of Thought* on the day of its publication. Although the party newspaper did not dare oppose the new line openly, it displayed its misgivings by giving only halfhearted support to the reformist campaign. The *People's Daily* editorial on the day after the publication of the Politburo's communiqué simply repeated what the Politburo had decided, adding only a small comment of its own—namely, that China should strive to maintain political, social, and economic stability. Later in March, when the *Shenzhen Special Zone News* published the first full account to appear in a domestic newspaper of Deng's trip to the city, the *People's Daily* was a day later than all the other Beijing newspapers in reprinting it.[53] Behind the scenes, extreme hard-liners tried to limit the circulation of Document Number 2. Party members in organizations under the hard-liners' control complained they learned of the contents of the document considerably later than their colleagues in more liberal departments. By the time the National People's Congress began its annual two-week session on March 20th, the political atmosphere in Beijing was electric. A spokesperson for the congress told reporters the day before the session that Li Peng would not be holding his usual televised news conference at the end of the session—fueling speculation that a fierce struggle was under way.

Li's state-of-the-nation address on the following day indeed confirmed that in spite of the Politburo's decision, there was far from a consensus in the leadership. Although Li parroted many of Deng's phrases, such as the need for the liberation of ideas and faster and bolder reforms, he conspicuously failed to repeat Deng's slogan that the main danger came from the left. Instead, Li focused on the opposite tendency. He said China should be on its guard against any ideological trend toward bourgeois liberalization, which would have serious consequences if allowed to run rampant. His omission was as clear as the political signal the former party leader Zhao Ziyang had given on May 4th, 1989, when he failed to repeat Deng's assertion that the student protests amounted to "turmoil." Zhao's omission was one of the main "errors" that led to his dismissal. In 1992, Li must have known he was taking risks, but he also knew that unlike Zhao he had powerful backing from elders such as Chen Yun.

It was not just on ideological matters that Li appeared out of step with Deng. Over the economy too, there was clearly a difference of approach. Whereas Deng had reportedly called for a higher growth rate, Li set the growth target for 1992 at 6 percent, one percentage point lower than the rate the economy had actually grown the previous year and the same as the growth target he had set for 1991. A month earlier the *Wen Wei Po* had quoted Deng as saying during his tour of the south that "quicker economic growth conforms to the people's needs and the requirements of increasing overall national strength and improving the people's living standards."[54] Li and his supporters were paying no attention.

Li's obvious deviations from the Deng line sparked an unusual furor in the normally rubber-stamp parliament. Xinhua News Agency quoted a military delegate as saying that the 6 percent target "does not accord with the spirit of speeding up economic development."[55] The *Ta Kung Pao* in Hong Kong said delegates "responded sharply" to Li's failure to mention the problem of leftism.[56] By the standards of Chinese politics, these were sensational revelations. Never in the past had a prime minister's address been criticized so openly by the handpicked congress delegates. Near the end of the session, the congress presidium delivered what amounted to a public rebuke to Li by voting to insert a line about the dangers of leftism into his report. This was one of 150 revisions to his original text. The *Ta Kung Pao* quoted delegates as saying that Li's report was "much better" after these changes.[57]

Li would not have adopted such a stance in public without backing from conservative veterans and indeed from other members of the Politburo who would have seen copies of his speech in advance. In spite of their climb-down on the question of including a warning about leftism in Li's address, they still managed to resist any revision to the 6 percent growth target. On the day after the congress, the *People's Daily* published an editorial hailing its outcome, but it left out one important point. It failed to mention the danger of leftism. In a political culture that places great emphasis on word-for-word repetition of the latest party line, particularly by the party's main mouthpiece, this was a glaring omission. The battle was clearly still raging.

The tit-for-tat struggle between the two sides continued through the spring and summer, with the hard-liners gradually giving up ground to a pro-Deng faction buoyed by a tremendous upsurge of popular support. In late April, the reformist deputy prime minister Tian Jiyun delivered a hard-hitting speech at the Central Party School, the party's main ideological training ground for top-level officials. It was an unusual move for a man who normally keeps in the background, but on this occasion Tian showed no sign of reticence. He accused the hard-liners of opposing almost every aspect of Deng's economic reforms, from stock markets to the rural responsibility system under which the state allocates plots of land to peasants to farm for themselves in return for a contracted amount of produce. "As soon as we mention the contract responsibility system, they say it's negating collectivization; as soon as we mention attracting foreign investment, they say it's betraying the country; as soon as we mention the shareholding system, they say it's capitalism," said Tian.[58] He warned against members of what he called the "wind faction"— opportunists who "spring up when the wind rustles the grass" and attack the reforms. "If these members of the wind faction gain a lot of power, it would be a disaster for China," he said. According to the *Ta Kung Pao*, Tian described getting rid of leftism among senior officials as "a major task. If one does not dare to touch it and does not touch it, reform and opening up will just be empty talk. Without thoroughly settling this problem, it will be questionable how long reform and opening up will last."[59]

Tian also suggested tongue in cheek that a leftist "special zone" be established where extreme hard-liners could re-create life as it was under Chairman Mao in the 1950s and 60s—complete with rationing and food shortages. Chinese sources said Tian's joke was greeted with rapturous applause. Though not originally intended for public circulation, details of the deputy prime minister's speech quickly became widely known. In the new no-holds-barred commercial atmosphere generated by the reformist comeback, employees of the Central Party School even sold bootleg videos of Tian's speech to Beijing intellectuals.

In late May, Deng made another appearance, this time at the giant Capital Iron and Steel Works in Beijing's western suburbs. Unlike his tour of the south, the trip was not reported in the official media, and it was several days before news of it first reached the ears of the foreign press, even though the plant employs more than 200,000 people. It is not clear why there was so little publicity. Perhaps Deng felt he had got his basic message across and simply wanted to fine-tune some of the details, knowing that whatever he said would be transmitted within the party leadership in the form of secret memoranda. Chinese sources said that during his visit Deng went as far as to criticize Li Peng and Jiang Zemin by name. He also heaped praise on his protégé, Zhu Rongji.

The hard-liners, however, succeeded in making their views known too. In April, they managed to impose a ban on a book called *Historical Trends,* which was published by a group of liberal intellectuals. Some of the essays in the book gave details of leftist opposition to Deng since 1989 and attacked by name the *People's Daily* and other newspapers controlled by hard-liners. Although many members of Deng's camp would have enjoyed seeing the hard-liners criticized so forthrightly, Deng himself might not have approved. The book stepped well beyond the bounds of acceptable political etiquette by publicly undermining the credibility of the party's leading propaganda organs. It was one thing for Deng to attack the *People's Daily* editor in front of select officials but quite another for intellectuals to do so in a book for public consumption. The appearance of the book was a sign that Deng's economic reform campaign was encouraging at least some long silenced liberals to test the waters again. Hard-liners also succeeded in restricting the circulation of some other books published that year related to Deng's southern tour, banning them from major bookstores on the grounds that the authors included dissident intellectuals or the contents named too many names in their attacks on the conservatives. But the books still sold briskly at private bookstalls on the streets.[60]

On May 1st, Chen Yun himself made a startling televised appearance in Shanghai—his first in nearly three years. The 87-year-old Chen was quoted as saying that Shanghai leaders should accelerate the pace of reform and opening to the outside world, concentrate on and take bold steps to develop the city's economy, and emancipate their minds. These were thoroughly Dengist slogans, and although Chen stopped short of praising Deng himself and made no mention of SEZs or the dangers of leftism, it marked a belated concession. The following month, in his eulogy marking the death of Li Xiannian in which he noted that he and Li had failed to visit the zones, Chen accepted that "certain effective ways of doing things in the past are no longer practical under the current new situation, characterized by reform and opening up."[61] Chen was far from gushing in his praise for the new line, but these were signs of a shift.

Also in July, the *People's Daily* editor Gao Di published a signed article in his own newspaper expressing strong support for Deng's reforms and even for Deng's attacks against leftism. At one point, however, the lengthy essay appeared to criticize the vehemence of the assault against hard-liners. "The problem with an overwhelming majority of comrades with either 'leftist'[62] or rightist ideological concepts is one of understanding and, therefore, fundamentally one of study, education, summing up experiences, and heightening awareness," Gao said.[63] "Comrade Xiaoping pointed out that 'in correcting either "leftist" or rightist tendencies, we must not wantonly upgrade problems into problems of principle. Do not subject each individual to the test of self-examination and do not launch campaigns.' The current problem is one of being alert to rightism and mainly guarding against 'leftism,' not one of launching a struggle against 'leftism' or rightism and much less launching campaigns."

Gao was clearly infuriated by the way his name kept being mentioned by the foreign media as one of the targets of Deng's antileftist campaign. In August, he used the *People's Daily* once again to print a self-defense. This time it had a comment attached to it by the editor of the magazine *People's Forum,* which had also published Gao's earlier prore-form essay. The note said Gao had been accused by the Hong Kong and Taiwan media and "certain people at home" of changing his tune in order to fit the new political mood.[64] "The rumors will be utterly scotched by facts that speak louder than words," said the comment. "We must guard against scandalmongers but need not be too nervous about rumors, still less should we slow our pace because of them." Gao's decision to vent his anger against his critics in such a personal and public way was a thoroughly unusual move for a man in his position. In what appeared to be a frantic effort to shore up his political reputation, he was sealing his own fate by violating party discipline.

Gao and the other extreme hard-liners clung to their jobs for a few months longer. But in addition to political pressure from Deng, and the death in June of one of the key hard-liners, the former president Li Xiannian, the leftist camp suffered humiliation at the hands of party members and ordinary citizens. In June, central Communist Party departments held elections among their party members to choose delegates to the 14th Congress. Gao Di, Wang Renzhi, Xu Weicheng (one of Wang's hard-line deputies), and the influential Deng Liqun failed to get selected, even though the balloting offered little choice of candidates.

On the day after Gao Di's first proreform article appeared in the *People's Daily*, Li Peng made a significant about-face. At a meeting with prominent noncommunist personalities, Li said China was now trying to exceed the 6 percent growth target he had set at the National People's Congress. It was a needless statement since in the first five months of 1992 economic growth had already surged to 11 percent, spurred on by the loosening of the government's purse strings under the influence of Deng's call for faster and bolder reforms. But it was the start of an embarrassing political climb-down for the prime minister. In July, a government spokesperson said China was now aiming for a 10 percent increase in GNP for the year, and that it was considering revising the conservative Five-Year Plan, which was adopted the previous year, to adjust the growth target during the entire plan period from 6 percent annually to 9 or 10 percent. The spokesperson confirmed that this was Deng's idea.[65]

As final preparations got underway for the party congress in October, Deng appeared to reign almost unchallenged for the first time in three years. But in Chinese politics, wishful thinking and reality are often confused by both Chinese and foreign observers alike. Just as five years earlier, after the party's 13th Congress, Western observers had largely written off the party's extreme hard-line faction as a political force, so too there was a growing tendency in 1992 to believe that the hard-liners were once again completely defeated. It was certainly true that Deng was on the ascendancy, but it would take more than a few dismissals to root out the deep-rooted conservatism that permeates the party structure.

The 76-year-old economist Yu Guangyuan, a member of the Central Advisory Commission, lamented in an essay written in 1992 that, although the hard-liners had been forced to stop airing their views in the national media, "their ideological influence . . . remains. A point of view that has been so widespread for so long is not going to disappear all of a sudden of its own accord. The people who've expressed these kinds of views have given no explanation of what they now think. People have no idea whether they've given up these ideas or not."[66]

The power struggle that intensified in the buildup to the party congress proved that deep divisions existed in the Chinese Communist Party over fundamental policy issues and the direction the country should take in the 1990s and beyond. Ultimately, it would have been hard for Deng to lose once he had undertaken such a high-profile gambit as his trip to the south. But the price of his strategy was the undermining of the credibility of the younger generation of leaders, who were proved by his actions to be too weak on their own to do battle with the hard-liners.

The "Deng whirlwind" may have bruised Deng's critics, but it also seriously disrupted his own careful efforts to establish younger politicians as the real leaders of the country and ensure a smooth transfer of power after his death. The *Beijing Review* perhaps unwittingly acknowledged Jiang's lack of credibility in its edition previewing the 14th Congress, saying that "while holding no official post in the state or party structure, Deng Xiaoping is still the helmsman of the country."[67] The death of Chen Yun in April 1995 may have been something of a relief to the pro-Deng camp. Without him, there was no obvious figurehead to lead the conservatives. But it was unlikely to be a long lasting respite. With Deng's own health failing, the future looked uncertain for his supporters too.

4

Revolution and Its Price

The Northern Expedition at the beginning of this century was the joint overthrow of the rule of feudal warlords by the Communist Party and the Kuomintang. Now at the end of this century, a second Northern Expedition has been launched by the south's new economic model. The reform and opening are revolutionary and so is the second Northern Expedition.
— Nexus: China in Focus *(official journal), spring 1993*

Nineteen ninety-two was a year of almost revolutionary fervor. Beijing appeared to experience a dramatic mood swing with the sudden opening up of new horizons of opportunity after three years of political and economic gloom. Extreme hard-liners in the party kept battling behind the scenes to limit the practical and psychological impact of Deng Xiaoping's tour of the south, but most ordinary Chinese ignored the mutterings of the crusty old guard and welcomed the advent of what they saw as a new era of unashamed capitalism. Many thought they had nothing to lose. Deng had not specifically threatened mass closures of loss-making state industries. He had not said the virtually free housing that the state provided most city dwellers would be privatized nor that many more state employees would have to start paying significant sums of money for health care and education for the first time in their lives. When Deng had spoken of bold reforms and the liberation of ideas, he had referred mainly to encouraging foreign investment and capitalist mechanisms such as stock markets and pursuing high-speed growth. He did not warn the public that the reforms would also accelerate the disintegration of the socialist cocoon many Chinese city dwellers had been living in for more than 40 years.

The managers of many loss-making state enterprises began actively encouraging their workers to find a second job in the private sector. For years workers had been doing so illegally, for until Deng's tour it was ideologically unsafe to suggest that state-owned enterprises—the pillars of the socialist state—needed help from the private sector to keep their employees happy. Now many workers could legally earn money on the side—sometimes far more than they were earning before—while continuing to draw their state salary and to enjoy the housing and welfare benefits provided by the factory. Few wanted to give up their original jobs entirely because the only way to get virtually free housing and health care was to be allocated it by state employers. In mid-1992, the Beijing city government introduced new rules allowing factory and office workers employed by the state, whose full-time services were no longer required, to go on indefinite unpaid leave to work in the private sector. The city also simplified procedures for obtaining business licenses. The factories had little to lose. Many workers in state-run enterprises were showing up for work for just a few hours a week or, if they did turn up more regularly, were idling their time away playing cards or chatting.

"One of the achievements of Deng Xiaoping's 'be bolder in reform' remark . . . is that peddlers and moonlighters appear in more and more Beijing streets like mushrooms after a heavy rain," gushed Xinhua News Agency.[1] It was an apt simile. Beijing's sidewalks became cluttered with people repairing bicycles, mending shoes, cutting hair, or standing with dirty rags in hand trying to flag down passing motorists to offer a cheap car wash. Hundreds of new open-air markets opened up, where moonlighting state employees peddled everything from clothes and snacks to arts and crafts.

Dissidents were not celebrating. Between May and July 1992, the authorities arrested dozens of students, intellectuals, and workers for their involvement in several small underground prodemocracy groups that had formed in Beijing and other cities in the previous few months.[2] According to members of these groups with whom I and other journalists had occasional furtive contacts, the police had long been keeping an eye on them. But the authorities had apparently refrained hitherto from rounding them up in order to give themselves time to build up as detailed a picture as possible of who was involved. It was the government's biggest move against organized dissent since Tiananmen and a clear signal to dissidents that Deng, in spite of his call for bolder reforms, did not mean to tolerate antigovernment activities. The crackdown, however, was hardly noticed outside the small community of urban intellectuals who paid close attention to such issues. Those arrested were little known to the outside world. Most of them were young former students who had been unable to get good jobs after Tiananmen because of their involvement in the demonstrations. The disappearance of the dissidents made little impact on the euphoria generated by Deng's southern tour. Since 1989, many ordinary Chinese had become accustomed to occasional repressive measures and knew how to keep their heads down. Most appeared to regard joining underground political groups as both foolish and futile.

Urban Chinese, in their conversations with foreigners, often denied any interest in politics. While some intellectuals monitored the power struggles that ensued from Deng's tour, many ordinary citizens appeared far more preoccupied with making money. "After Deng Xiaoping paid his visit to the south, his tour became a popular subject. People talked about it," one well-educated office worker, who before 1992 had been pessimistic about China's future, told me in October that year. "It has had a strong impact on people's lives. People used to be dubious about the future, but after Deng's speech they became clearer and more open and bolder and bolder. People have got more chances to do business. They've got more money. They don't care about politics. They have been suffering a long time, they have to be very cautious about politics. . . . People are more concerned with making money. Prices are going up and up. They want their salaries to be raised to keep up, that's all they care about. They like Beijing now because it's more and more like Guangdong."

Deng's gambit seemed to be working. Giving people greater economic freedom while continuing to restrict their political freedom looked increasingly like an effective formula for progress. Deng also wanted to loosen the grip of extreme hard-liners over cultural and leisure activities so that people could enjoy themselves in an environment less suffused with political propaganda. Hard-liners, in traditional Maoist fashion, saw control over the arts as crucial to maintaining political control. In August 1992, however, Li Ruihuan, an outspoken protégé of Deng in the Politburo's Standing Committee, attacked this view, saying no artistic work should be banned unless it actually violated the law or constitution and accusing unnamed leaders of having a "distorted understanding" of the purposes of literature and art.[3] Before Deng's southern tour, Li, who held the culture and propaganda portfolio in the Politburo, had effectively ceded control to the extreme hard-liners. But in 1992 he was on the attack. In his August speech Li criticized "undue and excessive emphasis on labeling literary and art works as 'socialist' or 'capitalist'" and said there should be less stress on the propaganda role of such works. "We must," said Li, "emancipate our minds to promote a literary and artistic boom."

Two days after Li's speech, the Press and Publications Administration said it had lifted restrictions that banned pictures of women in bikinis from appearing on calendars. From the point of view of publishers, the timing of this announcement could not have been better. By the end of the year, almost every newsstand on the streets of Beijing was draped with calendars, many of them sporting color photographs of busty, scantily clad foreign women. Li's speech was also followed a few days later in Shanghai by the staging of what the local *Liberation Daily* described as "China's first X-rated play."[4] The production of Harold Pinter's *The Lover* played to a packed house night after night. Publicity materials warned that the play was not suitable for children. With its theme of extramarital relationships, and its onstage simulation of lovemaking—albeit behind a semiopaque screen—the play was indeed daring by Chinese standards. Its first performance in China had actually taken place early the previous year at Beijing's Central Academy of Drama, but then no members of the public were allowed in to watch it. The *China Daily* newspaper said at the time that the Theater of the Absurd, the genre to which *The Lover* belongs, was deemed too risqué by Chinese directors because of its recurring themes of futility and hopelessness—not themes encouraged by hard-line Ministry of Culture officials.[5] Such plays, said the newspaper, "would be sure to spark some debate if they were ever staged in China."

The Lover was not exactly entertainment for the masses. Only a few dozen people at most could fit inside the tiny theater in an old colonial-style house in Shanghai's French quarter. Many of them confessed to being baffled by the play's surrealism—the two protagonists playing both themselves and their fantasy selves. "It takes time for people to understand," the director, Chen Shaoze, told me after one performance, looking both proud and a little nervous about the publicity surrounding his production. "Two or three years ago, among some playgoers this kind of performance would have been unacceptable. But along with the reforms and opening up to the outside world, I think more and more playgoers will think this kind of play is very normal, and they'll be ready to accept it."

These were heady times too for filmgoers. In August, the authorities lifted a ban on two movies directed by the country's best-known and most controversial director, Zhang Yimou. The films, *Raise the Red Lantern* and *Ju Dou,* had both been nominated for Oscars in the previous two years but had angered hard-liners because of their veiled criticism of China's backwardness, autocracy, and conservatism. The hard-liners preferred stirring epics such as *The Story of Mao Zedong* and *Decisive Battles,* which had dominated China's movie screens since Tiananmen. Zhang Yimou's films were not exactly light entertainment either, but those who failed to appreciate their subtle political themes could at least enjoy the beauty of his girlfriend and lead actress Gong Li, whose physical attributes were something of a legend in China. In late August, the authorities gave his latest film, *The Story of Qiu Ju,* the rare honor of a premiere showing in the Great Hall of the People with top leaders in attendance. Officials expressed uncharacteristic delight when the film, which ridicules the arbitrariness of the Chinese legal system, won the top award at the Venice Film Festival in September.

That month I visited Shanghai's People's Park, where every Sunday morning dozens of residents gather in the open air to practice their English. For the foreign journalist, such gatherings provide a rare opportunity to publicly interview citizens—albeit just the better-educated ones—at random without too much fear of eavesdropping. When talking in English, anonymously, in a forum where the presence of a foreigner is not unusual, people often seem less inhibited than they might be in other public situations. This was clearly the reason why, a few weeks after Tiananmen, the Beijing city authorities banned a similar weekly gathering in one of the capital's parks that previously used to attract hundreds of people. At Shanghai's English Corner, I was surrounded that Sunday by young and middle-aged residents, many of whom were excited by the latest signs of a cultural thaw.

"Now our country is opening more and more to the outside," enthused one young man in English. "We should learn something from Western countries. These films have been banned in China for at least three years. Now they are released, we are very happy. Our government has changed its mind and relaxed its policy for culture." The official press even aired the highly sensitive topic of press freedom—a taboo subject since Tiananmen. In early September the *Liberation Daily,* the Shanghai newspaper that had fired the first abortive salvos against the hard-line camp in 1991, published a commentary written by an outspoken delegate to the National People's Congress, Qian Bocheng.[6] Qian's article called for laws guaranteeing freedom of the press. "If we really want to become an open China in the eyes of the world, then we must first have an open press," said Qian's startling article. "That means opening up the press. Journalists have the right to interview, the media have the right to report, and the public has the right to know," said the delegate, who had not addressed such a controversial issue in public since shortly before the 1989 unrest, when he defended the principle of privatization at the annual session of the congress.

Qian's appeal for press freedom was not taken up by the national media, but another local newspaper, the *Shanghai Legal News,* did try to test the waters. In an unprecedented move, the newspaper attempted to sue the judicial authorities in the central city of Nanyang in Henan Province after a Nanyang court expelled one of the newspaper's reporters from a public hearing, seized his journalist's identity card, and confiscated his camera and film. Court officials said the journalist had violated rules by taking a photograph in the courtroom. The newspaper said the law allowed journalists to do so. What made the case particularly unusual was that both the *Shanghai Legal News* and the court are both under the ultimate control of the Ministry of Justice, which was doubtless embarrassed by this open feuding between its employees. "The media have been in a very passive state," the *Shanghai Legal News*'s editor, Ji Anguo, told me. "When the rights of journalists are violated, there's been no law to turn to ... so this case [we're fighting] is significant for the perfection of a socialist press law. It is significant for the protection of rights of journalists to conduct interviews and for educating journalists to carry out their jobs responsibly." The courts never accepted the newspaper's petition, but the fact that it was filed at all was a sign that the political ice was beginning to crack.

Later in the year, the journal *Future and Development,* which has a relatively small circulation, went several steps further in testing the limits of official tolerance, publishing astonishingly bold appeals for greater democracy by two prominent liberal intellectuals who had been in political disfavor since Tiananmen. "It is necessary to carry out democracy in order to achieve genuine political stability and unity and not the other way around," wrote one of them, Yu Haocheng.[7] "A situation where 10 thousand horses are muted and neither crows nor sparrows can be heard actually carries the seed of immense danger. This kind of situation cannot be sustained for long, and who knows, one day 'thunder may be heard in the place of silence.'" The other intellectual, Xu Liangying, compared China's pursuit of high-speed economic growth without accompanying political liberalization with the policies of Nazi Germany.[8] Leaders across the political spectrum must have felt this was going too far. The government hastily ordered the withdrawal of the journal from newsstands and libraries and forced the editor in chief to write numerous self-criticisms.

The magazine refrained thereafter from straying into such sensitive political realms.[9]

Rock music too enjoyed a renaissance in the more open cultural climate. In September of that year, I stood in a sports stadium filled with thousands of people listening to a concert given by some of the country's most controversial rock singers, some of them rarely heard in public since 1989. The youthful audience roared with delight to hear their favorite bands again—the longhaired leather and denim-clad musicians whose outrageous appearance, thumping rhythms, and aggressive nonconformism epitomized everything the hard-liners loathed. The police were there in force too—hundreds of them—but the audience vented its frustrations with nothing more illegal than screams, applause, and dancing on the seats. This was the new China Deng's tour had created. In the cultural sphere, almost anything was now acceptable, as long as it was not explicitly antigovernment.

One official newspaper revealed in September 1992 that a troupe had been putting on dance shows for peasants in Guangdong Province involving nude female performers.[10] On the evening the newspaper's correspondent attended one of these displays, more than 300 peasants had paid up to 15 yuan each for seats—the equivalent of five or six days' income for the average farmer. "Everyone is talking about openness now, so why don't we all enjoy The Dance of Openness," the compère was quoted as saying. The newspaper was less enthusiastic, describing it as a "twisted and sickening" performance. "What is difficult to understand is that this troupe has been giving these naked shows for some time and not in secret," the journalist wrote. "Everyone around there knew about it but so far no action has been taken to investigate and punish them." It is not known what became of the troupe after the newspaper's exposé.

In Beijing, as in other cities, bars, restaurants, and karaoke clubs multiplied exponentially in 1992. By the end of the year there were some 240 karaoke halls in the capital, compared with fewer than 40 two years earlier.[11] Many of the new bars consisted of a small, dimly lit room filled with cigarette smoke and a few tables screened from each other to facilitate intimate conversation between patrons and prostitutes. In a city of cramped apartments often shared by three generations of one family and with little of interest on television or at the cinema, these seedy new establishments provided welcome entertainment and escape for those who could afford it. The karaoke craze spread across the country, even into the more remote and backward areas. In Xining, the dismal capital of Qinghai Province on the edge of the Tibetan plateau famed for its prison camps, outdoor karaoke stalls became the rage. "This summer, numerous outdoor karaoke centers have popped up in Xining . . . which has turned the highland city into a singing Shangrila," said Xinhua News Agency.[12] "Outdoor playing has turned karaoke into a cheap recreation for the majority of low-income locals. Currently 42 open karaoke stands have sprung up along the city's 1,000-meter long main street attracting a large number of young karaoke fans, which adds a spectacular scene to the summer nights. Even in the normally calm outskirts, outdoor karaoke-goers have also found ideal places to entertain themselves by showing their own singing skill."

There were dark clouds on the horizon, but they still appeared very distant. As the economy boomed, credit controls slackened and spending by local governments and urban residents soared. The specter of inflation loomed again for the first time since the months preceding the Tiananmen Square protests, when the easing of price controls on some goods had prompted panic buying and a run on banks. The government appeared confident, however, that this time it had the situation under control and that inflation—running at about 10 percent in China's main cities by the end of 1992—would not lead to a repeat of the 1989 upheaval, which had been fueled in part by anger over price increases. So confident were the authorities in Beijing that twice in 1992 they took major steps to end decades-old controls on the cost of key foodstuffs in the capital. In April, the city government allowed retail prices of rice and flour to rise by more than 40 percent. In December, it completely removed controls on the prices of eggs, vegetables, and meat, prompting hikes of up to 30 percent. Some Beijing residents grumbled in private, but there was little sign of panic.

The pro-Deng camp thus had much to be proud of as nearly 2,000 delegates gathered on October 12th, 1992, in the Great Hall of the People for the opening session of the 14th Congress, the biggest party gathering in five years, and the event that Deng clearly hoped would set his reforms in concrete for eternity. Beijing greeted the occasion with typical communist fanfare. The authorities arranged millions of potted plants in multicolored clusters on street corners and pavements. Thousands of people flocked to Tiananmen Square to have their photographs taken in front of massive floral displays laid across the vast plaza. One of these took the form of a giant slogan saying, "The party's basic line will remain unchanged for a hundred years"—one of Deng's quotations from his southern tour. Red banners were draped down the sides of buildings and across streets with slogans hailing the convening of the congress. Plainclothes police patrolled in conspicuous force around Tiananmen and stepped up their surveillance of the small dissident community. It was a routine precaution. There was no sign of imminent trouble.

Just up the street from Tiananmen Square, Deng's own face—or at least an artist's rendition of it—beamed down on passersby from a recently erected billboard advertising a new film about his southern tour. Deng, who after coming to power had been so quick to remove public portraits of Mao and condemn the display of pictures of current leaders, apparently tolerated this particular aberration. Appropriately, the billboard faced a newly opened branch of McDonald's on the other side of the street, the fast-food chain's flagship outlet in the People's Republic and one of the most conspicuous symbols of China's increasingly liberal economic climate.[13]

The six-day party congress looked on the surface like a resounding victory for Deng. Jiang Zemin opened the meeting with a speech hailing Deng as the "chief architect" of China's reforms and modernization who had displayed "enormous political courage" in the blazing of new trails for the building of socialism. Much of his nearly two-hour speech echoed word for word what Deng had said in southern China, preventing leftism and all. For the first time in such a forum, the party leader called for the establishment of a "socialist market economy," which he described as "a long and difficult task of social engineering" requiring "sustained effort, a sense of urgency, and a firm direction."

Talk of setting up a market economy had been virtually taboo in China until Deng's tour, after which the term had become highly fashionable, though usually with the face-saving word "socialist" attached to it. It was not until 1980 that the party sanctioned even the limited application of market forces. Two years later at the 12th Congress, it formally decreed that central planning should continue as "the mainstay," with market forces acting only as "a supplement." In 1984, the party decided it should be a "planned commodity economy" with an undefined mix of both central planning and market forces. Now the word "planning" was being dropped from the description altogether. This was a clear rebuff to Chen Yun who had insisted, not long after Deng consolidated his grip on power in 1978, that "the planned economy should be the mainstay of socialism, with regulation by market forces playing a subsidiary role."[14] The *Ta Kung Pao* noted pointedly that the planning as "mainstay" formula adopted in 1982 was "in keeping with Chen Yun's line."[15]

Some Chinese economists quoted by the official media in the buildup to the 14th Congress said the word "socialist" should be dropped as well and that China should simply declare the establishment of a "market economy" as its goal.[16] But although Deng himself had never used the term "socialist market economy," most of his supporters were willing to put up with the phrase to placate the hard-liners, who were unhappy enough as it was. Three days before the start of the congress, the official *China Daily* newspaper quoted a senior government advisor as saying that "resistance to the socialist market economy should not be underestimated."[17] The newspaper predicted that during the congress "some who do not have the heart to see a planned economy discarded will continue to argue that adopting a socialist market economy will shake up socialist public ownership." But, the article said, "this is not expected to be the tone of the congress."

Jiang was careful to pay lip service to the traditional tenets of Chinese communist economic policy. In line with Deng's remarks in the south, he said in his speech that "public ownership," including collective ownership, would still remain the "dominant" feature of the Chinese economy. But this description was so vague as to be almost completely meaningless. Many "collective" enterprises are in fact disguised private enterprises that assume the name "collective" for the sake of reducing the risks of being engaged in private enterprise, such as, difficulty in obtaining bank loans and ideological campaigns by hard-liners. Many Chinese economists would have argued that at the time of Jiang's speech, the non-private sector controlled only half, if not less, of the national economy. Deng himself had hinted during his tour that he did not really regard the predominance of public ownership—whatever that actually meant—as crucial. "There is no need to be afraid of them," he said, referring to foreign-owned enterprises in China.[18] "So long as we keep levelheaded there is no cause for alarm. We have our advantages: we have the large- and medium-size state-owned enterprises and the rural enterprises." But Deng added a highly significant point. "More important," he said, "political power is in our hands." In other words, maintaining Communist Party rule was more important than worrying about the proportion of public ownership. This was the essence of Deng's philosophy. Party control mattered to him more than how control was exercised.

To Deng's supporters, one of the most important tasks of the congress was to revise the party constitution in order to make it reflect Deng's latest thinking on reform. The existing charter made no mention of Deng's policies, stating only that the party should uphold "Marxism-Leninism and Mao Zedong Thought." It did not even mention the concept of "reform and opening to the outside world." Changing the constitution to include Deng's thinking would make it more difficult for those who survived him to change his policies after his death. In line with Deng's wishes not to become the object of a personality cult, the congress kept Deng's name out of the revised version. But it filled the new constitution with Dengisms, including the principle that "while keeping vigilance against rightist deviation, attention mainly should be paid to guarding against 'leftist' deviation." This marked a significant change from previous versions of the constitution, which said, more neutrally, that the party should "oppose all erroneous deviations, whether 'left' or right." The new charter also dropped some of the Maoist rhetoric of earlier versions, such as the term "proletarian internationalism" and the statement that "the socialist system is incomparably superior to the capitalist system." It also changed the wording of the original assertion that "the course of world history during the past half century and more, and especially the establishment and development of the socialist system in a number of countries, has borne out the correctness of the theory of scientific socialism." Taking account of the almost complete collapse of communist rule elsewhere, the revised constitution said instead, without elaborating, that "the history of more than a century since the publication of the 'Communist Manifesto' proves the correctness of the theory on scientific socialism and the strong vitality of socialism." It sheepishly dropped the reference to other countries.

In the appointment of personnel during the congress and at the Central Committee meeting held immediately afterward,[19] Deng by and large got his way too. Several influential hard-liners were dropped from the Central Committee, including the *People's Daily* editor, Gao Di; the acting minister of culture, He Jingzhi; the head of the party's Propaganda Department, Wang Renzhi; and the former minister of education, He Dongchang—all of whom had been criticized by Deng early in the year. The Central Advisory Commission headed by Chen Yun was abolished, and contrary to widespread rumor in the buildup to the congress there was no attempt to set up a less formal body to replace it. Several hard-liners were removed from the Politburo, including Song Ping, Li Ximing, and Yao Yilin, while Deng's protégé Zhu Rongji was promoted to the Politburo's Standing Committee.

It was not a complete victory for Deng, bearing in mind the advice he gave to leaders during Tiananmen that "after the disturbances are put down" the leadership should take on an "entirely new look" with the most important consideration being that its members "should be perceived as reformers."[20] The hard-line prime minister, Li Peng, kept his seat on the now seven-member Politburo Standing Committee. But he was heavily outnumbered by Deng's supporters.

Any hope, however, that political victims of Tiananmen might resume top leadership positions were dashed that October. At a Central Committee meeting held shortly before the congress,[21] the party announced that it had completed investigations into the case of Zhao Ziyang and that the accusations made against him at the time of his dismissal in June 1989 were correct. During the congress, two radical reformists, Rui Xingwen and Yan Mingfu, who were stripped of their posts after the 1989 bloodshed, lost their seats on the Central Committee. The former Politburo Standing Committee member Hu Qili, who was also dismissed for allegedly supporting the student demonstrators, kept his Central Committee seat. But rumors in the buildup to the congress that Hu might be promoted to higher office proved unfounded. Rui, Yan, and Hu had all been partially rehabilitated in mid-1991, apparently because of their willingness to confess the error of their ways during Tiananmen. Hu had been appointed deputy minister of machine-building and electronics, Yan to the post of deputy minister of civil affairs, and Rui as deputy minister of the State Planning Commission. But developments of that month confirmed there was no chance of a full-scale comeback by any top politician purged after Tiananmen—especially Zhao—during Deng's lifetime.

In the weeks that followed, Deng's supporters pressed their advantage, forcing hard-liners to surrender control of key posts in culture and propaganda to more moderate figures. In early December, it was announced that Gao Di had been replaced as director of the *People's Daily* by the editor in chief, Major General Shao Huaze. It was also revealed that the head of the party's Propaganda Department, Wang Renzhi, had been succeeded by Ding Guan'gen, a liberal protégé of Deng Xiaoping. Later in the month, an official newspaper reported that Liu Zhongde, who had acted as press spokesperson for the 14th Congress, had taken over from He Jingzhi as head of the Ministry of Culture. None of these appointments, however, were followed by major purges of these bastions of conservatism. Perhaps Deng and his supporters felt that as the economy boomed, ideological and propaganda organs would naturally lose their importance and that it was therefore not worth risking a major political confrontation by pursuing their enemies too vigorously. Many Chinese observers believed that Deng did not want to rid the party entirely of leftists as this would give too free a rein to radical reformers.

The 14th Congress looked in some ways like a repeat of the previous congress in 1987, when the world declared an end to extreme hard-liners, only to find them still deeply entrenched, albeit in less conspicuous positions, in the party and government hierarchy.

In spite of all the leadership's efforts to project an image of openness and confidence during the congress, it revealed its continuing insecurity when, after the postcongress plenum, foreign journalists were invited to meet the new members of the Politburo Standing Committee in the Great Hall of the People. The exercise was in stunning contrast to a similar meet-the-press session after the 13th Congress, when a radiant Zhao raised glasses with some of the reporters and confidently and sometimes wittily answered their questions as he circulated around the throng of several hundred cameramen and correspondents, separated from them by a rope. This time, there were no cocktails. The seven Standing Committee members walked into the room, stood in line for photographs, were briefly introduced by Jiang Zemin, then walked out, ignoring the questions being shouted after them. The entire proceedings took five minutes. The leadership apparently did not want Jiang and Li Peng to face sensitive questions about that year's struggles.

Amid the jubilation in China and abroad over the dismissal of hard-liners, the ringing endorsement of Deng's policies, and the promotion of reformers such as Zhu Rongji, it was easy to overlook the congress's failure to reassure the country and the outside world that the post-Deng succession would be a smooth one. The meeting and the subsequent Central Committee plenum did little to reinforce Jiang's image as a man of authority in his own right. In theory, Jiang should have been the focus of the official media's attention during the congress, which was the most important party gathering since he took office in 1989. Jiang's predecessor Zhao Ziyang, after all, had put his stamp on the 13th Congress in 1987, which took place just a few months after he had been promoted to the party leadership. In practice, however, it was Deng who, in spite of his retirement and obvious frailty, dominated the 14th Congress proceedings, and delegates repeated his words from a few months earlier like mantras. According to official reports, Deng kept a close eye on the meeting from his home, assiduously reading reports and watching live television coverage. Deng reportedly clapped as he sat watching Jiang's opening address. "He's spoken well," Deng was quoted as saying. "I must applaud this speech."[22]

During the congress, the *People's Daily*—newly converted to the Deng cause—heaped praise on Deng, describing his theories as the party's "mightiest magic weapon."[23] It said the endorsement of Deng's policies by the congress was an event of equal significance to the party's decision at a congress in 1945 to make Mao Zedong Thought its guiding philosophy.[24] The Chinese people, it said, were fortunate to have the Communist Party and Mao Zedong Thought. "Now, with the unstable world situation and the difficulties and setbacks faced by socialism, the Chinese people are even luckier because we have the guidance of Comrade Deng Xiaoping's theory," said the lengthy front-page commentary.

As if to stress the point that this was his occasion, not Jiang's—the man for whose sake he had retired in the first place—Deng himself shuffled into the Great Hall of the People on the day after the congress to greet the delegates and members of the new Central Committee that had just convened. Chinese television showed Deng—in what the announcer described as "high spirits"—shaking hands with some of them to rapturous applause. It was Deng's first televised appearance since the southern tour. He walked sometimes unaided, sometimes with one of his daughters supporting his arm. The report quoted Deng as telling Jiang that the congress had been a great success—not surprisingly, perhaps, given that Deng had effectively written the script.

Personnel arrangements added to the uncertainty surrounding the succession plans. For years it had been widely expected by observers that President Yang Shangkun would be the kingmaker after Deng's death, keeping the army in line and making sure that Jiang adhered to Deng's policies. Yang, it was generally assumed, would be aided in this task by his younger half-brother Yang Baibing, who was then head of the military's General Political Department and secretary general of the Central Military Commission. But to the surprise of many observers, both men virtually disappeared from the political stage after the congress. Their fate demonstrated once again the outside world's sheer incomprehension of the forces at work in Chinese politics.

It was no surprise that the 85-year-old President Yang should lose his Politburo seat and, come the following year's annual session of the National People's Congress, his post as president too. This was in line with Deng's stated goal of promoting younger leaders to top positions. But eyebrows were raised when Yang not only lost these two jobs, but also the key post of first vice chairman of the Central Military Commission. Equally surprising was the removal of Yang Baibing, then 72, from his post as the commission's secretary general. The younger Yang gained a seat on the Politburo, but in November the Beijing-controlled press in Hong Kong confirmed that he had been removed from his concurrent post as head of the military's General Political Department. The younger Yang, it appeared, had been kicked upstairs.

But it was not until some weeks after the congress that the full significance of the Yangs' political demise became clear. It was not just the two men who had been sidelined. Within the armed forces, a full-scale purge of senior officers who supported them was launched. The first confirmation of the extent of the purge appeared in the Beijing-controlled *Wen Wei Po* in Hong Kong, which reported in December that the reshuffle of senior military officials "involved the biggest scale, the most personnel and the widest range" since 1949.[25] The newspaper did not give specific reasons for the changes but said the main purpose was "to ensure that the army will remain unanimous with the Chinese Communist Party Central Committee ideologically, in action and politically, to enhance its consciousness and resoluteness in implementing the party's basic line and to blaze a new trail in the army." Western diplomats said they believed that as many as 300 senior officers were sacked or demoted, mainly because of their connections with Yang Baibing.

It had long been rumored that the influence of the two Yangs—both of whose backgrounds are as political commissars rather than as fighting soldiers—was resented by many military officers. Since his appointment as head of the General Political Department in 1989, Yang Baibing is believed to have promoted many officers on the basis of loyalty to himself rather than professional competence. But this did not explain the suddenness of the Yangs' fall and the extent of the purge that followed. In the weeks after the congress, unconfirmed reports began to emerge that Yang Baibing had offended Deng by addressing officers about preparations for Deng's death without getting the elder statesman's clearance in advance. It was also rumored that Yang Baibing had attempted to pin the blame for the June 4th, 1989, bloodshed on Deng. According to this version, opponents of the Yang brothers used this as a pretext to persuade Deng to get rid of them. Even though he remained a member of the Politburo, Yang Baibing dropped almost entirely out of sight. The elder Yang, however, remained active behind the scenes and, as Deng's health deteriorated, began taking part in public activities. By 1994, some diplomats in Beijing were expressing the belief that Yang Shangkun—despite his lack of any formal positions—was once again a possible key player in Chinese politics after Deng's death. But it remained uncertain whether he would give his backing to Jiang Zemin, who succeeded him as president.

Not only were there question marks over the succession issue after the congress, but it was also far from clear how the party planned to proceed with the bold economic reforms it had been so stridently calling for. Although the congress embraced some radical terminology, it gave little indication of how the party planned to tackle such problems as inflation and the huge losses suffered by state-run industries. But to many ordinary Chinese, it was the mood of the congress that counted, not any specific policy announcements, and the mood was definitely encouraging for those trying their hands at capitalism. "Now we should no longer evade the use of the four characters meaning market economy, nor should we be afraid of being criticized for 'taking the capitalist road,'" one official account summarized reform-minded economists as saying at a "lively" meeting that year.[26]

It appeared to the outside world that, compared with its negative aspects, the successes of economic reform were so colossal that overall public support would ultimately ensure a successful transition to a market economy, even if there were occasional setbacks and disturbances along the way. Compared with the seemingly disastrous rush toward free market capitalism under way in the former Soviet Union and Eastern Europe, China appeared to have found the right formula by adopting a more cautious approach to the most sensitive aspects of reform while giving free reign to individual initiative. Foreign investors could hardly get enough of China's new "socialist market economy." Wary of crumbling ex-communist economies elsewhere, they poured into China in record numbers in 1992, signing contracts worth nearly $60 billion, twice the figure for the previous year.[27] "Go gold-rush [sic]," were the words used by Zhu Rongji to encourage foreign investors to profit from China's boom.[28] The words were apt. China was indeed becoming in many ways a vast, chaotic Klondike.

In his speech to the congress, Jiang Zemin said a "new revolution" was underway aimed at "fundamentally changing the economic structure." The term "new revolution" had been used before by Chinese officials to describe the reforms launched by Deng in the late 1970s, but after Deng's southern tour the phrase appeared with unusual frequency in the official press in contexts that implied it was only in 1992 that this "new revolution" really began. "The establishment of the socialist market economy structure is a great pioneering cause unprecedented in human history, a new revolution of self-perfection and self-development and a strategic move to resolve fundamentally various deep-rooted contradictions in China's economic sphere," said the *Liberation Army Daily* in a typical commentary.[29]

But China's economic revolution had its price. Although few observers paid much attention in 1992, it was apparent that China's explosive economic growth was also expanding the ranks of the disappointed and disillusioned, particularly among peasants and workers in state enterprises whose voices are rarely heard because they have little contact with the media. "Revolution is not the same as inviting people over for a meal or writing an essay or painting a picture or embroidering a flower . . . ," Mao Zedong once said. "A revolution is an uprising, an act of violence whereby one class overthrows the authority of another."[30] Deng certainly did not have violence in mind when he launched his "new revolution." But nor was it just a simple matter of giving the green light to capitalism. Deng was attacking the very foundations of China's economic structure, hoping thereby to unleash the pent-up entrepreneurial energy of hundreds of millions of people. But in the process, many would be hurt by the falling debris of the old order.

The city of Wuhan, where Deng reportedly spoke curtly to local officials during a brief stopover on his way to the south, epitomized the old order. Given its superb location on the banks of the Yangtze and China's main north-south railway line, it should have been doing far better. Typical of China's centers of state-owned heavy industry, however, Wuhan—famed for its iron and steel and vehicle production—was slow to learn the fast-paced entrepreneurial ways of the coast. One of its other important industries, textile manufacturing, largely relied on antiquated machinery, some of it abandoned by British businesses when they left Wuhan around the time of the communist takeover. By 1992, most of the city's textile plants were operating at a loss. If Shanghai looked backward and dowdy compared with booming Canton, Wuhan looked even worse. Big cities all along the Yangtze River, in fact, from Nanjing in the east to Chongqing in the upper reaches, were lagging far behind the coastal boomtowns.

During his southern tour, Deng said one of his greatest mistakes was not to have designated Shanghai as a SEZ at the same time as Shenzhen in 1980.[31] Had he done so, he said, the entire Yangtze River basin, and indeed the whole country's economy, would have looked very different. Inspired by Deng's words, the Chinese leadership came up with a blueprint for invigorating the economy of the 1,000-mile-long Yangtze River basin between Shanghai and Chongqing—an area about the size of Germany but containing more than twice Germany's population. In June 1992, Prime Minister Li Peng declared that Shanghai would be the "dragon's head," stimulating development along the serpentine body of the river. Cities upriver would be granted tax and other incentives for foreign investors similar to those enjoyed by the 14 open coastal cities and the five SEZs. The centerpiece of the plan would be Pudong, a colossal development project launched in 1990 and covering 130 square miles of semirural eastern Shanghai, which officials hoped would restore the city's pre-1949 status as a financial and commercial powerhouse of the Pacific Rim—"the Manhattan of China" as Deng described it during his southern tour. Although the Pudong project had been under way for more than a year by the time of Deng's trip, it was not until 1992 that foreign investors really began to take notice.

In the first eight months of that year, overseas investment in Shanghai amounted to nearly $2 billion, equal to the total of the previous 12 years. About half of the new investment poured into the Pudong area, turning it into a forest of cranes as new factories and office buildings sprouted alongside the disappearing remnants of ancient villages. Officials told me in September of that year that more than 1 million peasants would have to leave their homes within the next 20 years to make way for the new showcase. This figure was comparable to the number of people who would have to move out of the Three Gorges area of the Upper Yangtze to make way for the construction of a colossal hydroelectric dam there, a project that was finally approved after years of controversy in April 1992. One official report said some peasants in Pudong had staged demonstrations in protest against the relocation plans.[32] But they, like their counterparts up the Yangtze, were powerless to stop the juggernaut of development.

Five hundred miles inland, Wuhan was beginning to get a new lease on life. The vision of a mighty, modernized Shanghai emerging as a Hong Kong–style service center for a prospering Yangtze basin with Wuhan as its transportation hub and industrial powerhouse was an alluring one for many foreign investors. Unlike Guangdong, where massive investment over the years from neighboring Hong Kong and elsewhere in the world had pushed up the prices of labor and property, Wuhan was still virgin territory where prices were low, officials less canny, and big money could be made, especially if the Shanghai dream were to come true. With Deng's cajoling fresh in their minds, Wuhan officials began going all out to woo business. By the end of 1992 the city had signed contracts worth around $1 billion with foreign investors, more than three times the value of total contracted investment during the previous eight years. Although in China the actual amount of foreign investment is usually considerably less than the contracted figure, Wuhan was clearly making significant progress. In the same period, the city approved the establishment of more than 400 foreign-funded enterprises, twice as many as the number approved since 1984. Less than halfway into the following year, Wuhan had already attracted as much investment as it had in the whole of 1992.

The jewel in Wuhan's crown was a deal with Hong Kong's Wharf Group to build a multibillion-dollar container port on the edge of the city, which would turn Wuhan into central China's main entrepôt, taking in industrial goods from the Yangtze basin and shipping them downriver to Shanghai or by rail to Hong Kong. Wharf envisaged a new satellite town forming around this port, with hotels, residential blocks, and an industrial zone.[33] The official media gushed about Wuhan's resurgence as an "oriental Chicago." In 1993, Hong Kong's New World Development Co. Ltd. announced plans to invest a staggering $5.3 billion over the next five years in Wuhan, mostly in power, roads, bridges, and a new airport. The city had never had it so good.

But the money pouring in did not necessarily make life any easier for workers at the city's 4,000 state-owned factories. As often when reporting on China, it was only by chance that I learned of the complaints of these workers about the revolutionary changes underway in their city. So dazzling were the statistics and so efficient were the authorities at keeping dissent out of the public eye that it would have been easy to visit the city and notice nothing amiss at all.

I traveled to Wuhan in September 1992 to visit a large state-owned textile dyeing and printing mill that had sold a majority stake to a Hong Kong firm, the first state-owned factory of its size in Wuhan to cede control to a private company, let alone to a foreign one. It was the first publicized sale of its kind, in fact, anywhere in China outside the SEZs. For the Wuhan government's Textile Bureau, this was a daring attempt to rescue the industry, the kind of step that hard-liners would certainly have blocked before Deng's tour of the south. Privatization remains a politically sensitive word in China, and Wuhan officials I met steadfastly refused to use it to describe what had happened in the case of the Wuhan Number 2 Printing and Dyeing Mill. But privatization it was.

When the Hong Kong company Citiford bought 51 percent of the mill's shares in April, the factory was close to insolvency, with debts of some $15 million, only about $1 million less than the official value of its assets. Part of its "assets," however, consisted of stockpiles of printed textiles of such poor quality that the material was probably unsellable. In effect, the mill was bankrupt.

The head of the Wuhan Textile Bureau, Ling Shouqing, told me he first made contact with Hong Kong's Citiford in 1991 at an exhibition in Shenzhen. Ling enticed Citiford's manager, the 31-year-old Albert Wong, to visit Wuhan to take a look at the factory. "Wong came to Wuhan four times," Ling said. "He was very thorough. We welcomed him because we wanted a way out." So eager indeed was Ling for a way out that he offered Wong what looked like giveaway terms. The Textile Bureau would remain responsible for all of the factory's debts, while Wong could run the mill any way he liked and dismiss as many workers as he wanted. The Textile Bureau would pay for and arrange the resettlement of any workers Wong did not want. Wong replied that he wanted a 51 percent stake. Ling said he agreed immediately. Wong told me later, however, that the city government only approved giving control of the mill to Citiford after Deng's southern tour.

The deal nearly came unstuck over the question of how much the mill's fixed capital was worth. The city government told the Textile Bureau it had to be valued at $7.8 million. Wong balked at the idea of paying the Textile Bureau 51 percent of this sum for a factory consisting of outdated machinery and a slack, inefficient, and demoralized workforce. "For more than 20 days he gave us no reply," said Ling. "Work at the Number 2 factory basically came to a halt. A lot of workers didn't bother coming, thinking it would soon be turned into a joint venture. The situation was unacceptable." After convening several meetings to discuss the situation, the city government agreed to send Ling to Shenzhen to talk to Wong in person. There Ling agreed to slash the value by nearly 20 percent. Still Wong refused. "I told him we must have an agreement. We have made big concessions," Ling said. "We waited for four hours. We missed our lunch, waiting for Wong's reply."

In the end, Wong said he would only agree if Wuhan would reduce its valuation of the factory by another $350,000. Wong's wife insisted on this because 51 percent of this value would be RMB 16.88 million, a figure that, when pronounced in Cantonese, sounds like "keep on making money all the way." In Hong Kong, business deals often revolve around sums of money with what are considered auspicious homophones. Desperate to reach a deal, the Wuhan city government decided to cast aside its communist scruples and pander to the superstitions of Wong's 27-year-old wife.

"Within my bureau and at the factory, it's true to say that people had different opinions about all this," Ling admitted. "Even to this day, some of them can't see the advantage of having a joint venture. On the contrary, the way they see it there are a lot of problems." Many workers at the Number 2 Mill were indeed less than happy with the new arrangements. Under the agreement between Citiford and the Textile Bureau, fewer than 800 out of the original workforce of 1,900 people would be retained. Those not selected to stay on would be found new jobs by the Textile Bureau or given a stipend of about $15 a month, one-quarter to one-third of their original salary. On a rainy day in March, 1,900 anxious workers turned up at the factory to discover their fate. Ling said he told Wong and his wife not to turn up because it would be impossible for the couple to decide themselves which were the good workers and which were not. It was better, he told them, to let the Textile Bureau handle it.

The Wongs decided, however, that they would like to deal with the matter themselves. But they had seriously misjudged the mood of the workers. According to a factory source, when the couple arrived at the factory they were surrounded by hundreds of angry employees shouting slogans like "down with capitalism" and "traitors." Ling said some of the workers jostled the Wongs and shouted at him too, accusing him of selling the factory's assets to foreigners. Shaken by this reception, the couple retreated to their hotel, leaving Ling to deal with the workers. Later, Ling went to find the couple in their hotel room. "I said, today's incident was unfortunate, and we regret it. We didn't do our work well. But [Wong's wife] got extremely angry with me. For the next fifteen minutes I kept silent, while she went on at me saying the Textile Bureau had gone into partnership with them and should guarantee their personal security. She said, 'We're not going to carry on with this.' But then she began to feel that she'd gone too far, and she apologized, saying she shouldn't have lost her temper."

Wuhan officials held several meetings with the couple and managed to persuade them not to give up. Ling said Wong's wife simply did not understand what the situation was like in his city. "Wuhan is not the same as Hong Kong, it's not the same as Shenzhen," he told me. "If you come here to form a joint venture, you should be mentally prepared for it."

When I visited the factory some five months after the Wongs' encounter with the workers, tempers were still running high. Ling was annoyed about security guards at the factory who he said had threatened to tie up a former worker who had entered the factory grounds without authorization in order to fetch a newspaper that had been delivered there by mistake. The agreement between Citiford and the Textile Bureau stated that only people still employed by the factory could enter the grounds. Citiford enforced the rule with a civilian guard force that it had hired to replace the police who had previously manned the gates. "This is unbearable, this kind of cursing," said an indignant Ling of the new guards' behavior. "Is this the way people in Hong Kong behave toward their inferiors? Maybe they do. You should treat people with respect. He [the former worker] didn't do anything very wrong. This was a minor incident, but if too many incidents like this occur, it'll give a bad impression."

The alleged intimidation of the former worker occurred a few days before the factory's official reopening in June. What Ling failed to mention was that the guards had reason to be a little on edge. A factory source said that on learning they had been made redundant, many workers took their revenge by walking off with anything they could carry, from television sets to tools. Those who were chosen to stay on at the factory were not necessarily any happier either. Even though their wages were now slightly higher, they now had to work instead of idling their time away. Wong introduced a new regime aimed at instilling what he called the "Citiford spirit" into the workforce. This included playing the company song over the factory's public address system as the workers arrived in the morning and publishing a factory newsletter full of inspiring tales of model employees.

When I went to the shop floor, workers busy in the sweltering heat generated by the huge dyeing machines told me how much more efficient the operation now was and how they preferred the more disciplined atmosphere. Later, however, factory officials and my city government minder took me to the home of 52-year-old Chen Qianxi, a former worker who said he had left the mill because he felt he was not respected by the Hong Kong management. The Textile Bureau had found him another office job. His 42-year-old wife had stayed on at the factory but was later dismissed. The couple said no adequate explanation was given for the sacking. When I told them that workers I had spoken to at the mill professed to enjoy their work, Chen retorted, "The wages are higher than they were before, but when the workers talk about anything else they're very guarded. Because in my experience of Citiford, the directors are free to threaten people. If even my wife, who worked well and was very capable, could be dismissed so casually, then I don't think the workers would dare to say what's really on their minds."

Wong admitted he had encountered "far more problems" handling the workers than he had getting the Textile Bureau to agree to his terms for setting up the partnership. "It takes time for workers in a place like this that hadn't opened up before to accept new things. . . . In terms of personnel, in terms of changing people's attitudes, I think that's where we've had the biggest difficulties. The reaction of the workers who weren't selected had a direct impact on the development of the enterprise. This we didn't expect."

It was unusual that the Wuhan authorities were so willing to show me the problems encountered by their first bold experiment with reform. Normally, foreign journalists only get to see the best-run factories or, if they are very lucky, bankrupt factories whose former workers are being relatively well looked after. Wuhan might have been expected to be especially sensitive about negative publicity given that it was trying to woo foreign investors. But in 1992, thanks to Deng, openness had become the new official buzzword. Maybe Wuhan felt that a little glasnost would do its image good and perhaps make Citiford more understanding of the problems faced by the Textile Bureau. Whatever the case, Citiford's gamble appeared to pay off. Xinhua said that in 1994 the venture's pretax profits amounted to $1.2 million.[34] But the dyeing factory's experience revealed the potential for conflict in any attempts to rescue state industries with foreign capital.

Even before news of Deng's tour became known, the party-controlled trade unions in Wuhan had tried encouraging workers at loss-making state enterprises to supplement their incomes through a bit of honest capitalism. In mid-January, the unions opened a special market consisting of 200 stalls in central Wuhan where such workers could hawk food and other goods without having to pay any tax for their first year of business or any fees for the use of the stands.[35] These were attractive incentives, given that the alternative for many employees at deeply indebted enterprises was living on a government handout of only $10 a month, less than one-quarter of the normal wage for a factory worker.

But acquiring business acumen was not something that came naturally to workers who had been used all their lives to state handouts and whose experience of work had taught them that greater efforts did not necessarily bring greater rewards. Ling admitted that three months after the start of the new textile venture, more than 500 people from the former state-owned mill were still out of work. "There are too many people," he said. "We have to find work for them. This takes time. . . . Sorting things out for one person is difficult enough, but what about several hundred?" Ling said city officials were paying close attention to the joint venture experiment. "To tell you the truth," he said, "this is the first time this has been done in Wuhan. We were rather daring. We hope it will succeed."

The complaints of workers and former workers at the Wuhan Number 2 Printing and Dyeing Mill did not appear at the time to be part of a trend that might derail Deng's reforms. But even the state-controlled media, amid a blizzard of pro-Deng propaganda, gave occasional hints that not everyone was happy. Shanghai's police chief, Zhu Daren, said in June 1992 that "a small number" of workers in state-run enterprises had staged strikes and slowdowns and had applied to hold demonstrations in protest against economic reforms.[36] He said there had also been a few cases of workers assaulting their managers and "sabotaging production" for the same reason. In May, a Beijing-controlled news agency in Hong Kong said there had been an increasing number of cases of factory managers in northeastern Liaoning Province, China's industrial heartland, being attacked by workers who had been laid off or forced to accept pay cuts as a result of the economic changes.[37] "Production order has been sabotaged to differing degrees," it said. In the city of Jinzhou in Liaoning, "many workers seized the opportunity willfully to make trouble because they had been removed from their posts . . . or because their personal interests had been affected by the reform of the enterprise structure," the report said. "The glass doors and windows of the houses of many middle-level cadres of enterprises were broken . . . and many evil cases of assaulting and wounding enterprise cadres occurred in succession. In view of this, the cadres of many enterprises were filled with anxiety and had a lingering fear of implementing the measures for reform, and enterprise reform was very greatly affected."

The official organ of the chief prosecutor's office published a commentary calling for stern measures to protect reformist officials from acts of revenge by disgruntled employees.[38] The newspaper said there had been several cases of people making false accusations against their reform-minded superiors because economic changes had hurt their interests. It said reforms would inevitably effect people's way of thinking, their working habits, their lifestyle, and "some people's vested interests." The newspaper cited the case of a village official in charge of grain storage and two of his colleagues who put up posters outside government buildings accusing the reformist director of the county grain bureau of corruption. The newspaper said the director was in fact a staunch opponent of corruption among the village grain offices in his area of central Henan Province. It said the case was typical of several that had occurred recently in different parts of China.

The Beijing Youth News gave examples of what it called the "common social phenomenon" of violence against factory officials or their relatives.[39] In one instance in August 1992, an unidentified man threw sulfuric acid at the wife of the manager of a cement factory in Hunan Province. The manager had been trying to tighten discipline among workers at the factory, which had been running at a loss for a long time. Eight months after the assault on his wife, the manager himself was beaten up in his office by three thugs. In August 1993, the manager of a textile plant on the outskirts of Beijing returned home to discover his wife in the bathroom "naked and brutally murdered." The criminal turned out to be a 23-year-old worker who had been dismissed from his job at the plant as a result of the manager's efforts to reduce staff.

In the face of such resistance, the leadership decided in mid-1992 to abandon one of that year's favorite reformist slogans, "smashing the three irons," because of the anxieties it was arousing among workers in state-owned industries. The slogan referred to ending the system of guaranteed job security, with the "three irons" being "the iron chair" of the lifelong sinecure enjoyed by factory officials, the "iron rice bowl" of guaranteed jobs for all, and the self-explanatory "iron wages." Smashing the "three irons" was a herculean task, which if carried out effectively would involve laying off at least a quarter of all employees of state-owned industries, or between 20 and 30 million people on the state payroll but effectively redundant. "To smash the 'three irons' all over the country will not be an easy job," said Xinhua.[40] "It requires firm resolution and great courage. . . . It touches not only upon the interests of enterprise officials but also on those of government officials. . . . Another great difficulty is the loss to workers, who are supposed to be the 'masters' of enterprises. They have become accustomed to the notion of lifetime employment and fixed wages, and some of them even misread these as the hallmarks of a socialist society. A change in mentality will be required if change is to take place." Such warnings clearly terrified many workers, some three-quarters of whom in the state sector still enjoyed guaranteed jobs for life.

In June, an official newspaper said that even though the term "smashing the three irons" had been dropped from official parlance because it was "too simplistic," the campaign against guaranteed job security regardless of performance would still continue.[41] But it became clear that the government had decided to proceed far more cautiously, fearful of possible unrest. In the absence of a social security system, unemployed workers would face severe problems if their ties with their employers were completely severed. An unemployment insurance law introduced in 1986 required enterprises to pay into an insurance fund that would be used to pay workers in the event of bankruptcy. But this measure hardly allayed the concerns of employees. According to the law, the amount of money they would receive from such funds would only amount to a little more than what their local governments deemed to be enough to survive on, and they would only receive these payments for a maximum of two years.[42]

Although the state was legally obliged to find new state sector jobs for laid-off workers, in practice this proved an extremely difficult task given that most state enterprises were trying to trim their workforces, not expand them. To avoid unrest, therefore, the government discouraged mass layoffs. But many enterprises on the verge of bankruptcy, which applied to at least one-half of the 100,000 state-owned enterprises nationwide, still curtailed bonuses and other benefits, including medical expenses, normally provided to workers. The government did not directly encourage this, but it was imposing stricter curbs on credit to loss-making enterprises in an effort to make them reduce unnecessary spending. Many factories therefore saw cutting the payroll as the easiest option. The Politburo member Zou Jiahua admitted in December 1994 that "some enterprises continue to incur production and operational problems, with serious defaults in payments of wages to workers and staff members."[43] Some, he said, were also failing to pay pensions to their retirees on time, thus causing "financial distress."

Worried about the growing ranks of the unemployed and ill-paid workers whose incomes were being eroded by inflation, China reintroduced grain ration coupons in early 1995, some two years after the decades-old system had been discontinued. The coupons allowed the poor in 29 big cities to buy grain at about 5 percent less than the market price. Officials said soaring grain prices in 1994 fueled inflation that year, which reached an annual 24.7 percent, the highest level since 1949. From the beginning of 1995, under a new labor law workers across the country became entitled to a minimum wage, the level of which was to be determined by local governments. In Beijing, the sum was set at 210 yuan, less than half of what the average factory worker would receive. Nonetheless, some enterprises seemed unwilling to pay it. Beijing officials acknowledged in May that the number of labor disputes in the capital had risen by more than 50 percent to 321 in the first three months of the year, with most of the increase attributed to the failure of employers to meet the minimum wage requirement.[44]

Deng's southern tour hastened the polarization of urban society into the haves and the have-nots, with those in the latter category mainly those without the connections or skills necessary to adapt to the rapidly changing economic environment. Some intellectuals fared relatively well. Having long been at the bottom of the heap, with highly skilled doctors and university professors often earning less than ordinary manual workers, many of them gained new opportunities in 1992 to improve their lot. State-employed teachers could take on private students, quit their jobs to find work in the rapidly increasing number of private schools, or sell their services to state or private enterprises if they had technical expertise. Some were willing to abandon the Chinese intellectual's traditional disdain for commerce and go into business. A university professor in Beijing who sold meat pies in the streets during the summer vacation of 1992 became something of a cause célèbre in the official press. For many, of course, adapting to a new lifestyle was not easy. The *China Daily* newspaper described how a primary school teacher in the capital supplemented her income by selling corn on the cob from a street stall.[45] "Unlike the other sellers who are trying to outshout their competitors in attracting customers, she is sublimely demure," the newspaper said, adding that "it was painful for her to stand out in the scorching sun, let alone cry her wares aloud."

Many government officials, with their contacts in the bureaucracy, were well placed to make considerable profit out of China's new dog-eat-dog capitalism. By early 1993, about one-third of all government functionaries in Beijing had second jobs, according to the *China Daily*.[46] In Chongqing in Sichuan Province, the proportion was as high as 40 percent. The newspaper said government officials were working as consultants or in public relations—jobs in which their inside knowledge and ready access to market information would certainly stand them in good stead. But factory workers had far less to offer. They formed the bulk of the urban have-nots.

It was easy to overlook the plight of the urban poor amid the glitter of China's burgeoning prosperity. Foreign journalists found editors and the public more attentive to stories about China's nouveaux riches with their mobile telephones and beepers than to accounts of the misery of city dwellers who suddenly found the socialist rug pulled from underneath them. The poor did not make themselves conspicuous. In Chinese cities, rich and poor usually live side by side rather than in their own separate districts, as they do in many other countries. This is because the government has for decades owned and allocated most housing in urban areas. Although high-ranking officials often live in separate apartment blocks or old style courtyard houses, most urban Chinese are housed where their work unit happens to have space for them, often in the same building as people with very different income levels. The government is trying now to encourage people to buy their own homes and thereby relieve it of the colossal burden of housing more than 200 million urban residents. On the edges of some cities, housing estates of lavish villas are beginning to appear, inhabited mainly by foreign businesspeople and wealthy Chinese private entrepreneurs. But private ownership of housing remains extremely rare.

Because they still have state-subsidized accommodation, the urban poor are not sleeping out on the streets or in shanty towns. Many of them are people browbeaten by endless political campaigns and nervous about contacting foreign journalists. They do not have the experience that dissident intellectuals have of exploiting international public opinion to put pressure on the government. They pose, however, a considerable threat to social stability. Though wide-scale, concerted antigovernment action by impoverished workers appears unlikely given the ruthlessness of the security apparatus, if ever authority collapses as it did briefly in 1989, I believe the poor would be among the first to take to the streets.

To talk of a country being stable, as Chinese leaders endlessly do, when the gap between rich and poor is widening at a faster rate than in most other countries of the world seems wishful thinking. Even though there is little obvious sign of the hunger or deprivation that can be found in any city, say, in neighboring India, the fatalistic acceptance of one's lot that is pervasive among India's poor is also lacking in China. Many Chinese are resentful of the fact that others are getting much richer than they are. This feeling is reinforced by the lingering impact of three decades of enforced egalitarianism among city dwellers under Mao Zedong before Deng sanctioned the acquisition of wealth. Mixed in with their jealousy is often a feeling of contempt for the nouveaux riches, whom they regard as people with little formal education and social standing, exploiting legal loopholes, evading taxes, or simply ignoring the law altogether in their wheeling and dealing.

In its 1993 report entitled *The East Asian Miracle*, the World Bank noted that the high-performing economies of Asia had achieved "unusually low and declining levels of inequality."[47] Although China was not included among the high performers, the report said there were "striking parallels in the general pattern of growth" between China and its successful neighbors in Asia, including Japan, Taiwan, Hong Kong, South Korea, and Singapore. Through the early 1990s, however, the perception of many ordinary Chinese, and indeed government officials, was quite the opposite—namely, that the country's rapid economic growth was aggravating inequality, not reducing it. Statistics on income distribution in China can be very misleading, particularly given that those in the high-income bracket would be unlikely to declare their full earnings for fear of having to pay taxes—which few private citizens do. The concept of independent surveys is such a novel one to most Chinese that few would dare tell the truth even to the handful of nongovernmental research organizations that exist. According to official Chinese figures, however, the richest 20 percent of city residents in 1992 earned 2.8 times more than the poorest 20 percent, up from 1.7 times in 1981.[48] Although the ratio is about 11 to 1 if the rural population is taken into account,[49] the urban figures on their own would compare very favorably with overall income distribution in the high-performing Asian economies cited by the World Bank report, where the ratio is between 5 and 10. In Britain, the ratio is about 8. A report published by the Chinese Academy of Social Sciences, however, said the urban ratio in China would be 9.6 if people's assets were included in the calculation of wealth. The report said that although this ratio was considerably lower than in some developing countries, the "excessive" disparity in income levels was still causing public anxiety, particularly because of the illegal methods used by some people to get rich. "If steps are not taken to curb illegal income, there will be extreme polarization, which will affect the willingness to work of those whose incomes depend on their labor and will even cause feelings of dissatisfaction toward society and become a potential cause of social unrest," the report said.[50]

Official statistics on increases in the incomes of urban residents concealed the true story. Although the government usually highlighted figures that continued to show a rise after factoring in inflation—5.9 percent in 1992, 10 percent in 1993, and 8.8 percent in 1994—the true picture was less rosy. One official study published in 1995 acknowledged that "the rapid increase in the incomes of some households concealed the drop in living standards of other households whose incomes failed to keep up with inflation."[51] It said that in Beijing nearly one-third of households suffered a drop in their real incomes in 1994, a year of particularly severe inflation. In the heavy-industrial city of Shenyang in the northeast the proportion was higher than 45 percent, and in Xian in the northwest more than half of the city's households were worse off. A survey conducted in Sichuan found that 45 percent of town and city dwellers across the province experienced a decline in their real incomes in the first nine months of that year. The incomes of about one-fifth of Sichuan urban households were lower than the year before even before taking inflation into account.

The ostentation of the newly rich has exacerbated tensions between the rich and poor. At night, while the poor stay in their shabby apartments, the wealthy crowd into high-class restaurants, karaoke bars, or luxury international hotels. One of Beijing's glitziest new nightclubs opened along the road from where I lived and worked. Its huge neon sign of a multicolored butterfly lit up the sky over the crowded old courtyard-style houses and apartment blocks around it. The entrance ticket alone cost more than two weeks' wages for the average factory worker. Those who arrived by car could enjoy valet parking, an almost unheard of luxury in China. Inside, attractive young female waitresses approached guests' tables on their knees to take orders for drinks and requests for music to be played on the karaoke machines. The guests were not just a few Hong Kong businesspeople or their Chinese associates. Sometimes whole Beijing families occupied the tables.

A few hundred yards closer to my apartment compound was Beijing's biggest pet shop, a Hong Kong–owned establishment offering 24-hour medical services for dogs, "doggie hairstyling," and imported dog food. Dog ownership was then illegal in the inner-city areas of Beijing but that did not stop the well-to-do from acquiring expensive breeds and showing them off to their neighbors. A columnist in the *China Daily* newspaper said a dog-owning friend of his was ashamed to be seen in public with his pet because it only cost something in the region of a hundred dollars, about two months' wages for the average city dweller. Black marketeers made fortunes by selling pedigree breeds smuggled into China by train from Russia, by air from Japan, and by boat from South Korea. At open-air markets they would approach potential customers with tiny lapdogs stuffed under their overcoats to avoid detection by the police, offering to sell the animals for several hundred dollars each. At times when the authorities were not engaged in one of their periodic crackdowns on dog ownership, the black marketeers would openly display their wares on the pavement. There appeared to be no shortage of customers.

Just around the corner from where I lived a huge new restaurant opened up in what was once a warehouse owned by the Agricultural Museum behind it. Next to the entrance, on its own red carpet, was a Rolls Royce parked semipermanently just for show. It was one of only a handful of Rolls Royces in the city and cost in the region of 800 years' wages for the factory worker or low-level government functionary living in the apartment buildings nearby. A dwarf dressed in a red jacket was on hand to usher in customers, who were then escorted to their tables by hostesses, dressed in winter in long fur coats. One side of the restaurant, which could seat several hundred people, was lined with tanks containing exotic seafood of almost every edible species, from sharks to lobsters. The Cantonese owner, He Pinggang, told me he sold one or two fish every day costing RMB 2,000 each—about $250 or five months' wages for an ordinary worker. Based on the American working wage, this would be the equivalent of spending several thousand dollars on a single fish! The owner told me he did not know how much his own fortune amounted to, but his investment in the seafood restaurant alone was well over a million dollars. He also said he owned another restaurant and three villas in Guangdong Province. According to He's somewhat incredible account of his life, in the late 1980s he worked as an ill-paid driver in a state-owned enterprise. Then, with savings of a couple of hundred dollars, he went into the seafood trade and worked his way up to his present position in the space of only five years. "In a country the size of China you can't turn everyone into millionaires overnight," said He. "But in southern China a lot of people have become very rich. They have their own houses, they have their own cars. Their living standards are rising as fast as those of people in Hong Kong or Macao."

Luxury carmakers such as Rolls Royce and Ferrari scrambled to open showrooms in China. They expected to sell no more than a handful of cars a year at first, particularly given that with import duty included their vehicles would be more than twice as expensive as they would be in the West. But they knew that despite the bicycle-jammed roads and the lack of any garages capable of repairing such models, wealthy Chinese would still be willing to buy. Chinese officials, indeed, courted these symbols of Western luxury. In April 1994, when Rolls Royce Motors Ltd. signed a deal making the British company Inchcape Pacific the exclusive distributors of Rolls Royces in China, I drove in one of Beijing's seven Rolls Royces with the auto company's managing director, Mike Donovan, to the signing ceremony at the Great Wall north of the capital. Police outriders who accompanied our motorcade swore obscenely through their loud hailers at vehicles that got in our way. A deputy mayor of Beijing, Duan Qiang, was among the dignitaries who ascended the ancient monument to declare formally the arrival of Rolls Royce cars in China. "Rolls Royce is well known across the world," Duan said, "and Rolls Royces on Beijing's streets are an indication that China's reforms are creating a stable economy. If we step up our efforts, I believe that more and more Rolls Royces will be seen on the streets of Beijing." Duan, however, apparently did not think it would be appropriate for a communist of his rank to join the champagne toasts and disappeared after his speech.

It was not just the foreign media who paid disproportionate attention to the nouveaux riches. The official Chinese press also loved to dwell on stories of newfound wealth. The relatively liberal *Beijing Youth News* said that in the first half of 1993, Xinhua News Agency issued nearly seven times as many stories about the rich as it did about the poor.[52] The slogans of "hard struggle" and "self-reliance" that became all the vogue during the hard-line resurgence after Tiananmen all but disappeared from the official press from 1992 onward. A well-known Chinese fiction writer, Jiang Zilong, who specializes in true-to-life stories about China's working class, complained in an article published in mid-1993 that discussing poverty had become "as likely to cause trouble as talking about getting rich during the Cultural Revolution."[53] He said he knew of some families in his native city of Tianjin who had not eaten meat for several months and of several people who had committed suicide because of their poverty. After his article was published, Jiang, who is normally highly respected in official circles, received several phone calls from the intermediaries of local cadres who warned that his sources would get in trouble for giving him this information. "There are not that many people who have got rich," Jiang told me, "but they are a powerful force. There are many unemployed workers, but they don't have much power."[54]

Even the central government itself did not gain as much from the boom as might be expected. The country's total financial revenues amounted to less than 12 percent of the country's GNP in 1994 compared with more than 30 percent in 1978 before the reforms began. A senior Chinese legislator complained at the annual session of the National People's Congress in 1995 that the ratio was only one-third to one-half of what it was in leading industrialized countries. "As a result, the Chinese government lacks necessary financial capabilities to effectively exercise macroeconomic control," he warned.[55] Tax reforms in 1994 boosted the central government's share of overall revenue from 40 percent to more than 55 percent, but since then the rate of increase of the central government's revenue has remained considerably slower than that of local governments. One of the main problems is raising taxes. According to the official media, about a third of state enterprises evade taxes, 60 percent of foreign-funded enterprises, 80 percent of registered private entrepreneurs, and 100 percent of unregistered private businesspeople.

Some official estimates say the amount of tax evaded every year would easily pay off the country's growing budget deficit, which in 1994 was about $7.6 billion. The government also had to pay out huge sums to keep loss-making state enterprises afloat. The equivalent of about a quarter of 1994's budget deficit was spent on such subsidies. The government, however, preferred mounting debts to mounting unrest. By the end of 1994 it had allowed only about 500 state enterprises to go bankrupt out of at least 50,000 that were qualified to do so.

With the introduction of the new taxation system in 1994, officials expressed the hope that the budget deficit could be wiped out within three years.[56] In the past, provinces had negotiated with Beijing to pay a certain amount of taxes to the center every year. Any surplus they could keep. Under the new system, a fixed percentage of tax revenue would be allocated to the center. In theory, this would mean that Beijing would still profit if a province did exceptionally well, whereas in the past all the extra revenue would be pocketed by the provincial authorities. At the March 1995 session of the National People's Congress, the finance minister, Liu Zhongli, said that thanks to the new tax system, the budget deficit for the previous year was smaller than originally forecast, but the growth in expenditure in 1994 still considerably outpaced the increase in revenue, due in part to pay increases for government employees as well as the effects of inflation.[57] Liu predicted a more even balance of revenue and expenditure growth in the months ahead but cautioned that "we still face a grim situation in the finances that has not yet improved." Not only was the central government saddled with "huge debts," he said, but also "some counties and townships are still in an extremely difficult financial situation, with some still unable to pay wages . . . or even guarantee the issuance of wages on time." Liu warned that such problems were long-standing and would be hard to resolve "in a short period of time." The government's continuing difficulties did not bode well for efforts to narrow the gap in living standards by allocating more resources to underdeveloped areas and maintaining free or low-cost social services for the needy.

Determined to cut down on spending, and encouraged by Deng's green light to capitalism, government departments began turning to the market to generate extra cash. This represented one of the most dramatic and potentially destabilizing economic trends of 1992. Even the police, the courts, and the military raced to set up what were in effect private businesses managed by civil servants, with the profits going not to the central government but to the departments and very often to the individual bureaucrats in charge of the enterprise. "This has led to a huge amount of exchanging power for money, which has caused dissatisfaction among the broad masses," said the Chinese Academy of Social Sciences.[58] Although the idea of government departments doing business on the side was not a new one—some of Beijing's top hotels have long been controlled by the army, the police, or even in one case the Hong Kong and Macao Affairs Office—in 1992 a craze for such activity swept the country. So ill-regulated was China's economic transformation that the central authorities appeared powerless to intervene.

Evidence of the bureaucracy's new entrepreneurial energy was everywhere. In mid-1994, I walked down a street in Chengdu, the capital of Sichuan Province, where the city's police headquarters and law courts are located. Almost every shop along the way was run by the police. On sale was police equipment ranging from knives and electric cattle prods to police uniforms and insignia and the flashing lights used on top of police cars. The policemen selling the paraphernalia said I could buy anything on display. This was going on in spite of repeated warnings in the national media that "fake policemen" were everywhere, extorting money from ordinary citizens by demanding the payment of fines or bribes.

An enterprise set up by the police was involved in one of the most iniquitous yet legal commercial ventures undertaken by a government department that I encountered during my time in China. In October 1992, a Shenzhen-based company began selling what were described as ownership deeds for 50 square inches of land in America. The scheme began in the United States as a novelty gimmick, but many ordinary Chinese took the worthless pieces of paper extremely seriously, believing that the owners of these deeds would be granted U.S. visas or could use them as an investment and trade them in when real estate prices in America rose. There was, of course, no such possibility. A Beijing company run by the police acquired 5,000 of the deeds, which were priced at around $50 each in the United States. The company—one of several around the country that jumped on the same bandwagon—then hired a room in a luxury Beijing hotel from which it sold the pieces of paper to the public at $650 apiece, the equivalent of a year's wages for the average factory worker. With the help of some publicity in the official media, which conveniently failed to point out that these were just novelty items, the police-run company found no shortage of customers. Within a week, 300 Chinese had signed up to buy little pieces of America. Two of them had asked for 10 land deeds each. An engineer called Song Linjing told me she dreamed of going to America and even though her relatives called her stupid, she was still willing to pay the small fortune to buy the meaningless deed. In all, more than 100,000 were sold by various Chinese companies across the country. American consular officials received numerous phone calls from hopeful Chinese who had bought the certificates asking whether they could now have a visa to visit their property. Few had bothered to look at the small print in English that said the certificate was for novelty purposes and could not be resold for profit.

But many government departments, the police included, got into far bigger business than selling overpriced gimmicks. Some set up companies to sell resources to which they had cheap access—real estate, for example, or production materials. One Western businessman told me he paid the Chinese army to transport his goods by truck. The People's Armed Police, China's paramilitary antiriot and guard force, put some of its troops in civilian clothes and hired them out to foreign embassies as cleaners. By 1994, almost every government department or state-owned enterprise was engaged in some form of commercial activity. Early that year, the Foreign Ministry, which administers the housing compounds where all journalists and diplomats in Beijing are required to live, opened a modest grocery store in the lobby of my apartment building. State-owned factories raced to sell rights to their unwanted land on the booming real estate market. I visited a rural school in early 1993 in the northwestern province of Shaanxi that had turned one of its classrooms into a tiny shoe factory. The clattering and banging reverberated around the adjacent rooms where children were studying. Desperate for cash, most other schools in the country set up similar ventures.

State-run services such as education and health care were by no means immune from the new money-grabbing atmosphere. Although on paper state employees continued to enjoy free medical treatment and schooling for their children, in practice these services became increasingly expensive. To save money, loss-making government-owned enterprises often stopped reimbursing employees for their medical expenses. The cost of treatment, meanwhile, rose far more rapidly than the rate of inflation as corrupt hospital staff demanded ever higher kickbacks—"red packets" as they are known in Chinese—for good treatment. The Chinese press carried occasional stories of people dying when hospitals refused to admit them because they could not pay the fees. The official *China Business Times* said in early 1994 that one-third of all Chinese who needed hospitalization stayed at home.[59] In more than 50 percent of these cases, the cost of hospital care was the main reason for doing so. The newspaper said nearly one-quarter of city residents could not afford hospitalization. It gave no comparative figures for earlier years, but there was no doubt the proportion had risen considerably since the reforms began. In the countryside, where free health care almost entirely ended with the scrapping of the People's Communes, such statistics would not have been surprising.[60] But it was a more shocking revelation that city dwellers—who had long been much better cared for than people in the countryside—were also beginning to lose some of their traditional benefits.[61]

Meng Fanping and her husband Zhang Dongsheng were typical of those on the losing side of the economic takeoff. I interviewed them in early in 1994, a few months after they had been laid off by their loss-making, state-owned travel agency. Meng, 30, said she had received no severance pay at all and only limited medical coverage for herself. Her five-year-old son, however, still needed treatment for a heart condition. When he had undergone a heart operation while his mother was still working, half of the expenses had been paid by her employers. But now she was terrified of the possibility that he might require hospitalization again, given that the family no longer had any savings. "If the doctor told me he had to be admitted to hospital, I'd borrow money so he could get the treatment," Meng said. "I don't dare buy anything now, and the child doesn't eat as well as he used to." Her husband, who was also 30 years old, complained, "It's unimaginable for us to eat like rich people do in the restaurants," he said. "It's unimaginable for us to have a meal like them."

The disintegration of socialized medicine was mirrored by developments in education. Limited experiments with private education in the cities had begun in the mid-1980s. At first they were just specialist trade colleges, but after Deng's tour of the south private schools from kindergartens to high schools mushroomed in the cities. In 1993 alone, 10 private primary and middle schools were set up in Beijing. For the government, desperate to find a way of improving education without having to pay more money, it was an obvious way out. To make ends meet, state-run schools had been charging ever-higher sums, usually in the form of compulsory donations for books and other necessities rather than straightforward fees, which officially they were not allowed to levy. The emergence of private schools, however, exacerbated the problems faced by the state sector and highlighted the growing gap between rich and poor. Most of the new private schools charged colossal fees by Chinese standards, often several hundred if not several thousand U.S. dollars a year. In return, the schools generally provided good equipment and well-motivated teachers—a stark contrast with state schools where some teachers did not even bother showing up for class. Not surprisingly, the better conditions at private schools began to attract the best teachers from the state schools. Some worked for both while others gave up their state jobs entirely. In 1994, a teacher at the privately run Jinghua Primary School in Beijing earned about $115 a month, or about three times the salary of teachers in the state sector.

Most of these new private schools rented space from state schools, making it even more obvious to the have-nots what they were missing. In October 1992, no less a figure than the head of the Beijing government's Education Bureau formally attached the sign of the "Zhengze Private Middle School" to the gates of Beijing's first ever non-state-run secondary school. Next to the same gates was another sign, that of the Zaoying Middle School, a state-run establishment that actually owned the grounds and the buildings. The new private school occupied the top floor of the four-story schoolhouse. The two schools were not in direct competition—the state one being a junior high and the private one a senior high school. Nor, unusually, did the private school enjoy conspicuously better facilities. But its fees were not for the faint of heart. To enroll cost about $450—a year's wages for the ordinary worker. Tuition cost another $300 per year, and the Zhengze school prided itself on being one of the cheapest of its kind. In spite of the expense, parents told me they were attracted by the high quality of the teachers at Zhengze, and for every place available there were more than 20 candidates. While the state school downstairs was renting out the teachers' bike shed as a restaurant and running a metal frame factory to get some extra income, the private school was planning to move to new premises designed especially for them and funded by donations from wealthy Chinese overseas. "I learned in college that when you have money you can do anything, and when you don't have money, you can't," the parent of a pupil at the private school told me. "Certainly without money, it's impossible [to get a private education]. But it's not just a question of money. Even if you have money, if your boy isn't bright, even a millionaire can't enter." The official media, however, which thanks to Deng's southern tour were able to comment more openly on some social issues, said many Chinese regarded the private institutions as "aristocrats' schools." Xinhua News Agency said they were mainly "a kingdom for the children of people who have got rich fast" and quoted an unnamed educator as saying the "aristocrats' schools phenomenon" had caused "psychological imbalance" among the parents of children in state schools.[62] In other words, they were jealous and unhappy.

Private education and costly medical care are nothing new in other developing countries and indeed in most of the industrialized world. But in still nominally communist China these are highly divisive issues. Urban Chinese increasingly told me that the "new revolution" unleashed by Deng was in some ways turning the clock back to the days before the communists came to power. There were many winners and many losers. Bureaucratic power and raw capitalist instincts were often the passport to success in Deng's new order. The Communist Party hoped that ruthless policing would keep angry and frustrated urban residents under control.

5

The Virus of Corruption

Corruption is the virus that has eroded the healthy body of the party and the state. If we lower our guard and let it run wild, our party will be ruined, the people's power will be lost, and the great cause of socialist modernization will be forced off track. Our party, our cadres, and our people will never allow such consequences.
—Jiang Zemin, Communist Party general secretary,
August 1993

"Down with corruption" is a slogan that has been chanted by demonstrators and daubed on banners in almost every protest movement in modern Chinese history. Dissidents from KMT days to the present have tried to use popular anger against official corruption to goad the general public into revolutionary action. Communist historians identify corruption as one of the main reasons for the collapse of the Qing dynasty and of KMT rule on the mainland. As Jiang Zemin warned in 1991, "If we examine each dynasty in China's history, we see there existed corruption and struggles against it that were linked to the rise and fall and the life and death of a dynasty. . . . Historical experience tells us that if the anticorruption campaign fails, China's society cannot achieve integrity."[1]

Jiang, of course, had experience of the vehemence with which popular anger over corruption could express itself. In 1989, during the Tiananmen Square protests, slogans condemning corruption were more frequently seen and heard than those related to any other concern. One song particularly relished by the demonstrators was one that began with the words "*Dadao guandao* [down with profiteering officials], *dadao guandao, fan fubai* [oppose corruption] *fan fubai*," sung to the tune of the nursery rhyme *Frère Jacques*. Protesters said they felt corruption had become increasingly rampant since Deng Xiaoping launched his economic reforms, and although they did not openly attack the reforms themselves, some ordinary workers carried large portraits of Mao

147

Zedong and his prime minister, Zhou Enlai, as a way of showing their contempt for what they saw as social and moral decay under Deng.

Corruption of course is a problem common to many countries, including industrialized nations, but in few is the problem as threatening to social and political stability as it is in China. Corruption is at least as rampant in the Indian bureaucracy, for example, as it is in China's. Yet India has mechanisms whereby the general public can vent their anger, ranging from the ballot box to their frequently exercised right to stage public demonstrations. In China, ordinary citizens can only bottle up their frustrations. When they do find a rare opportunity to air their grievances, as they did in 1989, the outpouring of rage is all the more likely to be politically destructive.

Speaking to top party leaders just a few days after the crushing of the Tiananmen Square protests, Deng decreed that between 10 and 20 "major cases" of corruption should be publicly exposed "without delay" in order to "satisfy the people."[2] Deng warned that failure to curb corruption could jeopardize attainment of the party's "strategic goals." But although in response to Deng's urgings the party declared its renewed determination to crack down, the problem refused to go away, not least because it affected so many people at every level of the government. In late July 1989, the Politburo announced new antinepotism regulations banning the children and spouses of senior leaders from working in commercial enterprises. This was aimed at the many relatives of top officials who were taking advantage of their powerful connections to make huge profits in the business world. But the new measures were halfhearted at best, applying only to relatives of officials in the Politburo, Party Secretariat, and the State Council's Executive Committee. The relatives of retired revolutionaries—the real leaders of China—were not mentioned. Thus Deng's second son, Deng Zhifang, was able to keep his job as a senior executive in the China International Trust and Investment Corporation.[3] Similarly, in 1992, Bo Xicheng, the son of Bo Yibo, an influential party veteran who was then serving as vice chairman of the Central Advisory Commission, was able to resign his job as director of the Beijing Tourism Administration and start his own tourism business. The official media even portrayed him as something of a hero for doing so—failing to point out that he was effectively peddling his government contacts and connections with top leaders for commercial gain. In his resignation letter, which was published by the Chinese press, Bo Xicheng went as far as to describe himself as a "pioneer" who was "willing to leave my public office and earn a living just as any ordinary citizen."[4] Few ordinary citizens would have seen his move in such a heroic light. With his background, Bo could hardly fail.

Within a month of the Politburo's decision to bar the close relatives of top officials from doing business, the media announced that all those affected by the new rule had quit their jobs. But the official press did not say how many had done so nor who they were. For ordinary citizens, there was no way of checking. As far as the general public was concerned, few of the other anticorruption rules announced by the Politburo with such fanfare in July 1989 appeared to have much effect. For example, the Politburo banned the use of imported cars by top-ranking officials. Yet they were still allowed to use luxury—and just as expensive—foreign-brand cars made in joint venture factories in China. And the regulations allowed lower-ranking officials to continue using imported cars if they had them already, as long as they avoided "new waste." The Politburo announced the abolition of special shops selling luxury foodstuffs at low prices to top officials and their families. But any ordinary Chinese had only to walk around the car parks in front of Beijing's glitzy new department stores and see the disproportionate number of vehicles with official and military license plates to realize that rank still often went hand in hand with privilege and wealth. In the first five months of 1993, China spent about $1.7 billion on imported sedans, more than four times as much as during the same period a year earlier. Most of these were not for ordinary civilian use. Officials were clearly ignoring the regulations.

Deng's plan to expose 10 or 20 "major cases" of corruption ran into difficulties. There was no doubt the party could come up with many times that number of "major cases" if it really put its mind to it. But the task of exposing corruption inevitably became bogged down in factional politics. Hard-liners pursued corrupt reformers with greater vigor than they did members of their own ranks. One of the first victims was Liang Xiang, the reformist governor of the island province of Hainan off China's southern coast. In mid-September 1989, the authorities announced that Liang had helped his wife and one of his sons make money by speculating in property. They said Liang had illegally approved the importation of several cars and that the son had made a large sum of money from the deal. He was also accused of illegally letting another of his sons settle in Hong Kong and of using public money to buy his own clothing and give lavish private dinners. The leadership denied that

Liang's dismissal had anything to do with his reformist views or his close connections with the deposed party leader Zhao Ziyang, but many Chinese observers believed otherwise.[5]

It was widely rumored that after Tiananmen Liang had allowed dissidents to flee China via the island. He had also given permission to Zhao's younger son, Zhao Erjun, to set up a trading company in Hainan to which he gave the exclusive right to import foreign cars. After Tiananmen, both of Zhao's sons came under suspicion of corruption. The minister of supervision, Wei Jianxing, announced in April 1990 that the elder son, Zhao Dajun, was being investigated for allegedly "abusing power for personal gain."[6] During Tiananmen, demonstrators had accused the two sons of profiteering. After the crushing of the protests, hard-liners saw a chance to win back some public favor and get at Zhao, their political enemy, by pursuing his sons. In the end, however, no charges were ever formally made against them, perhaps because the leadership feared that doing so would expose the extent of wrongdoing among the offspring of other leaders still in power.

Another "major case" touted by the official media in September 1989 involved the dismissal of the deputy governor of Xinjiang, Tohti Sabir. He was accused of accepting several hundred dollars in bribes and of black marketeering. But in terms of the sums involved these appeared to be relatively trivial offenses. Less than two months after Sabir's dismissal the authorities declared him exempt from prosecution because he had "confessed to all the crimes he had committed and returned all the money." It was not a very convincing start to the anticorruption campaign. The cases of Sabir and Liang Xiang turned out to be among only a handful of "major cases" to come to light in the months following Tiananmen—fewer certainly than the quota set by Deng.[7]

It was impossible for the party to pursue the anticorruption drive with the vigor it deserved, not least because to do so would undermine the party's claim that only a small minority of officials engaged in malpractices. It was not in the party's interests to lend too much weight to the complaints about corruption aired by the demonstrators in 1989. A few days after the cases of Liang Xiang and Tohti Sabir were made public, the *People's Daily* said advocates of "bourgeois liberalization" were using corruption as an excuse to oppose the party. "They have described corruption . . . as 'astonishing,' posed as heroes in fighting against corruption, and taken advantage of the discontent of the broad masses of people with corruption in the party to create social unrest and antigovernment riots," the paper said. The party, it said, was "by no means rotten. On the contrary, it is a clean and honest party and a leading force in the fight against corruption. Grassroots party organizations and the majority of party members and leading officials believe in communism and subordinate their personal interests to those of the collective and resist corrosive and decadent ways of life and influences."[8]

But confirmation, if it were needed, that serious corruption extended to the very top echelons of the party came to light with the astonishing series of developments that began on April 4th, 1995, with the suicide of the deputy mayor of Beijing, Wang Baosen. Wang allegedly shot himself in the mountains outside Beijing just as investigators were about to begin looking into his involvement in corruption. The authorities posthumously accused Wang, who was responsible for approving construction projects in the city, of embezzling more than $40,000 of public funds and diverting another $25 million for use by his younger brother, mistress, and other associates. "He squandered without restraint public funds, building luxury villas, buying high-grade apartments, and booking hotel suites for a long time for pleasure-seeking. . . . He was morally degenerate and lived a rotten life," Xinhua News Agency said.[9] Officials failed to clarify why none of this had come to light until after Wang had killed himself.

Wang's unusual demise was followed less than four weeks later by the resignation of the Politburo member Chen Xitong from his concurrent post as party secretary of Beijing. Xinhua said Chen bore "unshirkable responsibilities" in the Wang affair. In early July, the party launched an investigation into Chen's role in "major issues" linked with Wang,[10] and in September expelled him from the Politburo and Central Committee. Chen thus became the highest-ranking official to be purged for alleged corruption since the communists came to power. But even though Chen was a central figure in the suppression of the Tiananmen Square protests, many Beijing residents greeted the news with cynicism rather than jubilation. Few seemed convinced by the assertion of Chen's successor as party secretary, Wei Jianxing, that the posthumous denunciation of Wang demonstrated that "under the leadership of the Party Central Committee, with Comrade Jiang Zemin as the core, our party is wholly capable of eliminating corrupt elements within its ranks and that our socialist system has the mechanism to eradicate corrupt phenomena in its body."[11] If Chen and Wang were involved in embezzling such huge sums of money and living such a lavish lifestyle, members of the Politburo must have known about it for years and condoned it. To most observers, Chen's downfall appeared more related to political struggles than to the party's avowed efforts to rid itself of corrupt elements no matter how high-ranking. Rumors swept the capital that Jiang had seized on Wang's suicide to hit out at Chen whom he saw as an ambitious political rival.

Many ordinary Chinese complain that corruption was more the rule than the exception. Taxi drivers moan about police routinely extorting money or cigarettes as "fines" for nonexistent traffic violations. A friend of mine in the police force told me that even a murderer could be freed from jail on payment of the right bribe. He himself managed to secure the release of a relative suspected of political crimes by bribing his relative's guards. To get a telephone or a better apartment, admission to a good school for one's children or decent medical treatment more often than not requires handouts of cash or gifts to the right officials. Foreign business-people often complain about increasingly blatant demands by their Chinese partners for gifts, overseas trips, or even the sponsorship of education abroad for their children. The foreign tourist might see little if any sign of such corruption, but any foreign resident in China knows how important it is to provide at least cigarettes and imported soft drinks or alcohol for the plumber or electrician to make sure the job is done well and promptly.

Less visible but far more serious corruption is rife in the higher ranks of the bureaucracy, among those who have access to or control over coveted resources such as building materials, coal, oil, steel, fertilizer, or means of transport. The gradual freeing of prices in recent years has helped reduce attempts to cash in on the difference between fixed and market prices, but profiteering remains rampant.

Much as he may have hoped to curb such practices, Deng only exacerbated the problem with his trip to the south in 1992. His calls for bold experimentation and a risk-taking spirit encouraged economic practices that in many countries would be illegal. In China, which only began to build up a legal system after Deng came to power, the law still lags far behind the pace of social and economic change. Officials and business-people who know next to nothing about stock markets see nothing wrong with insider trading. Many civil servants see nothing wrong with using state resources to generate some extra income for themselves and their departments by doing private business on the side. Indeed, many departments actively encourage it as a way of improving staff morale. This is, after all, a country long used to operating not according to the law but according to government or party dictate. Deng's instruction that officials should dare to take risks and boldly explore new paths in reform therefore carried as much if not more weight in the minds of many Chinese than any legal provision. To communist officials confused and demoralized by political changes in the former Soviet Union and Eastern Europe, Deng's words gave the green light to feather their nests while the opportunity still lasted. In the minds of many bureaucrats, the collapse of communism in Europe indicated that communism's days in China were numbered as well.

More than a year after Deng's tour, Jiang Zemin admitted that "negative and corrupt phenomena" had "seriously interfered with the work of reform and opening" and that ordinary citizens were "rather dissatisfied."[12] He said that unless the party adopted "resolute measures" to curb these phenomena, "they will bury the great cause of reform and opening and will finally lead to jeopardizing our party's ruling position." But the damage had already been done, and to many Chinese it appeared irreversible.

In the city of Shenzhen, the rapidly rising expectations of the general public collided head-on with burgeoning official corruption in 1992, triggering unrest that led to fears among reformist officials that Deng's new campaign might grind to a halt in the face of renewed hard-line resistance. Given Deng's hopes that affluence would bring stability, it was particularly ironic that the trouble occurred in Shenzhen, the most prosperous area of China. The trigger was the city's stock market, an experiment with capitalism that Deng had defended during his southern tour. "We allow people to reserve their judgment [about stock markets]," Deng had said. "But we must try these things out. If after one or two years of experimentation they prove feasible, we can expand them. Otherwise we can put a stop to them and be done with it. . . . What is there to be afraid of?"[13]

On August 9th, the Shenzhen city government began its annual sale of lottery tickets that would entitle those with winning numbers to buy shares due to be issued in the upcoming year. With huge numbers of investors chasing only a small number of shares on the Shenzhen and Shanghai exchanges—both formally opened in December 1990—there were fabulous profits to be made. Those who bought new share issues at the beginning of 1992 saw their investment increase more than seven times in value by the end of the year. The incentive to buy was made all the greater by low interest rates on bank deposits, which meant that, especially in years of high inflation, savers would effectively lose money by keeping their money in the banks. In 1992, interest rates were only about one percentage point higher than the national inflation rate, which meant that in big cities, where inflation tended to be higher than average, depositors lost money.[14]

Even though only one in 10 of the 5 million lottery tickets due to be sold would have winning numbers, investors poured into Shenzhen to buy them at 100 yuan apiece—the equivalent of a week's wages for the average factory worker. Officials estimated that a staggering 1.2 million people joined queues to buy the lottery tickets, of whom some 800,000 were from outside Shenzhen. Trains and planes bound for the zone were full to capacity, and vacant rooms at Shenzhen hotels were almost impossible to find. Some of those who flocked to Shenzhen were peasants who had brought with them stacks of identity cards in order to buy lottery tickets for their friends and relatives at home. Factory bosses and rich businesspeople paid workers to stand in line for them. Queues began to form two days before sales began, snaking for hundreds of yards in sweltering heat outside more than 300 banks and brokerages. Police used cattle prods, leather belts, and bamboo canes to keep the bad-tempered and impatient crowds in order. Dozens of people were injured in the crush, and many suffering from heat exhaustion were taken to hospitals.

The authorities had anticipated that the sale of lottery tickets would take two days. But within a few hours, almost all of the tickets were gone. The hundreds of thousands of people who continued to wait in line through Sunday night for the second day of sales realized on Monday morning that they had done so in vain. After three days and nights standing and squatting amid the spreading filth of human waste and discarded food containers, many investors could not control their anger. Simple arithmetic told them that even if everyone ahead of them in line had bought their full quota of 10 tickets, there should still be enough left for at least some of those still waiting. Rumors spread rapidly that bank officials, police, and other civil servants had kept many of the tickets for themselves or reserved places at the front of the queues for their friends and relatives. On Monday evening, August 10th, tens of thousands of enraged investors rampaged through the streets in protest. Thousands of them gathered outside the city government headquarters shouting "down with corruption." Some carried placards and banners with slogans such as "fight corruption" and "fight for justice."[15] The crowds overturned and burned several private cars and police vehicles, smashed shop windows, and attacked police. The authorities responded with water cannon, tear gas, and warning shots fired into the air. Aided by a heavy downpour of rain, the police managed eventually to disperse the demonstrators.

In an attempt to pacify investors, the government put another 5 million lottery tickets on sale. To prevent further unrest while this was going on, police in riot gear patrolled the city in trucks, while officers on foot forced investors to wait in a squatting position rather than stand and shove. One report said policemen pulled young men seemingly at random from the waiting crowds and beat several of them mercilessly.[16]

The rioting in Shenzhen was the most serious reported outbreak of urban unrest in China since the Tiananmen Square protests. Although the authorities were able to restore order relatively quickly, and with a remarkable lack of bloodshed, the violence was a sharp reminder of how suddenly public anger could erupt when ordinary people felt their economic interests were being threatened by a corrupt and callous bureaucracy. It was also an indication of potential danger ahead as Deng's economic reforms gathered pace, and corruption became increasingly rampant. The Shenzhen protesters' suspicions about the extent of corruption involved in the lottery ticket issue were borne out by the findings of an official investigation. A government report said the malpractices alleged by the demonstrators were "basically identical" to those discovered during the inquiry.[17] It said 10 of the 11 financial institutions authorized to sell the lottery tickets were involved in illegal practices. About 4,000 workers at these institutions appropriated an average of more than 15 of the tickets each. Police and other officials took another 20,000 of them, and a similar number were given away by officials as gifts. One senior banking executive in the city took no fewer than 3,250 tickets for himself. "Government sources say the Shenzhen share incident has become a reminder of how much corruption has seeped into the well of economic reform," said the *China Daily* newspaper.[18]

As a result of the fiasco, the mayor of Shenzhen, Zheng Liangyu, was transferred in November to the far less high-profile post of deputy governor of Jiangxi Province. Five months later it was announced that the party secretary of Shenzhen, Li Hao, had also been demoted. His new job was that of "advisor" to the Shenzhen government. The reasons for the reshuffle were never announced to the public. The leadership was probably worried that if it criticized the two men more openly or punished them more severely, it would be effectively declaring open season on any reform-minded officials who failed to curb corruption among their subordinates. To do that would risk halting the reform process altogether.

Deng was lucky the Shenzhen riots occurred at a time when his political star was on the ascendancy. Such was the euphoria generated by his
southern tour both inside and outside the party that it would have been
difficult for his opponents to use the incident as an effective weapon
against him. A Beijing-controlled newspaper in Hong Kong warned hard-
liners not even to try, saying that "on no account should one advocate
giving up eating for fear of choking just because some twists and turns
occur. This 'leftist' thinking is greatly detrimental to reform and opening
to the outside world. At present, we should devote our main efforts to
guarding against 'leftism'. This argument is applicable to the handling of
the issue of stock market chaos."[19]

Deng was also lucky that the riots broke out so far away from Beijing in a city with little record of political dissent. Had they occurred in
the capital itself, they might have triggered a chain reaction among the
wide array of disaffected groups in the city, leading to far more serious
unrest. The impact of the violence on the share market itself was short-
lived. The authorities closed down the Shenzhen exchange the day after
the rioting. When it reopened the mood was bearish but not panicky. By
the end of the week, the Shenzhen share index was back to nearly the
same level as before the unrest. Foreign investors, who earlier in the year
had been allowed for the first time to trade in designated shares on the
Shenzhen and Shanghai exchanges, showed little sign of alarm over what
was going on. Given the importance of developing stock markets to
China's efforts to establish a market economy, there seemed little chance
the government would go as far as closing them down entirely. But
among Chinese leaders of all political hues, the incident was undoubtedly
a sobering lesson in the dangers of rapid, ill-regulated economic change.

A few months after the Shenzhen riots, these dangers became apparent in the capital itself when the authorities exposed a web of corruption
surrounding the affairs of a privately owned firm in Beijing. The government declared that the enterprise, the Great Wall Machinery and Electronics Scientific and Technological Company, was incapable of redeeming the high-interest bonds it had issued to some 200,000 small-time
investors, many of whom had spent their life savings on the debentures.
When the official media revealed in June 1993 that the company was
being liquidated, hundreds of angry investors flocked to the company's
headquarters on the northeastern edge of the city. When I arrived with a
colleague to interview them, the police tried to stop us, saying we needed
permission from higher authorities. As we argued with the officers, some
people in the crowd jeered and hissed at the police. Dozens of investors

followed us as we walked away and crowded round us once the police were out of sight. Then they poured out their anger, speaking with venom and bitterness not so much about the head of the company who had been accused by the official media of grave financial wrongdoings but about the government itself, which only a few months earlier had been praising the Great Wall Machinery and Electronics Company as an incarnation of the new reform spirit and encouraging people to invest in it. It was the first time I had heard members of a crowd in Beijing speaking with such heartfelt vehemence since Tiananmen.

In many other countries, the scandal surrounding the Great Wall Machinery and Electronics Company might have led to the resignation of a top leader or even a change of government. The Chinese authorities lamely tried to pin the blame entirely on the 39-year-old director of the company, Shen Taifu. The official media said Shen had issued bonds without the proper authorization and had violated government restrictions on the fixing of interest rates. It also accused him of embezzling funds from his company. But the official account was full of holes. The angry investors who gathered outside the company headquarters showed us copies of articles published only a few months earlier by the official media that had heaped praise on Shen and his enterprise. One clipping from the *Science and Technology Daily* included photographs of the deputy prime minister, Zou Jiahua, and the minister in charge of the State Science and Technology Commission, Song Jian, visiting Shen's company. Another was a lengthy piece by a deputy chairman of China's parliament, Fei Xiaotong, which appeared in no less authoritative a newspaper than the *People's Daily* in January 1993.[20] Fei, who is a well-known social scientist and a staunch defender of the party line, said in his gushing article that the company's techniques could "promote the development of the socialist market economy with Chinese characteristics as well as the market for science and technology." Fei said the company had grown in the space of a few years from a tiny operation owning just one bicycle to the biggest nonstate enterprise of its kind in the country, with its main product—a "highly efficient, energy-saving electric motor"—widely used by Chinese industries. Fei said the sale of bonds by the company was being carried out "in accordance with relevant regulations issued by the State Council." He even suggested China should adopt the "Great Wall model" of bond sales in order to overcome its lack of funds for developing and marketing new technology and put to use the huge amount of money in personal savings. Fei also praised the company for "respecting old comrades" by hiring more than 160 former high-ranking officials. He said these old cadres were called on by the management to give their views on every major decision made by the company. This practice, Fei said, helped the company to avoid many problems and save a lot of time. No wonder, given this authoritative figure's ringing endorsement of Shen Taifu's enterprise, that many ordinary citizens rushed out to buy the company's bonds. Shen even had a certificate from the State Science and Technology Commission saying his fund-raising technique was legitimate.

Why then did the authorities arrest Shen, accuse him of fraud, and in April 1994 execute him by firing squad and sentence his wife, who was a senior executive in the company, to 15 years in prison? Some observers believe the authorities might not have treated Shen so severely had he not called a news conference shortly before his arrest at which he tearfully informed Chinese and foreign reporters that he planned to sue the People's Bank of China and its governor, Li Guixian, for $17 million for freezing his company's accounts. "Nothing we have done is illegal," he said. "We were simply following Comrade Deng's instructions to raise money and develop high technology." Shen said his dream was to turn his company into something on the scale of General Motors. "If they accuse us of illegally gathering funds, then our 200,000 investors are accomplices—they would not accept that verdict, and it could lead to social turmoil," he warned. Shen Taifu's lawyer described the lawsuit, which had been filed a few days earlier at a Beijing court, as unprecedented for a Chinese company.[21] In the eyes of many Chinese officials, however, any attempt to defy authority, even through the courts, is an unacceptable challenge. The court refused to accept the petition, and the day after the news conference Shen was arrested at Beijing's Capital Airport while attempting to board a flight bound for southern China, allegedly after presenting a fake identity card.

The authorities reinforced the impression that Shen Taifu was a scapegoat for higher-level wrongdoing by showing uncertainty over exactly what charges to lodge against him. In its first report on the case, Xinhua News Agency accused him of illegally raising funds and embezzling investors' money.[22] It said the bonds his company issued were "nothing but a fraud" and that Shen had violated regulations by refusing to tell investors what he planned to do with their money. The news agency said Shen had "squandered" funds by setting up 120 subsidiaries across the country, each of which spent huge sums on luxury cars, houses, and carpets. But when Shen was finally sentenced to death in March 1994, the main charges against him were bribery and embezzlement. "Illegally raising funds" had slipped way down the list of concerns.

The authorities appeared to have backtracked somewhat from their earlier attempt to portray Shen's crime as primarily that of issuing bonds without proper authority. Xinhua mentioned "illegal fund-raising" only in passing without explaining how Shen's scheme had supposedly violated the law.[23] One possible explanation is that they realized that too many investors had seen articles like Fei Xiaotong's in the *People's Daily* saying Shen's bonds were issued "in accordance with relevant regulations."

Shen's offer of 24 percent interest on his bonds was three times higher than the rate offered by state-run banks on deposits and about eight percentage points higher than the level of urban inflation. Official reports portrayed it as a pyramid scheme, pointing out that the 1 billion yuan worth of bonds Shen had sold since May 1992 was far in excess of the value of the company's assets. But the reports had remarkably little to say about what exactly was wrong with it, failing to repeat even the suggestion made by a Beijing-controlled newspaper in Hong Kong that interest rates on bonds should not exceed bank deposit rates by more than 40 percent.[24] Shen, it appears, had circumvented the interest rate rule by describing his bonds as "technical contracts." Clearly the authorities were stabbing in the dark, with only a very flimsy legal framework to back them up. Their case was made all the more difficult by the fact that Shen's company had honored its "contracts" with investors.

Shen was by no means alone in offering extremely high-interest bonds. The government's efforts in late 1992 to reduce inflationary pressure by restricting bank loans prompted many enterprises and local governments to raise money directly from the public by offering bonds at 20 or 30 percent interest. Investors' money often went straight into the booming real estate market or into car-smuggling rackets, both of which at the time were yielding fabulous returns. Investors had no worries because those issuing the bonds were mostly state-owned entities, which meant that if their ventures failed, higher authorities would usually step in to bail them out. But the government was apparently fearful that in the get-rich-quick atmosphere generated by Deng's southern tour, pyramid schemes would flourish and eventually, when they collapsed, trigger social unrest. "In China, people's anticipation is high," commented the *China Daily* newspaper. "It is so high that serious social uncertainty will result if the investment bubble is burst."[25]

The Chinese authorities pulled out all the stops to make sure that disappointed investors in Shen's company did not take to the streets. In order to avoid giving the impression that investors in similar schemes could get their money back come what may, the government vigorously denied that it used its own money to redeem the bonds. Most likely, however, the government helped make up some of the shortfall in order to avoid unrest. Officials said bondholders were able to recoup about 90 percent of their investment—in spite of the fact that Shen was alleged to have squandered and embezzled so much of the company's funds and that the company's assets were worth far less than the bonds it had issued. In its first report on the case, Xinhua said there had been "heavy losses" from the funds raised by Shen. It said only about 15 percent of the money he had collected by selling bonds in Beijing was found in his company's account when it was frozen by the central bank.

If Shen Taifu's operation was indeed illegal, the fact that he was able to sell his bonds so publicly amid so much positive publicity in the official media for 10 months before the government decided to stop him suggests there was high-level complicity in his crime. The only top-ranking official indicted in the case was the deputy minister of the State Science and Technology Commission, Li Xiaoshi. Li was sentenced to 20 years in prison for allegedly accepting a 40,000-yuan bribe from Shen Taifu and other bribes from Hong Kong businesspeople as well as for embezzling public money. Eleven other state functionaries, including a middle-ranking official, four reporters, and three bank clerks were also prosecuted for taking bribes from Shen Taifu. Two of the journalists were sentenced to seven years and six years in prison, respectively, for accepting payment to write positive stories about Shen's company. The fate of the others was not made public, nor was that of another 120 officials who a Beijing-controlled newspaper in Hong Kong said were being investigated for their alleged dealings with Shen.[26] It seems unlikely, however, that deputy minister Li Xiaoshi really was the only top-level official involved in the case. Questions certainly deserve to be asked about how Fei Xiaotong, the senior parliamentarian, came to write his glowing account of Shen's operation in the *People's Daily*. The official media never mentioned Fei's dealings with Shen Taifu, nor did they explain why other top officials who visited his company, including Song Jian and Zou Jiahua, failed to point out any wrongdoings. One of Li Xiaoshi's fellow deputy ministers in the State Science and Technology Commission was Deng Nan, the daughter of Deng Xiaoping. Could she have been unaware of what was going on? Obviously there was far more corruption or at best incompetence involved in the Shen Taifu case than the leadership ever admitted.

That top-level officials should turn a blind eye to or actively encourage Shen's dealings was not so surprising given Deng's instructions on his southern tour. "Once we are sure that something should be done, we should dare to experiment and break a new path," Deng had said.[27] "No one can ever be 100 percent sure at the outset that what he is doing is correct. I've never been that sure. . . . It will probably take another thirty years to develop a more mature and well-defined system in every field." As one Beijing University professor put it, some people interpreted Deng's new drive to set up a "socialist market economy" as meaning the economy should be free of all restrictions. "This view or practice has gone much further than the 'laissez-faire economy' put forward by Adam Smith in the eighteenth century," he said.[28]

The publicity surrounding Shen Taifu's alleged crimes and his execution failed to put a complete end to ventures of a similar nature. Remarkably, given Shen's fate, a pyramid scheme of even greater proportions was revealed by the official press in July 1995. The case involved an apparently well connected woman in the city of Wuxi in eastern Jiangsu Province who the media said had defrauded investors, including many government departments, to the tune of some $300 million by promising high interest rates. Her scheme had been running for five years—right through the Shen Taifu scandal—before it was halted by the authorities.

In early 1993 before Shen Taifu's problems came to light, the Chinese Academy of Social Sciences published a prediction that China would be plagued by increasing instances of rioting and other isolated "group actions" triggered mainly by "serious abuse of power among local officials" and the harming of people's economic interests by such problems as factory closures.[29] The report said corruption was being fueled by the increasingly widespread phenomenon of officials going into business without quitting their government posts. In 1992, as Deng's new reform campaign took off, more than 120,000 officials left their jobs to do business.[30] A far greater number, however, preferred to earn money on the side while still enjoying the security and prestige of a civil service job. One estimate put the total number of officials doing business by the end of 1992 at 10 million.[31] "Amid the pounding of the great wave of the market economy, the official class was the one most violently shaken up, with many of its members feeling a sense of loss or bewilderment about their future," said one Chinese commentator.[32] In a market economy, wealth would become as important if not more so than power. Many bureaucrats felt they had to change their way of life in order to keep ahead. Their privileged positions gave them ready opportunity to do so. "It seems as if overnight, power, perks, and rank have plunged in people's estimation," said the commentator. With funds, labor, and materials all increasingly available through nongovernment channels, many official positions were becoming obsolete. The rich could now simply buy on the open market the coveted goods to which once only officials had access.

The Chinese leadership, determined to thin the ranks of the country's 35-million-strong bureaucracy, actively encouraged officials to go into business. In 1992, Deng's reform campaign suppressed the lingering misgivings of hard-liners about reforming the bloated, inefficient bureaucracy, which for decades had recruited its members on the basis of political loyalty and personal connections rather than any publicly assessed standard of competence. The hard-liners feared the country would lose its political cohesion if expertise were given precedence over ideological purity. But at the 14th Congress in October, the party leader Jiang Zemin called for the introduction as soon as possible of a "national civil service system," which officials explained as being something more akin to the Western system of recruitment by public examination. "We should transfer a large number of personnel to tertiary industries[33] and other work posts that need to be strengthened, thereby turning these people into a vital new force for the modernization program," Jiang said. The plan that emerged in 1992 was to trim the bureaucracy by a quarter within the next few years, with at least 1 million people to go by the end of the following year.

Inspired by Deng's southern tour, government departments leaped at the chance to generate more money and get rid of unwanted staff. "After news spread in the autumn of cuts in civil service departments and staff, even those cadres who were not interested [in doing business] before could no longer sit still," said the Chinese Academy of Social Sciences.[34] "It was like adding oil to the fire. The heat went up and up, spreading to every town and village as far as the borders." In the northern province of Hebei alone, government units set up more than 5,500 businesses that year, employing some 50,000 former civil servants. In the first 10 months of 1992, the number of real estate companies in China increased tenfold and the number of trading firms one hundredfold—most of them run by officials or former officials.[35] Whereas long touted efforts to separate party and government functions were being pursued halfheartedly at best, the commercialization of the Chinese bureaucracy was carried out with revolutionary fervor.

This was not the first stampede by officials and government departments into business. As the economy boomed in the late 1980s under the guidance of Zhao Ziyang, there was a similar rush. Many turned to profiteering, a phenomenon that became one of the main complaints of demonstrators during the Tiananmen Square protests. In 1992, however, what the official media dubbed the "business fever" unleashed by Deng's southern tour was far greater in scope than anything experienced before in the course of reform. A Communist Party directive issued a few weeks after Deng's trip specifically allowed government departments to set up enterprises.[36] Many local governments rushed to issue their own guidelines in order to encourage the trend. Local regulations allowed officials to keep their government ranks and perks while engaging in business. The only minor inconvenience they sometimes had to suffer was the loss of their government salaries. Not surprisingly, many bureaucrats were more than willing to make that sacrifice when they could earn many times as much money in the private sector.

Having whipped up this "business fever," the authorities appeared at a loss as to how to regulate it. The sophisticated legal framework that governs the market economies of industrialized nations simply does not exist in China. In mid-1993, several months into the drive to set up a "socialist market economy," Liang Guoqing, China's deputy attorney general, admitted that it was becoming harder to distinguish between crimes and acceptable business practices.[37] "Problems involving the boundary between crimes of graft and bribery and noncriminal cases have increased," the *China Daily* quoted Liang as saying.

In July 1993, the central authorities belatedly tried to take action. The government issued a circular decreeing that party and government officials must not hold concurrent jobs of any kind in economic entities and must not moonlight. Enterprises set up by government departments to absorb excess staff must sever all ties with their parent organizations. The circular also banned government departments from deriving any kind of profit from enterprises they set up. In practice the new directive made little difference—the revolution Deng had unleashed proved unstoppable. One of my friends, a middle-ranking official in a state-run news organization, continued to run his own advertising and public relations company, exploiting the many contacts he had made in government and commercial circles while working as a journalist. One of his schemes was to act as an agent helping companies get endorsement from prominent high-ranking officials and other famous people. He said that normally, in order to invite a top official to attend an opening ceremony or the like, it was necessary to seek approval through a central department that schedules such activities. Approval, however, being very difficult to obtain, my friend hoped to make money as a middleman by using his extensive contacts with the secretaries of senior officials, which would enable him to bypass the regular channel. "These old men want some money to give their grandchildren," he said, "so they don't mind selling their calligraphy or other services." He said he had no choice but to do business on the side. His official salary of 400 yuan a month was not enough to cover his child's kindergarten fees, he complained. My friend and his associates showed not the slightest fear that the venture might be stopped. The government knew that to crack down effectively would dangerously undermine the morale of state employees. Its actions appeared largely confined to issuing stern-sounding but ineffectual directives.

Even official publications often drew attention to the abuses committed by bureaucrats-turned-businesspeople. One typical account told of how some Construction Department officials wanted to take over the management of a successful local restaurant.[38] When the establishment's owner declined, the officials told him not to worry, and they would remain on good terms. A few weeks later, however, the construction began of a public lavatory opposite the restaurant. The owner, realizing his business was doomed, changed his mind and agreed to cede management of the restaurant to the officials. No sooner had he done so than work on the lavatory mysteriously ceased. Other reports in the official press told of how bureaucrats who had gone into trade would order enterprises to buy their goods. Anxious not to get on the wrong side of officialdom, the enterprises would buy them even if the products were of poor quality. Sometimes when organizing launch ceremonies for new companies, officials would send out invitations to big factories they had dealings with, indicating on them a bank account number to which guests could make donations.[39]

Enterprises set up by officials were sometimes referred to in the press as "flipped nameplate companies"[40] because of their easily interchangeable roles as businesses and government departments. A book on corrupt officialdom published by hard-liners in 1993 quoted an economist as saying of these new companies, "Overnight, we've turned the clock back more than a decade. This is a major step backward for reform."[41] Many ordinary Chinese I met expressed similar sentiments.

The growing class of nouveaux riches officials made little secret of its wealth. In Beijing's most lavish restaurants, a significant proportion of the customers would usually be civil servants, wining and dining at the state's expense. Restaurant managers would complain quite frankly that anticorruption drives were bad for business. In Nanjing, the owners of about 20 percent of the city's privately run restaurants sold off their businesses at giveaway prices in the space of just three months in late 1993 because of a new campaign against graft.[42] By early 1994, at least a third of Beijing's karaoke bars and nightclubs were on the verge of bankruptcy thanks to the campaign. But one official report noted that many club owners expected the situation to change, believing that "campaigns come and go, and everything would resume just as it had been before the crackdown."[43]

Officials who preferred straight cash to lavish meals and entertainment could always buy fake restaurant and hotel receipts from black market receipt dealers who loitered around subway exits and other busy places in Beijing and other cities. These were particularly useful for the traveling official on expenses who could stay at the cheapest inn or with friends or relatives then use the receipts to claim much larger sums of money than he had spent.

In August 1993, the deputy attorney general Liang Guoqing admitted openly that corruption was worse than at any other time since the communists came to power.[44] "Crimes of graft and bribery now involve larger sums of money and more party and government officials than previously," he said. "More and more officials working in judicial departments and economic management departments now participate in such crimes. . . . [Corruption] has spread into the party, government administrations, and every part of society, including politics, economy, ideology, and culture."

The statistics underscored the extent of the problem. In the first nine months of 1993, about 10 percent of people prosecuted by the authorities were officials, even though bureaucrats make up only 3.5 percent of the population.[45] In the following year, Liang's office investigated more than 1,450 officials at or above the level of county chief or head of government department for suspected corruption.[46] This was a nearly threefold increase over the same period of 1993. The official press said "a considerable number" of those officials were "leading cadres in party and government bodies who had real power." Liang admitted that the authorities were sometimes fearful of investigating high-ranking officials. "But this does not involve a large number," he said. The popular perception was certainly otherwise. The common saying among ordinary Chinese was still that the authorities were "catching flies, not tigers."

The armed forces, once extolled by Mao Zedong as a bastion of ideological purity, were as much infected by what the media described as "hedonism and money-worship" as any other part of the establishment.

Ever since Deng came to power the military had been officially encouraged to set up its own businesses as a way of supplementing its budget. These ranged from tiny companies employing a handful of servicemen's dependents and retirees to huge conglomerates such as the Poly Group, a company headed by several close relatives of the country's top leaders and whose concerns range from arms exports to a multimillion-dollar hotel and office complex in northeastern Beijing. In many cases these companies help to finance bonuses and luxuries such as imported cars for ill-paid officers. The military has become increasingly involved in smuggling rackets along the coast, real estate speculation, and profiteering. So conspicuous has the problem become that China's two highest-ranking military officials, Generals Liu Huaqing and Zhang Zhen, warned in July 1993 that "decadent capitalist ideology and lifestyles" were threatening efforts to build up the army.[47] Their lengthy article, which was published prominently by the Chinese press, noted that "in both Chinese and foreign history, quite a few armies . . . were defeated by themselves as peace and prosperity filled the land, as the civil officials became indolent and the military officers became frivolous."

The Chinese military operated virtually outside the law. One common misdemeanor among army personnel was the sale of military identity cards for hundreds if not thousands of dollars each to criminals who regarded them as get-out-of-jail-free cards. In June 1993, the official press said the authorities had uncovered a racket involving as many as 300 military officials who allegedly sold demobilization papers to workers so that they could enjoy the better housing and employment opportunities given to ex-servicemen.[48]

Officials became increasingly open about the extent of the corruption problem. During the annual session of the National People's Congress in March 1994, many of the party-approved delegates fiercely condemned the phenomenon. One of them, the vice president of the Central Communist Party School, Xing Fensi, said corruption had led to "acute tension" between the public and party officials.[49] "If not dealt with properly, this will cause social unrest and political instability," Xing warned. He also noted that the widening gap between rich and poor was causing "the utmost dissatisfaction."

Corruption has always been a way of life in China. The exchanging of gifts and lavish meals is an established part of business ritual. Chinese journalists think nothing of accepting gifts from interviewees. News conferences are often accompanied by lavish banquets and many Chinese companies even offer cash to reporters, handing it out in envelopes at the start or end of a briefing.[50] In Taiwan, similar practices are common too. During the island's local and parliamentary elections in December 1989, officials handed out cameras to foreign reporters and hosted a banquet for them that included sharks' fin and abalone dishes—among the most expensive items of Chinese cuisine. What makes official corruption so destabilizing in China now, however, is that officials already have grossly disproportionate advantages in the race to set up a market economy. China may have given the go-ahead to engage in capitalism, but with land, property, and funds already concentrated in the hands of the state, the winners are bound to be those with bureaucratic connections. Japan and the "little tigers" of Asia began with somewhat more level playing fields. In China, officials can often take virtually whatever risks they like with the money at their disposal, knowing they would nearly always be protected by their positions and the party. They and not legal codes usually determine what is sound business practice.

In the countryside, corruption and abuse of power by officials is no less rampant than it is in the cities (a problem discussed in more detail in the following chapter). Rural officials may not have quite the same opportunities as their urban counterparts to make fortunes in the stock and real estate markets, but the economic boom and the continuing decline of central government authority has given them a freer hand than they have enjoyed in many years to build up their power and engage in graft. One example of this, noted by the official media, is the increasing appropriation by rural cadres of farmland for the building of factories. Peasants who had tilled the fields often receive little if any compensation in return. "Recently, the seizures of arable land by state-run and collectively run units has nearly run out of control," said the *China Daily* in April 1993.[51] A year later, the appropriation of farmland by village officials triggered riots by hundreds of peasants in Shitan County of Guangdong Province, about 50 miles from Canton. Police used tear gas to break up the demonstration, during which peasants waved banners saying, "Down with corruption."[52] Similar protests occurred in at least three other Guangdong villages that month. On December 31st, 1994, Guangdong police fired tear gas to disperse some 500 peasants in Zhuhai SEZ who were protesting over the confiscation of land for commercial development.

In the year leading up to Deng's southern tour, the party promoted a new movie about an honest rural official, Jiao Yulu, who as a county party secretary in the early 1960s led local people in fighting poverty and continued to work even though he was dying of cancer. Propagandistic though the film was, it proved enormously popular. The posthumous hero of the Cultural Revolution enjoyed a new lease on life in the popular imagination, with many moviegoers saying they knew of no official nowadays as selfless as Jiao Yulu. Some even wept as they watched the film. Buoyed by the public display of enthusiasm for a model communist, the authorities issued a Jiao Yulu postage stamp the following year, and in May 1994, on the 30th anniversary of Jiao's death, a senior Politburo member and other top officials attended the unveiling of a bronze statue of Jiao at a newly built memorial hall in the late hero's honor in his home province of Henan. The party's efforts to encourage rural officials to emulate Jiao, however, failed dismally. In January 1994, the *People's Daily* revealed that nearly 300,000 people in a flood-stricken area of southern Hunan Province were left starving after local officials sold their emergency grain supplies on the black market.[53] It said that some of the peasants had been forced to abandon their homes and go begging because of the food shortage. The head of the county's grain department and some of his colleagues allegedly sold most of the grain to firms and private individuals, making a total profit of nearly $100,000. The authorities confiscated the illegal earnings, imposed fines totaling $2,300 on those responsible, and said they would take further legal proceedings. The case, however, received no further publicity. Small wonder that the countryside, once the bedrock of Communist Party support and the showcase of Deng Xiaoping's reforms, was beginning to show signs of revolt.

6

Without Grain There Will Be Chaos

Historical experience and lessons indicate that whenever there are problems in agriculture and grain, the overall national economy and social stability will be affected. Without agriculture, there will be instability; without grain, there will be chaos.
— *Li Peng, prime minister, December 1992*

The 50-mile journey southward from the city center of Chengdu to the county of Renshou takes the traveler from a booming urban sprawl to backward rural China. The route begins on a brand new four-lane stretch of highway lined with factories, gaudy mock-Western-style villas, and karaoke bars. It ends on a narrow road that winds for several miles through vast expanses of lush paddy, past ancient villages surrounded by thickets of towering bamboo, and eventually into hills sculpted by narrow concentric strips of terraced fields.

Renshou lies beyond the prosperous belt of countryside surrounding Chengdu where the peasants work in the fields three months of the year and spend the rest of their time either working in village factories or sitting in roadside tea houses, playing cards or chess. The climate is good, the soil fertile, and Chengdu, the capital of Sichuan Province, offers plenty of job opportunities for young peasant women in the myriad bars and restaurants springing up in the city. They may not get much money by city standards for being waitresses, but for them it is riches beyond compare. Chengdu, deep in the interior, was slow to feel the effects of China's economic transformation. But then in 1992 after Deng's southern tour, the leadership selected it as one of the new "open cities," which meant it could offer foreign investors attractive incentives such as a two-year exemption from taxes. Its cheap land and direct air links with Hong Kong began to lure in droves of overseas businesspeople. Among them were many from Taiwan to whom Sichuan has a special significance as the province where they or their parents lived half a century earlier when the nationalist government had its wartime capital in Chongqing, southeast of Chengdu. But investors rarely got as far as Renshou, which had little to attract them. About 90 percent of the 1.5 million inhabitants of Renshou are peasants who raise pigs or use their tiny plots of land to produce rice, cotton, and cooking oil.

I was never given official permission to visit Renshou because from early 1993 onward it was the center of some of the most serious rural unrest ever reported in the history of communist rule. In the middle of June of that year, a spokesperson for the Sichuan government finally gave the first official account of rioting in Renshou, weeks after reports on the disturbances had begun to appear in the Hong Kong press. The slowness with which the news trickled out was a striking example of how impenetrable the Chinese countryside is for foreign journalists. Renshou is a mere 50 miles from the capital of China's most populous province, a city that counted that year an American consulate among its several dozen (now several hundred) foreign representative offices. Yet until the first reports of unrest appeared in Hong Kong newspapers, a few weeks after it had broken out, Beijing-based correspondents had no inkling of what was going on.

The Hong Kong newspaper *Ming Pao* reported that in early January 10,000 peasants had "staged a rebellion" in Renshou, burning two official cars and attacking court personnel.[1] The peasants' anger had been triggered by the local government's demands for contributions to repair a national highway through the county. In one of Renshou's several dozen townships, the local party secretary reportedly led a team of 60 people to the homes of peasants to demand payment. Those who refused to give cash were forced to hand over valuables or grain instead. "One peasant household's last three bowls of rice were taken away, and another woman was paraded through the streets," said the newspaper. The official account released three months after *Ming Pao*'s report did not confirm that Renshou officials had gone to these lengths to raise money, but it did admit that "some local cadres worked in an impatient and rude manner."[2]

The provincial leadership in Chengdu tried to ease tensions by ordering a halt to the levying of funds for the highway. According to the official account, the government agreed that the money already exacted from the peasants would be repaid to them, with interest, after the completion of the highway project. "Local peasants were satisfied with the decision. . . . A tense situation began to relax," the government report said.

But the trouble was far from over. According both to the official account and reports in the Hong Kong press, tension mounted again in early May when a little-known Chinese newspaper published a front-page story saying that some parts of Renshou had resumed the collection of funds for the highway and that one peasant who had spoken out against this practice had been "handcuffed and trussed to a tree for several hours." Peasants copied the article (which officials said later was "seriously untrue") and posted it in public places. Violence quickly erupted. One Hong Kong account said peasants kidnapped a local official in charge of land affairs and severely beat him. "Some peasants who had lost their senses began attacking cadres whenever they met them and smashing all the cars in sight," said the report.[3] The newspaper said 40 out of 60 officials in Fujia District where the violence mainly occurred were verbally or physically assaulted. Peasants reportedly surrounded the party and government headquarters of Fujia and rampaged through a vinegar factory and rabbit farm in the district, destroying and looting equipment. Of these latest developments, the outside world knew nothing at the time, but the leadership in Beijing was becoming increasingly alarmed.

"If economic trouble occurs in the 1990s, it is very likely to be in agriculture," Deng Xiaoping was often quoted by Chinese officials as saying. "If there is agricultural trouble, the country will not recover for many years, and the development of the overall economic and social situation would be severely affected." Trouble in the countryside was definitely brewing.

Worried about the prospect of growing unrest in Renshou and elsewhere, the party Central Committee and State Council issued an "emergency circular" in March 1993 warning that peasants were "very displeased" about the imposition of unfair or illegal charges on them by local governments.[4] It said some local authorities had disregarded Beijing's orders to "lighten the peasants' burdens" and were "surreptitiously" taking measures to make sure the orders were not carried out. The circular said such behavior, if continued, "would not only directly affect progress in agricultural production but would also adversely affect stability in rural areas and even in society as a whole." It described the reduction of fees and levies imposed on peasants as "an urgent political task."

The "emergency circular" proved ineffective, so two months later the leadership in Beijing tried again. On May 27th, the *People's Daily* published yet more regulations concerning the imposition of charges on peasants. Among these was a specific ban on the frequent practice of sending what it called "work teams" or "shock brigades" from door to door to collect fees. It also banned the seizure of grain, livestock, or furniture from those who could not or would not pay. In Renshou, however, this latest directive simply poured oil on the flames. On seeing the new regulations, Renshou peasants began demanding that the local authorities repay all fees exacted in previous years that did not conform to the new rules. According to the Hong Kong newspaper *Hsin Pao,* the May 27th regulations caused a "real intensification [of the unrest] into raids against district government and township government buildings, the burning of cars, and 'large-scale riots.' "[5]

By the beginning of June, it had not rained for more than six weeks, and Renshou was in the grips of a drought. On top of their anger over excessive levies, peasants were worried about the impact the weather might have on the rice harvest. On June 5th, tensions erupted into the worst violence the county had seen so far. It began when word spread among more than 10,000 people who had gathered for market day that police had arrested one of the ringleaders of the unrest. According to the official account, "villagers took some police on duty as hostages" and demanded the peasant's release. "More and more onlookers gathered, and more than 50 police on duty were encircled and held up on a road," said the report. "In order to prevent the situation from deteriorating, the police sent reinforcements of more than 130 unarmed [paramilitary] police to the scene to try to rescue their colleagues from the siege."

The official account played down the fierceness of the rioting that ensued. "A small number of people threw stones at the police and public security officers," it said. "The [paramilitary] police force was forced to fire a small quantity of tear gas in order to disperse the crowd and rescue the police. When that succeeded, the police rapidly withdrew from the scene. After the police left, a small number of lawbreakers set fire to five vehicles, including two police vehicles and three civilian vehicles."

The authorities said seven people were arrested in connection with the disturbances. The *Washington Post*'s Lena Sun said villagers told her the figure was closer to 30. Nonetheless, the crackdown was less intense than might have been expected given the scale of the violence. The leadership was clearly fearful of exacerbating the situation. Officials said the provincial government decided in the end to spend a million dollars of its own money on the highway project. It also dismissed or transferred more than 60 Renshou officials whose behavior had allegedly angered the peasants.

The Renshou riots were by far the biggest antigovernment protests reported in the Chinese countryside since the reforms began in the late 1970s. But by early 1993, rumors and occasional confirmations of other smaller-scale unrest in rural areas were becoming increasingly common. Ironically, it was Deng's southern tour that led indirectly to the upsurge of rural discontent. "It has been a proven fact that in the last more than 40 years since the founding of the country, every time the economy grows rapidly, agriculture is easily ignored," said the Chinese Academy of Social Sciences.[6]

Deng hardly mentioned agriculture during his trip to the south. His aim was to promote rapid growth, and he saw industry as a far more powerful and efficient engine than agriculture for achieving that goal. Industry was officially forecast to grow by more than 6.5 percent annually through the 1990s and agriculture only 1.5 percent. This would mark a considerable slowdown for agriculture compared with the period from 1984 to 1988 when the sector recorded average annual growth of 4.5 percent. In the early 1980s, when rural reforms first got underway, the growth rate was still higher. Following Deng's tour, however, many rural officials felt they had the green light to ignore agriculture altogether and reallocated their budgets to building up industries and setting up "development zones" that offered preferential terms for foreign investors. Money spent this way offered quicker and better returns than money spent on peasants. As far back as December 1991, in response to already simmering discontent among agricultural workers, Beijing had ordered that each peasant's contribution to the local government should not exceed 5 percent of that person's income, about half of what peasants were then paying on average. But local authorities routinely ignored this directive and turned to peasants to finance breakneck industrial expansion, exacting levies often amounting to two or three times more than the limit decreed by Beijing. Many local officials felt that in the absence of bigger contributions from higher-level authorities, not just for building factories but for the whole range of services provided by the grassroots bureaucracy, they had no choice but to turn to peasants for funding. By the end of 1992, most local governments in China had insufficient cash in hand to pay peasants for the grain and cotton the state had contracted to buy. Instead, they resorted to a time-honored practice in times of cash shortage—handing out IOUs. The problem was compounded by the inability of rural post offices to redeem the money orders sent by the fast-growing army of former peasants working in the cities to their relatives in the countryside. This was because rural state-owned banks had lent their money to local governments for industrial and infrastructure projects and did not have enough money left to lend to post offices. As the Lunar New Year approached, an avalanche of these postal orders descended on the countryside from migrant laborers who expected their peasant relatives to exchange them for cash to spend on the celebrations. The recipients were often sorely disappointed, sometimes having to wait several weeks or even months before the post offices had enough money to give them.

Chinese officials hinted that discontent in the countryside was becoming increasingly widespread. In December 1992, the party leader Jiang Zemin traveled to Wuhan, the capital of Hubei Province, to preside over a conference on agriculture attended by leaders of six rice-growing provinces in central and southwestern China from which reports of peasant unrest had been most frequent. Jiang demanded that no more IOUs—or "white slips" as they are termed in Chinese—be given to peasants. During a tour of the Hubei countryside, Jiang was told by local officials that peasants were "feeling a great burden," were "angry" and "resentful," and that relations between rural cadres and peasants were "tense."[7]

A few days later in Beijing, Prime Minister Li Peng called a video conference of provincial and municipal leaders across the country, telling them to exchange all the IOUs for cash in time to allow peasants to enjoy the Lunar New Year festivities.[8] Li was clearly worried about a possible explosion of unrest if local governments failed to pay peasants before the holiday. Although the IOUs-for-grain phenomenon had occurred from time to time in parts of China over the last several years, it had never been so widespread as it was in 1992 and early 1993.[9] Fearful of revolt, the central government rushed more than $500 million in emergency funds to the provinces, thereby allowing most peasants to cash in their "white slips" before the festival.

But the "green slips," as the money orders issued by post offices are known, remained a problem. In Nanchong Prefecture, Sichuan Province, about 100 miles east of Chengdu, about 60 percent of rural post offices were attacked by angry peasants in the buildup to the New Year holiday that fell on January 23rd.[10] This was by no means a small-scale disturbance. Nanchong consists of more than 100 large rural settlements and a far greater number of smaller villages with a total population of 1.3 million people in a hilly area some 50 miles from north to south and 40 miles from east to west. *China Daily* said seven postal workers were injured in the violence, and the doors and windows of several post offices were smashed.

The unrest in Nanchong occurred in spite of the Sichuan government's hurried efforts that month to get money out to the rural post offices. The money proved far from enough. An official newspaper cited the case of Qianjiang County, a remote and impoverished area of southeastern Sichuan.[11] Many of Qianjiang's inhabitants belong to the Tujia and Miao ethnic minorities, which have been living in the hills of central China for thousands of years. The newspaper said the provincial bank sent $350,000 to Qianjiang's post offices. Five months later, however, there were still more than $900,000 worth of money orders waiting to be cashed. The farmers desperately needed the money to buy seed and fertilizer. "From time to time, peasants run amuck through post offices, lay siege to them, or surround and attack post office personnel," said the report. "There is nothing the postal authorities can do about it." In one district of Qianjiang, more than 200 retired workers from a salt factory who received their pensions in the form of postal orders staged a sit-in at their local post office, "shouting curses and refusing to leave." An official report said Sichuan was among four central and southwestern provinces worst affected by the postal order crisis.[12] It said at least seven other provinces experienced similar difficulties.

Rather than resort to open confrontation with the authorities, some peasants simply fled their villages to escape the growing burden of taxes and fees. In July 1993, I interviewed a few of the thousands of peasants who throng the forecourt of Beijing Railway Station every day, some of them waiting for trains to take them to more prosperous cities, others newly arrived in Beijing hoping to find work. Standing amid one group of dirty and disheveled travelers, a 27-year-old man told me he had left his village in the northwestern province of Shaanxi because he had to pay a third of his income in taxes. "We have to pay all kinds of taxes as well as fees for education," he said. "This makes my life unbearable, so that's why I want to find a job outside my province. There are many people like me. I think everywhere in the countryside is just the same. The government has been saying that the burden imposed on peasants should be reduced, but at the grass roots officials ignore these regulations." Another man from the neighboring province of Shanxi said many of his fellow villagers grumbled about taxes. "They even disperse leaflets complaining about this problem," he said. A peasant woman, however, told me that many did not dare to protest. "Sometimes we think it's all just too much for us to bear," she said. "We don't want to pay all these fees, but I don't think people dare complain. When we do complain, the cadres say you just have to pay so we have no choice but to pay."

I was at the railway station no longer than about 20 minutes before I started noticing that two or three people who did not look like peasants were listening intently to my interviews, which I was recording for a radio report. One of them butted in and asked a peasant who I was and whether I had permission to be there. The eavesdroppers were clearly plainclothes police. In order to protect my tapes and avoid causing further trouble for my interviewees, I left in a hurry. The authorities were clearly nervous about what foreign journalists might learn from unbriefed peasants.

Very few foreign correspondents saw much of the Chinese countryside at all during this critical period. Lena Sun on her unauthorized trip to Renshou in Sichuan only stayed in the area for about an hour and a half before she sensed that local cadres were beginning to realize who she was and decided to leave. In mid-1993, Caroline Straathof of the Dutch newspaper *Das Volkskrant* and Kathy Wilhelm of the Associated Press visited a rural area of Henan Province in northern China. Their request to visit another province that reports indicated had been more badly affected by peasant unrest was turned down. But even in Henan, they had little freedom to find out what was really going on. "They wouldn't let us go into counties that we wanted to visit because we had heard reports of unrest there. We ended up in a place where we wouldn't have gone if we had had the freedom [to choose] ourselves," Straathof told me. "The two villages [we went to] were very well prepared for our visit. . . . We were assigned an official who got extremely upset the moment we left our hotel, so we had very little opportunity to go out on our own. We never got into really poor areas where people are dissatisfied." The two journalists' difficulties were typical of those experienced by other foreign correspondents.

The official Chinese press, however, gave plenty of hints of the scale of the problem. In April, the *Beijing Daily* newspaper admitted that the Communist Party's reputation in rural areas had "fallen sharply."[13] It said that in some places, officials armed with truncheons were stealing grain, animals, and furniture from peasants who could not afford to pay the levies. In many areas, peasants were being asked to contribute for newspaper subscriptions even though they never read newspapers. They were also being forced to buy insurance for their houses and crops. In one district peasants were told by local officials that if they did not buy insurance, they would receive no government aid if their property was destroyed by natural disaster. In another area, peasants who refused to buy "old age insurance" were barred from working outside their villages or taking up more lucrative jobs in rural factories. Many peasants were also being forced to make contributions for public showings of old films that few of them turned up to watch. Soaring school fees were forcing many peasants to withdraw their children from school.

The *Beijing Daily* provided one of the strongest indications of the rebellious mood in the countryside. An old peasant in northeastern China, who was in her late twenties when the communists took control, was quoted as saying, "They demand money from the peasants for everything, from having children to falling ill and dying, from tilling the soil to raising chickens, from building houses to getting married. The peasants really cannot bear it. If officials carry on behaving like this, we will definitely be forced to rebel." Another peasant beat his breast and said, "Some officials have no party spirit, all they do is demand money. If this carries on, I'll be the first to join an uprising." The newspaper quoted one peasant woman as uttering the traditional Chinese cry of despair in the face of an uncaring government—"heavens" (*tian ah*)—before drowning herself in May 1992. Officials had seized the 37-year-old woman's possessions after she failed to pay school construction and family planning fees.

A journal published in southern China said peasants in one village where officials were confiscating the property of those who failed to pay their taxes regarded the cadres as "even worse than the KMT."[14] The report said the peasants fondly recalled the days of Chairman Mao when local officials were more disciplined. "Recalling Chairman Mao's attitude to peasants when he was alive and looking [now] at these 'local tyrants' who only grow brambles instead of flowers for the party, we do feel that even our parents are not as dear to us as Chairman Mao," the article quoted the villagers as saying. In 1992, the authorities acknowledged that at least eight peasants killed themselves because they could not pay their taxes—a tiny number, perhaps, compared with the size of the rural population. Nonetheless, the fact that the government admitted to it at all was a shocking indictment of conditions in rural areas, particularly in a country where suicide is commonly regarded as a very potent form of protest.

The surge of antigovernment sentiment among peasants coincided with official reports suggesting that party and government control in some areas was seriously declining. Banditry was on the rise, ancient clan rivalries were erupting with increasing violence, and the authority of many rural party organizations was being eclipsed by that of religious leaders, the newly affluent, and gangsters. One of the more bizarre manifestations of this trend occurred in 1990 with the formation of a gang in a remote, mountainous area of central Henan Province.[15] The leader, according to an official report published two years later, was a peasant called Li Chengfu who wanted to overthrow communist rule and establish a new imperial dynasty with himself as its first emperor. Li's gang had 16 members, including 4 party members. The report said one of the communists was a battalion commander in the militia. Li allegedly ordered the militia leader to join the regular army and then use his influence to have troops stationed near Li's home who could then be used to support his planned uprising against Beijing.

It is not clear from the report how far the militia commander got with this part of the plan. The group's members were arrested in April 1992 after several months of undercover work by a policeman who infiltrated the gang posing as an expert in the ancient Chinese art of geomancy. Several dozen police and paramilitary troops walked and crawled during the night for several miles along a snow-covered mountain path, before bursting into the gang members' homes with machine guns at the ready. The journal quoted one police official as saying the group's alleged plot was "laughable." But he said the involvement of party members and the fact that the gang's activities spanned two counties was cause for vigilance. It is difficult to know how "laughable" the case of the would-be emperor really was. The journal said there was a trend among peasants in remote, backward areas of turning to superstition and, in some cases, of "taking the counterrevolutionary path."

Clearly, massive unrest could occur in the countryside without the outside world ever hearing about it. The Renshou riots in Sichuan were one example of how slow news is to trickle out. Another even more sensational example was the revelation late in the previous year that hundreds of paramilitary troops using armored personnel carriers and artillery had mounted a military-style operation against an enclave of well-armed drug and arms smugglers in Pingyuan, a remote district of southern Yunnan Province near the border with Vietnam. In this case it was not until nearly three months after the operation was launched in late August that the first terse report by Xinhua News Agency appeared in the press.[16] The scale of the military operation was not fully revealed by the Chinese media until late December, when the Legal Daily reported that a force of some 2,000 police and paramilitary troops had taken some two-and-a-half months to subdue the smugglers.[17] It said that over the previous few years, the traffickers had taken over control of grassroots party and government organizations in the Pingyuan area and had frequently fought off police who had tried to intervene in their activities. During the final crackdown, the security forces arrested more than 850 people and seized nearly a ton of narcotics, mostly heroin, along with more than 350 military rifles and 600 other assorted firearms. Seven of the traffickers were sentenced to death, including the deputy head of Pingyuan, which has a population of some 60,000 people.

These revelations were extraordinary enough. That criminals were able to take control of an area and successfully fight off the police for several years was an amazing admission. Although China had frequently acknowledged that there was a serious smuggling problem in Yunnan, never before had it been suggested that the province had become home to Colombian-style drug lords who could openly flout authority. That such a state had existed for several years without the outside world being aware of it raised further doubts about our understanding of China. How many other Pingyuan-style criminal strongholds might there be in the countryside out of sight of foreigners? How effective can party control of the countryside really be if it allows such open lawlessness to exist for so long? Even more sensational details of the operation, however, were yet to come.

In mid-January, a newspaper published in Guangdong Province, *Southern Weekend,* said the operation had been the Chinese government's biggest ever military operation against drug smugglers—which if true would mean it involved more military force than the campaigns launched to wipe out widespread drug production in the first two or three years after the communists came to power, when an estimated 10 million people were engaged in cultivating opium poppies.[18] Officials admitted that eliminating drug-related crimes, which the party said it had virtually achieved by 1952, was far more difficult in the 1990s because unlike in the years immediately after the communist victory, China's borders could no longer be sealed from the outside world. *Southern Weekend* said the war against drug smugglers in Pingyuan was so big, in fact, that American officials noticed satellite pictures of the troop deployment and warned Vietnam, fearing it could herald the start of another Sino-Vietnamese war. There has been no confirmation from Washington, however, of this possibly fanciful detail.

Southern Weekend said more than 14,000 people in Pingyuan, or about a quarter of the entire population spread over several villages, were engaged in criminal activities, turning the area into a "state within a state." The security forces found one trafficker, Ma Siling, living in a fortified villa in Pingyuan even though he had been sentenced to death for drug trafficking. The newspaper described the operation as "even more complex" than some of the toughest battles of China's border war against Vietnam in 1979, with the smugglers fighting back with antitank weapons and hand grenades. One of the biggest obstacles the government faced was that the villagers, most of whom are Muslims, feared a repeat of the "Shadian Incident" of 1975, when the Chinese army used artillery to crush a Muslim uprising in the village of Shadian in Yunnan, killing as many as 5,000 people. The newspaper said the villagers in Pingyuan were getting ready for a fight to the death, but the security forces managed to persuade a local Muslim leader to calm them down. According to officially released figures, seven policemen were killed during the operation, as well as two smugglers—a remarkably low death toll if true. The newspaper quoted Jiang Zemin as saying it was "a beautiful battle."

It will probably be a long time before the outside world finds out exactly how "beautiful" the Pingyuan battle was. Although Chinese television showed footage of the crackdown, with troops in camouflaged uniforms patrolling the streets and drugs being unearthed from hiding places, in the three years since the operation foreign correspondents have not been admitted to the area. The question of how 14,000 people who once derived much of their income from drugs and weapons smuggling now make their living remains unanswered. Most likely, within a few months, they began to return to their old ways.

The Pingyuan operation only achieved its apparent success because of intervention by the central government. At the grassroots level, party organizations have become so lax since the reforms began that it is becoming increasingly difficult for Beijing to ensure that its will is carried out in the countryside without sending in high-level official teams, sometimes even troops, to assert its authority. Chinese leaders are clearly worried about the party's declining strength in the countryside. A confidential circular issued to party officials in 1990 said many places in China were "blank spots" with no party members at all.[19] "In some remote or mountainous regions no party member can be found within a radius of scores of miles," it said. The report cited the case of Exi county in Hubei Province where more than 400 out of some 3,000 village-level party committees had not recruited a single member between 1979 and 1988. It said there were several other parts of the country with similar levels of recruitment. "If years go by without recruiting a single party member, as has happened in Exi and other places, it will result in the party having an increasingly aged membership of declining quality. It will cause the party to lose its vitality and vigor and seriously affect the party's performance as a fighting force and the role of party members as a model vanguard." The circular said some party cells in the countryside were only paying attention to the economy and ignoring the task of strengthening party organization.

The party leadership also expressed concern about the growing influence of religious leaders at the village level. Another confidential circular in 1990 said that "religious activities and party activities compete for participants, compete for time, and compete for space."[20] It said this phenomenon "damages the party's image, corrupts the will of party members, and seriously disrupts the building of grassroots party organizations in the countryside. . . . The result is extremely serious." The circular called for a "thorough reorganization" of party cells that had already come under the control of "religious forces." The document did not refer to any specific religious beliefs. Clearly the influence of Buddhism among Tibetan cadres was a worry to the party, as was that of Islam in Muslim-dominated areas. But the party was known to be concerned too about the rapid spread of Christianity among the majority Han population, particularly in areas where missionary influence was strong before the communist takeover such as Hebei Province surrounding Beijing. A middle-ranking party official in Beijing itself, whom I had known for several months, told me one evening that he had secretly converted to Catholicism. He did not, however, renounce his party membership, a move that would have jeopardized his career.

Also threatening to the party's rural base was the growing influence of the clan, which in precommunist days dominated the social and political structure of much of the countryside. After 1949, the communists tried hard to eradicate clan loyalties. During the Cultural Revolution, Red Guards destroyed what remained of clan temples and ancestral graveyards. But by the 1980s, many Chinese villages still consisted mainly of people with the same surname, making clan identity impossible to erase. I discovered the power of clan loyalty during a trip to the countryside in Shandong Province in late 1986. The provincial government arranged for me to stay in a village called Zhangjia Chedao, meaning literally "Zhang Family [side of the] Road." This was a community of about 700 people, most of them surnamed Zhang. It was separated only by a narrow dirt track from a community called Liujia Chedao, or "Liu Family [side of the] Road," which consisted of about 1,100 people mostly surnamed Liu. The 600-year-old settlement of Zhangjia Chedao, about 280 miles southeast of Beijing, was a showcase for foreign visitors.

In 1986, its peasants enjoyed an average annual income of 1,200 yuan, three times the national average and more than twice the average income of Liujia Chedao residents. Zhangjia Chedao had several highly successful factories, but they employed hardly any Lius. Most of the party committee members of Zhangjia Chedao were surnamed Zhang too, including the party leader, Zhang Mingyue. When I asked him why wealth was not spread more evenly between the two communities, he admitted that "even when we were part of the same People's Commune, there was no cooperation. They are named Liu and we are named Zhang, so we can't assign someone from our village to help them. The separation is a traditional custom. Even in 30 or 50 years you couldn't bind them together." In a nearby township, a senior party official told me there were several villages in the area where different clans were separated by only a road or a few fields but operated almost independently. He described this as a "feudal" custom. When I asked why the villages were not simply ordered to cooperate, he replied in surprise, "The more advanced village will not agree to unite with the backward one. . . . Would Britain agree to combine with China?"

In the years that followed, expressions of concern in the official media about the influence of clans became more and more frequent. One particularly alarmist article appeared in the *Legal Daily* in May 1994.[21] It said that in the previous year, 600 clan feuds had killed more than 100 people and injured 2,000 others. The newspaper cited this as an example of a general deterioration of social order in the countryside. "At present, village party branches and village committees in some rural areas are basically paralyzed," it said. "There are no authorities in villages, the masses are as disorganized as a plate of sand, and nobody is responsible for the comprehensive management of public order and other tasks and measures. Villages are powerless against local thugs and village brutes, and the evil tendency grows unchecked." The newspaper put much of the blame on the country's economic reforms. "The intense contrast between a rapid expansion of consumer consciousness and comparatively low incomes had caused some of the peasantry to lose their psychological balance and slide into crime." The report echoed the warnings given by many Chinese leaders. "If the rural economy is developed and the role of agriculture as the economic foundation is secure, the stability of the whole nation will be based on a solid foundation, and the further deepening of reform and opening up will have a powerful safeguard," it said. "Otherwise, there will be chaos and turmoil in rural areas, and the very

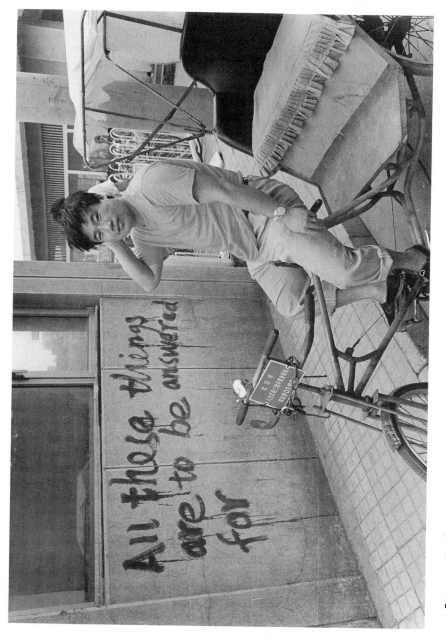

Four months after the violent suppression of the Tiananmen Square protests in June 1989, a rare sign of defiance appeared in the form of this graffito next to an expensive Beijing restaurant. (Photograph courtesy of Adrian Bradshaw)

Deng Xiaoping in a mural depicting urban development in southern China erected in Beijing during the lunar New Year festival, 1995. (Photograph courtesy of Adrian Bradshaw)

Left: Chen Yuan, deputy governor of the People's Bank of China. Chen is the son of the hard-line Party veteran Chen Yun, who died in April 1995. Chen Yuan is believed to advocate "neoconservatism." (Photo courtesy of Adrian Bradshaw)

Below: Exhibition of satellite dishes, Beijing 1994. Fearful of unrestricted access to foreign satellite broadcasts, China banned the private installation of dishes in 1993. Many, however, ignored the restrictions. (Photo courtesy of Adrian Bradshaw)

Above and facing page: The dissident Wei Jingsheng after his release from prison in September 1993, six months before he was due to complete a 15-year sentence for "counterrevolutionary" crimes. On the facing page, Wei is standing near the site of "Democracy Wall" where he and other activists posted handwritten bills in the late 1970s, calling for greater democracy in China. (Photograph courtesy of Adrian Bradshaw)

中國工商銀行
深圳市牙行
自動櫃員機
THE INDUSTRIAL & COMMERCIAL BANK OF CHINA
SHEN ZHEN BRANCH
A T M

The rapid growth of consumer culture is fueling demands for instant cash. Though still unusual, cash-dispensing machines like this one in Shenzhen are being introduced in the wealthier cities. (Photograph courtesy of Adrian Bradshaw)

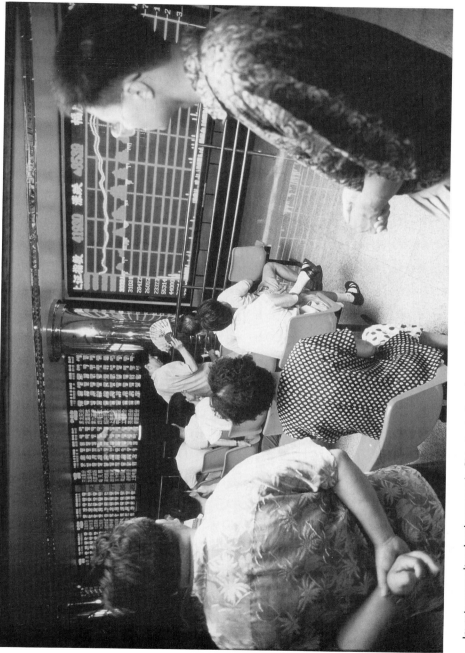

Investors monitor developments in China's stock exchanges at a Shanghai brokerage, 1994. (Photograph courtesy of Adrian Bradshaw)

Above and facing page: Migrant workers at Beijing Railway Station, 1994. The authorities blame these "blind drifters" for soaring crime rates in the cities. (Photograph courtesy of Adrian Bradshaw)

Police uniforms on sale in Chengdu, Sichuan Province, 1994. Despite government efforts to crack down on such business, some police departments see the sale of uniforms and other paraphernalia as a useful way of supplementing their budgets.
(Photo courtesy of G. A. D. Miles)

Lavish villas and luxury cars in Daqiu Village, Tianjin Municipality. Daqiu's party secretary, Yu Zuomin, was sentenced to 20 years in prison in August 1993 for "harboring criminals, obstructing public security personnel, bribery and unlawfully detaining people."
(Photograph courtesy of Adrian Bradshaw)

The Beijing Machine Tool Factory pays tribute to Deng Xiaoping's famous maxim, "It doesn't matter whether the cat is black or white, as long as it catches mice" by displaying appropriately shaded cats at its gates instead of the traditional lions. (Photograph courtesy of Adrian Bradshaw)

From left to right: Chinese leaders Yang Shangkun, Deng Xiaoping, and Jiang Zemin at a ceremony marking the completion of the drafting of Hong Kong's postcolonial constitution, the Basic Law, in February 1990. This was Deng's last appearance before the foreign media. (Photograph courtesy of Adrian Bradshaw)

The growing gap between rich and poor—an amusement park in Shenzhen with a shanty town in the foreground. (Photograph courtesy of Adrian Bradshaw)

A beggar in Haikou, Hainan Province. Once a rarity in Chinese cities because of strict government controls, beggars are becoming an increasingly common sight as peasants flock to urban areas in search of work. (Photo courtesy of Adrian Bradshaw)

From a publicity brochure produced by the village of Nanjie, Henan Province. Members of the village militia on parade. Extreme hard-liners extol Nanjie, where private ownership is all but banned, as a model of how rural reforms should be carried out.

Above and following page: The opening ceremony of the 7th National Games in 1993 became one of many festivities aimed at promoting China's bid to host the 2000 Olympics. Ultimately, the bid was unsuccessful. (Photograph courtesy of Adrian Bradshaw)

root of the progress of our country's socialist modernization will be jeopardized."

In October 1994, another official report quoted Chinese experts as saying that rural crime had become "one of the biggest social problems in China" in the 1990s.[22] "The dying embers of the strength of patriarchal clans are glowing once again, and activities of feudal superstition and secret societies have increased in a small number of rural areas." The dispatch said the failure of rural education to keep pace with economic advancement was fueling the problem. "Feudal superstition and secret societies have taken advantage of this, thus increasing crime in the rural areas."

One of the most dramatic recent examples of clan feuding occurred in Hunan Province in September 1993. According to an official report, some 200 police and paramilitary troops used tear gas to break up a pitched battle between thousands of peasants belonging to the rival clans of Liu and Li.[23] The violence erupted in a market town close to China's main north-south railway line. "The armed fight . . . changed the once bustling Matian marketplace and its neighboring graveyard into a battlefield," said the report.

"All over the long and narrow street, cement mounds or sand and stone bags were set up as bunkers. Large handmade guns were erected on the balconies of schools, hospitals, the supply and marketing cooperative building, and residential apartments. Large guns made from copper tubes, bullets made from cans and beer bottles, handmade grenades, explosive bags, pistols, knives, and spears all served as weapons. In the fighting and shooting, which lasted well over a day, 5 people were killed, 12 were seriously wounded, and 10 others were slightly wounded. After the fight, Matian township was in ruins, and several buildings were blown up." The report said feuding between the two clans dated back at least to the 1920s. The latest battle erupted after members of one clan beat up several members of the other. "Because of the influence of the traditional clan concept, some disputes over otherwise minor and trivial matters would often develop into fights between clans, and even in disputes involving clans of the same family name, factions would often have been formed along the lines of proximity or distance in blood relations and be engaged in acts of revenge," said the *People's Daily*.[24]

Rural clans, however, do not just fight among themselves. When they see their interests being threatened by officialdom they fight against the government too. A report from Hunan in 1995 said clan forces in rural communities near Dongting Lake, one of China's largest inland bodies of fresh water and a popular destination for tourists, were resisting the authorities' attempts to raise taxes and implement birth control measures.[25] "If the district- and village-level authorities are unable to satisfy the clans' demands, the clans dare openly to confront the grassroots government, either by preventing district and village cadres from doing their work or by beating up police officers carrying out their duties or even by organizing crowds to attack district and village government buildings and police stations," the report said. In 1991, members of the Huang clan in the area sent a force of 200 people to help out a couple of that surname whom the authorities were trying to force to adopt sterilization measures because they had already had two children (both of them girls).[26] The crowd beat up the family planning officials and besieged the local police station after officers detained the ringleaders.

The report said that in some villages clan chiefs were more powerful than the nominal village heads. "In the past the masses would depend on the collective, depend on [the party] organization, and depend on the government," it said. "Now some of them have begun no longer to trust the grassroots government. They do not support and they do not care about the work of the district and village [authorities]. They resist family planning measures and taxation. By contrast, they enthusiastically take part in clan activities. If they have money they contribute it, if they have no money they dedicate their labor."

Given how little the outside world knows about what is happening in rural China, it is quite possible that disturbances were erupting on a far wider scale than the official media acknowledged. The Chinese Academy of Social Sciences said the scale of rural unrest in 1993, including "parades, demonstrations, and attacks on local government offices," was unprecedented in the history of communist rule.[27] It was a profoundly embarrassing problem for a party that came to power on the back of a peasant revolt and many of whose veteran leaders, Deng Xiaoping included, were themselves from the countryside. It was particularly embarrassing for Deng personally because in the early years of his reform program the countryside had been China's success story. When urban reforms finally got under way in 1984, Deng hoped the cities would follow the rural model by encouraging free enterprise and changing the "iron rice bowl" mentality. "Our experience in the countryside convinces us that our urban reform will succeed,"[28] said a proud Deng that year. He said it had been essential to begin the reform process in the countryside because "China's stability depends on the stability of those areas. No matter how successful our work is in the cities, it won't mean much without a stable base in the countryside."[29]

Deng's "stable base" began crumbling not long after the urban reforms began. Between 1978, when Deng emerged as China's paramount leader and 1984, rural incomes rose on average by more than 15 percent a year in real terms. But after a record harvest in 1984, grain production recorded its biggest one-year drop since the communists came to power. Many peasants simply lost their enthusiasm for growing grain because of the low prices paid by the government and the rapid increase in the cost of production materials. There was no immediate danger of food shortages. There was plenty of grain still in storage. But it was nonetheless a worrying development for a party that had long equated grain production with political power and stability. For the next four years, grain output continued to stagnate. Rural incomes increased on average about 5 percent a year after taking inflation into account. But much of this growth was attributable to the rapid proliferation of rural industries in coastal areas. Many peasants working in these village and township factories earned fabulous sums by Chinese standards, as much as twice the average income of agricultural workers. Meanwhile in the inland provinces, those peasants still working in the fields saw little if any increase in their incomes.

In 1989, Chinese farmers managed to boost grain production back up to the level of 1984, but their incomes declined in real terms for the first time since the reforms began, dropping 0.7 percent. One of the main reasons for this decline was a dramatic slowdown in the growth of rural enterprises as a result of the austerity campaign launched the previous year. The credit squeeze of 1989 led to the dismissal of at least 3 million peasant workers. Between 1989 and the end of the austerity campaign in 1991, rural incomes increased by less than 1 percent annually. Thanks to a government decision to ease credit, rural industries quickly recovered after the slump of 1989. Thus, the average increase of nearly 1 percent in rural incomes included a rapid growth in income from the industrial sector and a considerable decline in income from agriculture. In at least 10 inland provinces, peasants' incomes in 1991 were lower than they were three years earlier. Nationwide that year, roughly half of the country's rural households were worse off than in 1988.[30]

The stagnation or at best slow increase in the incomes of those working on the land from 1985 onward does not necessarily mean that significant numbers of peasants were sliding back into a state of absolute poverty. Foreigners traveling around "open areas" of rural China throughout the 1980s and 1990s would hardly ever see signs of acute malnutrition. Indeed, by the early 1990s many of those rural areas foreigners were allowed to visit appeared to be flourishing. Most peasants had not only well-made houses but also electricity. Many even had television sets. Officials often give wildly different figures for the numbers of people living below the poverty line. The most commonly cited figure for 1990, which is also used by the World Bank, is 100 million people without enough to eat or wear, or just under 10 percent of the population. But when compared with the figure of 270 million for 1978, China appeared to have made stunning progress in feeding and clothing its people.

There is no doubt that the majority of Chinese peasants are substantially better off now than they would have been before the communist takeover. But given that it is very difficult for foreigners to visit poverty-stricken areas, official figures should be treated with some skepticism. The Chinese Academy of Social Sciences estimated that, in 1993, the number of peasants living below the poverty line actually increased by more than 9 percent to about 90 million.[31] Impressively low though the baseline was compared with the World Bank's estimate, for poverty to increase by that much in a year when GNP grew by a breathtaking 13 percent did not bode well. "For the last few years, the income gap between peasants has been expanding," said the academy. "At one extreme you have the 'rich and powerful' who own capital worth tens of millions or even hundreds of millions of yuan. At the other, you have ordinary peasants who can only just about get enough to wear and eat or have difficulty achieving even that. Although an extremely small number of people belong to the former category, and only a few belong to the latter, this has a very big impact on society."[32] For many of those living at the bottom end of the income scale, conditions were more wretched than the casual visitor to China might think. "In China . . . the prevalence of malnutrition among under-five-year-olds is hardly different from that of sub-Saharan Africa," said UNICEF's executive director James Grant in October 1991.[33]

It might be expected that the significant improvements in rural standards of living since the communist takeover would help the party to maintain its hold on power in the countryside. According to official statistics, life expectancy by 1993 had risen to about 71 years, higher than most of China's neighbors, including the former Soviet Union (70) and India (60). Adult literacy was nearly 70 percent compared with about 45 percent in India. But as often, China's seemingly impressive achievements are not necessarily reflected in the mood of ordinary people. I have never heard any Chinese peasants compare their lot with that of their counterparts in India. Of far greater importance to them is how other Chinese are faring. In the early years of the reform era, the comparisons were favorable. With agriculture achieving record growth rates, the income gap between city and countryside narrowed. According to official figures, when the reforms began in 1978, city dwellers were earning about 2.4 times as much as peasants. By 1985, at the peak of China's agricultural boom, the ratio had diminished to 1.9. But from 1985 onward, the trend reversed. By 1991, the ratio was the same as it was in 1978. In 1993, it was 2.6—a wider gap than when the reforms began.[34]

The situation, however, was far worse than these figures suggested. In 1978, both peasants and city dwellers received a considerable amount of income in the form of hidden subsidies for health care, education, and other services. But as the commune system broke up in the early 1980s, peasants lost many of these benefits while city dwellers continued to enjoy them. If the amount urban residents receive in the form of various subsidies is included in their income, their earnings in 1993 were at least four times higher than those of peasants. If the wages of those working in rural enterprises are excluded from the calculation of rural income, then the difference is greater still.

The widening gap between standards of living in the countryside and the cities goes against the trend established by east Asia's high-performing economies during their early days of high-speed growth. "In the developed world, the gap between urban and rural areas is narrowing," said the Chinese Academy of Social Sciences. "But in China it is getting bigger by the day, even bigger than in other developing countries. This is a strategic problem in China's modernization that must not be overlooked. It must receive the full attention of all departments."[35]

Chinese officials did not have to go deep into the countryside to witness the destabilizing impact of this growing gap between urban and rural incomes. The problem was more than apparent in the cities themselves. Perhaps the biggest social revolution to occur in China in the 1980s and 1990s was the breakdown of the decades-old system of enforced segregation between city and countryside, which in turn triggered a mass migration from impoverished rural areas into the cities. Since 1953, four years after the communist takeover, the government has advised people born in the countryside to stay there. In 1958 the authorities devised a registration system classifying people as either rural or urban residents, a system that, by the 1960s, was used by the authorities to stop peasants from migrating to the cities. Only registered city dwellers were allowed to live in urban areas, and even they often had great difficulty obtaining permission to move from one city to another.

This registration system has made a substantial contribution to the outside world's persistent misunderstanding of China. The foreign visitor is often impressed by the apparent orderliness of Chinese cities—the absence of obvious shantytowns, hordes of beggars, people sleeping in the streets, and other such normal traits of a developing country. One of the main reasons for this has been that rural poverty has been deliberately kept at a distance. Anyone caught in a city without an appropriate residence permit was liable to be detained and expelled. Around the time of major festivals and official occasions, city police would routinely round up unregistered peasants and send them back to their villages. Those who slipped through the net would find life difficult enough anyway. Only registered residents qualified for subsidized grain, oil, and other daily essentials. Admittance to a city school required a residence permit, as did free hospital treatment.

The sheer numbers of idle or underpaid hands in the countryside, however, combined with the ravenous demand for cheap labor in the cities eventually forced the government to relax the segregation and inch open the floodgates to allow the peasants in. In the mid-1980s, the government began allowing rural dwellers to seek temporary work in the cities, although permits remained difficult to obtain. Some were allowed in under agreement between their local governments and the city authorities to do menial work such as cleaning streets or dangerous work on construction sites, which city residents were unwilling to do. But by the early 1990s, peasants were pouring into the cities under their own steam. Chinese officials called them the "floating population" or, somewhat more disparagingly, "blind drifters"—a term used to conjure up the image of a mass of people drifting into the cities with no clear vision of what they would do there.

It is still not easy for a peasant to settle in a city. The biggest problem is housing, which city residents themselves have difficulty enough obtaining. It is quite normal to find registered city dwellers in their late twenties or thirties still living with their parents because there is no other accommodation available. Most people in cities live in housing provided by the state. There is hardly any private housing available, except at prices prohibitive to peasants and, for that matter, to most city residents. For migrants from the countryside, the best options are to find jobs that provide dormitory accommodation, such as on a building site, or to work as a domestic servant and live with one's employers. It is also possible to rent houses from peasants living on the outskirts of cities. Despite the difficulties, however, as many as 30 million peasants had moved into big cities or their immediate outskirts by 1994. An even greater number had left their homes to work in smaller towns. About half of the "blind drifters" headed for Guangdong to work in the thousands of factories turning out low-technology, labor-intensive products such as toys, shoes, and garments for Western markets.

In the suburbs of Beijing, peasants from different parts of the country formed their own communities, known colloquially as "villages" but which were in fact as big as towns. There is a "Zhejiang Village" consisting by the mid-1990s of some 100,000 people from eastern Zhejiang Province, most of whom turned the houses they rented from local peasants into tiny factories producing cheap garments—many of them illegal copies of brand-name clothes—for sale in Beijing markets. Tens of thousands of migrants from central Henan Province, Anhui in the east, and the far western region of Xinjiang established similar "villages" specializing in different trades. Many of those from backward, inland Anhui worked as housemaids. The Muslims from Xinjiang opened restaurants or street stalls selling kebabs, round flattened bread, and other regional food.[36] About half of the migrants worked on building sites. As many as 30,000 of them made their living scouring refuse dumps on the edge of the city and scavenging for odds and ends. Some turned to begging. By the end of 1993, according to official reports, Beijing had about 20,000 beggars, many of whom congregated in the areas where foreigners live. Some of them were small girls from the neighboring province of Hebei who gathered at the entrances to the new fancy department stores trying to sell bunches of flowers to shoppers.

In 1989, the Beijing city government tried to disperse the swelling communities of migrants, expelling more than a quarter of a million peasants working without permits from the city and imposing heavy fines on their employers. But the peasants kept on arriving. By the end of 1992, there were 1.5 million of them in the capital, six times as many as in 1978 and the equivalent of more than 10 percent of the total Beijing population.[37] Two years later, the official estimate of the capital's migrant population soared to more than 3.2 million. Similarly, in Shanghai, transients were estimated to make up about 20 percent of the city's population by the end of 1994.[38]

In theory, everyone staying in the city longer than three days has to notify the police, and apply for a temporary residence permit if staying longer than a month. New rules introduced in Beijing in mid-1995 required outsiders to obtain temporary dwelling and employment permits, banned anyone from hiring migrants without government approval, and required employers to provide accommodation for transient workers.[39] But there was no indication that these rules were any more likely to be obeyed by urban employers or rural migrants than similar measures adopted previously, such as requirements in some cities that peasants only take up jobs assigned by the city government and that they pay the authorities a "management fee" for finding them work.

In the late 1980s, unofficial "labor markets" began appearing in the streets of Beijing, where hundreds of peasants gathered to wait for city dwellers to offer them jobs, usually as domestic servants. From time to time the Beijing police cracked down on these open-air employment exchanges, but within a few days or weeks—sometimes within just a few hours—they would reappear.

The staggering scale of this human tide has been causing increasing anxiety among Chinese leaders. By the end of 1994, some 80 million peasants had moved permanently into towns and cities, more than 8.5 million of them in the previous year alone.[40] But in addition to these people, there were still an estimated 40 million farmworkers who remained in the countryside with no real work to do, a figure expected to rise to 120 million by the end of the century, assuming no more of them migrate—the equivalent of nearly half of the existing urban population. A large proportion of these rural residents, however, will inevitably head toward the cities, despite the growing problem of unemployment among registered residents. In 1994, the urban jobless rate was about 5.5 percent, including workers whose factories had suspended production—a higher proportion than in the United States as one official report pointed out in an uncharacteristically self-deprecating comparison with the capitalist West.[41] Officials admit the potential social impact of a further massive influx of peasants would be enormous. "It is . . . unavoidable that the movement of rural surplus labor will be blind and disorderly during a certain stage," Deputy Prime Minister Wu Bangguo told a national conference on rural migrants in 1995.[42] "However, if we let such a situation go on, it will jeopardize social stability and obstruct the progress of our reform."

Already by the mid-1990s, China's big cities were under severe strain. The authorities said migrant workers were to blame for soaring rates of theft, robbery, murder, and rape. The number of "major criminal cases" reported every year was increasing by between 20 and 40 percent.

Officials said migrants were responsible for as many as 70 percent of crimes committed in Beijing in 1994, compared with less than 25 percent in 1990.[43] Although China maintained its crime rate was still low compared with the developed world, many ordinary Chinese said they were increasingly worried about their own safety and the security of their property. In the early 1980s, most city dwellers in China were almost completely free of the paranoia about crime that grips many of their Western counterparts. But a survey of Beijing residents carried out in 1993 revealed that more than 15 percent felt "unsafe." Another 30 percent said their sense of security was only "so-so." Fewer than 10 percent said they felt very safe.[44] Those who said they felt unsafe cited the influx of migrant workers as the main reason for their concerns. "The number of major vile criminal cases and violent crimes has increased by a big margin," China's chief prosecutor Zhang Siqing reported to the National People's Congress in March 1994.[45] "The masses lack a sense of security."

The migration of peasants into the cities has disrupted one of the main mechanisms by which the Communist Party maintains social control. The residency permit system was not simply designed to protect the cities from the impoverished countryside. It also helped the authorities maintain order by keeping individuals in a specified place where their activities could easily be monitored. Neighborhood committees consisting of government officials and local volunteers, usually retired workers, keep watch on all comings and goings in their area. In theory, anyone moving into a neighborhood has to present a residence permit, and any visitor who is not a resident is closely watched by the neighborhood committee volunteers, who sit around in almost every alley and housing estate in Chinese cities, easily identifiable by their red armbands. But migrants from the countryside, living in Beijing's semirural outskirts, sleeping in the railway station or in jerry-built dormitories on building sites are not subject to the same supervision. There is no neighborhood committee official who can tell the police everything about them. For a city dweller, one of the greatest deterrents against committing a crime is the fact that any wrongdoing is recorded in the secret file maintained by the authorities on every individual. The file is usually kept by the individual's employers, and its contents play a crucial role in determining a person's career and benefits such as housing. A peasant with no file and no benefits has far less to fear.

Migrants have been playing a key role in the rapid increase of drug trafficking and the proliferation of pornography. Many of the peasant women moving into Chinese cities find easy work as prostitutes. By the early 1990s, prostitutes could be seen in large numbers in bars, discos, and in many hotel lobbies. The large numbers of peasants moving around the country with money in their pockets have been encouraging the resurgence of banditry on roads and railways. By 1993, a major case of robbery would occur almost every day on Chinese passenger trains, often involving gangs of robbers consisting of dozens of people armed with knives or guns. "Offenders, swollen with arrogance, have employed vicious and cruel means," lamented Xinhua News Agency.[46] "It is difficult to travel by train or bus. Can the situation go on like this?" When I traveled along it in 1994, the road between Chengdu and troubled Renshou county was among many rural highways festooned with official banners proclaiming war against "train bandits and highway robbers."

For the authorities the most worrisome time of the year is the Lunar New Year festival, when many of those peasants with jobs return home to celebrate with their families, bringing with them tales of the riches to be earned in the cities. After the holiday, many of their peasant friends and relatives return to the cities with them in the hopes of sharing the same good fortune. Most are unlucky. Driving through Guangdong Province after the Lunar New Year holiday one can see crowds of peasants outside almost every factory gate, waiting in vain for work. Canton Railway Station, where many of them arrive before catching buses to the boomtowns of the Pearl River delta, turns into a sea of humanity, as trains crammed to more than twice their official capacity disgorge thousands upon thousands of unkempt job seekers clutching canvas bags stuffed with their possessions.

Even in normal times, the "hard seat" compartments—as China describes the cheapest accommodation on trains—are usually full to overflowing with peasants on the move. But around the time of the Lunar New Year festival, the hard seat compartments turn into Black Holes of Calcutta on wheels. There is often no room even to sit in the corridors because doing so takes up more room than standing. The filthy, foul-smelling toilets are jammed with travelers as well. Getting on or off the train is often easiest through the windows. In early 1994, in the two-month period in the middle of which the Lunar New Year holiday falls, Chinese railways logged some 185.39 million passenger journeys—equivalent to shifting more than the population of Brazil. Every train carried at least twice as many passengers as it had seats. At some railway stations in the interior, crowds large enough to populate entire towns waited to squeeze themselves onto eastbound or southbound trains. Some died in stampedes, and many lost their belongings. The authorities' efforts to deter the peasants—by ordering factories not to take on new workers around the time of the festival or curtailing bus services from remote rural areas to the railway stations—have failed to stem what one official newspaper described as the "human avalanche."[47]

China's booming light industrial sector depends on this vast supply of cheap labor. Ordinary city dwellers have come to depend on rural migrants too, particularly to provide low-cost child care and other help in the home. But the large numbers of peasants who fail in their search for work are widely viewed by city dwellers long sheltered from rural realities as a deeply menacing force. In mid-1993, Shanghai's *Wenhui Bao* pointed out the political danger posed by jobless peasants in the cities who sleep in the open at railway stations, in parks, or on the streets "without any public health care, without any guarantee of their personal safety."[48] Such people, it said, could easily become disillusioned with society. "If this feeling is not dispelled in a timely manner," said the paper, "it will affect social stability." The article pointed out that jobless peasants in the cities are caught in a dangerous dilemma. If they return home they will have wasted their money. If they do not, they risk starvation. "If even 1 percent of this enormous mass of people has nothing to live on, there will be social chaos. . . . The floating population, in the absence of any controls, is fertile soil for the development of secret societies. If a large number of people who have lost their livelihoods form gangs and organize themselves, the threat to society will be even greater. If they join forces with the millions of unemployed in the cities, then the consequences will be more unthinkable yet."

Chinese officials and academics have long debated such dangers. The liberal *Economics Weekly*, which was closed down after Tiananmen because of its strong support for the students and its links with radical reformers, published several articles in 1989 warning of possible chaos as a result of the population transfer and growing tension in the countryside between peasants and officials. One article argued that the breakup of the People's Communes had put peasants and the government on a much more equal footing, giving peasants greater ability to defy authority by refusing to sell grain or growing less of it.[49] The article said peasants had staged occasional demonstrations and violent attacks against officials in 1988 because the government had tried to force them to sell their grain. The peasants were reluctant to sell because the government would only give them IOUs for their harvest. "The agricultural problem is already having an impact on social and political stability," it warned. Another article said mass migration could "trigger an explosion that would lead to nationwide turmoil." It called on the government to launch a huge public works program to soak up peasant labor and head off "large-scale social unrest."[50]

China Daily quoted He Xin, a well-known conservative intellectual, as warning in early 1989 that traditionally in China, people without livelihoods "formed a political force and under certain circumstances became rebels." He said the growing number of unemployed migrants was giving rise to such a force and that this trend could prove "potentially destructive."[51]

Chinese intellectuals have always been keenly aware of the ebb and flow of thousands of years of dynastic history. They often analyze the Communist Party's rise to power not in terms of an international trend that began with the Soviet Union and inspired revolution throughout the developing world but in the context of the ancient Chinese pattern of dynastic decline accompanied by peasant rebellion. Although they would not say so in public, some Chinese leaders clearly view China's modern history in much the same light. Mao Zedong is well known to have been a far more voracious reader of ancient Chinese histories than of Marxist classics. In the late 1980s and early 1990s, therefore, signs of growing restlessness in the countryside suggested to many urban Chinese that history was still in the grips of the traditional dynastic cycle and that the peasant protests augured the collapse of the communist dynasty. Much of this was wishful thinking on the part of dissidents, who particularly after Tiananmen were desperately looking for signs that the party was losing its grip. Objectively speaking, the riots in the countryside in 1993 did not bear comparison with the massive peasant rebellions that swept China in the nineteenth century as the Qing dynasty crumbled. And chaotic and disruptive though it was, the mass migration of peasants into the cities had not led to beggary and starvation on the scale witnessed in China's big cities before the communist takeover. But the fact that peasants rioted at all was a sign that communist authority in the countryside was in a state of serious decline. In a country as strictly controlled as China any public act of protest has greater political significance than the numbers involved might suggest. And nobody doubted that the influx of peasants was only in its relatively early stages. The worst of the "avalanche" was certainly yet to come.

By the mid-1990s, as Deng's death appeared increasingly imminent, the nightmare of political disintegration and chaos in the countryside became one of the main preoccupations of Chinese intellectuals and leaders as they tried to imagine how the country would survive without the "chief architect of reform." A book published in March 1994 entitled *Looking at China Through a Third Eye* reflected the apocalyptic visions of some Chinese.[52] The book claimed to be a translation of a work by a German sinologist described in the foreword as "the most influential expert on Chinese issues in Europe today." But this was a fiction aimed at giving the author—in reality an obscure Chinese novelist—license to discuss China's social and political situation without having to use endless party-approved clichés. The slim volume was banned within a few months of publication, but Chinese sources say many officials, including some top leaders, endorsed its analysis.[53]

The book said the diminishing influence of the party at the grassroots level in the countryside was creating a dangerous power vacuum and described this as "a disaster for society." It said the most serious mistake committed by the Communist Party since it came to power was the decision to conceal rural conditions from the outside world. The party, it said, thereby lost an opportunity to gain international sympathy and support for its policies. "If you do not understand the peasantry," it said, "you have no way of understanding the party's policies and the difficulties it faces." The author argued that the breakup of the People's Communes and the granting of greater freedom to peasants to choose their own jobs were "fatal for the Chinese government and its effective control over peasants." It quoted one unnamed official as saying that Deng's rural reforms of the early 1980s marked "the fall of the first domino." The "floating population" of migrant peasants unleashed by Deng's reforms, it said, was a "powder keg," with hundreds of thousands of people roving around aimlessly feeling ill treated and vengeful. "These kind of feelings shared by each individual add up to a powerful destructive force, which at any time could erupt into a leaderless, purposeless, and deadly movement."

Looking at China Through a Third Eye predicted that "if large-scale turmoil occurs in China again, unemployed peasants will certainly be active participants in the unrest and the main destructive force." Even more grimly, it warned that "if we look back over Chinese history, we will discover an obvious truth, that every dynasty without exception was destroyed by drifters. What we mean by drifters are peasants who have lost their land or do not feel safe on their land. If this vast army of ignorant, aimless, and extremely destructive peasants is ever organized into an antigovernment force, the government in power effectively will have already collapsed without any hope whatsoever of redemption."

Sobering though the upsurge of rural unrest of the early 1990s was for the Chinese leadership, the government's efforts to remedy its causes proved at best only mildly effective. When I visited Renshou county in August 1994, a year and a half after the peasant unrest that had so shaken the leadership, the peasants I spoke to were still far from satisfied. One young man described how a senior party official in the area was so wealthy his family did not bother working in the fields. "Every day he smokes two packs of cigarettes. One pack costs 20 yuan. His [official] wages are only 200 yuan a month," said the peasant, squatting on a dirt track in the blistering summer heat. "If you have power you have every-thing." He and a friend complained that while the authorities had suc-cessfully stopped the illegal raising of taxes in the area for a few months after the riots, the problem had started again. "These people are afraid," commented a former soldier living in Chengdu who had translated the peasant's Sichuan dialect into a more understandable Mandarin for me. "If they do anything they will be arrested. They're afraid of complaining, but the masses are angry. They are bitter but they can't express it."

Even the official media admitted that the complaints of peasants were not being alleviated by the directives issued in response to the 1993 crisis. One newspaper said in March 1994 that in "a small number" of villages, officials were ignoring the directives and increasing the illegal levies.[54] In official parlance, "a small number" often means many.

The outside world cannot truly know whether the dangers of peasant migration and rural unrest are overstated by fearful and perhaps even paranoid Chinese city dwellers. It is an aspect of change in China that foreigners can only guess at. The migration into the cities is a phenome-non on a scale never before encountered in communist Chinese history and only rarely in the history of mankind. But knowing that this huge movement of people is happening and what economic forces are driving them to leave their land, it would take a brave soul to reject the possibil-ity that peasants will become a major disruptive factor in Chinese devel-opment in the years to come.

7

Lighting the Fuse

Chaos is possible. Lots of small incidents have already occurred. Whenever a dynasty is ending it is like this. You can put down 99 out of 100 disturbances, but if you don't put down the last one it lights a fuse and there's an explosion.
—dissident Wei Jingsheng, January 1994

To avoid detection by secret police who might have been monitoring the telephone in my hotel room, I walked down the street to find a public phone. I decided to make only a brief call to the dissident whose number I had, just long enough to ask him to call me back from a public phone at a specified time so that we could both talk using the security of what I hoped would be an untapped line. It was not a foolproof plan. If the police were monitoring the dissident's phone when I called to give him the number of my public phone, they could trace that number, tap it and send someone to wait by the phone, find out who I was, and begin tailing me. This was August 1994, and I was in Chengdu, the capital of Sichuan Province, trying to arrange a meeting with the dissident, a key member of an underground labor organization in the city of Bengbu more than 800 miles to the east in the province of Anhui. Another leading member of the group had recently been arrested during a trip to Beijing and was being interrogated by the Anhui police. I knew that his fellow dissidents in Bengbu, including the one I wanted to meet, were fearful that their entire network was in danger of being discovered.

The authorities at the time were intensifying their crackdown on dissent. In Beijing and Shanghai, several activists had been detained in the previous few months and were being held incommunicado. One of those arrested in Beijing, the lawyer Wang Jiaqi, had been forced into a car by plainclothes police in March. The police put a hood over his head, pushed his head down toward his knees, and then threatened to bury him alive unless he cooperated. China is not a country where the authorities

197

are known for assassinating or arranging the "suicides" of their opponents, but Wang's experience suggested there might be exceptions. A few weeks later Wang escaped from the People's Armed Police camp where he was being held by taking advantage of a moment's inattentiveness by his guard to walk out of the front gate unnoticed. When I met him in Beijing soon after his escape he said he feared the police might kill him. A few days later he sneaked illegally into Hong Kong and was granted political asylum by a Western country. Wang was exceptionally lucky. It is extremely rare to hear of dissidents escaping from custody.

The authorities were nervous that August because unemployment was growing, inflation worsening, and public discontent deepening. Unlike foreign investors, the police did not take comfort from the country's spectacular economic growth rate. As they saw it, China was becoming increasingly unruly. Dissident intellectuals were trying to link up with disaffected workers and peasants in what they hoped would be the first broad-based antigovernment coalition in communist China's history. The dissident I planned to meet in Bengbu was one such intellectual.

I could not see anyone lurking in the shadows when the dissident called me back at the appointed time. The phone was in a small clock and watch shop that opened onto the street. The owner was just closing up for the day, so I was relieved that I had some privacy. I told the dissident, whom I shall refer to by the pseudonym Ding, that I would be visiting Bengbu at the end of the week. He told me to wait for him at midnight on the day of my arrival at Bengbu Railway Station.

Bengbu is a transportation hub of about 700,000 people on the banks of China's third-largest waterway, the Huai River, which winds through hundreds of miles of grain- and cotton-producing farmland before merging with the Yangtze near the sea. The city itself is about 200 miles inland and was still at the time of my visit a sleepy backwater compared with the coastal boomtowns and was plagued by the decline of its state-owned machinery, textile, glass, and paper industries. Many factories had virtually halted production or suspended work entirely because of competition from the booming private sector in southern China. The enterprises continued to give their workers up to 100 yuan a month and let them keep their housing, but this amounted to only a third or a quarter of a regular worker's income. To add to the region's woes, the countryside around Bengbu was badly affected in 1991 by one of the Huai River's worst floods in many decades. Moreover, as in many other parts of China, the living standards of peasants had hardly improved in years.

The authorities admitted that corruption was rife in Anhui. Since the start of a provincial campaign against graft in May 1993, about one in five, or a total of 300,000, Anhui officials had been accused of abusing their positions. Many were found to have siphoned off public money into their bank accounts or used it to pay for the education of friends and relatives, build private houses, gamble, and visit prostitutes. "These corrupt practices have sparked widespread public resentment," Xinhua News Agency noted.[1] For people like the dissident Ding, there was no difficulty finding fellow malcontents in this long-backward province.

At the appointed midnight at Bengbu Railway Station, I walked up and down the road in front of the forecourt, waiting for Ding. There were still a few food vendors and taxi drivers touting for business among the dozens of passengers milling around. I had not met Ding before and had no idea what he looked like, but he knew to look for a Caucasian face, and in a place like Bengbu there were hardly likely to be many of them.

After 15 or 20 minutes, a man approached me and asked me in a low voice whether I had come from Chengdu. I said I had, and he told me to follow a few paces behind him. As we walked along the dimly lit street, I looked around and saw another man walking at the same pace about 20 or 30 yards behind us. My heart beat faster. I had been followed on many occasions by plainclothes police in Beijing, and I had developed a sense for when it was happening. But there was nothing I could do without getting the man I thought was Ding in even deeper trouble. So I walked on. Two or three hundred yards up the road, with few people around, my companion stopped. I cautiously approached him, saying nothing to avoid making it too obvious that we were connected. The man who had been following us came up too, and with some relief I realized that the two knew each other. No words, however, were exchanged. They hailed a taxi and we got in, the two men on either side of me. One of them gave an address to the driver, but apart from that nothing was said as we drove through the darkened, near deserted streets toward the suburbs.

After about 15 minutes, we arrived at our destination. The two men led me in silence into an unlit apartment compound. We walked up several flights of stairs and then at last into a bare apartment where we began to talk. It turned out that the man who had followed us at the railway station was Ding. The other was a friend of his, also a key member of the underground labor organization. As the senior dissident of the two men, Ding had waited in the shadows at the railway station to see if the police would pounce when his friend approached me. Even though there had been no sign of the police as we drove to his apartment, Ding was still extremely nervous. He became all the more so when I told him I had already checked into a hotel in Bengbu. He wanted me to stay in his apartment and not emerge until it was time to leave. Ding was worried too because another dissident friend of his had told him I was on my way from Chengdu to Bengbu. I had not told anybody about my movements, so how could this person have known? Ding said his associates had many contacts in the police force who might have revealed this information. And the police would only have known if they had been tailing me or had tapped my call to Ding. Panicking, he suggested that I abandon my luggage at the hotel and flee the city in the morning. Eventually I persuaded him that I should check out of the hotel and leave by train before dawn. That gave us an hour or so to talk before I had to go.

Just as in most other major urban centers in China, protesters took to the streets of Bengbu in 1989. Most of them were students, who paraded through the streets, staged sit-ins, went on hunger strikes, and, in protest against the bloodshed in Beijing, set up roadblocks and demonstrated outside the city government headquarters. Among the protesters was Zhang Lin, one of Ding's friends. Zhang, then 25 years old,[2] had grown up in an Anhui village and, remarkably given his rural upbringing, obtained a degree in nuclear physics from Qinghua University in Beijing, one of the country's most prestigious academic institutions.[3] After graduating in 1985, Zhang was sent by the government, which at that time did not allow students to choose their own jobs, to Bengbu to work in the state-owned Bengbu Knitwear Mill. In the following year, he quit his job and started what he called a "democratic salon," a discussion group whose meetings usually attracted between 200 and 300 people and sometimes as many as 1,000. In December 1986 students in Hefei, the capital of Anhui Province, launched the first major student movement of the Deng Xiaoping era. In spite of the crackdown that quickly followed, Zhang's democracy salon kept going until the outbreak of renewed student unrest in 1989. He was arrested on June 8th, four days after the shooting in Beijing.

Anhui's provincial radio station described Zhang as "a criminal element" who had set up and led the "so-called" Bengbu College Students Autonomous Union during the 1989 demonstrations. In this capacity, according to the radio, Zhang "openly made an extremely reactionary speech" in the middle of Bengbu's Shengli Road, "instigated students to storm the Bengbu Cigarette Plant," and encouraged workers to go on strike. After the bloodshed in Beijing, it said, "Zhang Lin and others led a so-called dare-to-die corps to the streets to demonstrate and to storm the offices of the city party committee and the city government. . . . With a battery-powered microphone in hand, he frenziedly clamored for rioting, rioting, rioting throughout the city." Zhang was sentenced to two years in prison for "counterrevolutionary propaganda and incitement."[4]

After his release from jail, Zhang renewed his dissident activities with a vengeance. In early 1994, he was one of the main organizers of a new group called the League for the Protection of the Rights of Working People, which took the unusually bold step of petitioning the authorities for legal recognition. The league claimed an initial membership of more than 120 people nationwide, among them Ding in Bengbu. Within six months, its ranks were said to have swelled to some 300. It was impossible to verify the figure independently, but it sounded plausible given the degree of support expressed for the group among dissidents in Beijing and Shanghai, the two main centers of antiparty activity. The authorities, of course, refused to recognize the league and harassed and detained those members who had publicly declared themselves, Zhang among them. Ding, who unlike Zhang had kept his membership secret, remained, at least to begin with, undetected.

The authorities were clearly worried about the league, whose emergence coincided with signs of growing dissatisfaction among workers in loss-making state industries. The formation of the league was the biggest known attempt thus far by intellectuals to harness these grievances in opposition against the party. Zhang spent much of early 1994 traveling around the country recruiting members for the new organization, particularly those with "a long-term record of struggle." Zhang said league leaders would even go as far as investigating how potential recruits who had served time in prison had behaved during their incarceration. "If they were at all cooperative with the authorities, we have nothing to do with them," he said. Zhang moved quickly from place to place, trying to spend no more than three or four days at any address. When I saw him during one of his visits to Beijing in May, he had shaved off his distinctive beard in order to avoid recognition. The police finally caught up with Zhang in June 1994 and sentenced him without trial to three years of "reeducation through labor."[5] It was Zhang who, shortly before his arrest, suggested that I get in touch with Ding, one of his top lieutenants, to find out about organized dissent in Bengbu.

"I don't think we should rule out violence," said Ding, sitting in his barely furnished room on the edge of a bed covered with a bamboo mat. He was not speaking for the league, which stated as one of its "guiding principles" that it would "use legal means to carry out peaceful opposition to any violation of the rights of working people." Ding was venting his own frustration at the seeming impotence of the dissident movement as one after another of its members were picked up by the police. "If we could threaten their families or assassinate one or two of them, that would deter [the police]," said Ding. "Democracy activists have called for nonviolence. But there's a split in the democracy movement over this. I think there is a need for violence." Shortly before his arrest, Zhang Lin had also told me that some small dissident groups, particularly in his own province of Anhui and the southern province of Hunan, felt the same. Some of these groups, he said, had sworn to use peaceful means in order to join forces with the league but others had refused to do so.

Ding bemoaned the lack of funds available to dissidents to carry out their activities. "If we had money we could have collected you from the railway station in our own car, and then shaken off the police if they followed us," he said. "Another problem is that the democracy movement is like a plate of loose sand. There is no unified action." Ding said he was pessimistic about the future of organized dissent in China. Workers, he said, "openly curse Deng Xiaoping. But when they're needed [to take action], they withdraw. They don't want to take the initiative."

Luckily, even though it was well past one o'clock in the morning, we managed to find a taxi to take me back to my hotel. Ding told me to wait outside on the street while he went in to see if he could spot any police waiting for me. There were none in sight, and I collected my bag hurriedly, not bothering to wake the staff behind the desk to whom I had earlier given a deposit bigger than the cost of the room. With a packet of cigarettes, Ding bribed a railway official to let me onto an already overcrowded train. It was crammed with peasants on their way to Nanjing and Shanghai. I sat on my bag in the corridor, wedged in by people squatting and standing all around me, one man with his bare feet in the puddle of urine left by people stepping in and out of the filth in the lavatory next to him. The train arrived in Nanjing sometime after six o'clock in the morning.

My hasty retreat from Bengbu, it turned out, proved unwarranted. There was no sign that the police were on my tail. But Ding's caution was understandable. Many dissidents at that time were afraid. One of the reasons his friend Zhang Lin was back in prison was because he had introduced two foreign journalists to disgruntled workers and peasants in and near Bengbu earlier in the year. Zhang had spent much of his time investigating the complaints of peasants in villages around Bengbu, hoping to rally them to his cause.

Ding's pessimism about the future of dissent in China was widely shared by fellow activists elsewhere. Very few dissidents believed they could do much more than embarrass and irritate the authorities as long as Deng Xiaoping remained alive. Deng had shown fierce determination to stamp out dissent throughout his career, from the Anti-Rightist Campaign in 1957 to the crushing of the Democracy Wall Movement in 1979 and the suppression of the Tiananmen Square protests 10 years later. Although he condemned the Cultural Revolution, Deng stopped short of attacking the Anti-Rightist Campaign with the same degree of vehemence. Deng was the party's general secretary at the time of the campaign and therefore a key player in the purge of dissidents. Throughout his life, Deng had maintained that it was "necessary and correct" to launch the 1957 crackdown even though its scope had become "unduly broadened."[6] Many dissidents believed that while Deng's death might not bring any more liberal leaders to the fore, it might at least trigger a political struggle such as that of 1989, which would give them a window of opportunity to regroup and attack. Deng's increasing frailty, which was obvious from his rare televised appearances, was an incentive to the dissident community to intensify preparations for his demise.

The league came into being at a time when the euphoria surrounding Deng's southern tour was beginning to ebb amid growing public concerns about the negative aspects of rapid economic change, particularly corruption, inflation, and unemployment. Many dissidents who had been imprisoned for their roles in the Tiananmen Square protests had completed their sentences or had been released early as a gesture to Western governments. Some victims of the government's crackdown on Tiananmen were becoming increasingly bold and ingenious in their efforts to challenge the authorities, not through open confrontation but by attempting to take the government on through the courts. The former minister of culture, Wang Meng, was the most prominent pioneer of this tactic. Wang, who resigned from his post three months after Tiananmen amid efforts by hard-liners to tighten control over culture, attempted in October 1991 to file a libel suit against a literary gazette, the *Wenyi Bao*, controlled by the hard-line faction. Wang, who was then still a member of the party's Central Committee and a vice chairman of the government-sponsored Chinese Writer's Association, accused the journal of misrepresenting one of his stories as an attack against Deng Xiaoping.[7] The court refused to consider the case, a decision that Wang appealed against with equal lack of success in a higher court. Although Wang had never publicly associated himself with Tiananmen dissidents, one of the lawyers he hired to help him was Zhang Sizhi, who had courageously defended Wang Juntao, one of the alleged masterminds of the 1989 unrest.

Wang Meng's case was bound to fail. But as he clearly intended, it caused a considerable stir. Even though following Tiananmen, dozens of people had been vilified by the official media and hundreds of others labeled as politically suspect by their employers, there had hitherto been no reported examples of anyone trying to sue the authorities for misconduct or libel. Close associates of Wang told me that even though the former minister was rebuffed by the courts, his action achieved considerable success. Not only was there no sign of what some of his supporters had earlier feared would be an all-out attack on him and his allies through the official media, but several provincial newspapers had also broken ranks from the hard-line camp and published relatively objective accounts of Wang's case. The national circulation *Peasants' Daily* in Beijing even published an article by Wang himself indirectly defending the content of the story at the center of the dispute.[8]

In the following months, several dissident intellectuals tried similar tactics against their hard-line persecutors. Although the courts routinely refused to hear their cases, there was no direct retribution by the government, except perhaps heightened surveillance. Even though the domestic press studiously ignored them, the dissidents gained international media attention. The authorities, apparently anxious not to be seen to be denying citizens their right to sue, kept silent.

By early 1993, the government began adopting a more tolerant approach toward the handling of certain well-known political prisoners and dissidents in an effort to boost its bid to host the Olympic Games in the year 2000. Just as in 1989 the leadership ceded ground to dissidents because of the international media attention focused on the summit meeting between President Gorbachev and Deng Xiaoping in mid-May, so too to a lesser extent did it make concessions to the dissident community in the buildup to the International Olympic Committee's decision in September 1993 as to which of six competing cities would stage the 2000 Olympiad.

China was bitterly disappointed when it lost by only two votes to Sydney. Its bid, if successful, would have given it the chance to show itself off to the world as a self-confident, emerging economic superpower. But Beijing's defeat did not immediately lead to a renewed campaign against dissent. The leadership was still mindful of President Clinton's upcoming decision on the renewal of China's most favored nation (MFN) trading status. Clinton had warned in May 1993 that unless "overall, significant progress" was made on human rights by June of the following year, China risked losing its MFN status and with it billions of dollars worth of low-tariff access to the American market. It was a price that China did not want to pay.

It was an open secret that "significant progress" in Washington's eyes meant little more than releasing a handful of well-known political prisoners and refraining from rounding up too many high-profile dissidents. It did not mean that China actually had to implement the guarantees provided in its constitution for freedom of the press, speech, and association and the right to demonstrate. China had thousands of political prisoners from which to choose the lucky handful. The New York–based group Human Rights Watch/Asia, which has monitored the fate of Chinese dissidents more closely than any other foreign organization, documented nearly 220 arrests of dissidents in 1993. The group said it was in fact the worst year for political arrests since Tiananmen Square. Most of these cases, however, occurred in Tibet. In the rest of China that year, the severity of the repression appeared no worse than normal. In its bid to keep MFN, the authorities by and large kept their hands off the better-known dissidents, while some of those released that year helped to galvanize the fragmented and demoralized underground movement into renewed action.

To an extent China had no choice but to release some of its best-known political prisoners that year, simply because they had completed or nearly completed their sentences. The leadership had avoided imposing lengthy jail terms on the student leaders involved in the 1989 protests, handing out the longest sentences instead to older intellectuals and workers. This was in keeping with the leadership's assertion that the students were manipulated by instigators behind the scenes. Since the longest sentence imposed on any of those on the government's list of 21 most-wanted student leaders was four years (with the exception of the graduate student Liu Gang, who got six years), by 1993 most of those who had not escaped abroad had been or were due to be freed.

In what appeared to be a gesture to the United States, China decided to release the best known of the student leaders, Wang Dan, five months early in July. Wang was at the top of the wanted list issued after the 1989 crackdown. He became a national celebrity when he argued with Prime Minister Li Peng in a televised debate during the Tiananmen upheaval. When he was released "on parole," the gaunt, softly spoken 23-year-old said he had no regrets about anything he had done and that his greatest dream was to carry on his campaign for greater democracy. Later the leadership was undoubtedly to regret having let him go. Another student leader from Tiananmen days, Zhai Weimin, was released in September after completing a three-and-a-half-year prison term. He was the only student activist to have continued clandestine dissident activities on the mainland after the Tiananmen crackdown, setting up a small and short-lived underground group called the Democratic Front for the Salvation of China. He and its other main members were arrested in early 1990. Back on the streets in 1993, Zhai showed no signs of repentance whatsoever.

Equally unrepentant was Wang Xizhe who was released in February 1993 after serving nearly 12 years of a 14-year prison sentence. Wang, who lives in Canton, dates his dissident career as far back as 1974, when he and two others pasted up a famous wall poster calling for greater democracy. For that transgression he was kept in prison until three years after Mao Zedong's death. His first release coincided with the Democracy Wall Movement in Beijing, in which he became a leading activist. After not much longer than a year's freedom, his "counterrevolutionary activities" landed him in prison again. "What I did was worthwhile, and I have not changed my political beliefs," said an exhausted Wang after his release. "I don't mind going to jail at all. . . . I have been jailed twice already."9

Another giant of the Democracy Wall period, Xu Wenli, was released in May 1993, three years before completing his 15-year sentence. "I certainly committed no crime. What I did, I did for my country," Xu told reporters after emerging from 12 years in solitary confinement. From then on, however, Xu largely kept silent. In a rare public gesture, he issued a statement through his wife in February 1995 calling for, among other things, an official reassessment of Tiananmen and an end to one-party rule. But the former soldier and electrician appeared to prefer staying quietly at home with his family rather than plunging back into the dissident movement.

This was not the case with Wei Jingsheng, whom the authorities released in September 1993, six months before the end of his 15-year sentence. Wei, then 42, was by far the most famous political prisoner in China. During the Democracy Wall Movement, Wei wrote a famous article calling on the leadership to add a "fifth modernization," namely, democracy, to the "four modernizations" of industry, agriculture, science and technology, and defense, which were touted by the party as the chief objectives of the new era under Deng Xiaoping. Wei's article was pasted up on Democracy Wall in December 1978. The following March, Wei accused Deng in a wall poster of "metamorphosing into a dictator." Later that month, Deng ordered Wei's arrest and fiercely criticized the Democracy Wall dissidents. "Departure from the four cardinal principles[10] and talk about democracy in the abstract will inevitably lead to the unchecked spread of ultrademocracy and anarchism, to the complete disruption of political stability and unity, and to the total failure of our modernization program," Deng warned. "If this happens . . . China will once again be plunged into chaos, division, retrogression, and darkness, and the Chinese people will be deprived of all hope."[11] In a speech the following year, Deng attacked Wei by name as one of the "so-called democrats and so-called dissidents who flagrantly oppose the socialist system and the Communist Party leadership."[12] In 1993, there was no sign that either Wei or Deng had changed their minds about democracy.

Although Wei was not widely known beyond the dissident community at the time of his arrest, his trial and imprisonment turned him into a symbol of dissent in the eyes of many urban Chinese. Only a relatively small number of Beijing residents, mostly fellow dissidents, had even seen the former electrician who used to work at Beijing Zoo. Unlike the Tiananmen leader Wang Dan, he was never shown on national television. But while many Chinese know what Wei's "fifth modernization" refers to, few if any know of any political essays or the contents of any speeches made by Wang Dan. Wei's arrest was the first of a prominent dissident in the Deng era, and anyone with nonconformist political views watched closely to see what would become of him. Wei's spirited defense of his beliefs at his secretive trial in October 1979 became widely known among Chinese dissidents thanks to a transcript based on a tape recording furtively made by a sympathizer. The transcript was circulated by another Democracy Wall activist, Liu Qing, who spent 10 years in prison for his pains.[13]

The sentencing of Wei as a "counterrevolutionary" who had allegedly divulged military secrets to a foreign journalist—in fact, publicly known information about China's border war in early 1979 with Vietnam—created a martyr who would remain a thorn in the side of the leadership for years to come. Although Democracy Wall was closed down at the end of 1979 and dozens of other activists arrested, many dissidents were uncowed and continued for several months to publish underground journals. Wei's treatment was the subject of spirited debate among students at Beijing University in 1980 during campus elections to select student representatives for the local People's Congress, the powerless bottom tier of China's party-controlled legislative structure. Student radicals turned the elections into an unprecedented and never since repeated experiment in grassroots democracy, with candidates conducting Western-style campaigns—addressing rallies, giving interviews, and challenging each others' views. Some of them openly proclaimed that Wei's trial had been misjudged or that he had been sentenced too heavily. Hu Ping, who expressed the latter view, won the elections. But the government got cold feet about the whole exercise, fearing that it might lead to the emergence of a Solidarity-style alternative force in Chinese politics. Hu was not allowed to take up his post.

It was a demand for Wei Jingsheng's release that brought radical intellectuals together some eight years later in the first concerted act of defiance by dissidents in the buildup to the unrest of 1989. By the tenth anniversary of Wei's arrest on March 29th of that year, a total of 200 Chinese intellectuals had signed petitions, saying typically that an amnesty for Wei and other political prisoners "would be beneficial to the atmosphere of reform and in accordance with the increasing respect for human rights that is a pervasive trend in the world today."[14] Two weeks later, the Tiananmen Square protests began, led by younger students who would only have been about 10 years old when Wei was imprisoned. Older intellectuals by and large stayed in the background, and the campaign for Wei's release was sidelined by the more sweeping concerns of the students, workers, and other citizens who poured out onto the streets.

During most of Wei's incarceration, the authorities refused to give any details about his circumstances or whereabouts. His family avoided contact with the media and with other dissidents, making it even more difficult to learn news of him. Amnesty International even reported in late 1987 that it had received unconfirmed reports that Wei had died. It was not until early 1992 that the government gave its first public accounting, telling the American businessman and human rights campaigner John Kamm that Wei was being held in solitary confinement at a labor camp on the outskirts of the city of Tangshan, about 100 miles east of Beijing. Kamm said the officials made it very clear that Wei had not changed his views and still believed he had done nothing wrong. They said, however, that he was "basically" abiding by prison rules. The officials also insisted that Wei was in good health, contrary to persistent rumors that he had become mentally disturbed. After his release, Wei denied these rumors too. There was every sign that he was as mentally fit as he was 15 years earlier and just as defiant. It was a humbling experience meeting a man who had suffered so much for so long and yet who remained so good-humored, even-tempered, and clear-thinking.

Wei told me he believed it was Deng's daughter and personal secretary Deng Rong who finally convinced her father to let him go. There is no independent evidence to support this view, but it is plausible that Deng Xiaoping, who had been attacked more bluntly by Wei than by any other prominent dissident still in China, might have taken some persuading.[15] Nonetheless, it is clear that the authorities had long been preparing for Wei's return to public view. About four years before his release they moved him from the notorious prison gulag of Qinghai Province in southwestern China to the labor camp near Tangshan, where, according to Wei, they began treating him somewhat better during the last 12 months of his confinement, giving him more food and taking him on outings to show him how city life had changed under Deng's reforms. Wei said he thought the food contained some kind of drug to build up his bulk and that the improved conditions were aimed at giving the outside world a favorable impression of what China calls its "humanitarian" prison system when he was set free. Given that the improvement in Wei's treatment was not mirrored in the treatment of most other political prisoners around the country at the time, there can be no other explanation for the authorities' motives.

The leadership was clearly more nervous about freeing Wei than it had been about the release of any previous political prisoner. When Wang Dan was released, foreign journalists flocked to his parents' tiny apartment in western Beijing to interview him without encountering any police obstruction. It was only later, as Wang's continuing outspokenness began to worry the authorities, that the police began making periodic efforts to stop journalists from approaching his flat, citing rarely invoked regulations that all interviews with private citizens must be approved by their employers or by the city government. In Wei's case, the authorities waited for a week after his formal release before allowing him to return home, keeping him at a government guest house on the outskirts while dozens of foreign journalists camped outside his home waiting to see him. When he finally did appear, looking relatively fit but complaining of heart trouble and the loss of many of his teeth, Wei tactfully refused to comment on the current political situation in China, saying he needed more time to find out what was happening. But he soon lost his reserve.

When freed, political prisoners in China often find themselves under strong pressure from their families and friends to stay out of the limelight and avoid further trouble. Many of them do so. Their sentences always include "deprivation of political rights" for between one and five years after their prison terms are over. This sanction is automatically imposed on anyone convicted of "counterrevolutionary" crimes and includes deprivation of the freedoms supposedly guaranteed for other citizens by the constitution, including those of speech, correspondence, assembly, association, procession, and demonstration. A person deprived of political rights is also not allowed to hold a leading position in any enterprise, which in theory could include one's own private business. Some dissidents ignored these restrictions, but at the time of Wei's release there were fewer than half a dozen dissidents in the whole of Beijing who were willing to speak their minds on the record to foreign journalists on sensitive political subjects. Even Wang Dan, who frequently spoke out in spite of his one-year loss of political rights, was often guarded on certain issues and avoided talking about Tiananmen.

Wei, after more than 14 years in one of the world's most brutal prison systems, spoke freely and, befitting his image as the elder statesman of Chinese dissent, dispensed advice to the many younger dissidents who visited him. He only once betrayed a little nervousness during our meetings, when he got up during a conversation in his father's ground-floor apartment to close the window. "They might have long distance microphones," said Wei, looking at the trees outside. "They wouldn't put them in here because if they were discovered it would cause a big stir."

Wei's advice was not always to the liking of the younger generation. He thought it was a waste of time to confront the government openly by staging protests or writing petitions since any public act of defiance would simply lead to the arrests of the ringleaders and accomplish nothing. He believed more in quiet, behind-the-scenes organization in readiness for the day when dissidents could make their move and not be instantly crushed. Wei spoke contemptuously of some of his dissident colleagues, saying they looked down on workers as "riffraff and hooligans." "They want to become famous by meeting foreign journalists," he said. "They don't want to do practical work." He described Wang Dan as "a petitioner, not an organizer." Wei's work included frequent meetings with disaffected workers, some of whom came to find him to discuss their grievances. As a former worker and Red Guard activist, Wei had more in common with the ordinary citizen than did many of the young students who had led the Tiananmen Square protests. Although Wei came from a privileged background—his father Wei Zilin having worked as a senior official in the Ministry of Construction before his retirement—he spoke in a direct and simple manner devoid of arrogance and appeared at ease and good-humored with people from all walks of life.

During several interviews in early 1994, Wei painted a bleak picture of the mood of Chinese workers in state-owned factories, particularly in cities other than Beijing. "Outside Beijing, many people can't bear it," Wei told me. He said some workers were forming underground organizations, while others were showing their desperation by stealing factory property, attacking factory managers, or smashing up equipment. "These people stealing things [from factories] are people close to starving," Wei said. "You journalists are restricted in what you are allowed to do in Beijing. It's difficult for you to meet poor people. When people become poor they rarely leave their homes, they hide inside, so it's difficult for you to meet them." But Wei was not enthusiastic about introducing his worker contacts. They rarely liked to meet foreign journalists, he explained, because of the deeply ingrained fear among many Chinese that representatives of the foreign media are spies.

Official figures put the number of urban residents living below the poverty line at about 20 million in 1994, or over 5 percent of the total urban population.[16] That year, thanks to soaring inflation and the continuing poor performance of the state sector, the proportion of workers living in poverty increased from 5 to 8 percent.[17] Wei said he believed the situation was becoming increasingly volatile. "Chaos is indeed possible," he said. "Lots of small incidents have already occurred. There were lots of little incidents [involving worker protests] last year. Whenever a dynasty is ending it is like this. You can put down 99 out of 100 disturbances, but if you don't put down the last one it lights a fuse and there's an explosion."

Wei's words were echoed later in 1994 in a book published by the Central Party School.[18] It said that "even though the Chinese press usually avoids mentioning crises," disturbances were "constantly occurring," including protests by workers and peasant resistance to payment by IOUs. "These phenomena sound constant alarm bells for us," it said. "A slight problem in one area could affect the entire situation and threaten the overall progress of reform." The book warned that the Chinese people were living in a "political, economic, and cultural whirlpool" and that any slight disturbance could develop into "enormous social turmoil." Chaos in China, it said, was "a hidden danger" that should not be glossed over by reporting only good news.

Wei Jingsheng did not believe, however, that a worker uprising was necessarily imminent. "The Chinese are special," he said, "unless you push them right to the limit they won't rebel." Wei said government control was too tight. "If anyone comes out to talk about the problem [of poverty], even if they just use a few characters on a T-shirt saying 'we are very poor,' the police will come out and arrest them." He predicted that even after Deng's death, worker unrest would "take some time" to boil over. "The chaos will be within the party, not among ordinary people," Wei said. But he predicted that if the government continued to prevent workers from airing their grievances publicly, the eventual explosion of discontent would be all the more devastating. "If workers who are resentful or who have problems can go on strike or use other peaceful methods to solve their difficulties, there probably won't be any greater turmoil," Wei told me. "But right now the Communist Party doesn't even allow them to do this. It doesn't allow them to organize unofficial trade unions. So problems are likely to pile up . . . and lead to serious turmoil."

Perhaps rather wishfully, Wei said impoverished Chinese workers, unlike many of their counterparts in the former Soviet Union and Eastern Europe, did not constitute a conservative force who opposed market-oriented reforms. "A lot of poor people oppose economic reform, but what they oppose is not the speed of reform. In fact they wish the reforms could be faster," he said. "What they disapprove of is the nature of the reform process, the methods used. One of the hallmarks of reform in China is that wealth is concentrated in the hands of a very few people, people with power who have the best economic advantages. A large amount of state wealth has effectively become private wealth, so ordinary people are extremely angry about this. But they're not opposed to the market economy."

Leaders of the League for the Protection of the Rights of Working People said Wei was not a member of their organization. But they did say he supported it, and it was clear from the company Wei kept that he paid close attention to what the league was doing. The only organized work that Wei admitted to taking part in was that of his own public relations company, which he set up after his release using some of the $50,000 he was awarded in March 1993 by the California-based Gleitsman Foundation. The prize for human rights activism was conferred by a committee whose members included the Nobel Laureate Archbishop Desmond Tutu, the former United Nations Secretary General Javier Perez de Cuellar, and the exiled Chinese dissident Fang Lizhi. It gave Wei the equivalent of a lifetime's wages for the average factory worker and a degree of financial security such as few if any dissidents in China have ever before enjoyed. Wei hired a former Tiananmen student activist as his secretary and rented space in a shabby apartment block in northwestern Beijing. The dissident Zhai Weimin joined his informal staff. Zhai reticently described his work to me as "helping artists stage exhibitions."

Zhang Lin, the league activist from Anhui, is among Wei's biggest admirers. He told me that the democracy movement needed a "spiritual leader" like Wei in order to avoid fragmentation. "His release gave hope to many," he told me. Zhang was among them. During our meetings, he appeared full of revolutionary bravado, relishing his tales of danger and intrigue as a leading activist in the league. It was difficult to tell how much of what he said was braggadocio and wishful thinking, but given that he had been jailed five times in the space of eight years—six including his imprisonment in June 1994—Zhang had what seemed to be solid revolutionary credentials. During his two-year imprisonment after Tiananmen, Zhang was confined in a 20-square-meter cell with about 20 other inmates. The prisoners slept on the floor, jammed together so closely that they all had to turn over at the same time. Those who missed the cue to turn because they were fast asleep would be prodded awake. If an inmate fell ill, he would be taken to the clinic where an official would apply a cattle prod to the patient's hands. If the inmate subjected to this torture begged to return to his cell, he was considered not sufficiently ill for treatment.

As Zhang described it, the league had a complex organizational structure designed to withstand the inevitable arrests of those publicly associated with the group. In the "first line" of the league were its publicly acknowledged leaders: Liu Nianchun, the younger brother of Liu Qing, the dissident jailed for publicizing the transcript of Wei Jingsheng's trial; Yuan Hongbing, a Beijing University law professor and editor of the book *Historical Trends,* which was banned in 1992;[19] Wang Zhongqiu, a postgraduate student of law at Beijing University; and Zhang Lin, who was designated as the group's "liaison man." It was Liu Nianchun who handed in the formal application for registration at the Ministry of Civil Affairs in March 1994. The "second and third lines" of the organization were correspondingly less public in their activities, the third line being deepest underground. The smallest number of people belonged to the first line and, according to Zhang, were not necessarily the most influential people in the league. By the middle of 1994, most of the "first line" people had been arrested as had several other members of the organization in Beijing and Shanghai. But Ding in Bengbu and many others from the "second and third lines" remained free, though clearly in Ding's case scared.

The league was evidence of how far the dissident movement had progressed since the early days after Tiananmen. Although its self-declared membership of 300 was dwarfed by that of some of the short-lived prodemocracy groups formed during the Tiananmen Square protests, it was much larger than other known dissident organizations formed since June 1989. Most underground groups after Tiananmen consisted of little more than half a dozen friends who spent most of their time sitting around concocting statements to issue to the foreign media. Such groups were relatively easy for the police to monitor and round up.

Leaders of the league liked to think of their organization as a Chinese Solidarity. They saw the brightest prospects for their group not in Beijing and Shanghai, the traditional centers of dissent, but in the more backward provinces. Zhang Lin said Beijing and Shanghai were more conservative than other cities because their political climate was so repressive. "If you stay in Beijing a long time you lose your willingness to make sacrifices," he said. "It's different in the provinces."

Zhang said about half the league's members were workers and the rest mainly intellectuals as well as a few peasants and private entrepreneurs. Zhang's efforts to tap into rural discontent apparently were not very fruitful. The leaders themselves were all intellectuals. They said their aim was to unify as many smaller dissident groups as possible. Zhang's fellow organizer Liu Nianchun said the group did not want to confront the authorities aggressively to begin with. "It is better first to have a dialogue," he said. Liu said that even though individual members of the group might try to organize strikes, the group as a whole would not do so unless it gained official recognition. In one of its early statements, issued to foreign reporters, the league noted that ever since the start of the Tiananmen Square protests in April 1989, dissidents had continually carried out "small-scale activities" without achieving any concrete results. "The emergence of the league indicates that the Chinese democracy movement is becoming more organized, more open, and more in line with the law. As long as it does not suffer a crushing blow, it will surely provide an organizational basis for the rise of an alternative political force." It clearly still had a long way to go. Outside dissident circles it could hardly claim the same recognition that its model Solidarity did in the early years of that group's struggle with the communist authorities in Poland.

The league's leaders said the main slogans the group would use to rally popular support would be "down with corruption," "raise wages," and "stabilize prices." Zhang Lin described corruption as immeasurably worse than it was 1989 when it was one of the main catalysts of the Tiananmen Square protests. In one of its statements, the league said that a market economy based on fair competition would be impossible to create as long as officials continued to enjoy unfair advantages. "Rampant corruption," it said, "now constitutes the most direct and most harmful threat to the rights of working people." Such words would certainly strike a chord among ordinary Chinese.

The league knew that it was not the only force using the corruption issue in the battle for the hearts and minds of workers and peasants. Corruption was also a favorite theme of extreme hard-liners who believed, not without reason, that Deng's reforms were fueling the problem. The league's statement devoted considerable space to attacking "extreme leftists" who it said were also expressing concern about workers' rights and anger over corruption. "We must clarify the differences in principle between ourselves and the extreme leftist trend of thought," it said. The statement accused the hard-liners of wanting to restore Maoist egalitarianism, restrict economic freedom, and revive class struggle. There was no evidence to suggest that extreme hard-liners in the leadership were taking their message directly to the factories in the same way the league was trying to do. But the tone of articles published by leftist-controlled periodicals suggested that the two political extremes were indeed campaigning in the same constituency.

The league was not universally embraced by the dissident community. In Guangdong, the former student Li Minqi kept aloof. Li was trying to organize unions among joint venture companies and smaller enterprises. His was fertile ground. Some of China's most Dickensian working conditions are to be found in the myriad Guangdong sweatshops churning out labor-intensive products for export to the West. Reports abound of workers, most of them former peasants from other provinces, being effectively treated as slaves in these privately run factories, locked in and forced to work long hours, seven days a week. From time to time, fires sweep through these factories causing extensive loss of life because of the lack of safety equipment or ready access to emergency exits. The league appeared content to leave Li to his work in Guangdong—it was more interested in the bigger state-run enterprises. Li had been released from prison in 1992 after serving a two-year sentence for giving a "counter-revolutionary" speech at Beijing University to mark the first anniversary of the crackdown on the Tiananmen Square protests. But Zhang Lin, resentful perhaps of Li's refusal to join the league, referred to him dismissively as a "neo-Marxist." Dissidents often appeared no less prone to factionalism than the party they aimed to overthrow.

The league had a big advantage over dissident organizations formed five or ten years earlier. By 1994, China had developed one of the most sophisticated communications infrastructures of any developing Asian country. During Tiananmen, telephone ownership was a luxury that few intellectuals boasted. In the first half of 1994, however, the number of newly installed phones in urban residential buildings grew by nearly 70 percent compared with the same period a year earlier. Although in per capita terms telephone ownership remained extremely low—in Beijing, only 16 out of 100 families had their own telephones in mid-1994— many dissident intellectuals were among the lucky minority. They were also fast acquiring beepers, through which they sent coded messages to each other. In the first half of 1994, the number of beeper owners rose in China by almost 40 percent compared with the same period of the previous year. Computers loaded with Chinese character software were becoming more common too, making the task of producing leaflets and circulars much easier. Chinese department stores sold some 4,500 home computers between January and May 1994, a small figure perhaps, but still 10 times as many as in the first five months of 1993. In the whole of 1994, the number of personal computers sold nationwide, including those for business use, totaled some 600,000 units, a 30 percent increase over the year before.[20]

A few dissidents even had access to fax machines, although the use of these was in theory controlled by the Ministry of Post and Telecommunications, which required that all such machines as well as modems be officially registered. A few of those affiliated with academic institutions could use the Internet, the computer network that allows millions of computer users around the world to exchange uncensored information instantaneously at minimal cost. Almost unheard of in China in 1989, Internet usage was growing exponentially in the Chinese academic world by the mid-1990s, albeit largely in the closely monitored environment of the office rather than in the privacy of users' homes. Mobile telephones appeared to be the only communications luxury beyond the reach of dissidents, not because they were unavailable but because the price of between $2,000 and $3,000 per set charged by the Ministry of Post and Telecommunications made them prohibitively expensive. By the mid-1990s, however, mobile telephones were in common use among rich private entrepreneurs, and it is easy to imagine that in the event of another Tiananmen-style upheaval, they would quickly find their way into the hands of dissidents who, during the 1989 demonstrations, had enormous difficulty communicating with colleagues in other parts of the same city let alone elsewhere in the country.

The reemergence of veteran activists such as Wei Jingsheng and his fellow Democracy Wall activist Liu Nianchun in 1993 and early 1994 gave the dissident movement renewed impetus at a time when its traditional wellhead of support, the campus community, was drying up. In contrast with the months leading up to the Tiananmen Square protests, when students like Wang Dan organized informal discussion groups to discuss sensitive topics, Beijing's universities appeared more preoccupied with the market economy than with politics. Only a few senior graduate students had any direct experience of the 1989 unrest. Each passing anniversary of the crushing of the Tiananmen Square protests saw fewer and fewer commemorative activities. On the fifth anniversary in 1994, which was supposedly a particularly significant date because the anniversary was a multiple of five, there was no sign at all of any untoward activity on Beijing's campuses. The only people who appeared to pay much attention to the anniversary were foreign journalists and the police. The latter came out in their usual force for such occasions, checking vehicles in the campus area and trying to stop us from approaching the universities. In 1990, by contrast, about 1,000 students gathered at Beijing University, shouted slogans, and sang songs to mark the bloodshed a year earlier. Zhang Lin said he believed that while many students sympathized with the dissidents, they were afraid of organizing or expressing their views openly because so many of their colleagues were spies. The former student leader Zhai Weimin told me in 1994 that he still kept in touch with students, "but students won't be the initiators of the next movement."

Abroad, the dissident movement was in disarray too. Students who had fled the country after Tiananmen and formed dissident groups in the United States, France, and other Western countries were hopelessly divided. They bickered over questions of leadership and policy and in some cases led extravagant lifestyles that alienated many potential supporters among the tens of thousands of Chinese students overseas. Back in China, the dissidents-in-exile commanded little respect. By the mid-1990s, the Chinese authorities had begun to change their policy of not allowing dissidents to travel abroad, realizing that once overseas such people became far less dangerous. Dissidents abroad could lobby foreign governments to put pressure on China to improve its treatment of political opponents, but in order for their message to be effective foreign governments needed reliable and current information about the human rights situation in China. Such information most often came from the reports filed by foreign correspondents in Beijing, who in turn relied on dissidents still in the country to provide it. China clearly hoped its new strategy would stem the flow of information at its source. The dissidents it allowed to go abroad usually were placed on a secret blacklist circulated among Chinese immigration officials, which meant they could not return.

Thus in April 1994, in an obvious concession to Washington, the government put the former newspaper editor Wang Juntao on a plane bound for the United States after he had served only five years of his 13-year prison term, imposed on him for his role in the Tiananmen Square protests. Wang's release was one of Washington's main demands as it considered whether to renew China's MFN status. The Chinese government was willing to acquiesce but did not want Wang to rejoin the dissident movement in China. It had already learned its lesson from Wei Jingsheng. So it informed the American Embassy in Beijing that Wang would go straight from his cell to the airport. There Wang was handed over to a waiting American diplomat who accompanied the dissident, first class, on a flight to New York. Wang's colleague Chen Ziming, who was released on May 14th after serving a similar proportion of his 13-year term, was also asked to go into exile, but Chen refused.[21] So eager were the Chinese authorities to impress Washington in advance of President Clinton's decision on MFN that they did not insist that he go. But unlike Wei Jingsheng, who enjoyed six months of relative freedom before being detained again, Chen, who was suffering from heart trouble and other ailments, was immediately placed under virtual house arrest. Chen's release was the last major concession by the Chinese before Clinton decided in May 1994 not only to renew Beijing's MFN status but also to delink the issue henceforth from the question of human rights. In June of the following year, after Chen defied the police who kept close watch on his house by issuing an appeal for compensation for victims of Tiananmen and the release of political prisoners, the authorities sent him back to prison to continue serving his sentence.

With Clinton's decision, Beijing felt it was free to tighten the screws once more. But the leadership was powerless to stop the sweeping economic and social changes under way in Chinese society, which were creating increasingly favorable conditions for the growth of organized dissent. One crucial aspect of change was the diminishing effectiveness of one of the authorities' main instruments of control, namely, the *danwei* or "unit" to which every urban resident once belonged. The unit refers to the place where a person works. Each workplace has a party committee that once dominated the lives of every worker, deciding everything from promotions to housing allocations. Workers usually did not dare deviate from the political line for fear of losing benefits essential to their own and their families' welfare. By giving employees the green light to moonlight and find other work, however, the government undermined the unit's authority.

The unit's control mechanisms have by no means entirely crumbled. Most urban residents still depend on their units for housing. But this is slowly beginning to change too. In order to reduce its colossal spending, including depreciation costs, of $4.5 billion annually on public housing, the government has begun encouraging workers to buy the apartments they had been living in hitherto virtually rent-free. Few can afford to do so, and few see the point of buying a dilapidated apartment in a state-owned apartment block. But by the end of July 1993, 120,000 apartments in Beijing had been sold.[22] Their occupants had unwittingly—or perhaps intentionally—smashed one of the heaviest chains linking them to the state. One large state-owned enterprise in Beijing found that one in 10 employees submitted their resignation after taking advantage of the factory's decision to sell off housing under its control at cheap prices to the occupants. An official newspaper said many enterprises had similar experiences.[23]

Most students who were at the forefront of the Tiananmen Square protests were denied jobs in government offices or state-owned enterprises. But the rapid development of the market economy gave them plenty of other ways to make a living. Many headed to the southern boomtowns to work in joint ventures or private businesses. There nobody asked questions about their political backgrounds. Even in relatively backward Wuhan I came across a dissident I had known in Beijing who was working in 1992 as the public relations manager of a joint venture factory. In Canton, Wang Xizhe helped a friend export a tonic to Singapore. The police told him he should not engage in business and kept him under virtual arrest during the Canton Trade Fair in early 1994 to stop him from attending a press conference given by his friend to advertise the tonic. Wang said the police feared he would use the occasion to talk about human rights. "The police say I can't leave Canton," Wang told me. "I agree with that. But they also say I can't meet reporters and can't do business. That I can't accept. I would rather go back to prison." But Wang's difficulties appeared exceptional. Many other dissidents thrived in the relatively unfettered world of private commerce.

A friend from Beijing who had studied Marxism-Leninism and Mao Zedong Thought at a university in Beijing and spent several weeks in jail in 1993 for suspected political crimes became a wheeler-dealer in Canton, trading in smuggled cars. A former newspaper editor and party member, who supports the dissidents, told me in 1990 that he believed that going into business was a good way to maintain contacts with fellow activists. He himself was trying to set up a consultancy firm, which he said would employ people of like-minded political views. He said it would be relatively easy for him to do so because as a party member he would arouse less suspicion. "One of the biggest problems for these people [i.e., dissidents] is that it's impossible to speak out if you're completely dependent on the government for your livelihood," he said.

Particularly since the boom of 1992, the number of those living entirely on income derived from jobs in the state sector has decreased considerably. In early 1994, an unconfirmed story circulated among intellectuals in Beijing that the party leader Jiang Zemin had made a secret speech in which he drew attention to several manifestations of the dangers posed by "hostile forces." One example he gave was the running of 1,400 companies in southern China by former Tiananmen Square activists, a figure not publicly known or even rumored before. Jiang's reported remarks suggested that the government was well aware that economic change was weakening its grip.[24]

Even well before Tiananmen, the growth of nonparty-controlled organizations such as private businesses and research institutes had been providing breeding grounds for organized dissent. The post-Tiananmen crackdown slowed down this trend, but the loosening of economic controls in 1992 gave it renewed impetus. Among the pioneers in this emerging civil society were Chen Ziming and Wang Juntao. Chen and Wang's careers clearly demonstrated the potential political threat to the party posed by the rapid growth of independent institutions that at least outwardly have no political goals.

In the early days of their work, Chen and Wang described themselves as supporters of Deng Xiaoping.[25] Their political beliefs appeared far more moderate, even conservative, compared with those of the imprisoned rebel Wei Jingsheng. The two men would even have liked to work in the government had they not been barred from doing so because of their prominent involvement in the Democracy Wall Movement and the Tiananmen Square protests of 1976. Instead they decided to try to influence government from the outside by undertaking independent research into aspects of economic and political reform, the results of which they hoped would inform party policy makers. Thus in the early 1980s, Chen started building what was to become one of China's biggest, wealthiest, and most influential independent organizations.

Chen's empire began as a private trading company and quickly turned into a wholesale bookselling business at a time when private trading was still regarded as a risky and marginal occupation. Chen, then a researcher at the Chinese Academy of Social Sciences, found a few friends and relatives who were willing to join him in his novel enterprise. It was not until 1986, when he had been in business for about two years, that he finally resigned his research post. Chen borrowed the initial capital for his venture from a state-owned watch and clock-making company. Private enterprises at that time still had to find state-run firms to be their sponsors, a requirement that pacified die-hard Maoists who did not want to see the development of a completely private economy. The Watch and Clock Industrial Company agreed to be the sponsor of Chen's enterprise, but in practice it had no involvement in his business. State-run corporations were often willing to sponsor private enterprises if they knew they could make some easy profits without having to pay close attention to what the private businesses were up to.

Chen's Youth Books and Periodicals Distribution Agency was no ordinary book trading company. The books it sold were actually written by the company's own members. Chen and his colleagues would pay a state-run publishing house to print their works and then take charge of selling them. Chen's immediate priority was mainly to make money, but he also had broader political goals. One of his associates in the early days of his new enterprise recalled asking Chen how he saw his business developing. "His reply was roughly that he wanted to use the force of the private sector to promote democracy in China," the colleague said.

After running his book distribution agency for about a year, Chen turned his attention to a new way of making money—running correspondence schools. In 1985, when he embarked on this scheme, the thirst for knowledge among young and middle-aged people in China was intense. Many people had received almost no education during the Cultural Revolution. Universities and colleges, which had only reopened in the late 1970s, had far from enough places for all those who wished to resume their studies. Many people deprived of education during the Cultural Revolution now had full-time jobs and families and could not afford to give up everything to attend classes anyway.

Using their extensive contacts in the academic world, Chen and his colleagues set about finding professors in universities around the country who would be willing to supervise their courses. They then set up two correspondence universities. Through advertisements in the state-run press and flyers distributed by state-sponsored academic societies, Chen recruited well over 200,000 students for the two universities. Each student paid between 65 and 90 yuan for a two-year course or the equivalent of what was then about a month's wages for a young factory worker. In return, Chen and his associates sent out instruction materials including tapes and books, as well as examination papers. Those reaching a certain grade at the end of their course were given a certificate—recognized by the authorities—saying they had graduated from the correspondence school with an attainment equal to a college degree.

In 1988, the State Education Commission decided to exert tighter control over the education system and ordered the closure of correspondence universities. By then, however, Chen's colleges had earned more than 10 million yuan in profit, extraordinary riches by the standards of any Chinese. It is very difficult to translate such a huge sum of money into a figure that Westerners would understand. Millions of yuan might only be worth a few hundred thousand dollars if exchanged at the official rate, but in terms of what such a sum was worth then in China, where food, accommodation, clothing, transport, and other basic requirements were all heavily subsidized by the government, millions of yuan could be better compared with millions or tens of millions of dollars.

Two years before the State Education Commission's clampdown, Chen had already started up a far more significant if less profitable venture than his correspondence schools. He had used the money he earned from the schools to set up his own think tank, calling it the China Political and Administrative Sciences Research Institute. This was technically illegal. According to State Education Commission regulations, money earned from educational work was not to be reinvested in any other kind of business. But no one objected, and Chen at last began to fulfill his long cherished dream. "He once said that he wanted to turn his organization into something like the U.S. Rand Corporation, doing consultancy work for government decision-making bodies, providing top-level advice and strategies for reform," said one of Chen's associates. Among the group's founding members was Wang Juntao. The two men quietly built up an organization of extraordinary sophistication, quite independent of party control. Unlike more conventional dissidents they did not seek out the Western media, preferring instead to cultivate good relations with radical reformers working for the government. Their groundbreaking efforts thus went almost entirely unremarked by the outside world. "The two men's long-term aim was not to pursue scholarship," said an associate. "If they'd wanted to do that they could have done it in the Chinese Academy of Social Sciences. Their aim was to change the socialist system." It was only after Tiananmen was over, however, that most Western journalists and even many Chinese intellectuals learned their names.

In 1987, the think tank broke up because of personal disagreements, and Chen founded a new one called the Beijing Social and Economic Sciences Research Institute, using the prefix "Beijing" this time instead of "China" in order to pacify party hard-liners who had taken offense at the use of the "China" prefix by a nonparty-controlled organization.

The new institute's activities ranged from conducting public opinion surveys—a science then in its infancy in China—to publishing books on social and political issues. Within two years, the institute had nearly 50 employees and more than 100 associate researchers. It had office space consisting of 60 rooms, sophisticated computer equipment, and dozens of cars. By the time the Tiananmen Square protests erupted, it had launched nearly 40 research projects, organized 14 academic conferences, and published more than 100 books on the social sciences, including translations and works written by members of the institute. Hard-liners were deeply suspicious of the institute's activities, but thanks to the relative strength of reformist leaders at the time, the Chinese media gave the institute considerable encouragement by publishing some of the results of its surveys. In one of these polls, conducted in 1987, more than 3,000 respondents answered questions about their attitude toward highly sensitive political issues. A book based on the results contained what for China were embarrassing revelations about people's political views.[26] It said, for example, that more than a quarter of private entrepreneurs surveyed believed that it was right to rebel against the state "if the state caused you to lose hope." More than 15 percent of peasants gave the same reply and nearly 10 percent of intellectuals and officials. Even asking such a question would have been unthinkable a few years earlier.

Just as shocking was the survey's finding that fewer than 45 percent of peasants felt proud of living in a socialist country and only just over 50 percent of intellectuals. Officials showed the greatest enthusiasm for socialism, with more than 65 percent expressing pride in the system. Nonetheless, more than 10 percent of cadres replied that "there is nothing to be proud of." Asked whether they trusted the government, nearly 40 percent of peasants surveyed replied "No." Most respondents expressed dissatisfaction with the behavior of civil servants, including nearly 70 percent of officials themselves. A similar proportion agreed that "problems in the political system are the main reason why China is developing slowly." Fewer than half expressed satisfaction with the amount of freedom of speech and belief they enjoyed, and more than 60 percent of all respondents said they did not have enough freedom to stage rallies and demonstrations. To publish such controversial findings was daring indeed.

Chen and his employees exploited loopholes in the system and their own network of government contacts to the utmost. In early 1988, Chen suggested that a survey be carried out of the political attitudes of delegates to the National People's Congress, which was then holding its annual session in Beijing. Bai Hua, who was in charge of the institute's public polling section, the Opinion Research Center of China, agreed reluctantly to the suggestion. "He often wanted to do political things, and anything political was extremely dangerous," Bai Hua told me. "I didn't want my center to take any risks, so we often fought." No one had ever conducted a survey of congress delegates before, let alone an independent research group. The first problem was how to contact the delegates, whose addresses, like much seemingly routine information about public figures in China, were a secret. Bai Hua, who had studied journalism at university, knew a few reporters who were covering the congress. Chinese journalists have broad access to confidential information, and Bai Hua used her connections to get the addresses from them. When the session ended, she sent out questionnaires to 3,000 delegates from around the country. Remarkably, more than 1,000 responded.

"What we in fact intended to prove was that the National People's Congress was a rubber stamp, a Communist Party pawn," Bai Hua told me. She was not disappointed. The responses to questions about the duties and functions of the congress and its delegates revealed widespread ignorance. But the institute decided in favor of caution this time and kept these sensitive findings to itself. It also wanted publicity, however, so Bai Hua exploited her contacts in the media once again to call a news conference—an unusual move for a nongovernment organization—at which she announced some of the more positive findings of the survey, mixed in with a few sensitive tidbits. The People's Daily and China Youth News were among those that ran the story, crediting Chen's institute.[27] The China Youth News, in the spirit of relative daring then pervading the official media, even reported on the finding that many delegates were nervous about using their powers. The deputies, it said, had been asked by Chen's group to comment on the case of one delegate whose wife had called him long distance to ask him not to be too outspoken because he had once got into trouble after expressing disagreement with the official line at a congress forum. The newspaper said more than half of the delegates replied that the wife's worry was reasonable.

"All the news about us published by the *People's Daily* and so on was written by my friends," said Bai Hua, who fled to the United States after Tiananmen. "The editors looked at the reports with cool detachment and couldn't see anything wrong. They didn't know what the Beijing Social and Economic Sciences Research Institute was. So no matter how tightly controlled things were, there were still loopholes we could exploit."

Perhaps most remarkably of all, Chen's institute owned its own newspaper, the *Economics Weekly*. Private newspaper ownership is, of course, banned in China. But the institute was not, as far as the authorities were concerned, private. It was technically under the supervision of the Beijing Municipal Science and Technology Commission. In fact this was a polite fiction—one of Chen's friends happened to belong to the commission and arranged the formality of registering the institute as an affiliate—but it was a good enough cover to enable them to buy the newspaper in 1988 for 300,000 yuan from an organization under the Chinese Academy of Social Sciences. Chen made Wang Juntao its deputy editor. "Everyone realized this was a very important step," said a key member of Chen's institute. "With your own newspaper and your own outfit, people would listen to you."

Chen subsidized the newspaper with profits from his other ventures. Under Wang Juntao's guidance, it changed from a crusty academic journal into one of the most outspoken mouthpieces of the reformist camp, attracting many admirers from among the party leader Zhao Ziyang's circle of liberal-minded advisers. Zhao's reformist predecessor, Hu Yaobang, who retained his seat on the Politburo after being forced to quit his post as general secretary in January 1987, was among the paper's supporters. Shortly before his death in April 1989, Hu asked his wife Li Zhao to write a letter to the newspaper. The letter said the weekly was "not only scholarly but also practical and to the point." It would, she said, "enjoy the confidence of society." After Hu's death, the weekly published these words of praise on its front page with a large photograph of Hu above the article. Party hard-liners saw the newspaper differently. One post-Tiananmen diatribe described the *Economics Weekly* as one of three journals under the "control" of Zhao's advisers who used them "to publicize the ideas, theories, and views of bourgeois liberalization."[28]

Like many other Chinese newspapers, including even the *People's Daily,* the *Economics Weekly* showed strong support for the students during Tiananmen. Its penultimate edition, published on the day of the bloodshed, June 4th, 1989, carried a front-page commentary by Chen

Ziming, written under a pseudonym, saying that the use of armed force to resolve "contradictions among the people" could only backfire and "disrupt the progress of development."[29] The last edition appeared two weeks later, feisty to the end. "The creation of a market economy and the pluralization of the political system are the two most important hurdles that all socialist countries face," the newspaper quoted a Chinese legal scholar as saying. "Whether or not they can cross these hurdles will decide the fate of socialism."[30]

The then mayor of Beijing, Chen Xitong, said in his June 30th, 1989, report to the National People's Congress that the *Economics Weekly* had "coordinated" with a "drive to topple Deng and protect Zhao" in the months preceding the Tiananmen Square protests. The mayor accused the journal of trying to "whip up public opinion to cover up Zhao Ziyang's mistakes, keep his position and power, and push on with bourgeois liberalization with even less restraint." Surprisingly, perhaps, the mayor did not mention Wang Juntao by name and referred to Chen Ziming and his institute only in passing in a speech that was otherwise peppered with the names of organizations and individuals who had allegedly manipulated the students from behind the scenes. At the time, the mayor appeared more concerned with the role of Zhao's official think tanks than with Chen and Wang's activities.

But in the months that followed, the leadership decided Chen and Wang deserved the toughest punishment of all the dissident intellectuals the authorities succeeded in capturing. It was rumored among their friends and relatives that the leadership had come to the conclusion that the two men were the "black hands behind the black hands" responsible for orchestrating the demonstrations and that they were "veterans of four dynasties"—meaning the four major outbreaks of prodemocracy unrest since 1976[31]—who should therefore be regarded as particularly dangerous. At the secretive trials of the two men in February 1991, officials accused them of trying to "overthrow the government" during the Tiananmen demonstrations. They focused on the formation of a group by Wang and Chen called the Protect the Constitution Committee that gathered together leaders of several worker and student organizations involved in the protests. The prosecutor said the committee appointed someone to organize the blocking of troops who were trying to enter Beijing to enforce martial law and issued a declaration describing martial law as a "fascist terror tactic" and calling for the removal of Prime Minister Li Peng. It was a poorly argued case, with no evidence cited that Wang or Chen had done anything more conspiratorial than hundreds of other intellectuals involved in Tiananmen. The 13-year prison sentences imposed on the two men probably had more to do with what they represented—the emergence of an organized, independent intellectual force—than with anything they actually did in 1989. As Wang's wife Hou Xiaotian put it, "People like Wang Juntao, who have no party to back them up, who are unwilling to advertise themselves, and who are not as famous as Wang Dan, these people have done a lot of work. They have been pioneers in the course of Chinese democracy. I cannot but respect the Communist Party's insight, their ability to see at a glance who are their real adversaries."[32]

The leadership would almost undoubtedly have meted out similar punishment to the private businessman Wan Runnan had he not fled the country after Tiananmen. Wan was to the business world what Chen Ziming and Wang Juntao were to the research community. Just as Chen wanted his company to become China's Rand Corporation, so Wan said his aim was to create China's answer to IBM. "When Wan established [Stone Corporation] with 20,000 yuan [$5,400] in a two-room office provided by a rural factory, nobody could imagine this humble 'stone' would become a computer empire with 30 million yuan in fixed assets and a turnover last year of 300 million yuan," gushed Xinhua in 1988, when Wan was still a model entrepreneur lionized by the official media.[33] "Some people call these new entrepreneurs China's 'red capitalists' of the 80's," the agency said.[34]

Unlike Chen and Wang, Wan, who was in his mid-forties by the time Tiananmen erupted, was not a man with a long record of political activism on the wrong side of the party line. Wan was, in fact, a party member. But that did not stop him from sharing some of Chen and Wang's interests. When one of his employees proposed setting up a think tank, Wan readily agreed. In 1988 he established the small but influential Stone Social Development Research Institute, appointing the well-known political and legal scholar Cao Siyuan as its head. Cao, a former researcher in one of Zhao's think tanks, had extensive contacts in the official world thanks to his role as the chief drafter of China's first law on bankruptcy, the most fiercely debated piece of legislation ever considered by China's normally docile parliament. The law was adopted in 1986 and went into effect two years later, providing a legal framework for the winding up of loss-making, state-owned industries that for decades had been propped up by massive state subsidies.

One of Cao's jobs as director of the Stone think tank was to do consultancy work on the new law. But his activities also strayed into the more sensitive realm of politics. Cao had long been an outspoken advocate of giving the National People's Congress greater clout and removing overtly political jargon from the constitution. In March 1989, not long before the student protests erupted, Cao's institute organized a large-scale conference on constitutional reform attended by many of the country's radical intellectuals. Among the constitutional amendments Cao wanted to see were provisions that those brought to trial should be presumed innocent until proved guilty and that the secretive proceedings of the National People's Congress should be broadcast live and published in full. Cao wanted ordinary members of the public to be admitted to the Great Hall of the People to observe the meetings. His suggestions fell on deaf ears. The only part of the congress the government was prepared to broadcast live was the carefully scripted opening address by the prime minister. This was not a concession to Cao. Such broadcasts had been introduced several years earlier. The government was not prepared to take even the remote risk of a dissident voice being heard by publishing a full record of debates, and it certainly did not want members of the public observing the sycophantic behavior of the "people's representatives" close up.

By the time of Tiananmen, Wan's Stone Corporation employed more than 700 people, many of whom eagerly joined the demonstrations. Unlike Chen and Wang, who preferred to stay in the background, Wan threw himself and his company into the movement, donating large sums of money to the students and organizing meetings of protest leaders. As the *People's Daily* put it, "Wan Runnan picked up a big stone—'the entire company'—and threw it at Beijing."[35] Cao Siyuan and his think tank helped Hu Jiwei, a liberal member of the National People's Congress Standing Committee, collect the names of fellow members on a petition calling for an emergency session of the Standing Committee to discuss the unrest. The authorities later accused Hu and Stone of including the names of people who had not agreed to give their support and of plotting to use the Standing Committee to dismiss Li Peng and rescind martial law. Hu was stripped of his post and expelled from the party. Cao also lost his party membership and was imprisoned without trial for nearly a year.

In retrospect, it seems extraordinary that the leadership of such an authoritarian state should allow the emergence of large, wealthy, independent institutions such as those operated by Chen Ziming and Wan Runnan. It is particularly remarkable given that, at least in the case of Chen Ziming and Wang Juntao, the authorities had been keeping close watch on their activities throughout the 1980s. Bai Hua quoted a police-man as telling one of her colleagues in 1989, "Do you think we haven't been keeping track of people like Bai Hua and Wang Juntao who've been up to all these antiparty activities? I can tell you, my office has been responsible for monitoring the activities of Chen Ziming and Wang Jun-tao for the last 10 years." If this was the case, it is puzzling that the authorities allowed the two men to set up their independent empire. "I still don't understand," Bai Hua herself admitted. "One reason perhaps is that the government began allowing the creation of independent orga-nizations, and all the procedures they went through were legal. There was no way they could say we won't let you do this. Besides at the time they didn't constitute much of a threat to the government. It was, after all, just a research organization." Bai Hua's explanation did not sound convincing. Had the leadership wanted to it could easily have found a pretext to close down the institute. But for much of the 1980s reformists led by Hu Yaobang and his successor Zhao Ziyang appeared to have the upper hand, and in spite of the vigilance of the police they apparently wanted to encourage constructive input into the policy-making process by nongovernmental experts.

So it was that in the hurly-burly of economic reform in the late 1980s, even under the noses of the police, the two men were able to cre-ate the fabric of what could well have become an influential nonparty structure in Chinese politics. In the chaos of reform in the 1990s, there are undoubtedly many such structures in the making, quietly taking shape just as Chen and Wan's organizations did without drawing the attention of the foreign media, ready to emerge when the next political crisis erupts. As the *People's Daily* rightly put it, "It may be hard for everyone to imagine that Wan Runnan, a gentle and cultivated entrepre-neur, dressed in Western suit and with enormous wealth, also picked up a 'stone' [to throw at the government]."[36] China in the 1990s has many more wealthy private entrepreneurs than it did in 1989. Together they represent a potentially powerful new interest group.

By punishing Chen and Wang so severely and attacking Wan so harshly, the authorities clearly wanted to prevent the emergence of others like them. But the economic changes already underway before Tiananmen that gave these men such leeway appeared unstoppable. Thanks to the resurgence of extreme hard-liners, the pace of change may have slowed for a while after the crackdown, but Deng's southern tour removed the last fetters. Stone Corporation, after issuing a ritual denun-ciation of Wan, was allowed to continue operating. In 1993 one of its subsidiaries, Stone Electronic Holdings, listed on the Hong Kong stock market, the first nonstate Chinese entity to do so. Earlier in the year, America's Compaq Computer Corporation signed a distribution agreement with Stone giving it access to the more than 1,000 Stone outlets across China. After a post-Tiananmen slump, Stone's profits surged. In 1994, the company announced an annual sales target of 10 billion yuan ($1.15 billion) by the year 2000, three times the figure attained in 1993.

Even Cao Siyuan managed to revive his bankruptcy consulting business—independently of Stone—after his release from prison. The official media, which had once portrayed him as an archvillain of the 1989 unrest, started to quote him once again as an authority on bankruptcy.[37] Official think tanks staffed by Zhao Ziyang's supporters such as the Research Institute for Economic Structural Reform, the Research Center for the Reform of the Political Structure, and the Rural Development Research Center may have been closed down for good because of their perceived involvement in the Tiananmen unrest, but there was still room for independent thinkers to maneuver, albeit with greater circumspection than before 1989.

It is hard to imagine a rich private entrepreneur openly confronting the government as long as the leadership remains at least superficially united. But in the event of another open split in the leadership such as occurred in 1989, many independent organizations including private businesses will inevitably take sides, backing those forces that they see as most likely to protect their interests. Those who come down on the side of antigovernment groups, as Wan Runnan did in 1989, could play a significant role given their resources and networks of contacts, more than they did in 1989 when the development of private enterprise was still in its relative infancy.

Mu Qizhong is typical of the post-Tiananmen wheeler-dealer who is careful to appear politically correct but whose business empire symbolizes the rapid social and economic changes that in recent years have been eroding rigid party control and creating a more pluralist society.[38] Mu himself cultivates party leaders and, according to former advisers, dreams of becoming a political leader himself—although he is not a party member. Mu was catapulted to national fame in 1992, the year of Deng's campaign tour, when he concluded the biggest commercial deal ever conducted by a nonstate enterprise in China. The transaction involved the purchase of four TU-154M passenger jets from Russia in exchange for 500 freight cars filled with consumer goods ranging from clothing to canned food. Mu sold the planes to the state-owned airline in Sichuan, his native province, for a profit of some $20 million.

Mu clearly revels in publicity. Although his company, the Land Economic Group, declined my requests for interviews—perhaps because of concerns about the BBC's troubled relationship with the Chinese government—he met several other foreign journalists and even reprinted their articles about him in his company brochure for no other apparent reason than to show off his fame. One publicity leaflet produced by Land describes Mu as "a legendary figure." His story is indeed a remarkable one. A year before the death of Chairman Mao—to whom he bears a striking physical resemblance—Mu was sentenced to death for calling for a market economy in a lengthy essay entitled "Where Is China Going?" The timing was fortunate—before the authorities got around to shooting him, Chairman Mao died, the Gang of Four was arrested, and in 1979, after Deng's rise to power, Mu was released.

In the remote town of Wanxian in the middle reaches of the Yangtze, Mu, a former factory worker, began a small trading business with a startup capital of just 300 yuan borrowed from friends and made a healthy profit by selling Sichuan-made brass clocks in Shanghai. In 1983, he was imprisoned again—this time on charges of profiteering. He was released a few months later, apparently because the Beijing leadership decided that keeping him in jail would discourage private business, which it was then eager to develop. Those were particularly perilous days for the private sector. Although individuals and families had long been allowed to engage in small-scale private enterprise, it was not until 1988 that China revised its constitution to give official sanction to companies employing eight or more people, even though by that time there were many tens of thousands of them.

After his second release, Mu moved his company up to Beijing. Aided by an adviser with good connections in the Ministry of Foreign Economic Relations and Trade, Mu began working on the Russian plane deal in the late 1980s, studiously avoiding the Tiananmen upheaval. Indeed, he repeatedly emphasized his disapproval of the protests, a stance that probably enabled him to survive the hard-line backlash against private entrepreneurs in the months after Tiananmen. "Lots of other private companies were supporting the students . . . and I was about the only one to stand out against them," Mu said in a company newsletter. "My reasoning is really simple. Mass movements can't save the country, they can only make things even more screwed up. China's future lies in economic progress, in a new economic system—a commodity economy. Only when you've got a good base and stable economic growth can you talk about democracy or reforming the political system."[39] Even the official *China Daily* newspaper acknowledged Mu's political savvy. "The question has to be asked: Why has Mu survived where many other renowned private moguls have not managed to grasp success in China and keep it?" the newspaper asked. It answered its own question with a quotation from Mu. "I'm economically radical but politically I don't rock the boat. . . . I hold that China can only choose socialism."[40]

By the end of 1993, official news reports said Land's assets were worth about $260 million. Mu's motto, emblazoned on company literature, is "There is nothing you can't achieve in the world, only the things you can't imagine." The plane deal with Russia revealed how much could be done by sheer brazenness. In that case, he was able to persuade the Russians first to send the planes to Sichuan, then, using the jets as collateral, he borrowed money from the bank in order to buy the consumer goods to pay for them. It was an operation that required no assets at all apart from daring and good connections. Mu clearly had plenty of both.

Mu's best contacts appeared to be in the military. According to former employees, he wined and dined top army officers. "Military contacts are extremely useful," Reuters quoted Mu as saying in an interview in 1992.[41] "Our army is involved in a lot of businesses—beating swords into ploughshares, you know. . . . Why should we cooperate with them? They have the power—all kinds of power." One of Mu's aides added, "What we need is their chop [official seal]. . . . With one chop they [the military] can earn millions and millions of dollars." Mu also cultivated the civilian leadership. During the party's 14th Congress in 1992, he convened a celebratory gathering of 80 top economists and other scholars at which he described the congress as an event of "epoch-making significance to the future of China." Mu said he would have liked to set off firecrackers three days in a row to hail the meeting had not the use of fireworks in urban Beijing just been banned. "Deng Xiaoping's theory on building socialism with Chinese characteristics will usher China into a genuine golden period," he said in his fulsome oration, which was summarized by Xinhua. Mu even sponsored a bridge competition for senior officials in 1991 in the Great Hall of the People that was attended by the then chairman of the National People's Congress Wan Li, who, like Deng, is an avid bridge enthusiast. Mu had clearly thought carefully about which sports to sponsor. In another gesture to Deng, Mu told one of his aides that he hoped to build a 100-story building in Shanghai and name it "Xiaoping" after Deng or "Gaige," meaning "reform."

The list of Mu's extraordinary dreams is as endless as it is bizarre, ranging from launching the country's first private satellite to running his own television station to buying a Russian battleship for conversion into a Yangtze passenger boat. Whether he achieves them or not, Mu represents an important new force in a country where power and money are becoming increasingly interchangeable. One of Mu's former advisers recalled telling his boss, "You are not an entrepreneur, you want to be a dictator, a Mao Zedong. Now is not the time, and even if it was you wouldn't succeed. In politics you must have ideals, you must have the trust of the people. But you have no group of supporters. No one trusts you." Mu, he said, did not take this tirade in a positive spirit.

Although there is no evidence that Mu himself is actually trying to gain political power, the party has acknowledged that other rich entrepreneurs are doing so. A confidential memorandum circulated among party members in November 1990 warned that wealthy businessmen in some rural areas had been trying to buy votes in elections to local People's Congresses or village committees in order to secure victory for candidates sympathetic to their cause or even to get themselves elected.[42] "Most of these people have been involved in some kind of wrongdoing, taking advantage of loopholes in the reforms of the last few years to get rich by evading taxes or by some other abnormal means," said the document. "When their moneybags are full, they want to 'get some clout' in politics." It cited the case of one village election in which a wealthy businessman bought nearly 50 percent of the votes for 5 yuan each, the equivalent of about two days' income for the average peasant in exchange for one vote. In another small town, a private tailor offered 20 yuan to any People's Congress delegate who would vote for him to become the deputy chief of the town government or as much as 100 yuan to any official who would support him. "Due to the interference of such people, some low-quality individuals, including some people who have committed crimes in the past and have not corrected their ways, have been elected as township and village officials," said the circular. It said that in places where this had occurred, economic progress had come to a halt, and social order had deteriorated. The document called for a "clear-cut, resolute struggle" with "individuals who are vying with us for power in the countryside."

In the cities, one of the biggest organized threats to party control is presented by triad-type secret societies, which officials admit have grown enormously both in size and sophistication in recent years. The aims of these groups are quite different from those of triads in the nineteenth and early twentieth centuries, which until the collapse of the Qing dynasty dedicated themselves at least ostensibly to the overthrow of the Manchu imperial household. In the 1990s, secret societies are mostly criminal gangs with no specific political aims that thrive on the rapid spread of prostitution, gambling, and drug abuse. As the ranks of the unemployed swell, and peasants flock to the cities, there is no shortage of potential recruits. Triad activity appears particularly widespread in the south where criminal gangs based in Hong Kong have the greatest influence. In Guangdong, officials say many of the province's bars, karaoke clubs, brothels-cum-barbershops, illegal gambling dens, and drug-dealing operations have links with triads.[43] But to judge from official reports, the problem has spread across the country.

In the late 1980s and the 1990s, the official press published news of the smashing of triad societies with increasing frequency—the "True Dragon Gang" in the northeast, the "Ten Stars Gang" and the "Sea Spring Gang" in Shandong Province, the "Changing Times Gang" in Hebei, the "Sleeping Dragon Gang" in Shanghai, and the "Butterfly Gang" in the scenic tourist resort of Hangzhou.[44] In 1993, the police said they smashed 150,000 criminal gangs, a nearly 25 percent increase on the year before.[45] In the first eleven months of 1993, the police caught over 780,000 members of such gangs, an increase of more than 55 percent.[46] Officials said secret societies were becoming increasingly well organized and well equipped, with members often using their own cars, mobile telephones, and beepers. "They have clear divisions of responsibility, and they have their own gang rules and regulations," said one report.[47] It said that no sooner had one gang been smashed than another would spring up.

Many triad members have ready access to firearms, which have become increasingly easy to buy on the black market. From time to time gun sellers in the market town of Baigou in Hebei Province close to Beijing offer their wares even to foreign visitors, except, that is, when the authorities are mounting one of their periodic clampdowns. Many of the weapons are surplus sold off by legitimate gun manufacturers. A few are stolen from army, police, and militia units. In southern provinces, villagers have easy access to weapons including sometimes even submachine guns and rocket launchers smuggled across the often ill-guarded borders with Vietnam, Laos, and Burma.[48] In a major crackdown between September 1992 and June 1994 the police seized more than 390,000 illegal firearms.[49] But this did not prevent the number of crimes involving guns from rising by nearly 40 percent in the first half of 1994 compared with the same period a year earlier.[50] "Illegal firearms and ammunition have become a major malignant tumor endangering all of society," said one official newspaper.[51]

To judge from Chinese press reports, triads often operate in cooperation with corrupt officials. In 1991, the authorities in the northeastern city of Harbin announced the smashing of five triad-type organizations, all of which were headed by wealthy private entrepreneurs. They said the groups used legitimate private businesses as a cover for their crimes and bribed government and party officials to protect them.[52] A newspaper in Guangdong warned that secret societies there had infiltrated grassroots party and government organizations and that if the authorities failed to tackle the problem resolutely, "the scene will be terrifying—no peace in the cities, no peace in the towns, no peace in the villages, and no peace among the people."[53] There is little evidence of any connection between political dissent and triad activities, but the authorities are doubtless mindful of the assistance given by secret societies, criminally inclined or otherwise, to both sides in the conflict between the communists and nationalists before 1949.[54] After its formation in 1921, the Communist Party devoted much attention to winning over secret societies, which then wielded considerable influence among urban workers and peasants.[55] After the communist takeover, Chairman Mao made it a priority to eradicate them.

It is important to bear in mind that many Chinese have considerable experience with organized rebellion, not only thanks to the 1989 unrest but also, at least in the case of middle-aged and older Chinese, thanks to the Cultural Revolution. During the height of the Cultural Revolution in the late 1960s, almost every urban Chinese was caught up in the violence and terror unleashed by Mao when he encouraged the young Red Guards to overthrow authority and take over running the country from those he saw as hidebound bureaucrats who had lost their revolutionary fervor. The Red Guards split into many factions, some of which fought their rivals with guns and hand grenades, prompting Mao in 1968 to disband them and reimpose order through Revolutionary Committees run by the military. Some of the young rebels of the Cultural Revolution were the spiritual predecessors of the students who led the demonstrations of 1989. Even though their methods and aims were quite different, they were inspired by the same idealism and youthful contempt for the established order. The Red Guards may have chanted Maoist slogans, but some of them at least were fired up less by ideology than by the pleasure of wreaking revenge on the oppressive local officials and corrupt bureaucrats who were dominating their lives.

The political skills and alliances formed by Red Guards were not quickly forgotten. Many veterans of the Democracy Wall Movement are people who cut their political teeth as teenage rebels in the factional struggles of the Cultural Revolution. Wei Jingsheng was one such—he and his Red Guard friends ransacked party offices in Beijing in the late 1960s. At around the same time, his friend Wang Xizhe was in command of a Red Guard unit in Canton. Wang was shot and wounded in one fight. He told me he believed that in the event of political turmoil in China, former Red Guard leaders, now mostly in their forties or fifties, would play a role, not as cheerleaders for a Maoist revival but on the side of liberal dissidents.[56] "During the Cultural Revolution, workers were organized," said Wang. "Their leaders are still around. If independent organizations surface, these people will resurface. They are waiting for the right moment. That means huge political change at the top. Mass movements in China always have something to do with top-level politics, like the Cultural Revolution, for example. Democracy Wall was a struggle between Deng Xiaoping and [then party chairman] Hua Guofeng. June 4th [1989] was a struggle between Deng Xiaoping and Zhao Ziyang. When Deng Xiaoping dies and various factions struggle, one faction will stir up the masses."

Realizing the potential importance of hardened veterans like Wei in any effort to do just that, the leadership apparently decided in the end that it could no longer afford to allow him to remain free, no matter what the diplomatic costs of detaining him might be. In the early evening of April 1st, 1994, Wei was in a car with his assistant Tong Yi heading toward Beijing along the highway from Tianjin. He was on his way home after a month-long tour of the provinces. Before he reached the city, however, his car was stopped by half a dozen police vehicles. An officer showed Wei a warrant informing him that he was being detained for interrogation. His arrest was part of a renewed clampdown on organized dissent. One by one the police picked up the leaders of the League for the Protection of the Rights of the Working People and of an unofficial human rights group in Shanghai consisting of more than a dozen activists, many of them veterans of the Democracy Wall era.

Dissidents were once again in retreat. But the authorities were clearly jittery. They were trying to deal with a problem that had become far bigger than just a relatively small group of diehard antigovernment radicals.

In the buildup to the fifth anniversary of the June 4th bloodshed, police in Beijing cordoned off the homes of every major dissident in the city, preventing any foreign journalist from visiting them. It was the first time such a tactic had ever been used. The authorities also banned any kind of unofficial public gathering—no matter how seemingly innocent—around June 4th of that year. The government's nervousness may not have been visible to the casual visitor to Beijing. There were no troops on the streets. But plainclothes police swarmed over Tiananmen and around the campus area. It was obvious to most people living in the city that the government was just as mindful that something might detonate China's social time bomb as Wei Jingsheng so clearly was. Dissidents like Ding in Bengbu felt they had only to keep their heads down and wait for something or someone to light the fuse.

Greater China Risks

The problem now is that a tiny minority is trying to use Hong Kong as a base to overthrow the people's government of China. These people openly call for the overthrow of the central government and seek to transplant the so-called 'democracy,' 'freedom,' and 'human rights' found in the West. . . . These activities aimed at undermining China contradict the wishes and interests of the Chinese people and as a result harm Hong Kong's stability and prosperity.
—People's Daily, *December 1989*

Standing in the grassy quadrangle in front of Canton's main public library, young well-educated residents of the city crowded round me to discuss the future of Hong Kong. It was a Sunday morning in August 1993, just past the halfway point between Tiananmen and the handover of the British colony to China on July 1st, 1997. Hong Kong was in the grips of a fierce debate over efforts by Governor Chris Patten to make the territory's political system more democratic as a bulwark against the possibility of heavy-handed interference by Beijing come the British withdrawal. Apart from one or two former students overseas, most of my dozen or more interlocutors had never been to Hong Kong, a mere 100 miles down the Pearl River which flows languidly through Canton on its way toward the British enclave. Without a lot of money or a sound pretext such as official business, it is extremely difficult for most Chinese to complete the British and Chinese paperwork necessary to visit Hong Kong. But in many ways the territory has more impact on the lives of Guangdong Province's 60 million inhabitants than does the leadership in Beijing.

The Chinese authorities had been waging a strident propaganda campaign against Patten's proposals, saying they would create chaos in Hong Kong and were part of a plot by London to make sure that British sympathizers would continue to dominate the territory after the handover. Relations between London and Beijing were more strained than they had ever been under Deng's rule. Many of the young Chinese who discussed this with me outside the library, however, did not side with their government in this dispute. It was a scene almost unimaginable in most other Chinese cities—young people airing dissenting views about their leadership's foreign policy in a public place with a foreign journalist conspicuously making a tape recording of their words. In no other city, at least, had I had such an experience except during times of political upheaval. But Canton, the Guangdong provincial capital, is different. Its residents may express more interest in making money than in politics, but when they do talk politics it is often with less inhibition than their counterparts in other more tightly controlled parts of the country would show.[1]

"I think Chris Patten's suggestions are useful for Hong Kong people," one young man declared in broken English. The British, he said "want profit for the Hong Kong people. Hong Kong people don't care about the Chinese government."[2] Another man agreed, saying, "I think from the point of view of democracy, human beings should have the power to choose their own future. Why don't the Hong Kongese have it? I think it is very unfair for the Hong Kongese. I think the Cantonese will learn lessons from this case because they will realize [the fulfillment of] human rights depends on them. It does not depend on any government." A third man chimed in: "Chris Patten's intentions are good!"

The views of these young people who had gathered to practice their English were by no means entirely supportive of Patten. Like the public in Hong Kong itself, they seemed divided into three main camps—those who unreservedly supported Patten's proposals, those who endorsed his motives but believed it was best to avoid confrontation with China, and those who believed Patten's proposals were ill-intentioned, destabilizing, and harmful to Hong Kong as well as, by extension, to the flourishing hinterland of Guangdong. "Democratic reform is new to China," said one student. "We need more experience, we need valuable experience from abroad. But we have to pay attention to tradition, we can't be too anxious. We have to slow down our speed so we can really make everyone accept the reforms. Chris Patten simply judges the situation by [his experiences] in Britain. He thinks Britain is so democratic, and therefore China should do the same as Britain. . . . I think the Chinese government always pays attention to Hong Kong's prosperity and the happiness of its people. I'm sure the Chinese government will act according to the declarations it has made."

But although there were several people in the crowd who supported the government line, the fact that anyone was willing to speak out openly against it was a sign of how easy it was becoming for political debate in Hong Kong to influence the thinking of people inland. It was particularly striking that Guangdong residents openly sided with a member of the British colonial establishment routinely condemned by the official Chinese press as an imperialist troublemaker. Although relatively few ordinary people I met in Beijing appeared interested in the furor over Chris Patten's proposals, it was certainly provoking some debate among educated people in the far south.

It is difficult to know how accurately my own straw poll outside the Canton Library reflected the mood of Guangdong citizens in general. Ten months earlier, however, Hong Kong's *South China Morning Post* conducted what it described as an "unprecedented" opinion poll in Guangdong to gauge the level of support for Patten's plans.[3] Out of 456 residents of Shenzhen and Canton who took part in the survey, 33 percent expressed support for the governor's proposals, and 28 percent said they opposed them. The remainder gave no opinion. Asked whether they approved of Patten's performance since taking office in July 1992, more than 60 percent said they did. Fewer than 50 percent gave a similar endorsement of their own provincial governor, Zhu Senlin. The newspaper's survey, conducted by telephone from Hong Kong, did not claim to be based on a representative sample. Most ordinary people and students in Guangdong do not even have a telephone. But it was all the more extraordinary that so many businesspeople and officials—who have the readiest access to telephones and who might be expected to be among the staunchest supporters of the status quo—expressed such support for Hong Kong's controversial new governor. The poll suggested the Chinese leadership was justified in its fears that political change in Hong Kong could have wider ramifications than its impact on the territory alone.

It was not until after the crushing of the 1989 demonstrations that Chinese officials began openly expressing concerns that Hong Kong might pose a political threat to the mainland government. This was because Tiananmen marked the first direct and open involvement by the Hong Kong public in antigovernment unrest on the mainland since the communist takeover. The idea that a territory of about 6 million people more than 1,200 miles from Beijing (whose population alone is twice that of the British colony) could jeopardize communist rule might sound absurd. But in 1989, communist governments around the world began to collapse one after the other, and public support on the mainland for the ruling party sank to an all-time low. The leadership in Beijing became terrified that Hong Kong residents, who had shown such fervent support for the Tiananmen students, could turn the colony into a haven for organized dissent and foment unrest across the border. With control so tight on the mainland, it seemed unlikely that Hong Kong activists could do much more in practical terms than help mainland dissidents to flee. But the leadership feared the spread of prodemocracy ideas from Hong Kong, and it feared that in the event of another upheaval in China, the territory would provide important logistical support for mainland dissidents. As the handover loomed, Hong Kong looked to Beijing like something of a Trojan horse.

It might have appeared that after the handover China would not have to worry so much about anti-Beijing dissent in Hong Kong because it would be in control of the territory and would therefore be able to silence any malcontents. As Deng told visitors from Hong Kong and Macao in 1984, Chinese troops stationed in Hong Kong after 1997 would be there not only to demonstrate that China exercised sovereignty over the territory but also to quell disturbances.[4] "If there are any disturbances there will have to be intervention," said Deng. "Not only the central government but also the people of Hong Kong will have to take action. . . . Knowing that there were Chinese troops present, people who intended to incite disturbances would have to think twice about it. And even if there were disturbances, they could be quelled immediately." Deng's failure to mention the role of the Hong Kong police suggested he had little faith in their ability to do the job. In 1986, Deng modified his remarks somewhat, saying that "intervention of some sort" would be necessary if people tried "to convert Hong Kong into a base of opposition to the mainland under the pretext of 'democracy.'" But he said this could involve "the administrative bodies in Hong Kong" and that mainland troops would only be deployed if there were "serious disturbances."[5]

Some observers believed that in spite of Deng's tough words, China was fearful of having to intervene in Hong Kong to crush unrest. "They are terrified of creating another Tibet [in Hong Kong]," a British diplomat involved in negotiations with China over Hong Kong told me. "They don't want to have to be looking over their shoulders all the time." It might be easy for China to find a pretext to detain a few key activists in

Hong Kong after 1997 but to do so would risk permanently alienating the Hong Kong public. According to the diplomat's analysis, China will try its utmost to avoid a backlash in Hong Kong such as occurred in Tibet in 1959 when rumors that the Chinese were preparing to arrest the Dalai Lama triggered an uprising involving tens of thousands of people that led to a bloody crackdown and heightened tension ever since. Such a scenario, if repeated in any form in Hong Kong, would not only make it much more difficult for China to maintain political control over the territory but would also incur a tremendous loss of face for Beijing internationally. China would also have to consider the impact of any military intervention on economic confidence in a territory that is China's biggest source of foreign investment, handles one-third of China's external trade, and in which China is the largest investor after Britain. No less important, Beijing would be highly reluctant to scuttle any chances it might have of convincing people in Taiwan that its "one country, two systems" policy is workable. The reunification of China under this formula is a highly cherished goal of the Beijing leadership.

Unlike on the mainland, where indirect pressure through the work unit is still a valuable—though diminishing—asset in the fight against dissent, in Hong Kong China would have few such levers to pull after 1997. Given how Beijing's police often appeared weak and hesitant in the face of unrest in the capital in 1989, China is unlikely to trust their Hong Kong counterparts to be any more resolute in the suppression of dissent or popular protests in the territory after 1997. In the case of Tibet, the authorities can at least rest assured that most Chinese do not identify with the cause of a people whom they regard as racially and culturally quite different from themselves. In Hong Kong, however, Beijing after 1997 would be dealing with fellow members of the ethnic Han majority. Beijing's actions in the territory would therefore be watched far more closely by officials and general public alike in the rest of China than the quelling of separatist unrest in Lhasa. Given these possible restraints on China's actions in Hong Kong after 1997, it is not surprising that the Beijing leadership is fearful of any development in the territory that might ultimately force it to intervene.

For months after Tiananmen, Chinese officials seized the opportunity of any meeting with their British counterparts to complain about the participation of Hong Kong residents in the 1989 unrest. In Tiananmen Square itself, this involvement had manifested itself in not much more than the somewhat surreal form of neat rows of brightly colored collapsible tents donated by Hong Kong supporters that appeared on the plaza a week before the bloodshed. These stood out in stark contrast to the foul-smelling filth and squalor of the makeshift tarpaulin shelters, the abandoned public buses, and the sleeping bags laid out in the open air that most of the protesters had been using hitherto. There were only enough of the new tents to shelter a few dozen people out of the thousands camping on the square, but they took pride of place on the flagstones between Chairman Mao's mausoleum and the Monument to the People's Heroes.

The tents, however, were only a tiny part of Hong Kong residents' material contribution to the demonstrators' cause. The unrest in China stirred up unprecedented passions in the colony. People from hitherto procommunist organizations joined hands with prodemocracy liberals to form the Hong Kong Alliance in Support of the Patriotic Democratic Movement of China, the biggest grassroots movement of its kind in the territory's history. The Hong Kong Alliance raised well over $2 million on behalf of the mainland demonstrators. Although only a few thousand dollars actually reached the students in Tiananmen, the willingness of Hong Kong residents—traditionally regarded as politically apathetic—to donate money to such a cause was remarkable. Hundreds of thousands of people joined a series of parades organized by the Hong Kong Alliance, including top Hong Kong businesspeople, the staff of mainland Chinese enterprises in the colony, and even low-ranking Chinese officials. As news of the bloody crackdown reached the territory, more than a million people took to the streets—one-sixth of the population.

After the crushing of the protests, the alliance helped dozens of Chinese dissidents flee the country and provided them with temporary shelter in Hong Kong while they sought asylum in third countries. It also donated money to Chinese dissident organizations abroad, including more than $150,000 to the main group set up after Tiananmen by prodemocracy activists in exile, the Front for a Democratic China headquartered in Paris.

There is no evidence that support from Hong Kong affected the development of the 1989 unrest in any significant way. But the then mayor of Beijing Chen Xitong expressed concerns about the territory's role in his June 30th, 1989, report on the demonstrations. "To ensure that the situation on the square could be maintained," he said, "they [the students] used funds provided by reactionary forces both at home and abroad to improve their facilities and install advanced telecommunications devices, spending 100,000 yuan a day on average. They even started illegal purchase of weapons. By using the tents provided by their

Hong Kong supporters, they set up 'villages of freedom' and launched a 'Democracy University' on the square." The protesters, he alleged, had "strong financial backing" from "hostile forces overseas" including people in Hong Kong.

A month later, the *People's Daily* published a fierce denunciation of the Hong Kong Alliance that, though exaggerated in its claims, revealed the extent of the Chinese leadership's fears. "In order to turn their program into actions, in the period of turmoil, the alliance sent some people to bring huge amounts of money and large quantities of materials to Beijing to support the illegal organizations," it said.[6] "Some members of the alliance even joined the illegal organizations and participated in plotting the counterrevolutionary rebellion. More seriously, some members of the alliance even called for Hong Kong to be turned into a front position for supporting the subversive activities and delivering weapons and ammunition to the counterrevolutionary rebels on the mainland!"

When Britain and China reached their agreement on Hong Kong's future in 1984, one of their basic understandings was that Hong Kong and China would not interfere in each other's politics after 1997. Chinese officials were quick to remind Hong Kong of this after Tiananmen. "The central people's government will neither change the capitalist system nor implement socialist policies in Hong Kong and Macao," said the then director of China's Hong Kong and Macao Affairs Office, Ji Pengfei, two weeks after the bloodshed.[7] "Hong Kong and Macao should not interfere in or attempt to change the socialist system in the mainland either, not to mention allow some people to use [the two territories] as a base for subversion of the central government." Chinese officials often summarized this idea using the saying, "well water does not intrude into river water," in other words, "I'll mind my own business, you mind yours."

In China's view, adherence to this unwritten pact was essential to the success of Deng Xiaoping's "one country, two systems" formula. Tiananmen, however, proved, if proof was necessary, that this formula was unworkable. Hong Kong cannot possibly become a part of China yet ignore the politics of Beijing. Not only will Beijing appoint the chief executive and the territory's top officials after 1997, but Hong Kong residents will also, for the first time, elect representatives to the National People's Congress in Beijing. Many residents of the territory already feel they have a stake in the politics of mainland China, as the mass demonstrations in support of the Tiananmen protests amply demonstrated.

A month after the bloodshed in Beijing, top Chinese officials responsible for Hong Kong affairs met in the capital to discuss their response to the perceived threat from the colony. According to Xu Jiatun, who was then the director of Xinhua News Agency's Hong Kong office and as such Beijing's top representative, the meeting focused mainly on how to deal with the Hong Kong Alliance.[8] Xu said that at the meeting, Ji Pengfei expressed the belief that the alliance, led at that time by the popular Hong Kong legislators Martin Lee and Szeto Wah, was an organization dedicated to the overthrow of the Chinese government and which wanted to turn the colony into an "anticommunist base."[9] Ji demanded that the British government revoke the group's official registration and declare it illegal.

Xu—despite his reputation as a liberal—agreed with Ji that the British should ban the alliance, arguing that since plotting to overthrow the Crown was against the law, "we can make representations to the British about open calls in Hong Kong for the overthrow of the Chinese government." He said some people had all along wanted to turn Hong Kong into an anticommunist base and that Tiananmen had encouraged them to come out into the open. Xu said Chinese intelligence had determined that the alliance was involved in helping Tiananmen activists flee the mainland. But in a note of moderation, he said most people who had taken part in the alliance's activities during Tiananmen had done so in the heat of the moment and efforts should be made to win these people over. In the end, however, the meeting agreed that Hong Kong's Basic Law, the post-1997 constitution for the territory, which was to be ratified by the National People's Congress the following year, should include various provisions aimed at curbing anti-Beijing activities in Hong Kong.[10] These allow the imposition of martial law in the territory in the event of a major breakdown in order and require the post-handover government to outlaw "subversive activities" and ban Hong Kong political parties from forming ties with overseas political groups.[11]

In his memoirs, Xu expressed regret that he had supported efforts to outlaw the alliance; a policy, he said, that would prove impracticable even after the handover. "If [after 1997] strong-arm measures are used to ban it, not only will the Chinese Communist Party and the Chinese government pay an even greater political price," Xu said, "but also it will put the government of the Special Administrative Region [of Hong Kong] in an extremely difficult position and undermine the people's faith in it."[12] It would be better, Xu argued unsuccessfully, to tolerate it and try thereby gradually to change the minds of its supporters.

Sir Percy Cradock, the foreign policy adviser to the then Prime Minister Margaret Thatcher, said in his memoirs that British officials had argued strenuously against the subversion clause.[13] But it appeared that London was in fact more preoccupied with trying to persuade China to increase the number of directly elected seats in Hong Kong's Legislative Council, a move for which there was a considerable demand among Hong Kong residents as a result of the bloodshed in Beijing.[14] During an off-the-record briefing for British correspondents in Beijing in early 1990, a senior British diplomat who had played a key role in the talks with China revealed in an unguarded moment that he was not even aware of the widely reported fact that the final version of the Basic Law included the provision requiring the future Hong Kong government to adopt legislation against subversive activities. To Chinese officials, however, this was one of the most crucial parts of the document. Since Deng's rise to power, the authorities had been gradually building up a body of law that could be used to justify the suppression of dissent in China, including regulations on public demonstrations and the keeping of state secrets. Chinese officials clearly felt that in Hong Kong too, legal backing would make it easier to silence critics.

In March 1990, in his opening address to the annual session of the National People's Congress, Prime Minister Li Peng reinforced China's message. "We should," he said, "enhance our vigilance against a small number of people with ulterior motives who use Hong Kong and Macao as a base of subversion against the central government and the socialist system." Although Li was only repeating what Chinese officials had been saying for several months, it was a significant change from the tone of his keynote speeches at previous congresses. Never before had menacing language like this been used in such addresses when referring to Hong Kong. So great was the outcry in the colony over Li's words that the congress deputies—under orders from the leadership, of course—amended his speech to add the supposedly reassuring words "the broad masses of compatriots in Hong Kong and Macao are patriotic." Few people in Hong Kong, however, derived much consolation from this description.

The British authorities in Hong Kong did not agree to China's requests to ban the Hong Kong Alliance. But they did try to pacify Beijing by declaring in October 1989[15] that they would not allow Hong Kong to become a base for subverting the Chinese government—a statement that must have made it very difficult for China to take seriously Britain's objections to the provision against subversion in the Basic Law. The then governor of Hong Kong, Sir David (now Lord) Wilson, tried to convey a similar message directly to the Hong Kong public in his annual policy address that month, saying residents of the colony should use their freedoms "with a sense of responsibility and self-restraint" and noting that "for many years our community has recognized the importance of not becoming directly involved in China's often complicated domestic politics."

These statements were part of Britain's attempts to defuse a potentially catastrophic dispute with China over the case of a Chinese swimmer who had defected to the United States via Hong Kong that month. The Chinese authorities accused the British of "conniving at" subversive activities in Hong Kong and for more than two weeks stopped allowing the colony to repatriate the dozens of Chinese illegal immigrants who try to sneak into the territory every day. Even though both sides backed down, the row underlined the seriousness with which China viewed Hong Kong's role as a haven for dissidents. Hitherto, Beijing had always stopped short of directly attacking Hong Kong in its efforts to secure British compliance. This time, however, it had effectively threatened to flood the territory with illegal immigrants in order to force Britain to stop helping dissidents. The popular theory that China would never "kill the goose that lays the golden egg" lost some credibility during the dispute. As one British diplomat put it to me at the time, "China's aim was to show that it has Hong Kong over a barrel, and not vice versa."

As time passed, passions in Hong Kong subsided and activities organized by the Hong Kong Alliance and other organizations supportive of China's democracy movement drew less and less attention. On the sixth anniversary of Tiananmen in 1995, about 4,000 people at the most (fewer than half that number according to the police) turned up to the alliance's candlelight vigil at Hong Kong's Victoria Park to mark the occasion. This compares with some 150,000 who attended a similar occasion on the first anniversary. The alliance's occasional demonstrations outside the Hong Kong branch of the Xinhua News Agency calling for the release of political prisoners in China would often attract only a dozen or so activists. The organization looked increasingly marginal. Indeed, the "office" of its 20-member secretariat consists merely of one desk and a filing cabinet crammed into the corner of an office used by the Hong Kong Professional Teachers' Union. The alliance's only permanent space of its own is a small room in another somewhat rundown commercial building nearby where it allows members of the public to peruse its collection of books and documents relating to the 1989 unrest. By 1995, the organization was losing more than $100,000 a year and had only about $650,000 left of its savings, about a quarter of what it had in 1989. Some of the money was being spent on mailing tens of thousands of leaflets about the dissident movement in exile to random addresses across China and sending thousands of Christmas cards to mainland political prisoners. Only about a dozen or so people a year on the mainland replied to these missives. With the help of its full-time staff of just two people, the alliance was also giving money to the families of political prisoners in China and to help Chinese dissidents stage what one alliance official called "small acts of rebellion" on the mainland such as the making of T-shirts with veiled antigovernment slogans printed on them.

Amid the barrage of hard-line Chinese rhetoric, prominent Hong Kong politicians who once had been outspoken supporters of the students in Tiananmen began to take a more cautious approach, preferring to confine their criticisms of Beijing to issues of direct relevance to Hong Kong rather than take up cudgels on behalf of mainland dissidents. To many people in Hong Kong, exercising a degree of self-censorship appeared preferable to provoking Beijing's wrath.

But in spite of the alliance's considerably diminished profile in Hong Kong, the Chinese authorities showed no sign of changing their attitude toward it. Chinese officials shunned all contact with its leading members and refused them, as well as Martin Lee, visas to visit the mainland. Their fears stemmed at least in part from the continuing strong public support for politicians such as Lee and Szeto Wah. In August 1995 the Beijing-controlled newspaper *Wen Wei Po* said that Lee's Democratic Party, the biggest party in the Legislative Council, was simply an offshoot of the alliance[16] and that both organizations aimed to overthrow the Chinese government.

Although China has referred less and less to Hong Kong's role as "a base of subversion," this is more a reflection of Beijing's desire to put Tiananmen behind it and calm public nerves in the colony than a sign that Chinese leaders have reassessed their view of Hong Kong as a political threat. The Beijing media may have stopped talking about "subversion" in Hong Kong, but Beijing-controlled newspapers in the colony itself have continued to do so periodically. In May 1994, *Wen Wei Po* published a particularly strident editorial.[17] "If some people attempt to change the system of socialism using the system of capitalism, they are bound to cause clashes and confrontation between Hong Kong and the mainland, which would spell disaster to Hong Kong," it said, stressing that Hong Kong should be an "economic city" rather than a political one. "The implication of Hong Kong's being an economic city is that it plays a positive role in the development of the Chinese economy. If Hong Kong becomes a political city and is used by some people as a base for changing the mainland's political system, the mainland will certainly consider responding to the act of one system interfering in another. . . . Respect is mutual. Only when two systems respect each other can 'one country, two systems' be implemented. If one system does not respect the other system and tries to bring it down, the implementation of 'one country, two systems' will suffer." The editorial accused the "impenetrably thick-skinned" alliance of continuing its efforts to use the territory as a base to confront China. "This is like playing with fire that will make Hong Kong and the people of Hong Kong suffer," it said.

By 1995, the number of dissidents escaping from China with the help of the alliance had slowed to a trickle of half a dozen or so a year. This was more a sign that dissidents remaining in China were no longer so eager to flee the country than it was of any more effective policing by the Chinese authorities. The continuing operation of the "underground railway," more than six years after Tiananmen and in spite of strenuous Chinese efforts to smash it, was a considerable embarrassment to Beijing. The smuggling of dissidents into Hong Kong highlighted how difficult it had become for Beijing to enforce its political will in the distant south, where activists on the run have only to pay a few hundred dollars to triad gangs to smuggle them into Hong Kong in high-speed boats. John Sham, a Hong Kong entrepreneur and former actor sympathetic with the dissidents, who has been accused by the Chinese of being one of the main organizers of "Operation Yellow Bird" as the "underground railway" is sometimes known,[18] told a BBC reporter that the triads "were ideologically sympathetic to the democratic movement" and that "it was certainly not because of the money" that they agreed to help out.[19]

China itself apparently has been trying to win over Hong Kong's triads, perhaps out of a desire to ensure their cooperation during the transition period. At a news conference in April 1993, the Chinese Minister of Public Security, Tao Siju, caused an uproar in Hong Kong—where triad membership is illegal—by saying that "as for organizations like the triads in Hong Kong, as long as these people are patriotic, as long as they are concerned with Hong Kong's prosperity and stability, we should unite with them. I believe that the more people we unite with the better." Tao even revealed that a group "similar to triads" had deployed 800 members to protect an unidentified Chinese state leader on an overseas trip.

During his tour of southern China in early 1992, Deng Xiaoping was not solely preoccupied with attacking his hard-line enemies and revitalizing his economic reform program. He also delivered a strong warning to people in Hong Kong to stay out of Chinese politics. Clearly referring to the Hong Kong Alliance and its supporters, Deng said "certain people" in the territory were wrong to hope for chaos in China.[20] "If China fell into chaos, Hong Kong would be the first to meet with disaster," Deng said. "If 200,000 people fled to Hong Kong, it couldn't stand it. If a million people did, it would collapse." Deng was clearly implying that he saw these "certain people" in Hong Kong as potential agents of turmoil on the mainland.

Undoubtedly exaggerated though China's fears are, given the tiny number of Hong Kong residents actively involved in seeking political change in the mainland, I believe that on the part of many officials in Beijing they are genuinely felt. Memories of the overwhelming support shown by Hong Kong residents in 1989 for the prodemocracy campaign led by these same few Hong Kong politicians and activists will long continue to haunt the leadership just as will memories of Tiananmen.

With hundreds of thousands of people, mostly Hong Kong residents, crossing the land border between the colony and China every day and with Hong Kong radio and television reaching tens of millions of people in Guangdong Province, the nervousness of Chinese leaders about political trends in Hong Kong becomes easier to understand. The Hong Kong media have already had a profound impact on their counterparts in Guangdong. Once lackluster state-owned newspapers and radio stations, now increasingly reliant on advertising revenue, are trying as best they can within China's political constraints—and sometimes beyond them—to mimic the style of Hong Kong. Guangdong residents may not show the same interest in politics as their urban counterparts from the north, but they do complain frequently and vociferously on Guangdong's increasingly daring live phone-in radio programs about problems such as soaring inflation and rampant corruption. In 1986, the province became the first in the country to introduce this kind of program in an effort to woo listeners away from Hong Kong's talk radio.[21] Radio audiences in Guangdong are now frequently regaled with comments such as that of a Ms. Liu, who complained to the *Today's Hotline* program of Radio Canton in January 1994 that official motorcades drive other road users off the streets like "emperors' and senior mandarins' convoys in imperial China."[22] A senior official at Radio Canton told me with pride how one of the first programs aired by the station after its 1992 launch included a live broadcast from a Canton neighborhood where the police were forcibly evicting residents to make way for a construction project. "We had the sound of houses collapsing and interviews with residents who opposed the project," said the official with an open relish for controversy rarely expressed among senior journalists on the mainland. Radio Canton is in theory controlled by the Propaganda Department of the city's party committee but sounds hardly anything like most Chinese radio stations, which generally shun live news and current affairs programs as too risqué.

Under Hong Kong's influence, Guangdong's newspapers too have become the raciest in the country. Although they follow the government line on political and national stories, they frequently carry bold exposés of social conditions in Guangdong and indulge in the same passion for gossip about the rich and famous as their counterparts over the border. Some of these newspapers make extensive use of a growing contingent of freelance reporters whose lack of affiliation to any official work unit makes them particularly fearless by the normally timid standards of Chinese reporting.

So extensive is the impact of Hong Kong television in Guangdong that the dissident Wang Xizhe found that many people recognized him in the streets after his release from prison in 1993 because they had seen him on news programs broadcast from the colony. Shopkeepers even offered him discounts. While few people in Beijing would be able to identify their own city's top dissidents—including the much renowned Wei Jingsheng—Wang is something of a celebrity in Canton. A taxi driver who picked me up near Wang's home saw me bidding farewell to the dissident and recognized him immediately. "That was Wang Xizhe, wasn't it?" he asked as if he had just seen a movie star rather than a former enemy of the people. "Canton is more open than Beijing," Wang told me. "It's a lot to do with Hong Kong television. Even at the police station they watch Hong Kong TV. Policemen say to me that if they weren't wearing their uniform they would support me. Guangdong people don't care about politics. But they do have views about people who support human rights. They respect them."

Wang also believes that most Guangdong residents respect Chris Patten. "Patten is now pushing democracy ten steps forward," he said. "In 1997, it will go backward two or three steps at the most. So Hong Kong's relatively democratic climate is bound to have an impact on the mainland. Hong Kong will play a bigger and bigger role in China. Hong Kong influences Guangdong, and Guangdong influences the rest of the country."

Hong Kong's reabsorption into China in 1997 will significantly change the political structure of the country. Hong Kong will, on paper at least, enjoy far greater independence from central government interference than any other region of China. This will be an unprecedented experiment for a Leninist government that, like all communist governments, emphasizes the paramount importance of "democratic centralism," in other words, unquestioning obedience to directives from the top. Allowing politicians, no matter how distant they may be from Beijing, to take a line different from that of the center goes against the grain of Chinese political thinking. Even Deng, the architect of the "one country, two systems" policy, was clearly aware of the astonishing mental leap that it required. "Has any government in the history of the world ever pursued a policy as generous as China's?" he asked. "Is there anything recorded in the history of capitalism about any Western country doing something similar?"[23] Deng even gave his express permission for Taiwanese organizations in Hong Kong to continue criticizing the Communist Party after 1997. "That won't bother us," he said, "because the Communist Party cannot be toppled by criticism."[24] Deng must have known, however, that his assurances flew in the face of established communist practice and would be impossible to put into practice without causing enormous anxiety among the leadership in Beijing.

Even Shenzhen's battle in the 1980s to gain legislative independence from Guangdong—a trivial concession compared with what Hong Kong was being offered—aroused considerable controversy within China. Shenzhen argued that it needed to be able to introduce its own laws in order to ensure that the city's legal framework kept pace with the fast-growing sophistication of its economy. Under its original constitution, any new laws for Shenzhen had to be formulated by the Guangdong provincial government and passed by the provincial People's Congress, a time-consuming process that became increasingly annoying to Shenzhen officials. But in March 1989, when the National People's Congress finally passed a bill that gave Shenzhen the same lawmaking powers as Guangdong itself, more than 1,000 delegates or about 40 percent of those present either voted against the move or abstained from voting. At the time it was the largest display of opposition in the normally rubber-stamp parliament's history. Some of the delegates had no objection to the bill itself but believed it should have been the Guangdong People's Congress rather than the national legislature that granted Shenzhen such authority. Others, however, believed Shenzhen was simply becoming too powerful.[25]

Envy of and the desire to emulate Hong Kong's autonomy could become an increasingly disruptive factor in Chinese politics after 1997. While Beijing officials directly involved in reaching agreement with Britain on the territory's future might understand why Hong Kong should be a special case, there is hardly likely to be a consensus on this issue among provincial officials, many of whom would resent seeing a part of China enjoying far better treatment at the hands of Beijing than themselves, just as they resent favoritism toward Shenzhen and the other SEZs. British officials say that even getting Deng and his aides to agree to the terms of the Joint Declaration on Hong Kong's future was a tough battle, with the Chinese preferring a far shorter and more vaguely worded agreement that would give them maximum latitude to behave in Hong Kong as they wanted. Thus, if Beijing does indeed adhere to its promise to give Hong Kong a "high degree of autonomy," it could face growing demands from provincial officials for more autonomy for their own regions—demands that would be difficult for Beijing to resist without being accused of slavishly adhering to an agreement reached with a colonial power while ignoring the requests of its own people. The most likely outcome of this tension is that Beijing will cede even more of its authority to the provinces, particularly those with economic clout.[26]

Despite the risks involved, however, the return of Hong Kong to China in 1997 and that of Macao two years later will be enormously gratifying to those in power in Beijing, who are united at least in their desire to put a final end to what they see as more than a century and a half of humiliation at the hands of foreign powers that formally began with the ceding of Hong Kong to Britain in 1842.[27] Even more gratifying for the older generation of leaders would be reunification with Taiwan, which, come the end of the century, will be the last significant piece of territory claimed by Beijing but not under communist control. Inherited memories of the Opium Wars may be strong in the Chinese consciousness, but memories of the civil war with the nationalists are far more vivid. Before Hong Kong was pushed to the forefront by the then British prime minister Margaret Thatcher's visit to Beijing in September 1982, Deng said the "three major tasks of the 1980s" were to "intensify socialist modernization, to strive for reunification and particularly for the return of Taiwan to the motherland, and to combat hegemonism and safeguard world peace."[28] In public, at least, Hong Kong was not a major item on the agenda. For much of the 1980s Chinese leaders hinted on and off that they saw the end of the century as a reasonable target for reunification with Taiwan. Deng Yingchao, the influential widow of Zhou Enlai, predicted "with confidence" in 1980 that she would be having "cosy chats" with "former colleagues and friends" in Taipei by the end of the decade.[29] Hu Yaobang, then general secretary of the Communist Party, said in 1983 that "if [reunification] does not come in the

1980s, it will come in the 1990s."[30] Hu did not live to see the 1990s, and Deng Yingchao died on July 11th, 1992, without fulfilling her dream. Deng Xiaoping cautioned in 1987 that reunification "may . . . take decades or even a century instead of a few years,"[31] but the issue nonetheless remained a highly emotional one for Beijing's leaders.

Hong Kong's return to China will transform Beijing's relationship with what it regards as the renegade offshore province of Taiwan. The outcome of this transformation is one of the biggest and most worrying uncertainties in the region. In 1983, Hu Yaobang listed the separation of Taiwan from China as first among the destabilizing factors in Asia, ahead of the division of the Korean peninsula.[32] The possibility of armed conflict between the two sides still haunts the region in spite of the rapid growth of economic and semiofficial contacts since 1987 when Taiwan ended four decades of martial law.

Taiwan's president, Lee Teng-hui, who took over after the death in January 1988 of President Chiang Ching-kuo, the son of Generalissimo Chiang Kai-shek, has overseen the rapid liberalization of Taiwan's once rigidly authoritarian political system. He has allowed the de facto abandonment of what since the Chinese civil war has been Taiwan's "three no's" policy toward the mainland—no contact, no negotiations, and no compromise. Since the late 1980s, the Taiwan government has been allowing its residents—including some senior officials[33]—to visit China and has been sanctioning Taiwanese investment in the mainland. In 1991 Taipei even began negotiations with Beijing, using the cover of what it described as an unofficial organization, the Straits Exchange Foundation, to do the talking. The discussions between this body and its mainland counterpart, the equally "unofficial" Association for Relations Across the Taiwan Straits have focused mainly on practical problems affecting the burgeoning unofficial contacts between the two sides. These include the legal status of the hundreds of thousands of Taiwan tourists, businesspeople, and fishermen who now visit the mainland every year as well as how to deal with cross-straits crime such as the hijacking of mainland planes by would-be defectors to the island, an all-too-common problem.

The growth of contacts has been fueled largely by the force of the marketplace, which has driven the two complementary economies to interact and intermesh despite their huge political differences. Taiwanese businesses have been lured by China's cheap labor and land. China in turn needs Taiwanese investment, which has been fueling the economic boom along the southeastern coast. By the mid-1990s, the mainland authorities said there were more than 20,000 Taiwanese firms operating in China with a total investment of around $20 billion. The Taipei government's estimate of total investment was considerably lower at around $4 billion, but with a colossal amount of Taiwanese money flowing across the straits without the island government's explicit approval, the mainland's figure is the more plausible one. Although Taiwan only formally began allowing indirect investment on the mainland in 1991, it is now the biggest investor in China after Hong Kong. Most of the Taiwanese money goes to Fujian Province, which is directly opposite the island and to which many of the islanders can trace their ancestry, or to Guangdong, which has the advantage of being closer to Hong Kong, the main conduit for Sino-Taiwanese business dealings.

Xiamen, Fujian's SEZ, is within sight of the nationalist-held cluster of islets known as Quemoy just a couple of miles off the communist shore, but the nail-biting days of 1958 when China showered the archipelago with shells are long over. The once tense military standoff—punctuated until the late 1970s by desultory exchanges of artillery fire—has been all but forgotten by Xiamen residents amid an invasion of tourists. Taiwan even apologized when troops on Quemoy accidentally fired shells at a Fujian village in November 1994, injuring four people. Since 1993, when martial law was finally lifted on the islands, Quemoy has been playing host to hordes of Taiwanese holidaymakers eager to see the tunnels, tank traps, minefields, and other paraphernalia of the Cold War days.

On the other side, the tiny communist islet of Gulangyu, which occupies a strategic position in Xiamen harbor, has also been cashing in on the more relaxed climate. Once home to more than 5,000 troops, there is now hardly a soldier to be seen. Beaches off-limits to civilians in the early 1980s are now open to all, and tunnels once reserved for the military provide useful shortcuts across the island where motor traffic is banned. In Xiamen itself, there is no shortage of customers for the boat tour that, every half-hour during the day, takes dozens of tourists out into the harbor to gaze at the nationalist-held islands through binoculars. "These are islands controlled by the Taiwan KMT," the tour guide declares excitedly every few minutes. Xiamen officials say they hope to start trading with Quemoy as a way of undermining Taiwan's ban on direct commercial links. For several years already, fishermen from the two sides have been meeting in the middle to swap contraband goods.

But fast-developing contacts between Taiwan and the Chinese mainland present dangers as well as blessings for the communist authorities. Although Taiwan's cultural impact on the mainland is less conspicuous than Hong Kong's, it is growing exponentially. In Xiamen and other cities of Fujian Province, the obvious wealth of the Taiwanese business-people and tourists who frequent the karaoke bars and expensive restaurants of coastal China provokes a combination of resentment and envy—resentment of what mainlanders often describe as the arrogant and boorish behavior of Taiwanese visitors and envy of their economic success. Among mainland dissidents, the liberalization of Taiwanese politics since the late 1980s is often discussed as a potential model for the communists to adopt. Very few Chinese, dissidents included, would dare express public support for the KMT. Even during the Tiananmen Square protests Taiwan's achievements were rarely discussed openly by demonstrators. But in private it is not uncommon to hear ordinary Chinese speak of their government's number one rival with some respect. In Canton, the dissident Wang Xizhe told me the communists should allow the KMT to come back to the mainland and compete as a legal party. "This is not a great possibility now," he told me in 1994, "but it is a possibility if you look at the trend of history. The Communist Party looks very strong now, but in fact it's very weak politically. When the KMT first went to Taiwan, everyone thought it was finished, but now it has won popular support [in Taiwan]."

Fujian, the destination of at least a quarter of all Taiwanese visitors to the mainland, does not have any dissident as outspoken as Wang. Despite the huge influx of Taiwanese and other overseas Chinese visitors, the province has yet to take on the politically liberal air of freewheeling Guangdong. Residents jokingly compare Fujian with Guangdong in the rhyming ditty, "*Guangdong ren chao gupiao, Fujian ren gao shejiao*"—the Cantonese play the stock market while the Fujianese propagate socialism. Nonetheless, Fujian is no stranger to dissent. The antigovernment unrest of 1989 affected many of the province's cities, including Xiamen where residents applauded, displayed banners of support, and set off firecrackers as thousands of students and journalists from the state-run media marched through the streets.[34]

The Taiwanese authorities have generally avoided displaying overt support for dissent on the mainland, and there is no equivalent on the island of the Hong Kong Alliance. Even during Tiananmen, the Taipei government refrained from cheering on the demonstrators, partly because of their concern that by appearing to back the protesters they would give Beijing an excuse to crack down and partly because Taipei, for all its anticommunist rhetoric, is worried about the possibility of chaos on the mainland and its impact on the island's stability.[35] Unlike the people of Hong Kong, who have long been aware that they will come under Beijing's control in 1997 and therefore have a natural interest in mainland affairs, most people in Taiwan are less interested in Chinese politics. The response of Taiwanese to Tiananmen was not nearly as emotional as it was among ethnic Chinese in the British colony. When the prominent student leader of the Tiananmen unrest Wuer Kaixi visited Taiwan in 1990, a senior official told him that the KMT would not "take the initiative" to involve itself in the dissident movement on the mainland and would provide only "moral support."[36] At the back of Taipei's mind is the fear that a breakdown of authority in China could trigger an exodus of refugees to Taiwan, harm Taiwanese economic interests on the mainland, and, perhaps most importantly, unleash dangerously unpredictable forces that might threaten the island's security. In addition, with many residents of Taiwan preferring to describe themselves as Taiwanese rather than Chinese, any attempt by the KMT to get involved in mainland politics would be widely resented on the island itself.

It is interesting to speculate what might happen in Taiwan if authority does indeed collapse in Beijing. It is always possible that despite the Taiwan government's current standoffishness, it would find itself sucked into the vacuum since it would by default represent the only relatively coherent force with a direct interest in China's political future. Also possible, however, is that political turmoil on the mainland would push Taiwan even further toward a declaration of formal independence, whether as the "Republic of China" or as the "Republic of Taiwan" as the more radical proindependence activists on the island would prefer to call it. Supporters of such a move would argue that formal separation from the mainland would allow the island's leaders to concentrate on their own affairs and avoid being dragged into the maelstrom of Chinese politics. The international community would, in their view, be more likely to intervene to protect Taiwan if the island was widely recognized as an independent country.

The main backers of independence for Taiwan come from the opposition Democratic Progressive Party (DPP), which draws its support mainly from the 80 percent of people who were born on the island and have no close blood ties to the mainland. Since its founding in 1986, however, the DPP has toned down its rhetoric on the independence issue in order to avoid alienating voters who fear that the party's stance might push Taiwan into confrontation with China. The DPP knows that Beijing's occasional saber rattling does have a significant effect on voters.

Elections in early December 1994 for the powerful post of Taiwan governor as well as for three mayoral seats revealed continuing strong support for the KMT, with more than 50 percent of voters backing the ruling party and about one-third voting for DPP candidates. The only significant upset for the KMT was in Taipei, where the DPP captured the mayoralty, but the elections showed that as long as voters continue to fear military moves by China, the KMT would continue to predominate despite its reputation for corruption and its past record of discrimination against native Taiwanese.

Within the KMT, however, there are also increasingly powerful forces in favor of formal independence for Taiwan, not at the cost of all-out confrontation with China but at least as a long-term goal. Since the early 1990s, the KMT has been expressing its desire to rejoin the United Nations, so that there would in effect be two Chinas represented there. This idea is anathema to Beijing, which as a permanent member of the Security Council has the power of veto and can therefore block Taiwan's moves as long as it wants. But Taipei, though formally recognized by fewer than 30 nations—most of them countries with little international influence—still hopes to boost its profile in other world bodies and establish official contacts if not diplomatic relations with countries that recognize Beijing. This tactic is condemned by Beijing as a "two Chinas" policy[37]—a concept almost as sacrilegious to the communist mind as formally declaring the island's independence and abandoning the goal of reunifying the country.

The spread of proindependence sentiment on Taiwan has been viewed with growing alarm in Beijing. Even in his much publicized overture to Taiwan in January 1995, China's president, Jiang Zemin, maintained the right to use force. "Our not undertaking to give up the use of force is not directed against our compatriots in Taiwan but against the schemes of foreign forces to interfere with China's reunification and to bring about the 'independence of Taiwan,'" Jiang said in deliberately ambiguous language that did not exclude the possibility of an attack against the island itself.[38]

China's concerns reached a new peak following President Lee's unprecedented private visit to the United States in June 1995. Beijing regarded the trip as evidence that the international community, backed by Washington, was moving toward acceptance of Taiwan as a separate political entity from the mainland. In an outburst of fury unparalleled since Lee took office, Beijing withdrew its ambassador from Washington, suspended its semiofficial dialogue with Taiwan, and announced the staging of missile and artillery tests in the East China Sea about 90 miles north of the island. The *People's Daily* published diatribes against President Lee, filled with unusually bellicose rhetoric. One editorial accused Lee of "attaching Taiwan compatriots to his war chariot and driving them all to the battleground of fierce confrontation between the two sides of the Taiwan Straits."[39] Another warned that "the issue of Taiwan is as explosive as a barrel of gunpowder. It is extremely dangerous to warm it up, no matter whether the warming is done by the United States or by Lee Teng-hui. If this happens it will explode some day, and the consequences will be unimaginable."[40] And a radio commentary aimed at Taiwan said that if the island declared independence, "the 1.2 billion Chinese people . . . will certainly defend our country's territorial integrity with their blood and lives. Chinese people mean what they say."[41]

In his memoirs, Xu Jiatun, who as head of China's operations in Hong Kong was also in charge of dealings with Taiwan, states that in Beijing's view the chances of a military takeover of Taiwan have been increasing ever since Lee became president.[42] "The activities of the Taiwanese independence movement as well as its very existence and growth are the result of Lee Teng-hui's connivance," he wrote. "The gradual consolidation of Lee's power and position is resulting in diminishing prospects for peaceful reunification." Xu said Deng Xiaoping reevaluated the Taiwan situation after Lee became president and reached the conclusion that "the possibility of using armed force to resolve the unification issue is becoming greater and greater." As a result of this assessment, according to Xu, Beijing has been giving higher priority to making preparations for a military takeover than it has been for peaceful reunification, even though it is keeping up "strenuous efforts" to persuade Taiwan to accept peaceful terms.

Xu's comments on this issue are remarkably blasé given the implications for regional and indeed global security—not to mention the livelihoods of Taiwan's more than 20 million people—if what he says is true. The Taiwan Relations Act passed by the U.S. Congress in 1979, which still provides the framework for Washington's unofficial ties with Taipei, says that any military threat to the island would be of "grave concern" to Washington and that the United States would maintain its capacity "to resist any resort to force or other forms of coercion that would jeopardize the security, or the social or economic system, of the people on Taiwan." It is not an explicit promise to back Taiwan militarily against China, but it would certainly be difficult for any U.S. president to ignore the obvious implications of the act's wording. Xu said that the use of force by the mainland might simply involve a blockade of Taiwan, but if Beijing senses that the United States is unlikely to intervene, then "there will be a rather strong possibility of a direct assault." He pointed out that Beijing does not regard proindependence forces in Taiwan as belonging to the "Taiwan people," a point that considerably diminishes the value of Jiang Zemin's early 1995 assurance that military force would not be used against "Taiwan compatriots."

Hawkish though Xu Jiatun may sound, his views are worth taking seriously as China enters a period of heightened political uncertainty with contestants for power anxious to prove their nationalist credentials. The son of a Politburo member told me without hesitation that China would attack Taiwan if the island declared independence. "China would react emotionally, out of a sense of nationalism," he said. "Any government that failed to take action would have to step down." My own straw polls among Beijing residents found a remarkable degree of support for military action against Taiwan in the event of a declaration of independence by the island. They included well-educated friends of mine who are often critical of the government and who would be among those who would suffer as a result of what would be the considerable economic impact of any conflict. Concern about the growth of proindependence forces in Taiwan is shared across the political spectrum in Beijing. It is a worry undoubtedly aggravated by a feeling among Chinese leaders that if Taiwan were allowed to become independent, it might accelerate a trend toward regionalism and separatism on the mainland itself.

It is difficult to imagine how in practice China might go about taking Taiwan militarily. Although Beijing has a distinct advantage in terms of weaponry and sheer numbers of military personnel, maintaining political and social control in Taiwan after a military takeover would be a herculean task, not least because of likely fierce resistance from the native Taiwanese majority who have long resented domination by mainlanders. The pros and cons of military action would be fiercely debated within the Chinese leadership. At risk would be not only Taiwan's prosperity and by extension the prosperity of parts of coastal China that have large amounts of Taiwanese investment but also economic and political confidence in Hong Kong and China's image in the rest of the region and beyond. A strong incentive for pragmatism in Beijing is the phenomenal economic potential of the increasingly integrated economies of the mainland, Hong Kong, and Taiwan. The World Bank predicts that by early next century, "Greater China" (as this triangle is often called), will constitute the world's biggest economy. Multinational corporations dominated by ethnic Chinese from the three regions as well as the 50 million-strong Chinese global diaspora could easily overshadow the once seemingly unbeatable Japanese. But while the economies of Greater China are growing in power, so too are proindependence forces in Taiwan. For Beijing, the stakes are ever more gargantuan.

9

The Third Generation

The imperialists are pushing for peaceful evolution toward capitalism in China, placing their hopes on the generations that will come after us. Comrade Jiang Zemin and his peers can be regarded as the third generation, and there will be a fourth and a fifth. Hostile forces realize that so long as we of the older generation are still alive and carry weight, no change is possible. But after we are dead and gone, who will ensure there is no peaceful evolution?
—Deng Xiaoping, early 1992

The village of Nanjie[1] in the backward inland province of Henan is a microcosm of a China run the way Deng Xiaoping's conservative critics would like it to be run when the "chief architect of reform" is no longer around. Battered though they were by Deng's southern tour in early 1992, the hard-liners have continued pressing their case for an alternative approach to reform. Nanjie is their showpiece, a community of 3,000 permanent inhabitants and more than 8,000 temporary workers in the central plains conveniently located on the edge of Route 107, the country's main north-south highway. To the conservatives, the Nanjie Village model represents the best approach to fighting "peaceful evolution." Nanjie's story, as told by its supporters, reads like a manifesto for China's future.

Banished from the pages of the mainstream press after 1992, the hard-liners had to rely mainly on a clutch of little-read theoretical journals still under their control in order to get their message across. But given the leadership's emphasis on the need for stability and unity, the fact that they were able to publish their views at all was a sign that they still enjoyed considerable influence. In June 1994, one of these hard-line magazines, the bimonthly *Contemporary Trends of Thought,* carried the story of Nanjie Village as its lead feature under the headline "A Bright Red Flag in the Great Central Plains."[2] As China prepared to enter the twenty-first century, it said, "there is a trend of thinking that holds that Mao Zedong Thought is no longer effective and that socialism is useless." This view, it said, had become a hot topic of discussion, and amid this debate, "the village of Nanjie in the Great Central Plains has raised high the great red banner of Mao Zedong Thought and has kept to the socialist way of collective prosperity in accordance with Mao Zedong's guidance."

Very few ordinary Chinese would have seen the magazine, but party officials—the journal's main readership—would immediately have picked up the political point being made, namely, that Deng was turning his back on Maoism and for that matter on the socialist way. The little-known village of Nanjie was being touted by the magazine's backers as the remedy to China's growing social dislocation and ideological confusion.

In August 1994, posing as a businessman in order to circumvent the government's restrictions at that time on provincial visits by BBC correspondents, I traveled to Henan Province to see the village where, in the words of its propagandists, "the sounds of revolutionary songs reverberate all around." In the provincial capital Zhengzhou, where the changes wrought by Deng's reforms are manifest in the signboard of one cinema advertising films "not suitable for children" such as *Virgin's First Time* and *The Great Rape,* some residents at least were full of praise for the village. Even though most national newspapers were low-key in their coverage of Nanjie, its existence was obviously well known in Zhengzhou thanks to extensive publicity in the local press. The man close to retirement age who was assigned by Zhengzhou's official travel service to drive me to the village was among Nanjie's supporters. He explained to me that the size of China's population and the quality of its leaders were the biggest obstacles to the country's development. "The main thing about Nanjie Village is that it's got good leaders," he said wistfully.

The village is about 70 miles south of Zhengzhou on the edge of the town of Linying. Although Linying is the seat of the local county government, its shabby streets stand out in contrast to the immaculate appearance and seeming opulence of Nanjie. The village the hard-liners chose to extol is a far cry from the dismal leftist "special zone" spoken of so mockingly by the reformist deputy prime minister, Tian Jiyun, in his speech to the Communist Party School in April 1992.[3] While other villages surrounding it have narrow, potholed roads overshadowed by old, dilapidated houses, Nanjie's main thoroughfare is a broad tree-lined boulevard more typical of the kind seen in big cities than of anything in rural China. The road is lined with shops, newly constructed office buildings, and factories. The village, in fact, looks far more like a miniature version of a coastal boomtown than a semirural community deep in the interior.

Unlike Shenzhen, however, which erected a 3,200-square-foot poster of Deng Xiaoping after his southern tour as a gesture of respect to the zone's great protector, Nanjie gives pride of place to a no less imposing representation of Mao Zedong. To commemorate the 100th anniversary of Mao's birthday on December 26th, 1993, the village spent 200,000 yuan on a 30-foot-high white marble statue of the late chairman and erected it in a traffic circle on the main thoroughfare. A village militiaman in green army fatigues stands around the clock beneath the towering figure that gazes down the length of the road with right arm outstretched and left arm tucked behind the waist in the typical Mao pose. The only other Chinese village known to have erected a Mao statue in recent years is Shaoshan, Mao's own home village. Shaoshan's golden likeness of the Great Helmsman was unveiled by the party leader Jiang Zemin, also in commemoration of the 100th anniversary, but such a gesture to the country's founder was only to be expected on such an occasion. Elsewhere in the country, once ubiquitous Mao statues are being gradually and without fanfare pulled down, with the notable exception of Nanjie.

During my visit to Nanjie, I saw no sign at all of any tribute to Deng Xiaoping, in spite of the fact that the elder statesman was at the time the object of a mini-personality cult whipped up by the official media in response to his southern tour. The slogans pasted on walls or suspended across the road were far more redolent of the Mao era. Many of them called on residents to learn from Lei Feng, the model soldier posthumously extolled by Mao for his selfless devotion to the party. "Use Mao Zedong Thought to Guide the Market Economy," said one slogan in a factory courtyard, as if to say that if we must follow Deng's path, let us at least not abandon our communist ideals.

According to *Contemporary Trends of Thought,* Nanjie Village was inhabited by vagrants and beggars before the communist takeover. Under Mao, life improved somewhat, but the village remained mired in poverty. As a result of Deng's rural reforms, which gave peasants more control over the land and what they grew on it, a few households prospered, but the majority still had only just about enough to eat and wear. With the help of donations from residents, the village built a flour factory in 1981, but this was not enough to transform the backward community. Finally in 1986, some of the peasants decided that it would be best to pool their resources rather than farm the tiny individual plots of land—about one-tenth of an acre per head of population—allocated to them under Deng's program. "In practice," said the journal, "everyone realized that each household separately doing their own work meant they had little ability to fight natural disasters, they lacked the wherewithal to boost production, and because everyone was engaged in agriculture they could not run factories even if they wanted to." Or, as Nanjie's own self-promotional literature puts it, "the output-related responsibility system[4] that once enabled [the villagers] to put an end to hunger, had clearly lost its popularity." So much, it implied, for Deng's agricultural reforms, once hailed by the official media as the best thing to happen to rural China since the early days of communist rule when the landlord class was wiped out and the land divided among the peasants.

The village party committee called a meeting in 1986 to discuss what it called the "grim situation." Some of the officials present feared that recollectivizing the land would violate national policy. But then one of them pointed out an escape clause in Deng's rural program—namely, that it was up to individual localities to decide whether or not to introduce the responsibility system. Although most had done so, Nanjie would be acting within the rules by deciding to farm the village's land collectively. So the officials agreed that any Nanjie household that handed over its land to the village would receive about 45 pounds of flour every month for every member of the family. Within three years of the meeting, most of the peasants had joined the scheme. The village built factories on about 50 acres of the newly acquired land. The rest it farmed collectively. With the help of four combine harvesters, nine tractors, and other assorted new machinery, a mere 80 people were able to do what it had previously taken virtually the entire village to accomplish. In 1993, wheat output per acre reached two-and-a-half tons compared with just one-and-a-half tons 10 years earlier. "They are laboring conscientiously to create a little communist society," said the chief of propaganda from a nearby city in a foreword to a book about Nanjie published by the village, *Central Plains Style: Stories Told by the People of Nanjie.*[5]

Nanjie's story may sound like the gushing propaganda that once accompanied Mao's disastrous People's Commune experiment of the late 1950s, when he took back the land from the peasants and forced them to join huge collectives. But Nanjie today is clearly no Potemkin village. Judging from my own brief visit, Deng's critics chose their model wisely.

Nanjie boasts the biggest instant noodle factory in the country, with a daily output of 230 tons. The noodles are sold across China and even exported to Russia. The village also has factories turning out flour, packaging material, beer, cakes, and crispy rice. It has a printing factory run as a joint venture with a Japanese firm. The Japanese side invested $700,000 in the plant, which the village says made $2 million in profits within six months of starting production in 1992. "This is not the same as the production team days," said an old villager quoted in *Central Plains Style,* referring to the People's Communes. "Although it was a collective system then too, there weren't so many enterprises, and so the collective economy didn't prosper. Now, as far as I can see, we have nothing to worry about."

Socialism Nanjie-style certainly appears to have its advantages compared with the situation in most other parts of the Chinese countryside. Nanjie villagers enjoy almost everything free, from housing to fuel to education. At the time of my visit, nearly half of them lived in apartments in brand-new six-story buildings. Officials said all of the villagers had new Panasonic TV sets, provided gratis by the collective. In line with their policy of trying to do away with private ownership, village officials insist that people moving into the new accommodation give up all their personal possessions except for bedding, clothing, and cooking utensils. Everything else—family heirlooms included—has to be thrown away or given away. Unlike their old houses, the new apartments belong to the collective. The occupants have no right to sell them. With so much provided free by the village, salaries are low. In 1994, most villagers earned less than 125 yuan a month, or about a third of an urban factory worker's wages. There is no overtime pay and no weekends off. But annual benefits and handouts amount to an average of 1,000 yuan per person, more than the yearly income of most Chinese peasants and more than twice the average annual income of peasants living in Nanjie's neighboring villages.

Central Plains Style illustrated the benefits of collective life with the story of a 16-year-old boy in the village who was diagnosed as suffering from heart disease. Doctors in the county hospital insisted that the family pay a deposit of 10,000 yuan—the equivalent of six years' income for the average Nanjie villager—before they would operate. In desperation, the boy's father went to all his friends and relatives trying to borrow money but could only raise about 3,000 yuan. Finally he went to the party secretary of Nanjie, Wang Hongbin, who told him simply to ask the village Finance Department for the money he needed. The father "was stupefied with amazement. He couldn't believe his own ears. He looked up at Secretary Wang, who gave him a warm smile," the book said. Elsewhere in rural China, where most peasants lack health insurance, the boy might well have been allowed to die.

Although Party Secretary Wang presides over one of Henan's most prosperous villages and has the moneymaking instincts of a capitalist, when it comes to ideology he is an avowed Maoist. In spite of its modern factory buildings, new school, and apartment blocks, Nanjie has the air of a bygone era. Many of the younger villagers walk around in army fatigues. This is because they have to undergo at least three months of training in the village militia before they can work in the factories. According to *Contemporary Trends of Thought,* the main purpose of this is not only to train the villagers how to fight but also to indoctrinate them politically. "Studying the works of Mao and learning from heroic personalities, taking part in the collective life of the military, performing deeds for the public good, and doing volunteer work helps them to establish a firm and correct political orientation," it said. In the courtyard of one village factory I visited, I saw workers lining up at the end of their shift in military formation. The official showing me around said this was so they could listen to party documents read to them by their bosses, receive instructions, and "sing revolutionary songs." Unfortunately he whisked me away before I had a chance to confirm their choral skills.

"Nanjie Village insists on using Mao Zedong Thought to educate its people," said one village leader quoted in Nanjie's promotional book, "and it insists on using politics to regulate the production of its enterprises." In the rest of Deng's China, one of the main thrusts of economic reform in recent years has been to separate politics and the party secretaries who engage in it from the real work of factory management.

After the Tiananmen Square protests, Nanjie's party committee published a book containing five of Mao's most famous essays and gave a copy to each of the villagers, apparently as an antidote to any reactionary ideas spread by the demonstrators. Thereafter, the village organized frequent mass meetings at which residents were required to study and discuss the book. Nanjie schoolchildren had to learn by heart Mao's "Old Three Articles,"[6] the core of the Maoist canon that every Chinese citizen was required to study during the Cultural Revolution. Every morning, Nanjie villagers go to work to the sound of one of the classic Cultural Revolution songs in praise of Mao, "Sailing the Ocean Depends on the Helmsman," blaring from loudspeakers. Nanjie's song and dance ensemble, which consists of several dozen people, specializes in Cultural Revolution–era operas. "Through the study of Mao's writings, the villagers of Nanjie have widely displayed the lofty traits and ideals of loving the collective, of selflessness, of taking a responsible approach to one's work, and of daring to make contributions to the collective and the country," said *Contemporary Trends of Thought.*

The village's methods of enforcing law and order and ensuring that everyone pulls his or her weight smack of the Cultural Revolution too. Above the door of every household is a metal plaque with up to 10 stars on it.[7] Each star represents the occupants' compliance with certain rules or standards of behavior, such as adherence to family planning regulations, good neighborliness, or industriousness. Only those with all 10 stars receive all the benefits and handouts provided by the collective. A family with nine stars loses the free flour allowance. Eight stars entails the additional loss of free oil, and seven stars means the free coal allowance is suspended as well. A family with six stars or less loses everything, although officials say this sanction is extremely rare. Each household's rating is decided once every three months by a committee of villagers, with the village leadership having the final say. Private entrepreneurs often come out badly since they automatically lose a star for failing to "contribute to the village's prosperity." In mid-1994, there were only about a dozen private businesspeople in Nanjie.

The newspaper *China Youth News,* in rare coverage of the Nanjie phenomenon by a national newspaper, reported that anyone who "harms the interests of the collective" or who "acts contrary to public morals" can be summoned before a mass meeting of villagers who subject the wrongdoer to "vigorous and fierce" public criticism—a means of punishment reminiscent of the mass "struggle sessions" of Mao's days.[8] A more severe form of discipline involves being banished to one of the village's remaining dilapidated, old style dwellings and being forced to haul bricks in the village's construction sites, with only vegetable soup and corn bread to eat. Those undergoing this sentence have to wear a yellow vest to identify their status as wrongdoers to their fellow villagers. The newspaper said this punishment was aimed at shaming the miscreant and making him or her appreciate how good life had become in the village. It is not known how often such sanctions have been imposed, but Nanjie claims to have been crime-free since 1988.

The village also has no time for the kind of adults-only entertainment to be found in the provincial capital. Maoist austerity is the norm. In true

Cultural Revolution fashion, no courting at all is allowed below the age of 23. Nanjie residents have to get permission from the Communist Youth League to get engaged. An outsider who wants to marry a Nanjie villager has to be "smart in appearance, a high school graduate, and 'without any problems' in their behavior."[9] Both partners have to be members of the league in order to tie the knot. Mass wedding ceremonies are held once a year on New Year's Day. The collective pays the bill, including the cost of a set of Mao's works presented to each couple. No one is allowed to hold their own private wedding ceremonies, except for those remarrying after the death of a partner.

Party Secretary Wang Hongbin, who left school when he was 14 and became Nanjie's party chief at the age of 26, one year after Mao's death, boasts a spartan lifestyle befitting his Maoist beliefs. He also enjoys a personality cult in the true Maoist tradition. Many Nanjie villagers display Wang's photograph in their homes. Some display several. Wang himself claims to spend two or three months of every year doing manual work in the factories. His monthly salary is a mere 250 yuan, the same as the other top party officials in the village. Wang's salary has not increased since 1988, and he receives no bonuses. He does not even own a car. Yet Nanjie is the kind of village where mobile telephones and beepers are a common sight, a five-story office-cum-hotel complex is under construction, and visitors such as myself are treated to lavish banquets. "Because we rely on Mao Zedong Thought, there is no corruption," said a village schoolteacher introduced by my guide. "Secretary Wang is very reliable, very capable. Everyone listens to him." Wang's aides try to emulate his habits. According to one report, they usually carry two packs of cigarettes with them—one expensive brand for smoking with business contacts and another ordinary brand for their own use or to smoke at party meetings.[10]

The village's promotional literature describes how Wang has the only key to five suggestion boxes that are attached to electricity poles around the village. Once a week, he opens them up, reads the complaints and opinions of villagers, and tackles any problems raised. "The reason why our party branch has become a powerful fighting force is because we have two treasures," says the literature. "One is the five-volume set of Mao's works, the other is the suggestion box."

Where reality ends and propaganda begins is, as often in China, difficult to determine in the case of Nanjie Village. But its importance lies not so much in what it actually is, but in the ideal it represents to its hard-line backers. While there are no national leaders who have publicly championed the Nanjie experience, the village's supporters would likely include most of the same conservative figures who emerged with such force after Tiananmen and who were the target of Deng's offensive in early 1992. Although the deaths in recent years of several hard-line veterans such as Chen Yun, Li Xiannian, Wang Zhen, and Yao Yilin have deprived this group of important figureheads, there are other less exalted figures like the dour former Politburo Standing Committee member Song Ping as well as the former propaganda chief Deng Liqun who remain vocal supporters of the conservative line. To them, China should be a state with a backbone of firm ideological principles, in which the party is absolutely supreme, in which everyone can expect to enjoy certain basic necessities provided by the state such as housing, education, and health care, and in which the arts and entertainment play a political role. Market economics are fine, as long as everyone gets a share of the benefits and the party remains in control of the means of production. Central to this vision is the leadership of a vigorous, charismatic individual like Secretary Wang. There is no room for any organized opposition. Because the party is free of corruption and attuned to the needs of the public, it enjoys universal support.

In the struggle for power after Deng's death, this is a vision of China that some in the leadership will try to promote. It is a view that will attract many of the older generation who are imbued with the ideals that brought the communists to power. It is potentially attractive too to many ordinary people who have lost out in the dog-eat-dog world of Deng's reforms. In a relatively objective article about Nanjie, a liberal newspaper in southern China, *Guangdong and Hong Kong Information Daily,* told of how some elderly visitors would, after touring the village, "express their nostalgia for the old times, their anger and grievances about today's society, and their great hopes for the future of Nanjie."[11]

Those at the more liberal extreme of the political spectrum do not share the nostalgia of the old-timers. The newspaper *Southern Weekend* published a commentary describing the complimentary coverage of Nanjie's achievements in some official newspapers as "lunatic raving." Although it did not dispute Nanjie's wealth, it said its success was by no means unique and was the product not of adherence to Maoism but of the environment in which the village operated, namely, reform and opening to the outside world. The author said many of Nanjie's practices violated "the principles of modern civilization." The mass meetings held to criticize aberrant villagers, it said, showed "a lack of respect for human dignity," and the marriage regulations were a "gross violation of the freedom of citizens." The commentary accused the editor of *China Youth News*—ironically, a newspaper normally regarded as relatively liberal—of having "fantasies" about the Cultural Revolution. It said coverage of Nanjie showed that leftism was still a significant force in the media.

In July 1994, *Guangdong and Hong Kong Information Daily* published several letters written by readers in response to the articles about Nanjie carried by the newspaper earlier that month. One letter praised the village, saying it was "a sign that people are having second thoughts about reform and opening to the outside world. This is because reform has not fully addressed all the problems that exist in Chinese society. In addition, certain defects in the system have caused a series of new problems in society and have led to what could be described as a loss of control over the way society as a whole functions. Nanjie's government, on the other hand, . . . has set up an effective regulatory system that has ensured both that the leadership functions normally and that people's enthusiasm is brought into play. This is definitely worth thinking carefully about." [12]

Most of the other letters, however, were critical, as might be expected given the newspaper's own reformist stance. One reader said that Nanjie's excessive emphasis on the collective would suppress the will of the individual and inhibit creativity. Two officials from a party propaganda office in a city near Canton said Nanjie was overdependent on its leader, Wang Hongbin, and that without him its stability and prosperity might be jeopardized. A reporter from *Southern Weekend* wrote to say that Nanjie lacked any concept of law as shown by the "inhuman methods" used to punish wrongdoers and the village's "exploitation of legal loopholes" to do business. The Nanjie leadership, the reporter said, "should keep a clear head and realize that tactics like these are basically illegal. What is regrettable is that not only have they failed to realize this but are even proud of what they do." Another journalist from Canton said sarcastically that the fact that Nanjie was allowed to behave in this "regressive" manner while China was promoting reforms and the market economy was at least a sign of some progress. "It is hard to imagine," the journalist said, "a style of development different from the mainstream model being permitted to exist in the 1950s or 60s."

While those in the Chinese leadership who are attracted by the Nanjie model might prove a disruptive force in the struggle for power after Deng's death, their lack of a charismatic leader puts them at a strong disadvantage. At the national level there is no Party Secretary Wang. Until his death in April 1995, Chen Yun at least enjoyed some respect among ordinary people for his tough stance on corruption if not for his political views. Prime Minister Li Peng, one of the younger followers of the Chen Yun camp, is so despised both inside and outside the party for his role in the suppression of the Tiananmen Square protests that he is unlikely ever to emerge as the country's paramount leader. The retired veteran Deng Liqun equally commands little respect outside traditional bastions of conservatism such as the Propaganda Department and Ministry of Culture. But even if none of these figures look like serious contenders for supreme power, they will still constitute an important force in the maelstrom of Chinese politics after Deng's death, just as they have done for much of the 1980s and early 1990s.

The man Deng hopes will keep opponents of his policies in check, Jiang Zemin, appeared at least superficially to be gaining political strength as Deng's physical health declined. At a Communist Party plenum in September 1994, Jiang secured the promotion of two of his allies in Shanghai to important party posts.[13] The mayor of Shanghai, Huang Ju, was given a seat on the Politburo, and Wu Bangguo, the city's party leader and a Politburo member, was given an additional job in the secretariat of the Central Committee. At the National People's Congress held the following March, Wu was made deputy prime minister too. The surprise resignation of the Politburo member Chen Xitong from his concurrent post of Beijing's party chief in April 1995 and the subsequent investigation into Chen's alleged involvement in corruption led to further speculation that Jiang's authority was waxing. It had been widely rumored that Chen was one of the party leader's main rivals. Chinese with ties to the leadership told me that Chen had supported some provincial leaders in opposing Jiang's promotion of his former colleagues in Shanghai to top positions in Beijing.

It is hard to determine, however, how much Jiang's maneuverings were evidence of his personal leadership skills as opposed to manipulation by other key figures such as the chairman of the National People's Congress Qiao Shi. Chinese sources said Jiang was only able to move against Chen thanks to support from Qiao, a fellow member of the Politburo Standing Committee. Qiao objected, however, to Jiang's suggestion that Chen be replaced by the party leader's close ally, the Politburo member and Shanghai Party Secretary Huang Ju. Instead, Qiao installed his own protégé, Wei Jianxing, as the new Beijing party chief.

In China, rank often bears little relation to a person's real power. The sudden and sweeping purge of General Yang Baibing and dozens of his appointees in the military in late 1992 and early 1993 underscored the ineffectiveness of any political or military grouping centered around a person who lacks great authority in his or her own right. When Yang Shangkun's authority declined, as it appeared to in late 1992, Yang Baibing's power, which depended not so much on his rank but his relationship with Yang Shangkun, evaporated.

The addition in March 1993 of the title of state president to Jiang's already impressive array of posts did little to enhance his actual power, even though the new title made him the first Chinese leader since Mao Zedong to hold the top positions in the party, state, and military simultaneously. The main advantage to Jiang of being state president was that it brought him into more contact with foreign leaders and gave him a chance to display his diplomatic skills. But Jiang the diplomat drew a mixed response. His first chance to shine after assuming the presidency came in November 1993 when he paid a groundbreaking trip to Seattle, Washington, for a summit meeting of Asia Pacific Economic Cooperation (APEC)—the highest-level visit by a Chinese leader to the United States since Tiananmen. In a move calculated to appeal to his American audience, Jiang visited the suburban home of a worker from Boeing. Ignoring shouted questions from journalists, Jiang, accompanied by the Foreign Minister Qian Qichen, played up to the cameras, eating homemade cookies, and presenting stuffed toys to the two children. Jiang displayed a human side of the Chinese leadership that the American public had not seen for years. American officials, eager to encourage the impression that the tide was beginning to turn in Sino-U.S. relations, told reporters that Jiang appeared well briefed and in control. Other observers, however, were less impressed by Jiang's skills. When Mortimer Zuckerman, the publisher of *U.S. News and World Report,* interviewed Jiang earlier that year, the party leader persistently referred to notes when giving his answers—a common practice among relatively junior officials who are worried about straying from the party line but unusual for someone of Jiang's rank when talking just to a small group consisting of a foreign visitor and his or her aides.

Beijing-based diplomats often joked about Jiang's sometimes overzealous attempts to impress his guests with his knowledge of English, Russian, Romanian, French, and Japanese.[14] Sometimes Jiang even tried to entertain visitors with snatches of song in some of these languages. One of his favorite routines was to recite parts of Abraham Lincoln's Gettysburg Address, which he says he memorized as a high school student in the 1940s. By parroting such phrases as Lincoln's "government of the people, by the people, for the people," he apparently hoped to project an image of a leader in tune with Western thinking, cut in a different mold from the typical Chinese apparatchik.

But while Jiang's public relations efforts may have impressed some foreigners, they did not appear to enhance his image enormously among cynical Beijing residents. In one particularly clumsy attempt to enhance Jiang's popularity among ordinary Chinese, state-run television showed the party leader singing a Uighur folk song over the intercom system on board the plane taking him back from his November 1993 trip to America, Cuba, Brazil, and Portugal. The aim was apparently to show that the party boss was not above relaxing with his subordinates and that like Mao he could touch the hearts of the masses. But among several Chinese I spoke to in Beijing, the footage inspired more ridicule than reverence. This was not the behavior many Chinese seemed to expect of a top leader returning from a crucial diplomatic tour. The footage showed Jiang unsuccessfully urging the more demure Qian Qichen to join him in song. The normally taciturn Qian did, however, take the microphone to recount a joke, the punchline of which unfortunately was not broadcast.

In 1989, after the crushing of the Tiananmen Square protests, Deng made it clear that he wanted Jiang to become the country's next strongman after Mao and himself, describing him as the core of the "third generation" of Chinese leaders. He admitted that the people he had previously chosen to succeed him—Hu Yaobang and Zhao Ziyang—had failed to stay in power for long. "At the time . . . they were the best choices I could make," Deng said, apologetically. "Besides, people change."[15] Deng did not explain why Jiang should last any longer than his two predecessors, but by handing over his chairmanship of the Central Military Commission to Jiang in November that year, he gave him a public seal of approval the likes of which he never bestowed on Zhao or Hu, who had always remained junior to Deng in the military hierarchy. Jiang was, Deng said enigmatically, "well qualified to be chairman of the military commission because he is well qualified to be general secretary of the party"[16]—a remarkable statement given that Jiang had been a member of the Politburo for less than two years and had never served on its standing committee. Jiang himself admitted, albeit with ritual modesty, that he did not feel qualified for his new role. "I thank you comrades for trusting me," he said after the Central Committee had endorsed his appointment as military chief.[17] "I said at the previous plenary session that I was not fully prepared when I was elected general secretary of the Central Committee. This time, I am not fully prepared either. I have no experience in military work, and I feel my abilities fall far short of what the position demands."[18]

Jiang's career in Shanghai was certainly undistinguished. A senior Western diplomat based in the city expressed astonishment when I asked him about rumors that Jiang was about to be appointed party leader just a few hours before the news was confirmed. In Deng's eyes, Jiang's main redeeming features must have been his tough approach to dissent, his acceptability to rival factions in Beijing, and his ability to charm foreigners and convince them of his commitment to reform. During the 1989 unrest, Jiang incensed demonstrators by firing the outspoken editor in chief of the Shanghai-based *World Economic Herald* and closing the newspaper down, thus depriving the party's liberal wing of its main mouthpiece. In the buildup to the June 4th bloodshed, as it became clear that Zhao was in serious trouble, Jiang was summoned to Beijing to oversee the party's propaganda work. On his arrival at Capital Airport, Jiang reportedly pretended to be a doctor in order to avoid detection by protesters who were stopping government cars at roadblocks along his route.[19] In his new role, Jiang must have been kept abreast of the decision making that led to the bloodshed. But he kept a low profile, thus avoiding becoming directly tainted in the public eye by the military action. This probably enhanced his suitability as a candidate for the party leadership. With his hands seemingly clean, Jiang would be in a better position than the widely despised Li Peng to restore the party's image at home and abroad after Tiananmen.

In early 1994, *China Youth News,* the mouthpiece of the Communist Youth League, published an unusual article written by a prominent Chinese academic suggesting that the transfer of power from Deng to Jiang might be less than smooth.[20] The author, Lu Jianhua, said 1994 would mark a "crucial period" in the handover from the second generation to the third generation. "History proves that . . . in contemporary China, the issue of unity during the period of transference of power is the most difficult to tackle," said Lu. "Once an obstacle to unity arises, it will elicit massive personnel changes or even policy reversals, thus leading to turbulence in the social situation." Lu warned, without elaborating, that "inappropriateness in the course of transference of power will lead to disastrous consequences." The only way to ensure political stability, he said, was to establish "checking and balancing mechanisms" in the central government. "A protracted and institutionalized stability must rely on a more flexible form of control in society, which can effectively mediate various acute social contradictions and remove factors for potential social conflict in a timely manner," Lu said. "Of course, a relatively long process is necessary for the establishment of this new form of control."

That such an article should appear in such a prominent newspaper suggests a significant lack of confidence in official circles in Jiang's ability to hold the country together. Unlike Mao and Deng, Jiang is a politically uncommitted man without any obvious vision of the way forward for China. After Deng's death, he will be vulnerable to attack by any politician who is better able than he to inspire and motivate the public and bureaucracy or simply better able to impose his or her will. From one extreme of the political spectrum, advocates of a China run like Nanjie Village will attack him or try to control him. From the other extreme, Jiang will face demands for all-out privatization and moves to liberalize the political system.

It is widely believed that Jiang's own preference, as well as that of most other leaders of his generation, is for a path somewhere between these two extremes, but in Chinese political culture the will of the majority often fails to carry the day. Jiang's sympathies appear to lie with those described as neoconservatives—advocates of strong dictatorial control and a more cautious pace of reform than Deng has pursued but with far less emphasis on Maoist ideology than the Nanjie Village supporters would like to see.

The controversial book *Looking at China Through a Third Eye* presents some of the arguments favored by neoconservatives.[21] Although the book was marked for "internal circulation," meaning it should not be sold to foreigners and ordinary members of the public, it became an instant favorite, with pirated editions selling briskly on the streets to all and sundry. Chinese sources told me that Jiang Zemin spoke highly of it to party colleagues, before he became aware that its author was not, as claimed in the foreword, an eminent German sinologist but its purported translator Wang Shan, the then 42-year-old deputy director of the Beijing Opera Troupe who makes a living on the side by playing the stock markets and writing novels about China's criminal underworld. In a scathing critique of the book, the liberal former Minister of Culture Wang Meng said "some comrades are weeping tears of joy [over it], as if they have discovered some treasure. Clearly this 'German scholar' has said something they themselves wanted to say but which was not convenient for them to enunciate."[22]

Wang Shan's book warned of the dangers unleashed by Deng's

reforms, referring to the country's 800 million peasants as "a living volcano" who had been kept under control by Mao but thanks to the breakup of the People's Communes under Deng now posed a major threat to stability. Chinese people, the book argued, were overly optimistic about their country's situation. "China is already well into a phase of violent social change. There are signs of increasingly fierce confrontation between interest groups," said the author. He insisted that "China today still needs Mao's talent, boldness, and unparalleled skills as a ruler." The book had little to say about Mao the ideologue. Mao the dictator was clearly Wang Shan's model. "China needs a new idol," he said, "but it seems to have missed the opportunity."

Wang attacked Deng's strategy of trying to preserve stability by pushing for high-speed economic growth. "This is a very dangerous trap," he said. "Although sluggish economic growth would lead to a political crisis of confidence, high-speed economic growth will intensify society's inherent contradictions and give rise to new problems with which the Chinese Communist Party is completely unfamiliar." The book said that because of its size and poverty and the extent of illiteracy, China could not follow the path of Asia's "four little dragons."[23] The only way forward, it said, was to "follow in Mao's footsteps and explore its own path."

Wang's book was particularly negative in its assessment of Deng's southern tour, saying that even though economic growth had surged, economic efficiency had remained static. It said Deng "had seemingly legitimized all kinds of wild and reckless behavior" with his pronouncement that the way to decide whether something is "surnamed capitalist or surnamed socialist" is simply to look at whether it helps boost production, makes the country stronger, and increases living standards. "The question is, once the surging flood waters [unleashed by Deng's southern tour] have receded, what will be left behind on the great expanse of land they once swept over?" the author asked. "The latent crisis in society is extremely serious. The rapid speed of the economic train might delay the explosion of this crisis, but it cannot diminish it. On the contrary, it will only serve to aggravate it. The Chinese people and Western countries alike do not wish to see a repeat of the Beijing Incident of 1989. But subjective desires and objective reality are, in the final analysis, two different things."

Many of these views would be endorsed by extreme hard-liners and neoconservatives alike. But in a clear rebuttal of the former category, the book said party propaganda should be more honest in order to dispel the "erroneous fantasy" that socialism is superior to capitalism. The alternative to ideological control, it said, was to use the military to maintain order. "This is another fact of life," said the author. "Only when there is authority can stability and order be maintained, because order is partly a spontaneous creation and partly a product of fear." In a concession to traditional ideology, however, the author warned against allowing a new capitalist class to emerge. "If different social strata appear, they will have difficulty living with each other, and the struggle between them will very likely be a savage one. This would be a disaster for China and the rest of the world."

In his final summing up, Wang Shan said the situation in China was "even more perilous than that in Russia." He said this was because Russia was far more advanced than China in terms of economic development, educational standards, and political sophistication and also had a far smaller population.[24] In China, he said, there were "so many layers of complex contradictions—between foreign and Chinese capital, between developed and impoverished regions, between central government control and the devolution of power to the regions, between the foundations of society and the methods used to stimulate the economy, between the beneficiaries [of reform] and ordinary citizens. And all this is happening amid an enormous, densely packed mass of ill-educated, underemployed, and impoverished people. One can say that whatever the central government does is bound to be at least partially wrong. A crisis could occur at any time. Danger will be ever present."

Gloomy though it is, much of Wang's analysis sounds very plausible. In the mid-1990s, as Deng's death appeared increasingly imminent and the country's future looked correspondingly uncertain, the book must have gone down particularly well among the many Chinese officials disillusioned with Maoism yet fearful of the chaos that might be unleashed if the party were to loosen control. The neoconservative group has a broad constituency upon which to draw.

Among those most inclined toward neoconservative thinking are many of the offspring of the country's elderly leaders. This younger generation fears that the political and business empires they have built on the basis of their parents' prestige might crumble without a firm, dictatorial hand to keep the party together and prevent political dissidents and other malcontents from stirring up potentially disastrous trouble. The foreign media often refers to the powerful children of the country's elders as the "party of princes," or *taizidang* in Chinese. One of the key figures in this group is Chen Yuan, the son of the late Chen Yun. Shortly after the failed coup in Moscow in August 1991, the younger Chen is believed to have organized the drafting of a 14,000-character essay suggesting ways that China should respond to developments in the Soviet Union. The document, entitled *China's Realistic Response and Strategic Options after the Dramatic Changes in the Soviet Union,* was published by the *China Youth News* in a restricted newsletter circulated among senior officials.[25] Its contents read like a manifesto for the neoconservatives, boldly challenging some of the basic tenets of Deng's approach to reform. As deputy governor of the People's Bank of China, not to mention Chen Yun's son, Chen spoke with considerable authority. In his position he could express his views with virtual impunity as long as he did not openly challenge party rule itself.

The essay said that events in the Soviet Union had undermined the credibility of the party's ideology. The party, it argued, should therefore place less emphasis on ideology in order to avoid playing into the hands of radical reformists and the party's critics among the public at large—a view his pro-ideology father would not have endorsed. But Chen Yun would have sympathized with his son's complaint that while the party had successfully checked demands for radical political change since Tiananmen, it had not done enough to curb equally radical demands in the economic sphere. The document warned that the privatization of state property would weaken central government control and increase regionalism. It said that while a few small, nonessential, state-owned enterprises could be privatized, successful ones must remain in the hands of the party. The article attacked the decentralization of economic control—a key feature of Deng's reforms—and called for a "new start" aimed at creating a "new centralism." The essay said it was "extremely important" that the party rather than the government should identify itself as the owner of public property. This would enable the party to maintain control over the nation's assets and thereby put a stop to protectionism and waste on the part of local governments, which currently regard themselves as responsible for state-owned industries in their area. Instead of exerting direct control over state enterprises, local governments would have to seek approval first from their local party committees.

The essay suggested countering demands for radical economic reform by stepping up propaganda focused on the country's fundamental problems—its poverty, its huge population, its history of civil war and foreign domination, and the inadequacy of its natural resources. The document explicitly praised "neoconservative philosophy," which it said could help to combat the views of radical reformists who were agitating

for all-out privatization followed by political reforms that would ultimately destroy the party. It defined neoconservatism as "an approach to
reform that is different from that of traditional hard-line conservative
forces." The document said "neoconservatives" advocated "making use
of the reasonable elements both of the traditional and contemporary
order as well as gradually introducing the reasonable components of the
Western system in order to bring about China's modernization." It also
praised "Western rationalism," which it defined as rejecting romanticism
and stressing order and gradual change. Intellectuals should not be con-
strained by ideology, it said, but at the same time they should be kept
under control in order to avoid a repeat of the 1986 or 1989 demonstrations. The police and courts should be strengthened in order to combat
any "unconstitutional" activity—a common code word in China for dissident behavior.

Chen Yuan's document stressed the importance of traditional Confu-
cian culture and its emphasis on the collective rather than the individual.
The Asian economic takeoff of recent years, the essay said, was proof of
the "great contribution" of Confucianism. It suggested that in response
to the formation of economic blocs such as the European Community or
the North American Free Trade Agreement, China should join with Taiwan, Hong Kong, and Singapore to form an economic group based on
Chinese ethnicity, with the smaller, more prosperous members of the
group complementing China's pool of cheap labor and broad industrial
base—in other words, a Greater China bloc.

There is little sign, however, that the "party of princes" represents a
coherent faction within the party. There is also considerable opposition
within the party ranks to the influence of these "princes." This was
clearly demonstrated when, in December 1987, Chen Yuan failed to be
reelected to the Beijing party committee of which he had been a standing
committee member for the previous four years. That year's elections for
the new party committee were the first held by the city with more candidates than the number of seats available. It was therefore difficult for
Chen to ensure his success in the "princes'" traditional manner, by
pulling strings.[26] At the party's 14th Congress in 1992, both Chen Yuan
as well as Deng's daughter Deng Nan were unexpectedly excluded from
the new Central Committee. Their two fathers may have represented very
different political camps, but the idea of promoting their children
appeared unpalatable to a broad section of party and public opinion
alike. Although Deng Nan was among the nearly 2,000 delegates to the
congress, Chen Yuan did not even win that honor. The two were the most

prominent of more than half a dozen members of the "party of princes" who had been widely expected to be appointed to the new Central Committee but failed to make it. It is likely that Deng himself decided to bow to widespread demands inside and outside the party that such people be barred from promotion, realizing that failing to do so would only serve further to undermine public confidence in the party. Nepotism, after all, had been one of the main grievances of the demonstrators in 1989.

Though they may have been denied top positions in the party, the offspring of top leaders remain close to the center of power by virtue of their powerful parents and networks of contacts and are still likely to be among the important players in the struggle that follows Deng's death. The neoconservatism many of them espouse appeals to many leaders. Even many of Zhao Ziyang's key advisers advocated what they described as neoauthoritarianism, a view that differed somewhat from neoconservatism in that it espoused fast-paced reform but similarly backed the idea of having a dictatorial figure oversee the country's evolution from old style communism. Supporters of neoauthoritarianism pointed to Asia's "little dragons" as examples of how authoritarian regimes could, after a period of rapid economic growth, successfully evolve into democracies.

Some of Zhao's supporters pointed out, however, that such a scenario could not be repeated in China because so much of the country's wealth is in the hands of the state rather than privately owned. An economy based on private ownership, they argued, was essential to the process of building up a civil society that would in turn provide the foundations of a democratic system. Authoritarianism in a China dominated by state ownership, they said, would simply foster corruption. A better option would be to decentralize power and build up democratic institutions at the same time as boosting private ownership.[27] Ironically, given Zhao's reputation as a liberal, one of the main charges leveled by the hard-liners against him was that he himself hoped to be the enlightened dictator called for by advocates of this philosophy.

In post-Deng China, however, it is difficult to see any figure who has the authority and charisma necessary to play the role of dictator at a time when the country is undergoing a painful and potentially turbulent metamorphosis. The vacillating Jiang Zemin does not appear to be the man nor does the uncharismatic Li Peng. Deputy Prime Minister Zhu Rongji would be a possible contender, but although Zhu has acquired a reputation as a forceful, determined, and highly intelligent leader, he, like his former boss in Shanghai, Jiang Zemin, lacks any obvious power base in the party or military.

Zhu's main strength as a politician is his popularity. In Shanghai, he enjoys a far better reputation among ordinary people and business leaders than Jiang. Zhu first arrived in the city as deputy party secretary in 1987. The following year he was appointed mayor and in 1989 assumed the additional and more prestigious title of municipal party secretary when Jiang was elevated to the top party post in Beijing. During his tenure in the city, Zhu became widely known as a man who could cut through red tape, impress foreign businesspeople, and solve intractable problems. It was under Zhu's direction that Shanghai drew up plans for the development of Pudong,[28] one of the country's most grandiose projects, which would in effect create a whole new city east of old Shanghai. Many residents also praised Zhu for having made vigorous efforts to improve housing and infrastructure and tackle pollution.

Even before his promotion to the central leadership in 1991, Zhu was sometimes referred to as "China's Gorbachev" by the Western media because of his reformist views and leadership potential. It is not a sobriquet that Zhu relishes, given that Gorbachev is anathema to the party elders. "I'm not happy [about the description]," Zhu told an American journal in 1990. "I'm China's Zhu Rongji, not China's Gorbachev."[29] Whatever his economic views, Zhu, like other Chinese leaders, is certainly not an outspoken defender of political liberalization. But his stance during the demonstrations was somewhat ambiguous. After Jiang Zemin flew to Beijing to prepare to take over from Zhao Ziyang, Zhu found himself in charge in Shanghai. Faced with escalating chaos triggered by the bloodshed in Beijing, the mayor kept his cool. Even after demonstrators set fire to a train that had ploughed into a group of their colleagues blocking the tracks, killing six of them, Zhu refrained from giving vent to the kind of rage that Li Peng had earlier expressed in response to the unrest in Beijing. On June 6th, the night of the train disaster, there appeared more rationale for calling in the troops than there had been two days earlier in the capital. Yet the army stayed out of Shanghai, and the crisis subsided. Two days later, Zhu appeared on Shanghai television to make a direct appeal for calm—a tactic his Beijing counterparts had not attempted. "Comrades," he said, "why did the government not take forceful measures to restore the legal system to deal with such a grim situation? It was not because I did not have the power in my hand."[30]

Zhu explained that among the Shanghai protesters, good and bad people were mixed up together. "If we take forceful law enforcement measures at this time, it is quite possible we might harm the good people by mistake. If so, we will not be able to win the understanding of the masses. . . . Many comrades asked me to use armed police and even troops. Our municipal party committee and government have studied this question. As mayor, I would sternly announce here . . . the municipal party committee, the municipal government, and I have never considered using troops or exercising any military control. This is really the case. We have never considered those things."

Coming just four days after troops had opened fire on demonstrators in Beijing, presumably also including a mixture of "good" and "bad" people just like the crowds in Shanghai, Zhu's remarks seemed especially pointed. The words "turmoil" and "counterrevolutionary rebellion," which officials in Beijing used so often to describe the unrest, were conspicuously absent from Zhu's address. Zhu told the Shanghai people not to believe in "rumors" from abroad about what had happened in Beijing. But with what could have been deliberate ambiguity, he added: "Things that occurred in Beijing are history. No one can conceal history. The truth will eventually come to light."

During Deng Xiaoping's trip in May 1992 to Beijing's Capital Iron and Steel Works, Chinese sources say the elder statesman described Zhu as one of the few people who understood economics. Zhu's subsequent career suggests Deng certainly had enormous confidence in his ability to supervise his reform program. Although as prime minister Li Peng remained technically responsible for managing the economy, it appeared increasingly that Zhu was in day-to-day control.

Zhu's first assignment after his appointment as deputy prime minister was to tackle one of the thorniest problems besetting the economy, namely, the interlocking chain of debts between state-owned industries. Many of these enterprises have to sell their products and buy raw materials at prices set by the government and in quantities dictated by the government. A steel factory might therefore be required to sell steel to a nuts and bolts factory that cannot afford to pay for it because it in turn has to sell its output to a truck factory, which itself is in debt because it has to sell its trucks at low prices to government departments. The leadership's efforts to make state-owned enterprises more responsible for their own profits and losses instead of relying on subsidies encouraged debt-ridden factories simply to refuse to sell their products to other state enterprises, except at market prices for cash. Officials estimated the debt chain amounted to some $55 billion in June 1991 when Zhu formally declared war on the problem—a sum equivalent to nearly 90 percent of the government's total revenue that year.

Some official reports, reflecting no doubt the political sympathies of the journalists, portrayed Zhu as a savior who would rid the nation of a crippling burden—even though at the time he was not even a full member of the Central Committee. "There is a popular saying that 'once Rongji takes personal charge, he himself can do the work of two people,'" said the proreform *Liberation Daily* of Shanghai.[31] "The new officer, known for his 'resolute and rigorous work style,' gallantly took up the challenge. After carefully examining and studying the problem, he promptly designed a plan to 'cut the Gordian knot.'" Using the kind of language often used in official descriptions of communist heroism during the civil war of the 1940s, the newspaper described Zhu as engaging in "decisive battles across the country." Xinhua quoted Zhu as urging local leaders to "storm the heavily fortified positions" of indebted industries.[32]

The deputy prime minister toured the country, warning managers that they would be held personally responsible for their factories' debts and that they could expect no new loans if they failed to cut production of shoddy, unmarketable goods. Zhu berated local governments for exacerbating the debt chain problem by launching overambitious construction projects for which they could not afford to pay suppliers and contractors. By the time he declared the completion of the antidebt campaign at the end of 1992, Zhu had organized the clearing of more than two-thirds of the debts that were outstanding when he first started. This he had achieved partly by organizing nearly $10 billion in loans to help enterprises pay their bills. It was a short-term solution and a potentially inflationary one. The problem had not gone away by any means—to have eliminated it entirely would have required far more drastic surgery than Zhu was authorized to perform. But the official media still hailed his efforts as "remarkably successful."[33]

By the end of the campaign, Zhu was not only a full member of the Central Committee but also a Standing Committee member of the Politburo and head of the State Council's Economic and Trade Office. Hong Kong's *Wen Wei Po* reported in November 1992 that Zhu Rongji and Li Peng had been appointed deputy heads of a newly formed Leading Group on Finance and Economics, a secretive party body headed by Jiang Zemin and responsible for formulating economic strategy.[34] This implied that Zhu was at least on an equal footing with Li.

Zhu continued to shine in 1993, acquiring in May of that year yet another position as head of the party's Leading Group for Agricultural Work and in July the job of governor of the People's Bank of China, the central bank.[35] These new portfolios presented him with yet more herculean tasks—soothing the growing anger of peasants, curbing inflation, and restoring order to a chaotic financial system in which controls on bank lending had all but disappeared and local governments were borrowing massively in order to gamble in the booming stock and property markets. When Li Peng disappeared from public view from late April to mid-June of that year because of heart trouble, Zhu as his senior deputy became all the more prominent.

But even though he was spoken about with awe by foreign diplomats and businesspeople and managed to impress many people in Hong Kong during a visit to the still jittery colony a year after the 1989 bloodshed, Zhu's stellar performance and meteoric rise to the top did not necessarily win him many supporters at home. His efforts to revitalize moribund state industries involved confrontation with profoundly conservative bureaucrats and increasingly independent-minded provincial officials. Zhu does not believe in charming his opponents into submission. Unlike other Chinese officials who often conceal their feelings with banal generalities and formulaic responses lifted directly from party handbooks, Zhu prefers to speak his mind, even to the point of losing his temper—a style of behavior frowned on in a society where preserving face and striving for consensus are considered cardinal virtues.

During a visit to the Yungang Coal Mine in Shanxi Province in November 1992, officials showed me a videotape of a visit Zhu had paid to the huge state-owned pit six months earlier. His was no ordinary propaganda tour replete with smiles, handshakes, and platitudes of the kind so often shown on Chinese television. The video showed Zhu berating a room full of mine officials, telling them in nitty-gritty detail how they should drastically cut the mine's workforce in order to save money. As a result of his intervention, the colliery withdrew more than 3,000 miners from relatively well paid jobs at the coal face and put them to work above ground in service sector jobs with less guaranteed incomes. This amounted to one-third of the underground workforce. Zhu acknowledged his abrasive style. "My criticism is sometimes too serious. That is not a good thing," one official journal quoted him as saying.[36] "But why does someone not do his duty until the leader loses his temper? Some things are not very difficult to do, but they are not done."

To the hard-liners, Zhu's "Gorbachev" tag is more worrying than his curt manner. Alone among the current top leaders of China, Zhu is a victim of the 1957 Anti-Rightist Campaign. His alleged offense was criticizing China's economic policy. Although many leaders were victims of the Cultural Revolution—a badge of honor among high-ranking officials—those labeled as "rightists" in 1957 are often still regarded with some suspicion by the old guard, even though most "rightists" were formally rehabilitated after Deng came to power in 1978, Zhu included. For 23 years after 1952, Zhu held only one rather ignominious job, that of deputy chief engineer of the Electric Power Communications and Engineering Company run by the Ministry of Petroleum. It was hardly a solid foundation on which to build a career in the top party leadership.

By 1994, Zhu's fortune had begun to wane as inflation surged, debts mounted again among state industries, and peasant dissatisfaction remained widespread. Although he was among those best qualified to pursue Deng's policies after the veteran leader's death, he appeared to have made little headway in building up a power base of his own. At the National People's Congress in March 1995, Li Peng openly hinted that Zhu was at least partly to blame for the country's economic difficulties. Li noted that a year earlier he had proposed that inflation be kept to 10 percent in 1994 but that in the end it had risen to nearly 22 percent. "For price rises of this magnitude, there were objective reasons as well as shortcomings in the work of governments at all levels," Li said.[37] Though Li himself represented the top level of government, it was his deputy Zhu who had exercised day-to-day control over the economy for the previous two years. Li went on to say that inflation was partly the result of the government's—for which read Zhu's—decision to increase considerably the prices of grain, cotton, and crude oil and its moves toward making the Chinese currency freely convertible. "The measures were necessary for rationalizing price relations and arousing the initiative of producers, especially the masses of farmers," Li said. "The measures drove up the general level of prices to a certain extent. This was a price we could hardly avoid paying in carrying out reform. The problem was that we failed to adequately assess the related effects of these measures."

Li's words were reminiscent of the report he delivered to the National People's Congress in March 1989, shortly before the outbreak of the prodemocracy unrest. Then too China was reeling from the effects of a surge of inflation the year before. The then party leader, Zhao Ziyang, had been the man responsible for pushing through price reforms that had led to a run on banks and panic buying in the summer of 1988. Li suggested in that report too that problems were inevitable. But, he added, "there are also shortcomings and mistakes in our work guidance. Generally speaking, there does exist a trend of being overanxious for quick results in economic construction and social development."[38] Less than two months later, acrimony between Li and Zhao erupted into open warfare.

Of China's top political leaders, one of the men most often mentioned abroad as a likely strongman after Deng is Qiao Shi, a member of the Politburo's Standing Committee who for much of the 1980s and early 1990s was the party's head of security, responsible for police and secret intelligence work, including the investigation of senior officials. In 1993, Qiao was appointed head of the National People's Congress. Many foreign observers speculated that Qiao would try to turn the traditionally rubber-stamp body into an independent power base. There is no real evidence that he has done so, but Qiao appears to have more potential staying power than most of his other colleagues on the Politburo Standing Committee. Key to this is the support he appears to enjoy among party veterans both reformist and hard-line. He was the first senior Politburo member to give public support to Deng's call for faster and bolder reforms in early 1992. Yet the hard-line former president, Li Xiannian, who died in June of that year, once described Qiao in glowing terms as "a young cadre of rare qualities" who was "capable but not proud." Li noted in particular that Qiao had "joined the revolution very early" and had been "tempered by the struggle with KMT rule."[39]

Qiao's career in the party is certainly longer than that of any other Standing Committee member of the Politburo apart from the Long March veteran and Deng ally General Liu Huaqing. Qiao, indeed, was Jiang Zemin's superior when the latter, then nearly 20 years old, joined the underground Communist Party in Shanghai in 1946. Qiao had joined six years earlier, at the age of 16. During Tiananmen, he played an ambivalent role, appearing to support the crackdown while reportedly showing signs of sympathy with liberals such as Zhao Ziyang, who opposed both Deng and the extreme hard-liners. In his memoirs, China's former chief representative in Hong Kong Xu Jiatun quotes Zhao as saying he believed Qiao supported the former party leader's views on the unrest.[40]

Like Jiang, Qiao is a figure without any obvious political vision and certainly one capable of bending with the political wind. Although he may have had his reservations about the imposition of martial law, he did not express these in public. Eight days after the killings, Qiao visited the martial law troops and toured a hospital where injured soldiers were being treated. Qiao thanked the troops profusely for making "great contributions" in the "recent struggle to quickly quell the counterrevolutionary rebellion" and for "fighting bravely to safeguard the interests of the People's Republic and the people and the capital's social stability."[41] When Qiao met the then East German Politburo member Egon Krenz in

Beijing in September of that year, he praised the East Germans' "full understanding of and support for our struggle to quell the counterrevolutionary rebellion."[42] He was no less forthright in his condemnation of liberal ideology. "Our struggle against imperialism's reactionary strategy to effect peaceful evolution in China and against bourgeois liberalization will be a protracted one. We must not, in the slightest degree, relax our efforts in this connection at any time," Qiao warned cadres at the Central Party School that same month.[43] He even paid a visit to Nanjie Village and, according to the village's brochure, repeatedly told officials there "you're doing a good job, you're on the right path."

As Tiananmen receded into the past, Qiao's speeches focused increasingly on the need to strengthen the legal system and fight corruption, issues that were of course dear to him as the country's security chief. But the normally taciturn Qiao projected little sense of passion. His air was more that of a highly efficient and intelligent apparatchik than of a leader who could inspire a vast nation.

After Deng's death, the "third generation" of leaders will still have to play to a gallery of elders. China's political culture is such that top leaders only cease to exert influence when they die or are purged. The lack of any formal title can be a hindrance to wielding power but by no means an insuperable one. During the 1980s, the elders of Deng's generation who controlled Chinese politics from behind the scenes were often referred to by the foreign media as "the eight immortals." This was a reference both to their longevity and to the much revered "Eight Immortals" of the Taoist pantheon, a group of wise men who, according to legend, attained eternal life after drinking an elixir. The group of "immortal" communists has dwindled since the first of their number, Li Xiannian, died in June 1992. A fellow archconservative, Wang Zhen, died in March of the following year. Chen Yun—the most influential after Deng himself—died in April 1995. But at least some of the remaining elders, though very rarely seen in public and equally rarely quoted, still play a role in shaping party policy if not in day-to-day decision making.[44] Their absence from public view makes it almost impossible to assess the extent of each "immortal's" influence. But their physical decline has not necessarily led to a corresponding reduction in their political clout.

The continuing authority of some of these "immortals" was highlighted in November 1994 by a lengthy interview with one of their number, Bo Yibo, which was published in the *People's Daily*.[45] In most Western countries, an interview with a retired leader might be noteworthy but usually would not be read as a statement of policy to which the nation should adhere. But the *People's Daily* is the party mouthpiece, and the words it prints are assumed by readers to have the endorsement of the Central Committee. Though he had long since ceased to hold any official posts, Bo's blunt reminders in his interview about the dangers of ignoring party discipline and failing to follow directives from the top therefore carried considerable weight. Bo warned that China's economic progress might be short-lived if the party neglected efforts to ensure tight discipline in its ranks. He implied that the challenges the party now faced were as big as they were in 1948 on the eve of the communist takeover and in 1978 when Deng came to power. Bo admitted there was now a possibility that "we may not fulfill our tasks so smoothly or well" and hailed the examples set by Mao and Deng who had saved the day in 1948 and 1978, respectively, by stressing the need for regional officials and indeed every party member to toe the party line.

In an implicit comparison with the present day, Bo said that if Mao had failed to crack the whip in 1948, "all localities would have sunk into a state of decentralization where each of them would have gone its own way. Even if the situation was good then, there still existed a great possibility that it would deteriorate, resulting in an unfinished war of liberation and an unfinished revolution across China."

But by far the most active of the "immortals" is the former president Yang Shangkun, who appeared by the mid-1990s to have recovered from the political buffeting he suffered around the time of the party congress in 1992.[46] On December 30th, 1994, Yang arrived in Shenzhen on a well-publicized two-week trip during which he visited many of the same sites that he and Deng had visited during the famous "southern tour" three years earlier. He repeated the same appeal for a faster pace of reform and praised Deng's "foresight" in setting up the SEZs.[47] The prominence given to Yang's remarks by the national media suggested that he was no longer on the political sidelines. Many Chinese believe that of all the "immortals" Yang is likely to have the most significant influence on the future direction of Chinese politics after Deng's death. This is because of his long career as Deng's right-hand man as well as his intimate links with the military, which is still believed to play a kingmaking role even though it stays in the background of the political process. This role was symbolized by the appointment of then 76-year-old General Liu Huaqing to the Politburo's Standing Committee in 1992 even though this went against the party's stated goal of promoting younger leaders.

There have been persistent rumors that since stepping down from the presidency in 1993, Yang has been cultivating ties with the disgraced

Zhao Ziyang, which if true would suggest that he might support a political future for China that would be more liberal than Deng's regime. A Western diplomat who attended a meeting between Yang and a visiting foreign leader in late 1992 told me that Yang appeared to be at pains to highlight Zhao's name. Yang told his guest that Zhao had made a trip as prime minister to the visitor's country. On hearing Zhao's name, other Chinese in the room looked nervous, and Yang's interpreter avoided translating that part of the president's remarks. Noticing the response, Yang repeated very clearly what he had said with a smile, referring to Zhao as "comrade," the only title he still officially holds as an ordinary party member. The diplomat said he had the clear impression that Yang was trying to convey to his guests the sense that he was a liberal figure at heart, despite his reputation during Tiananmen as an advocate of ruthless action against the demonstrators.

Of the surviving "immortals," Yang is the only one to have embarked on a high-profile trip outside Beijing and Shanghai since Deng's southern tour. This could be important in post-Deng China as the leaders of affluent provinces acquire increasing clout relative to the center, and economic liberalization sucks power away from Beijing. Any would-be paramount leader is likely to have to court provincial leaders even more assiduously than Deng had to. As Bo Yibo hinted in his *People's Daily* interview, it is becoming increasingly difficult for the leadership in Beijing to give orders and expect them to be carried out across the country. Provincial support, particularly from independent-minded regions like Guangdong, could therefore be crucial.

Among Chinese dissidents, ever hopeful of fundamental political change after Deng's death, much speculation focuses on the future political role of the man who was once supposed to be the leader of the third generation, Zhao Ziyang himself. Zhao's inability to stand his ground in 1989 was evidence of his political weakness at the time. Like those third-generation leaders now in power, Zhao had few links with the military. Without such links, any effort to stand up to Deng and the other party veterans was bound to be futile. But what Zhao lacks in terms of a power base he makes up for to a significant degree as a symbol of opposition to the use of military force in 1989, a stance that has probably won him many supporters within the army itself as well as among the general public. Zhao's conspicuous absence from political life and indeed from public view since Tiananmen is one of the most telling signs that the 1989 upheaval remains a key unresolved issue in Chinese politics. In a political culture that places so much emphasis on consensus and projecting an image of unity, Zhao's failure to reappear can only suggest that Tiananmen is still such a divisive problem that his return even in an honorary role is considered by party leaders to be too potentially destabilizing. Rehabilitation for Zhao would be a major first step toward a reassessment of Tiananmen, a process that could rock the foundations of the current leadership.

Asked by a foreign reporter to comment on rumors that Zhao might return to politics, Li Peng said in April 1990, "I do not believe that that is the prediction of the majority of the Chinese people."[48] There have been occasional rumors since then that Zhao has in fact been offered a minor position but has refused. If this is the case, it is likely that he himself believes his political reputation could only be enhanced by refusing to compromise with his critics.

The relatively liberal press under Beijing's control in Hong Kong has hinted at Zhao's continuing popularity after Tiananmen, at least in Sichuan where he served as party boss from 1975 to 1980. Zhao's pioneering role in introducing the agricultural reforms that were later to sweep the country was so much appreciated by Sichuan peasants at the time that they coined the rhyming phrase, *Yao chi liang, zhao Ziyang,* meaning "If you want to eat grain, look for Ziyang"—Zhao's surname and the word for "look for" having similar sounds in Mandarin. *Wen Wei Po* said that after Tiananmen, residents of one county where Zhao had first carried out the reforms "dared not to attend some of the scheduled criticism meetings" of the former party leader.[49] Xiao Yang, the reformist governor of Sichuan, told the newspaper, "As far as the issue of reform is concerned, Comrade Zhao Ziyang scored considerable achievements and accomplished a lot of work.[50] His achievements cannot be denied. As we speak of someone's achievements and contributions, only when he stands for the will of the masses can he be described as making a contribution. It is not the case that the people's will for reform no longer exists because he [Zhao Ziyang] is not in power now."[51]

The only substantial clue we have to Zhao's thinking after Tiananmen comes from a "self-criticism" he made shortly after his dismissal, details of which were leaked to the Hong Kong media around the fifth anniversary of the Tiananmen Square protests.[52] The document, which amounts to more than 7,000 words in its English translation, shows Zhao to be a man committed to the party's traditional code of behavior, even though he opposed the use of force to crush the demonstrations. He expresses his support for "the four basic principles" of party dictatorship and the need to fight "bourgeois liberalization." His difference with the hard-liners is that he believes that "bourgeois liberalization" is best fought against not by waging campaigns but by improving the lives of citizens so that they support the party's dictatorship of their own accord.

There are other important liberals who could emerge as backers of a Zhao comeback. Deng's bridge partner, Wan Li, who was chairman of the National People's Congress until Qiao Shi took over, is one example. The Politburo Standing Committee member Li Ruihuan is another. But my own prediction is that without a strongman like Deng around to keep rival factions in their place, competing visions of how China should be run—from the Nanjie Village model to laissez-faire capitalism and everything in between—and by whom it should be run, will alter China's political landscape so rapidly that placing bets on any individual would be dangerous. Undoubtedly regional leaders whose names are hardly known now outside China will play an increasingly important role as central authority continues to wane. In the event of an East European–style political upheaval, Zhao could emerge as an important transitional figure, but he would face such colossal popular demands for political change that he too would likely be rapidly swept aside, not least because of his age (he was born in 1919) and health (he suffers from heart disease).

Indeed, Zhao's death could well have more impact on Chinese politics than anything he might do while still alive. Just as the death of his predecessor, Hu Yaobang, triggered the nationwide upheaval of 1989 and the death of the popular prime minister Zhou Enlai led to the Tiananmen Square protests of 1976, so too could Zhao's demise spark demands for political change. Zhao himself warned in his self-criticism after Tiananmen, "facts in many countries show that economic development does not automatically make people satisfied and contented and does not automatically bring about social stability." His death, if it occurs before an official reassessment of Tiananmen, could reopen the political and social wounds of that period.

Sudden, unpredictable unrest is one of the biggest challenges to the third generation of leaders. Whatever their political platform, there is probably a general consensus among them that any disturbances should be quickly nipped in the bud. All of them would want to avoid the possibility of another Tiananmen-style upheaval that could cost them not only their jobs but even their lives if events develop as they did in Romania. In May 1992, the army issued new regulations clarifying under what circumstances troops could open fire on demonstrators and how lethal force should be deployed.[53] The rules gave soldiers permission to open fire without seeking higher-level approval if "there is no time or communications have been cut." They stressed that the army's duty was to "protect the party and the socialist system" and that the military should "support the party's absolute leadership over the armed forces." Soldiers, they said, should be subjected to "political examination" to ensure their "purity." But the rules did not, of course, address the problem of disunity within the party. While there may be general agreement on the need to control dissent, opening fire on demonstrators—particularly in the hallowed grounds of central Beijing—would still be an extremely divisive issue, not only in the party but in the military as well. Faced with large-scale unrest, whoever is in charge would either have to order the army to assert control forcefully or risk a disastrous breakdown of order. Neither Jiang Zemin nor any of his third-generation colleagues look like leaders who could act decisively in such a situation and be sure of keeping the party and the army together.

Sheet of Loose Sand?

Without powerful, spiritual support based on a correct theory, our party, our country and our people will be like a sheet of loose sand, will not have rallying power, fighting power, creative power and cannot have a wonderful future.

—Jiang Zemin, July 1993

As the twenty-first century approaches, Western policy makers will have to pay increasingly close attention to developments in China, from the country's economic growth to its military ambitions and its treatment of Hong Kong and Taiwan. Faced with the reality of an economically vibrant China with a huge potential market, a permanent seat in the United Nations Security Council, an arsenal of nuclear weapons, and a huge military-industrial complex offering missiles and other hardware to overseas buyers, Washington has decided to favor "constructive engagement" with Beijing rather than attempt to isolate and coerce an increasingly assertive member of the international community.

Western governments fear that if shunned by the outside world China could return to the dangerously unpredictable xenophobia that characterized its foreign policy under Chairman Mao. They fear too that political collapse would not only destabilize China but the rest of the region as well. With the return of Hong Kong imminent, most officials in London, Washington, and other capitals with a stake in the territory's future consider stability in Beijing particularly vital no matter what reservations they may have about the communist government in power there. Deng's warnings of tens of millions of refugees flooding the region, deliberately alarmist though they may sound, do frighten China's neighbors, which already, even in these times of relative stability, are worried about growing numbers of illegal Chinese immigrants. Deng knows well the rhythms of Chinese history—the rise and fall of dynasties punctuated by civil war and rebellion—and so does the outside world.

In 1924, the Chinese revolutionary Sun Yat-sen described his country as a "sheet of loose sand."[1] His words were intended to convey an image of a country hopelessly weak and disunited. China was, he said, "the fish and the meat" and the rest of the world "the carving knife and the serving dish." The reason China was unable to unite in the face of foreign aggression, Dr. Sun argued, was that "the Chinese people have shown the greatest loyalty to family and clan with the result that in China there have been familyism and clannism but no real nationalism." He warned that in order to avoid the "destruction of our race," China must "earnestly promote nationalism."

More than 70 years later—and with a population three times as large—China still frequently recalls Dr. Sun's words. Its leaders warn that without the party, China would once again become a "sheet of loose sand," a state that they say could have as devastating implications for the rest of the world as for China itself. The fight to instill a common sense of purpose and national identity among the Chinese people is still regarded by the party as a crucial one. "Patriotic education," focusing on the humiliation of China by foreign powers before 1949 and the strength and respect the country has gained under communism, is a significant part of every Chinese schoolchild's upbringing. Patriotism and support for the party are portrayed as one and the same thing insofar as the party believes that its fate and that of the nation are inseparable.

The party's campaign to boost patriotism can only have been helped by the growing awareness in the West of China's formidable potential. Former U.S. President George Bush, who was head of the U.S. diplomatic office in Beijing in 1974 and 1975, predicted in late 1993 that the twenty-first century could well be the "China century." Bush envisaged a "promising scenario—China as open, responsible, a global economic superpower."[2] The former Secretary of State Henry Kissinger echoed this remark two years later, describing China as "on course to emerge as an extraordinary superpower within 20 years."[3] In 1993, the International Monetary Fund (IMF) introduced a new method of evaluating a nation's GNP that showed that China's economy was nearly four times larger than previously calculated. The method was based on the domestic purchasing power of a country's currency as opposed to the old system of simply converting GNP into U.S. dollars at market exchange rates. The old method put China's GNP per head in 1990 at $370 compared with $410 in 1976, a nonsensical result given that the country's economy had grown by 7.5 percent annually since 1978—double the average growth rate of the world economy. The new system ranked China as the third-largest economy in the world after the United States and Japan rather than tenth as previously determined.

The Chinese leadership clearly both relished such prognoses and worried about them. While the state-controlled media eagerly reported them, at the same time Chinese officials were clearly concerned that such descriptions would fuel antagonism toward China among hawkish politicians in the West and reduce Beijing's eligibility for the low-interest loans and trading concessions normally offered to developing countries. The Chinese foreign minister Qian Qichen said foreign claims that China had already become the world's third-largest economy "do not correspond to reality."[4] He said China was still "among the less well-off developing countries" and that it would take "the efforts of several generations" to make it a medium-developed nation. This stance also suited China's argument that, as an economically backward country, its priority in the field of human rights was to feed and clothe its people rather than to ensure freedom of speech, association, assembly, and the press—freedoms that Western countries only began paying much attention to relatively late in their development.

But even though Chinese officials accused the IMF of distorting the facts, Beijing's own economic and social development targets for the year 2000 were impressive enough. Already in 1995, five years earlier than planned, the country fulfilled the target set in 1982 of quadrupling the country's 1980 GNP. By the turn of the century, China also aimed to eliminate poverty, begin narrowing the income gap between urban and rural areas, and ensure that, despite the burden of a population growing by more than 15 million people a year, the country would remain self-sufficient in grain.[5] Another no less ambitious goal was to wipe out illiteracy among young and middle-aged people by the year 2000.[6] In 1991, China predicted that within a decade it would reach or surpass the level of medium-income countries in terms of health, nutrition, average life span, and literacy rate.

Based on the statistics and the visibly rapid transformation of China's cities and parts of the countryside, the leadership had reason to feel some degree of pride. But it was also worried by signs that breakneck economic growth was undermining the political cohesiveness that the communists had tried so hard to achieve and fueling a resurgence of the "familyism and clannism" that Sun Yat-sen had spoken of so despairingly.

In 1990, Prime Minister Li Peng described some predictions by Western analysts that imbalanced economic development in China could aggravate friction between regions and lead to the growth of localism as "incorrect" or at least "a misunderstanding."[7] He said this could not happen because "China is a unified country, a unified market, and an integrated whole, and because the Chinese nation has a strong rallying force as a result of its history of several thousand years." But frequent reports in the state-controlled media conveyed a very different picture, namely, that of a once highly centralized political structure jeopardized by growing regionalism and provincialism. A senior provincial official warned in 1994 that "the whole country" could fall into "a situation where there are local regimes and departmental blockades."[8] In confidential analyses, some Chinese scholars have gone as far as to predict that China could break up like the former Yugoslavia within a few years of Deng's death.

Many observers argue against the possibility of a Soviet or Yugoslav-style breakup on the grounds that the country is far more ethnically and culturally homogenous than these two countries were before their disintegration.[9] The nationalist sentiments of Chinese leaders and the general public are certainly strong enough that any effort by Tibet or other minority regions, or for that matter Taiwan, to gain outright independence would be fiercely resisted. But nationalism alone has never in Chinese history proved capable of preventing regions from gaining de facto independence while remaining nominally part of the Chinese state. As long as Taiwan does not formally sever its links with China or challenge the ideal of a unified Chinese nation, most people on the mainland are probably quite content to let it go its separate way politically, economically, and even militarily. Beijing's "one country, two systems" formula for reunification with Hong Kong, Macao, and Taiwan does not appear to offend nationalist sentiments in China, even though in theory at least those regions would remain virtually as autonomous as they are now and just as much off-limits to most Chinese. The only guarantee that the mainland itself will not break up into any number of Taiwans or Hong Kongs is the existence of a strong central government backed by a united army. How long China will continue to enjoy such a guarantee, if indeed it has it now, is questionable.

The decentralization of power under Deng has transformed the traditional Maoist relationship between central government and the provinces. Economic decisions made in Beijing are now increasingly the product of compromise between Beijing's interests and those of provincial governments. Hardly a Central Committee meeting goes by without rumors of provincial leaders vigorously defending their region's interests against what they perceive as efforts by Beijing to claw back some of the authority the center has lost since the late 1970s. Provincial leaders are still appointed by Beijing, and even though they may fight their corner their careers still depend on loyalty to the central leadership. But once in place, the leader has considerable control over the appointment of subordinates, over state-owned industries located within the province, and over spending within the province's budget. A few top provincial leaders have strong personal ties with their regions, through birth or upbringing or through having served in them for a considerable part of their careers. One such leader, Ye Xuanping from Guangdong, sometimes appeared to identify more strongly with the interests of his native province than with those of the central government. The reform-minded Ye, the son of the late communist Marshal Ye Jianying, acquired enormous power during his term as governor of Guangdong from 1985 to 1993. It is widely believed that the central leadership had great difficulty in persuading him to leave his post and move to Beijing to take up the sinecure of vice chairman of the Chinese People's Political Consultative Conference. When he finally did so, he made sure his successors were people to his liking.

Provincial officials occasionally make remarks to journalists that appear to be out of keeping with Beijing's line, complaining about austerity measures, for example, or ideological campaigns. But the main evidence for what is widely believed to be growing regional assertiveness comes from reports on the problem that appear in the official press. In an article published in mid-1995 by a conservative journal, two Chinese economists warned that "the political authority of the central government" had been "damaged" as a result of "excessive" devolution of fiscal control to the provinces during the reform era.[10] "There are quite a few examples in history of the decentralization of fiscal control leading to political collapse," they warned. "In recent history, the failure of the [1911] Revolution and the collapse and breakup of the former Soviet Union were both closely related to the lack of centralized control over finances."

The state-controlled media have admitted that some provinces have increasingly attempted to stop the outflow of commodities to other parts of the country where they might fetch a higher price as well as to curb the importation of products from other provinces that might hurt the sales of locally made goods. Such protectionism has long existed under communist rule, but officials say it has become especially serious since the 1980s.

In 1990, a Chinese economist said local protectionism had become "a major obstacle to economic development."[11] Some regions have issued directives banning the flow of specified goods across their borders, enforcing them by setting up checkpoints and even deploying troops to patrol interprovincial highways. The official press reported that in the hilly border area where the central provinces of Hunan, Hubei, and Jiangxi converge, several cities and counties issued their own "currencies" in 1990 in order to restrict residents to buying goods in their own area.[12] City and county governments in the region used the illegal money to pay the salaries of officials and workers and buy crops from peasants, with the result that by mid-1990 about 40 percent of the currency in circulation in the region was not the official renminbi.

Chinese newspapers often describe how peasants trying to sell their produce in the cities encounter checkpoints set up illegally by local governments every few miles along their route at which they are forced to pay taxes. In 1992, a farmer taking a truckload of garlic to Beijing from one of the country's main garlic-growing areas of Shandong Province 500 miles away had to pass no fewer than 20 checkpoints at which he would have to pay taxes totaling more than 1,000 yuan—well over one year's income for the average peasant. "Some bold farmers who can't put up with such blackmail have charged through the checkpoints but many others silently swallow 'the unlucky situation' and reluctantly give up marketing their surplus products in urban areas," said the *China Daily*.[13]

Driving through the countryside northeast of Beijing in 1990, I encountered one example of how easy it is for localities to extort money from road users. Finding the highway impassable at one point because of flooding, I followed a detour along a dirt track. Enterprising peasants along the route stopped all the cars passing through their village and demanded 10 yuan from each, handing out official-looking receipts in return. The driver of a police jeep in front of me paid up like the rest of us. He was probably out of his jurisdiction and therefore powerless to protest against what was almost certainly a scam backed by officials in the area.

China Daily said economists "occasionally" warned that the country would fail to fulfill the target of providing sufficient clothing and food for the entire population by the year 2000 if commodities could not flow freely between rural and urban areas.[14] Despite a government drive in 1990 to crack down on the problem, it has refused to go away. In January 1995, Xinhua admitted that it had resurfaced in many provinces. "Because there are no explicit rules against their actions, some provinces and cities have relied on wanton highway fee collections to boost their income or dispense more material benefits to certain departments," the news agency said.[15]

Interprovincial rivalry has even escalated into violence. In a rare admission of the extent of provincial feuding, the *China Daily* said in August 1989 that more than 800 battles between neighboring counties or provinces had occurred in the previous decade, a "dramatic increase" compared with the 30 such fights reported in the 1950s, 40 in the 1960s, and 130 in the 1970s.[16] Casualties, it said, numbered in the "tens of thousands," although it did not say since when. Most of the 800 reported fights in the 1980s occurred in remote regions of western China. *China Daily* said the discovery of a rich asbestos reserve in a disputed border area between Qinghai and Xinjiang in the far west had led to several large-scale battles, including one in 1985 that left 130 people dead or injured.

Most of the skirmishes erupted because of disputes over boundary lines between rival provinces, counties, towns, or villages. In 1989, more than 32,000 miles of provincial borders had yet to be mapped. "The boundary line for one province is not necessarily the same as shown on the map drawn for a neighboring province," *China Daily* said. "No one wants to give an inch, and if contested land is valuable, it can become a battlefield."

That such clashes should occur even in spite of the country's centralized and tightly controlled political system suggests trouble ahead should Beijing's authority crumble. The biggest nightmare of the central leadership is the possibility that regional military commanders might align themselves with provincial interests and precipitate a return to the warlordism that ravaged the country for most of the first half of the twentieth century. It is simply a matter of guesswork how likely this scenario is given how little is known of the inner workings of the Chinese military. But it is clearly one to which Deng Xiaoping has devoted a lot of attention. When he briefed top party leaders in September 1989 on arrangements for his retirement, Deng was at pains to stress the importance of strengthening Beijing's authority and preventing factionalism within the military. He pointed out that during the Cultural Revolution, Chairman Mao had rotated the commanders of the military regions. "He did so because he knew the art of leading the army, that is, not to allow any leading cadre to form a circle and have a sphere of influence," Deng cautioned his successors.[17] "It is a tradition of the army to have its leaders transferred frequently. During the wars the army was divided into mountain strongholds. But because of our understanding of Marxism and our organizational sense of discipline as communists, we did not form factions. Even so, the 'mountain-stronghold mentality' has had bad effects and a special campaign was launched to combat it. Local cadres may present the same problem; when they have been in one place too long, they should be transferred elsewhere."

The Chinese armed forces cannot be assumed to be immune from the gradual process of atomization now eroding the country's once monolithic political and social structure. As the late Chen Yun put it in 1990, "the army is extremely, extremely, extremely important." Without the army, he said, "this affair in Tiananmen, Beijing, wouldn't have worked out. We certainly must do a good job of strengthening the army."[18] Although there is no evidence that regional military commanders harbor ambitions to become latter-day warlords, there is plenty of evidence to suggest that rapid economic changes are having much the same impact on officers and men as they are on the general public, with some profiting enormously, others losing out, and discipline generally slackening.

In mid-1992, as the country plunged into a money-grabbing spree triggered by Deng's southern tour, the head of the navy's political department, Admiral Tong Guorong, warned of the effects this was having on morale in the armed forces.[19] Some soldiers, Tong said, feared that allowing some people to get rich before others would lead to the polarization of Chinese society or that opening up further to the outside world would have a negative social impact. Other soldiers feared that efforts to trim the staff of government departments and state-run enterprises would make it more difficult for them to find work on returning to civilian life as well as limiting job opportunities for their relatives. Tong said some soldiers who saw civilians getting rich wanted to leave the army in order to earn more money. Some, he said, had been affected by "corrupt ideology, culture, and lifestyles," which had been spreading during the reforms, and some had turned to crime. The admiral said such problems had existed for a long time but had become "even more prominent" as a result of Deng's latest campaign or, as he diplomatically put it, "in the wake of a faster pace . . . of reform and opening up."

A common belief among China-watchers is that as long as the party remains united, the army will rally behind it and defend it even at the cost of more Tiananmen-style bloodshed. This belief is based partly on the impression that the People's Liberation Army has become more professional and much less of an active player in politics under Deng. Military representation in the Central Committee and the Politburo, though increased somewhat at the 14th Congress in 1992, is still considerably lower than it was in Mao's day. The theory is that a more professional army follows the orders of its civilian masters no matter what the political inclinations of individual military commanders. To some extent, the crushing of the Tiananmen Square protests bore out this view. But it is impossible to say how the military would respond should one part of the leadership advocate military intervention in a crisis and another equally strong faction oppose it. In such a situation, fault lines in the military structure of which we now have little inkling might suddenly become far more apparent.

Since Tiananmen and the collapse of communism in the former Soviet Union and Eastern Europe, the party has been desperately searching for a new sense of purpose with which to inspire and unite the nation. An important part of this was the campaign, which ended in failure in September 1993 after more than two years of effort, to promote Beijing's application to host the Olympic Games in the year 2000. This was communist China's first ever attempt to stage the Olympics, and the leadership poured colossal resources and energy into the bid. One motive was China's desire to improve its image abroad and counter the diminishing but still persistent negative publicity it was suffering because of Tiananmen. But it was also clear that the leadership saw the bid as a chance to whip up patriotic fervor and give the party and people alike a common goal on which everyone could agree. In the year 2000, Hong Kong and Macao would be part of China again, and the games would be a chance to celebrate the reunion.

Chinese officials maintained that more than 90 percent of the population supported Beijing's application. The claim appeared to be a reasonable one. Most dissidents I spoke to even said privately they supported holding the Olympics, despite the heavy-handed methods used by the authorities to make Beijing look presentable to inspectors from the International Olympic Committee when they toured the capital in March 1993. To impress the visitors, city officials turned off heating in some parts of the city to cut down on pollution caused by coal-burning boilers, ordered children and office workers to clean the streets, moved streetside food peddlers away from the main thoroughfares, and imposed heavy fines on taxi drivers who failed to display Olympics stickers in their car windows. Only one dissident in the whole country, a little-known former Democracy Wall activist called Qin Yongmin from Wuhan, spoke out against the games. His argument was not so much that China's human rights record made the country an unsuitable host for such an event but that Beijing could not afford the expense.

Chinese officials spoke with pride of how the Olympics bid reinforced the *ningju li*—the cohesive strength—of the Chinese people. When Sydney won the race, many Beijing residents were clearly very disappointed. Chinese officials accused the United States and Britain of ganging up to sabotage the bid and insisted that, in the words of the Beijing-controlled *Ta Kung Pao* in Hong Kong, "the more [Western countries] bully and oppress us, the more cohesive the Chinese nation becomes and the higher aspirations the Chinese people have."[20] But the government's preoccupation with "cohesiveness" suggested that it perceived a serious threat.

The dramatic arrest in April 1993 of the party secretary of Daqiu Village, about 70 miles southeast of Beijing on the outskirts of Tianjin, highlighted on a miniature scale the problem of newly rich localities going their own way in defiance of Beijing. For years, the official media had been heaping praise on Daqiu for its astonishingly rapid transformation from dirt-poor backwater to the richest village in the country. Yu Zuomin, a semiliterate peasant who had been the village's party secretary since 1954 when he was in his mid-twenties, was hailed by the government as a hero. Yu decided in the early 1980s that the best way out of poverty was to develop industries rather than concentrate on farming as in the past. By 1992, Daqiu boasted no fewer than 280 enterprises ranging from real estate businesses to factories producing electronics and machinery. Some 60 of these were foreign-funded ventures. Its total output that year was officially valued at nearly $800 million. Yu himself was reputed to have amassed a personal fortune amounting to some $18 million. He wore Pierre Cardin suits and drove a Mercedes, as did several of his top aides. The other 4,500 permanent residents enjoyed the luxury of three-story apartment buildings with modern amenities and standards of living more in the style of the industrialized West than the rest of rural China.[21] This was the reformist version of the conservatives' Nanjie Village in Henan. No *Selected Works of Mao Zedong* or curbs on private ownership here. It was the embodiment of Dengist capitalism. Top leaders toured Yu's village and congratulated him wholeheartedly.

With fame and wealth came power and independence. After his eventual sentencing in August 1993 to 20 years in prison, the authorities revealed that Yu had effectively turned Daqiu Village into a private empire. After one of his cousins and six other villagers were arrested for beating a man to death in 1990, Yu organized more than 2,000 people to write letters to the court demanding the murderers' release.[22] He also arranged for donations to be made to the families of the killers, called meetings to denounce the man who was slain, and dismissed several relatives of the deceased from their jobs. Although Yu's actions must have caught the attention of the authorities, he clearly had high-level support. The official media said nothing. Then, in late 1992, Yu ordered an investigation into a village company he suspected of corrupt behavior. Instead of entrusting the job to the relevant authorities, Yu and his henchmen—including one of his sons—did the interrogating, turning a conference room into what Xinhua called "a clandestine court, equipped with video and audio recording equipment, electric truncheons, and whips."

Over a period of more than two weeks, about a dozen employees of the company were interrogated and detained. The suspects were kept in handcuffs, kicked, clubbed, and whipped. Some were stripped above the waist during interrogation in the bitterly cold room. Yu himself "flew into anger and slapped" one of the detainees. Under the party secretary's "instigation," a group of villagers brought one of the suspects into the conference room and demanded that he confess to having embezzled company funds. When he refused to do so, no fewer than 18 people stripped off the detainee's clothes, beat him with clubs, and whipped him "for seven hours without interruption." The victim later died in a clinic.

When the local police heard about the murder, they sent six officers to investigate. Yu, however, ordered that the officers themselves be detained. The police were clearly so worried about offending such a famous person that rather than sending a rescue party they arranged for the mayor of Tianjin himself to ask Yu to set the officers free. Xinhua said it was only after the mayor intervened that Yu ended the 13-hour confinement of the policemen.

It was widely rumored that Yu was on good terms with someone in the Politburo or even with Deng Xiaoping himself. Even if this was not true, it was undoubtedly an extreme embarrassment for the leadership to move against someone who was being held up as a model practitioner of Deng's reforms. It was therefore not until mid-February 1993, more than two months after the murder, that the authorities began to take decisive action. Official reports said the Tianjin authorities sent 400 paramilitary police to the village. To avoid confrontation, they kept at a distance, sending in a small team to try to persuade Yu to cooperate. But according to the official account, Yu "spread rumors" that more than 1,000 soldiers with "cannons, police dogs, tear gas bombs, and other weapons" had surrounded Daqiu. Yu summoned all the villagers to a meeting and told them to take a month off work with full pay and "take up arms to protect Daqiu Village." He gave out steel bars to be used as weapons and blocked the approach roads with trucks, tractors, carts, and oil tanks. Xinhua said he also "made secret arrangements" for the four main suspects in the murder case to flee.

After a few hours the troops withdrew, but the villagers kept up their barricades. A few days later, Yu did allow in a team of investigators from the Tianjin party committee—presumably believing that he himself was still immune. The Chinese leadership must indeed have been divided over how to handle the affair because Yu was allowed to attend the annual session of the National People's Congress in March. It was not until April 21st, five months after the murder, that he was finally arrested. Yu would not have gone as far as he did had he not believed he had top-level backing. But his showdown with hundreds of armed troops showed that he was prepared to do battle even when the political tide was turning against him. As Xinhua said Yu admitted, the "growth of wealth and fame had sent him dizzy and made him so arrogant and imperious that he indulged in going his own way and even went so far as to override state laws." Yu's was a more spectacular example of what was going on all over the country—officials who for decades had been following the party line losing their moorings in the race to get rich. As a rural party cadre, Yu was supposed to be part of the bedrock of the party structure. But as a result of Deng's reforms, that bedrock was fast crumbling.

"Some people familiar with Daqiu Village commented that there was no law in the village and what Yu Zuomin said was [equivalent to an] 'imperial edict,'" commented Xinhua. "Many people had been resentful of Yu's behavior. They called Daqiu 'a fortified village,' Yu Zuomin 'the chieftain,' and his second son Yu Shaozheng 'the junior chieftain.'" Heaping abuse on those out of political favor is, of course, part of China's political culture. But Xinhua's comment appeared to be close to the mark in Yu's case.

Extreme hard-liners were among the few who articulated the threat to political unity posed by the economic changes, but many Chinese intellectuals agreed with their analysis if not with their proposed remedies to the problem. In May 1994, the hard-line monthly journal *Pursuit of Truth* published one of the most strident warnings ever openly published on the potential dangers facing the country.[23] It said some senior party and government officials in the provinces were "going their own way, failing to carry out orders, ignoring bans, neglecting the overall national situation, and paying no attention to laws and regulations." If this continued, it said, "it would be very dangerous. Decentralization and regionalism would lead to separatism."[24] The journal said that even though people "posing as reformers" had dismissed the possibility that China's communist system might collapse as it had in the Soviet Union, there was a "considerable amount of social evidence" that China might follow "the same disastrous road" and "be destroyed overnight." The article said the privatization of state industries, the failure since 1989 to curb "bourgeois liberalization," inflation, corruption, and the growing gap between rich and poor were among the main potential causes of turmoil. It said the Tiananmen Square protests of 1989 were still "fresh in people's minds," and everyone wanted to preserve stability. But it reminded readers of Deng Xiaoping's assertion that one of the main causes of Tiananmen was the failure to uphold the basic principles of Chinese communism. In the five years since then, it said, what Deng had once described as the party's "greatest failing" during the reform years, namely, ideological education, had not been corrected.[25]

A study circulated by the Chinese Academy of Sciences in 1993 went further still, predicting that Deng's death could "in the worst-case scenario" lead to "a situation like post-Tito Yugoslavia," referring to increasing demands for economic and later political autonomy by the Croatians and Slovenes after the death of the Yugoslav leader in 1980.[26] In such a scenario, "within a few years—at the earliest within a decade and at the latest between 10 and 20 years—economic collapse would lead to political division and finally the disintegration of the country," said the 86-page report by a Chinese political scientist at Yale University and a researcher at the Chinese Academy of Sciences.

Writing before the introduction of the new center-province tax-sharing system in 1994, the authors said they were "extremely worried" about the declining share of the country's GDP that found its way into the central government's coffers. They predicted that the central government's revenue would drop from 7 percent of GDP in 1992 to 5 percent in the year 2000, a proportion they described as "equivalent to the financial strength of the central government under the Kuomintang in 1934, and even lower than the financial strength of the government of the former Yugoslavia before 1989." They said this meant the center was losing control over the economy and that this could have "extremely serious short- and long-term consequences." The early months of the new tax system did not appear to signal a dramatic reversal of this trend.[27] As one of the authors of the confidential study noted in a subsequent article, the central government's revenues in 1994 accounted for only about 6.5 percent of GDP, compared with more than 20 percent in the United States and 15 percent in India.[28] "China's central finance remains extremely weak and fragile, and its revenue has fallen to the lowest level in history," he said.

The Chinese Academy of Sciences report, which was distributed among senior government officials, observed that during negotiations between the provinces and the central government over economic policy, "it is often the provinces that gain more than they lose, while the center loses more than it gains." It said Chinese policy makers either "have not fully realized the danger of the central government's rapidly declining power, or they have realized it and have no effective way of halting the continuing downward trend." The central government's declining ability to control the economy, it said, was giving rise to "economic fiefdoms," trade protectionism, and economic blockades between provinces. "The economy is the foundation of the political system," said the authors. "Economic strength determines political strength. 'Economic fiefdoms' will weaken the political structure. The continuing decline of central authority and power is an important potential cause of the collapse of Chinese society and the breakup of the country. This must not be overlooked."

This grim analysis was not openly publicized in China, but one of the authors, the economist Hu Angang from the Chinese Academy of Sciences, delivered a similar if somewhat less explicit message through the official media. "Regional economic disparity is sure to have a serious effect on China's economic development and social stability," Hu was quoted as saying by the China News Service.[29] He pointed out that the per capita GDP of Shanghai was 7.4 times that of the southwestern province of Guizhou in 1991, rising to 8.4-fold in the following year. "In 1988, the regional disparity in Yugoslavia before its disintegration was seven- to eightfold. In comparison to China's condition, this should arouse the vigilance of the people concerned," said Hu, whose calls for stronger central government are believed to be well received among "neoconservatives" in the Chinese leadership.[30] China News Service said 84 percent of middle-ranking officials studying at the Central Party School surveyed by Hu believed that "an excessive disparity in regional economic development will affect China's social stability." The remainder supported either the view that the phenomenon would simply lead to "unfair social distribution" or, at the other extreme, to "the breakup of the country."[31]

In an article written for a Singapore newspaper, Hu described the anger felt by the leaders of relatively backward provinces over the taxation and other privileges enjoyed by the SEZs along the southern Chinese coast.[32] Hu noted how the SEZs of Shenzhen and Zhuhai had "taken to spending huge sums of money on barbed wire fences to prevent large populations of the poor from swarming in. The SEZs have virtually become nations within a nation, nations within a province." This he said was "a rare phenomenon in any part of the world, strictly forbidden in any industrialized country with a market economy." Hu said that in mid-June 1994, he addressed a group of some 30 top provincial officials at the Central Party School in Beijing and told them the SEZs should no longer receive preferential treatment. The response was "sensational," Hu said. "Many leaders said that I had expressed what they had always wanted to say but dared not. Leaders from underdeveloped regions said the SEZs were getting the best of both worlds, for they took cheap resources from underdeveloped regions and sold them at good prices, and imported products after little or no taxation to sell them at bargain prices. It seems that in China, reform means preferential policies, and market economy means SEZs. . . . What manner of market economy is this? Is it not one that is monopolized by the few? I do not see how it passes for fair competition. Such unfair trade drove everyone crazy. One leader from Zhejiang Province told me that they saw no reason why others could enjoy favorable policies while they could not." Ironically, Zhejiang is one of China's most prosperous regions.

Hu noted that the SEZs, however, had powerful backers who believed the zones should enjoy even more preferential terms so they could continue to play a role as a bridge to the outside world. He said supporters of this view belonged to "special interest groups" motivated purely by "self-interest," which he said were now emerging in China. The animosity Hu described between different parts of the country does not bode well for the country's future cohesiveness. If provinces are jealous of each other's economic advantages, they are likely to be equally so of each other's political advantages. When Hong Kong returns to China, it too could find itself the subject of interprovincial rivalry and jealousy.

Chinese officials also express concern about the widening economic gap between regions with large ethnic minority populations and the rest of the country. Many of China's ethnic minorities are concentrated in relatively remote and barren parts of the country, making it extremely difficult for them to keep pace with the rest of the country. In a 1994 survey of senior provincial officials responsible for ethnic minority issues,

Hu Angang found that most believed the gap would continue to grow in the coming decade and would pose a growing threat to social stability.[33] Nearly 70 percent of those surveyed said they believed that ethnic tensions would become "increasingly acute."

Even the casual foreign visitor to Tibet or to those parts of Xinjiang dominated by Turkic-speaking Muslims is likely to encounter some evidence of tension—whether in the form of unusually tight security in public meeting places or through occasional chance meetings with local residents seemingly desperate to convey their misgivings about life under Chinese rule. In other parts of China, dissatisfaction may be widespread but is rarely expressed openly to the non-Chinese-speaking foreigner who is not looking out for it. But in Tibet, foreign tourists are often approached in monasteries or temples by monks who whisper a few dissenting words in English. "Chinese, bad," muttered one young monk I met during my 10-day trip to Tibet in August 1994. "They do this," he said in English, gesturing toward some nearby policemen and grabbing my wrist as if arresting me. "We are oppressed. We want the Dalai Lama to come back," said a museum caretaker who drew me aside for a long conversation in English about the "oppression" of Tibet by the Chinese authorities. Frequent incidents like this, combined with reports of almost daily small-scale protests by monks or nuns in the center of Lhasa, suggest the region remains highly volatile. These protests are broken up by the police within minutes and the participants escorted to jail.

It is hard to imagine that ethnic unrest either in Tibet or Xinjiang will ever result in independence for those areas. For one thing, both regions, as well as the somewhat less volatile province of Inner Mongolia, are of enormous strategic significance to Beijing. For another, few members of the ethnic Han majority show any sympathy for the separatist movements among the minorities. Beijing can continue using heavy-handed methods to maintain control in the border regions without significantly affecting the public mood in the interior or, perhaps more importantly, exacerbating tensions within the ranks of the party. But the seeming futility of their cause will not deter supporters of independence from stepping up their campaign. In 1995, the authorities admitted that "the situation concerning splittism" in Tibet remained "grim" and that there had been an increasing number of "counterrevolutionary cases" in the region. In 1994, they said, 164 people were arrested in Tibet on charges of counterrevolution, an increase of more than 90 percent over the previous year.[34]

China today thus presents a paradox. It is a country achieving phenomenal growth whose citizens enjoy unprecedented economic freedom and which is playing an increasingly important role as a world power. Yet at the same time it is a country in growing disarray, deeply unsure of itself. Its leaders feel threatened both by the "hostile" West and by the slightest sign of open dissent at home. Yet China is now a major international trading nation whose brash new breed of self-confident executives wheel and deal on stock exchanges from Hong Kong to Wall Street and which attracts more investment from the capitalist West than any other developing country.

If the direction of China's development is confusing to the outside world, it is equally so to many Chinese. Many even look to natural phenomena such as floods and earthquakes for portents, an ancient form of superstition that thrives in times of uncertainty. Even many well-educated Chinese friends of mine appear to believe or at least half-believe that natural disasters are omens of impending change. Faith in this theory was strengthened in 1976 when the Tangshan earthquake, which left a quarter of a million people dead, was followed six weeks later by the death of Chairman Mao and within another month by the arrest of the Gang of Four. In late 1989, an official report revealed that frequent rumors of impending earthquakes had caused "serious damage" to production in recent years. It said such rumors were fueled partly by horrific memories of Tangshan and partly by "social and cultural" factors—an obvious reference to the superstitious link between natural disasters and political change. After the floods that swept over one-fifth of China's arable land in 1991, killing hundreds of people and affecting some 200 million others to varying degrees, many ordinary Chinese I met at the time talked with excitement about the political upheaval they felt must surely follow. Even the earthquake of January 1995 in the Japanese city of Kobe that left 5,500 dead caused some Beijing residents to speculate about possible upheaval in their own country in the near future, particularly given that it was only five days earlier that Deng Xiaoping's daughter had spoken so forthrightly to the *New York Times* about her father's declining health—an interview that many Chinese knew about thanks to foreign shortwave broadcasts.[35]

In February 1995, as speculation that Deng's death was imminent swept the country, the *People's Daily* itself tried to calm nerves, saying that the fact that an extra eighth month would be added to the Chinese lunar calendar later in the year was no cause for alarm. Leap eighth months have been inserted into the 12-month lunar calendar four times this century in order to bring it back into line with the solar calendar. The last time was in 1976, the year of the Tangshan earthquake and Mao's death. The preceding two occasions were in 1957—the year of the Anti-Rightist Campaign—and 1900, the year of the Boxer Rebellion and its suppression by an international invasion force. In Taiwan, where super-stition—and uncertainty about the future—is no less widespread than on the mainland, the publication in 1994 of a book entitled *The Leap Eighth Month of 1995* caused a considerable stir with its graphic account of how Deng's impending death and growing economic and social problems in China might trigger a military invasion of Taiwan.[36] The author sug-gested that September 1995 would be a particularly risky period because of the insertion of the extra lunar month at that time and the approach of Taiwan's first direct presidential elections in March 1996. Some 50,000 copies of the book were sold within six weeks.

In a similar vein is the book *Yellow Peril*.[37] This 500,000-word fan-tasy about China's collapse after Deng's death and the outbreak of nuclear civil war was written in China and smuggled out to Taiwan, where it was published in June 1991. Clandestinely produced photo-copies of the crudely written work were eagerly sought by Beijing intel-lectuals. Even though the book did not claim to be anything more than a work of fiction, some aspects of the scenario it presented sounded vaguely plausible to Chinese readers after the bewildering series of events in the Soviet Union and Eastern Europe.

In *Yellow Peril*, the party's general secretary decides after Deng's death to try to win back public support and attract Western economic aid by overturning the party's official assessment of the 1989 unrest. A hard-line general, however, angered by the government's stance, organizes the assassination of the party leader and seizes power. In order to protect their interests from being undermined by the new leader, the provinces of southeastern China declare independence, triggering a civil war between north and south. Taiwan's army joins in on the side of the south and comes close to taking over Beijing. The northern general retaliates by destroying Taipei with a nuclear missile and thereby regains control of the country. Taiwan, however, manages to buy its own nuclear weapons but fails in its attempt to destroy Beijing, hitting the Soviet Union instead. The Soviet Union—which still existed at the time the book was written—together with the United States responds by firing nuclear missiles at China's nuclear facilities and sending troops to arrest the general. In the chaos that follows, hundreds of millions of Chinese refugees flood Europe and North America. One of the general's supporters, however, fires 10 nuclear warheads at America from a submarine that escaped detection during the Soviet-U.S. attack. Washington assumes the missiles to be Soviet, and a nuclear war erupts between the two superpowers. In the end, the Chinese refugees form "self-salvation" groups that help restore order and democracy in the postholocaust world. Most of the book is completely implausible, but it plays successfully—to judge from the popularity in China of pirated copies—on widely and deeply felt fears of division and chaos.

On streetside bookstalls across China, the work of a Chinese Nostradamus entitled *Tui Bei Tu* is among the best-sellers of the mid-1990s. This seventh-century classic—long banned under communist rule—is supposed to contain clues to China's future conveyed through a series of 60 mostly surreal drawings, each accompanied by a few lines of equally obscure poetry. Across the centuries, the book has gained particular popularity during end-of-dynasty turmoil, with rebels using it to prophesy victory for their cause and thereby drum up public support. As the introduction to one mainland version of the book explains, *Tui Bei Tu* is "a way of shaping public opinion used by feudal rulers to seize power or consolidate power. It is also similarly used by oppressed people to overthrow their rulers."[38] A university-educated Chinese man in his twenties told me he was quite convinced by what he said was the ancient book's "prediction" that civil war would break out around the time of Hong Kong's return to Chinese rule. Not surprisingly, popular interpretations of the book do not place much credence in the long-term survival of communism.

In the mid-1990s, the outside world appeared to be undergoing one of its periodic mood swings in its assessment of China. The euphoria generated by Deng's southern tour had begun to dissipate as inflation soared, unemployment worsened, corruption spread, foreign investors complained about the untrustworthiness of their hosts, and Deng's death appeared imminent.

Symptomatic of this mood swing was a study commissioned by the U.S. Department of Defense in August 1994 on possible scenarios for China in the coming seven years.[39] Based on the assumption that Deng dies and no strong leader succeeds him, roughly half of the 17 American business analysts and academics involved in the study believed the transition would lead to the "breakup" of China in some fashion, with possibilities ranging from a period of unresolved factionalism at the center to greater regionalism to total collapse. Only one-third of the group believed China would remain much the way it was in 1994. The "liberal reform scenario" hoped for by Western powers was considered the least likely. The study did not exclude the possibility that one person might struggle for ultimate power after Deng's death but concluded that "this effort was doomed to failure and would become a pathway to collapse" and that only a "group leadership" could hold the system together.

Fifteen years before the Pentagon organized this study, some of the dissidents who took part in Beijing's Democracy Wall Movement were asking themselves much the same questions about China's future. In May 1979, a crudely mimeographed journal called the *Spring of Peking*—one of the most influential of the dissident publications of the time—published a short story called "The Tragedy of the Year 2000," the first political fantasy of its kind to appear since the communist takeover.[40] Wei Jingsheng, Democracy Wall's most outspoken activist, had been arrested two months earlier, but many intellectuals were still full of optimism about the new age of Deng Xiaoping. The short story's author, however, identified only by the pen name of Su Ming, sounded a note of caution. His story described how a top leader, whom the author does not name but who is clearly Deng, dies in 1998. In the subsequent year, several other leaders die under mysterious circumstances. Extreme hard-liners, who the author implies were actually responsible for the deaths, take control and try to reimpose orthodox Maoism. Crowds gather at Democracy Wall in protest, but the dissident movement is crushed by the authorities and the wall knocked down. A year later, however, in 2002, Beijing residents, among them a member of the Politburo, place flowers on the site. The story ends ambiguously, with party officials meeting in the Great Hall of the People surrounded by troops from a distant province.

The point of the story is that China's future is in the hands of individuals and that policy changes no matter how popular are no guarantee of long-term continuity. As a speaker at Democracy Wall declares in the year 2000, "People have to die sometime. The older generation of revolutionaries who lead us forward now will die sometime. Will these purely physiological changes threaten the great cause that has just been undertaken? Will these historic reforms be buried because of a struggle for power? It's not impossible." Fifteen years later, in the twilight days of the Deng era, the question remains just as valid, and the answer is no clearer.

My own reporting in China spanned the most tumultuous years thus far of the reform era as well as the years of greatest social and economic change in urban Chinese society since the Cultural Revolution. Bearing in mind the barriers to understanding these changes as outlined in the introduction to this book, my own prediction is that China in the early twenty-first century will be a country increasingly preoccupied with the uphill battle to maintain order and control. To achieve this, its leaders might well exaggerate external threats, making Chinese foreign policy increasingly unpredictable and threatening to the country's neighbors. I believe China will be a better place materially to live in for many millions of people, but it will also be a more dangerous one as crime rates continue to soar, riots erupt among the growing number of have-nots, and political uncertainties continue to hang over the nation. Foreign investors will find themselves in an ever more hazardous and unpredictable environment as central authority declines, corruption spreads, and each locality makes its own rules. But the temptations of the world's largest market will remain irresistible.

This book has focused on some of the fundamental problems the country faces in an era of economic and political transition. It will, I believe, take enormous political skill on the part of the post-Deng generation of leaders to prevent these problems from plunging the country into the turmoil that so many fear.

Notes

The abbreviation *SWB*, used throughout these notes, represents the BBC's *Summary of World Broadcasts*. To assist readers who might wish to refer to the original sources, I have used the Chinese titles of news agencies and periodicals cited. Their English translations are as follows:

Ban Yue Tan	*Fortnightly Chat*
Baokan Wenzhai	*Periodicals Digest*
Beijing Fazhi Bao	*Beijing Legal News*
Beijing Qingnian Bao	*Beijing Youth News*
Beijing Ribao	*Beijing Daily*
Cankao Ziliao	*Reference Materials*
Dangdai Sichao	*Contemporary Trends of Thought*
Dushu Zazhi	*Reading Magazine*
Fazhi Ribao	*Legal Daily*
Guangming Ribao	*Guangming Daily*
Henan Ribao	*Henan Daily*
Jiefang Ribao	*Liberation Daily*
Jiefangjun Bao	*Liberation Army Daily*
Jingji Ribao	*Economic Daily*
Jingjixue Zhoubao	*Economics Weekly*
Liaoning Ribao	*Liaoning Daily*
Liaowang	*Outlook*
Minzhu Yu Fazhi	*Democracy and Law*
Nanfang Zhoumo	*Southern Weekend*
Nongmin Ribao	*Peasants' Daily*
Qiushi	*Seeking Truth*
Renmin Gong'an Bao	*People's Security News*
Renmin Ribao	*People's Daily*
Renmin Ribao Haiwaiban	*People's Daily Overseas Edition*
Shanghai Fazhi Bao	*Shanghai Legal News*

Shenzhen Tequ Bao	*Shenzhen Special Zone News*
Shijie Jingji Daobao	*World Economic Herald*
Shoudu Jingji Xinxi Bao	*Capital Economic Information*
Weilai Yu Fazhan	*Future and Development*
Wenhui Bao	*Wenhui News*
Wenyi Bao	*Literature and Art News*
Wenzhai Bao	*Digest News*
Xin Guancha	*New Observer*
Xin Shiji	*New Century*
Xinmin Wanbao	*Xinmin Evening News*
Xizang Ribao	*Tibet Daily*
Yangcheng Wanbao	*Yangcheng Evening News*
Yuegang Xinxi Ribao	*Guangdong and Hong Kong Information Daily*
Zhenli de Zhuiqiu	*Pursuit of Truth*
Zhongguo Jiancha Bao	*China Procuratorate News*
Zhongguo Qingnian Bao	*China Youth News*
Zhongguo Tongxun She	China News Agency
Zhongguo Xinwen She	China News Service
Zhonghua Gongshang Bao	*China Business Times*
Zhonghua Yingcai	*China's Talents*
Zhongliu	*Midstream*
Zugong Tongxun	*Organization Workers' Newsletter*

Introduction

1. By August 1995 there were 12 outlets in Beijing and 40 nationwide.

2. See *Hong Kong in China: Real Estate in the Economy* by Anthony Walker (Hong Kong: Brooke Hillier Parker, 1995).

3. "Talks in Wuhan, Shenzhen, Zhuhai, and Shanghai," *Selected Works of Deng Xiaoping,* vol. 3 (Beijing: Foreign Languages Press, 1994), 368.

4. "Long March to the Market: Deng Xiaoping, China's Reformist Leader, Is the FT's Man of the Year," *Financial Times,* December 29th, 1992.

5. The Foreign Ministry rarely gives explicit reasons for turning down an application, but officials usually drop clear enough hints in private. My wife, Catherine Sampson, was a victim of this selection process. Having worked in Beijing for five years as the correspondent of *The Times* of London, she was offered a new job as the *Guardian's* correspondent. Having surrendered her accreditation for *The Times,* however, she was unable to get Foreign Ministry approval to write for the *Guardian.* Officials made it clear that this was in retaliation for her "unfair" reporting as well as for the editorial stance of *The Times.* She managed to continue writing for other publications using pseudonyms, but it was more than a year before *The Times* was able to send in a new correspondent to succeed her. The poor state of Sino-British relations and London's disinclination to take up the issue with the Chinese government did not help in this case. By contrast,

the former *Washington Post* correspondent in Beijing, Lena Sun, was allowed to continue working in China even after the police had discovered "secret" documents in her apartment. Beijing's fear of Washington's reaction undoubtedly restrained China from expelling her.

6. Between August and November 1991, my wife and I maintained a list of the license plate numbers of our followers. We counted 26 unmarked cars and motorcycles, some of which we spotted on more than one occasion. The cars used for the purpose would often be black sedans and would always contain at least three people, including the driver. The vehicle would try to keep two or three other cars between itself and our car to avoid detection. On a long journey across the city, several vehicles would be assigned to tail us, with each covering a particular sector of the city before handing over to the next. The purpose of our journey made no difference. We were often followed even to official briefings. The aim appeared to be to intimidate. Although the followers themselves never physically intervened to prevent us from meeting someone, Chinese contacts of foreign journalists would occasionally be approached by police or by officials in their work units and warned not to have dealings with correspondents.

7. "More Chinese Counties Open to Foreigners," Xinhua News Agency, May 9th, 1995. The report gives the total number of open cities and counties *(xian)* as 1,176.

8. According to the "internal" *(neibu)* Chinese police handbook, *Gong'an Neiqin Gongzuo Shouce,* edited by Zhen Yuegang and Guan Shuguang (Beijing: Jingguan Jiaoyu Chubanshe, 1993), the top three levels of classification are, in descending order, *"juemi"* (top secret), *"jimi"* (secret), and *"mimi"* (confidential or secret). The normal period after which secrets in these categories become declassified is 30 years, 20 years, and 10 years, respectively. The manual says the *mimi* category should include figures for the number of people arrested and in labor camps, unless a decision has been made to publicize them. It says some secrets can remain classified longer than the normal periods, such as "counterrevolutionary incidents and statistics concerning such incidents that have not been made public" and "details concerning the handling of riots or acts of rebellion that it would be improper to reveal."

Chapter 1

Epigraph from "Zhongguo Yongyuan Bu Yunxu Bie Guo Ganshe Neizheng," *Deng Xiaoping Wenxuan,* vol. 3 (Beijing: Renmin Chubanshe, 1993), 361. Deng was talking to Pierre Elliott Trudeau, the former prime minister of Canada. For stylistic reasons, I have used my own translation here rather than the official English version.

1. In mid-1995, dozens of dissidents in Beijing signed petitions calling for a reevaluation of the Tiananmen Square protests. At the other end of the political spectrum, the extreme hard-line journal *Zhongliu (Midstream)* in its June 1995 edition attacked the failed attempt five years earlier by dissidents overseas and

their supporters to broadcast news about their movement from the *Goddess of Democracy* radio ship. *Zhongliu* described the attempt as a "repercussion of the bankrupt political rebellion" of 1989 (" 'Minzhu Nu Shen' Jiu Bu Liao Fan Gong Qijian," *Zhongliu*, June 1995, p. 45). Though its circulation is small, *Zhongliu* is housed in the offices of *Guangming Ribao*, one of China's leading official newspapers. Its backers are believed to be a group of ultraconservatives, mainly consisting of officials working in propaganda and cultural departments or who have retired from such posts.

2. The party's fears of reopening the wounds of Tiananmen were evident after the forced resignation in April 1995 of the Politburo member and Communist Party secretary of Beijing, Chen Xitong, who was later placed under investigation for his alleged involvement in corrupt activities. As mayor of Beijing during the Tiananmen Square protests, Chen played a prominent role in the suppression of the unrest. Many Chinese wondered whether Chen's disgrace might signal a change of heart by the leadership over the 1989 demonstrations. Chen's successor, Wei Jianxing, however, was careful to put a stop to such rumors. In a speech published on June 30th, 1995—just four days before the announcement that formal investigations into Chen's activities were underway—Wei noted the "outstanding contributions" made by the Beijing municipal leadership in "stopping the turmoil and quelling the counterrevolutionary rebellion of 1989" ("Jin Yi Bu Jiaqiang he Gaijin Dang de Jianshe Ba Beijing Shi Gaige Kaifang he Xiandaihua Jianshe Shiye Jixu Tui Xiang Qianjin," *Beijing Ribao*). This rare mention of the unrest by a top official was clearly intended as a forceful reminder that as far as Tiananmen was concerned, nothing had changed. It remains to be seen whether, after Deng's death, Chen and possibly his onetime backer Li Peng are made scapegoats for Tiananmen. One plausible scenario is that they might be blamed for having misinformed Deng about the nature of the protests, thus absolving Deng of some of the responsibility. For more on Chen's resignation and subsequent dismissal from the Politburo and Central Committee, see chapters 5 and 9.

3. The KMT, or Nationalist Party, ruled the Chinese mainland from 1911 to 1949 and continues to hold power in Taiwan.

4. The official tally is 3,000 civilians wounded and more than 200 killed. The government also says more than 6,000 security personnel were injured and several dozen killed. These figures are undoubtedly conservative, but the real number of dead and injured may never be known. There are strong arguments in support of figures ranging from 400 to 2,600 for the number of people killed. Chinese Red Cross sources quoted by the Japanese news agency Kyodo on June 4th, 1989, said the death toll was 2,600. The Chinese Red Cross, however, denied this figure as "sheer fabrication" in a report by Xinhua News Agency on June 15th. The *New York Times* correspondent Nicholas D. Kristof, who has devoted much attention to this issue, says he believes that between 400 and 800 civilians died. His arguments are contained in "A Reassessment of How Many Died in the Military Crackdown in Beijing" (*New York Times*, June 20th, 1989). Amnesty

International reported in August 1989 that it believed more than 1,300 people had been killed in Beijing.

5. The initial student death toll given was 23. A month later it was revised to 36. Such a precise figure for the numbers of other civilians or security personnel killed has never been revealed.

6. "Today's Cultural News Briefs: Monument Unveiled," Xinhua News Agency, June 4th, 1990.

7. Xinhua News Agency, December 8th, 1990. *SWB* FE/0944/B2.

8. Jiang was speaking in an interview with Barbara Walters of ABC's *20/20* program. Xinhua quoted Jiang as telling Walters that after the crackdown on the unrest, there was "some lack of understanding of or unfriendly attitude toward China. To use a Chinese proverb, it can be described as 'much ado about nothing.'" ("CPC General Secretary Jiang Zemin's Interview with ABC Anchorwoman," Xinhua News Agency, May 24th, 1990.)

9. Li Peng was addressing a news conference at the annual session of the National People's Congress in April 1990. The full text of his remarks can be found in *SWB* FE/0733/C2.

10. Amnesty International and some news reports said that 300 people were killed when the police intervened to stop the demonstrations in Chengdu. I have found no evidence to support such a large figure and am inclined to believe estimates of around 20 people killed.

11. Details of these provincial demonstrations are difficult to confirm since there were very few journalists reporting on events at the time from cities other than Beijing, Shanghai, and Canton. These accounts are based partly on official descriptions of what happened in the provinces, for example, *Liang Xin Dong Po de 56 Tian,* edited by Leng Quanqing and Miao Sufei (Beijing: Da Di Chubanshe, 1989).

12. Yuan Mu was speaking to Chinese journalists on June 6th, 1989. The full text can be found in *SWB* FE/0477/B2.

13. *SWB* FE/0469/B2.

14. "Beijing Children Celebrate International Children's Day," Xinhua News Agency, June 1st, 1989.

15. The statement issued on June 5th in the name of Mayor Chen Xitong was important too, but his failure to appear in person was a telling sign of continuing political uncertainty. After an event of such magnitude as the June 4th bloodshed, a confident government would have been far quicker to assert its authority in the form of visible leadership.

16. The White House press secretary Marlin Fitzwater was speaking to reporters in Washington. See "Army Units Said to Clash in Beijing," United Press International, June 6th, 1989.

17. "We Can Handle China's Affairs Well," *Selected Works of Deng Xiaoping,* vol. 3, 315.

18. *Deng Xiaoping Wenxuan,* vol. 3, 360–61.

19. "Address to Officers of the Troops," *Selected Works of Deng Xiaoping,* vol. 3, 294.

20. "Talks in Wuchang, Shenzhen, Zhuhai, and Shanghai," *Selected Works of Deng Xiaoping,* vol. 3, 368.

21. In his speech to the Fifth Plenum of the 13th Central Committee, November 1989.

22. Yang Shangkun was succeeded as president by Jiang Zemin on March 27th, 1993.

23. By the time of President Yang's retirement in 1993, China-watchers had reached a very different verdict on his political outlook—seeing him as a reformist rather than a conservative. This about-face highlights the problem with using such labels. In the face of the challenge to their rule posed by the demonstrators in 1989, some "reformist" leaders turned "hard-line," Deng and Yang Shangkun among them. In this book, I use "hard-line" to refer to those who place far greater emphasis on the dangers of "bourgeois liberalization" than Deng normally would and who have strong reservations about the pace and scope of Deng's economic reforms.

24. Zhongguo Xinwen She, May 22nd, 1989. *SWB* FE/0464/B2. The news agency said the contents of the letter were broadcast in Tiananmen Square. Demonstrators had set up their own public address system on the plaza.

25. See, for example, Nicholas D. Kristof, "Standoff Persists in Beijing; 7 Top Ex-Commanders Warn Army Must Not Enter City," *New York Times,* May 23rd, 1989.

26. "Court-Martialed Chinese General Said to Be Pardoned," Reuters, July 24th, 1990.

27. Zhongguo Xinwen She, November 12th, 1989. *SWB* FE/0614/B2.

28. *Jiefangjun Bao,* quoted by Reuters, February 13th, 1990, "China Says Enemies Want Control of Army."

29. "Address to Officers of the Troops," *Selected Works of Deng Xiaoping,* vol. 3, 295.

30. "Zhao Ziyang on Combating Bourgeois Liberalization," Xinhua News Agency, March 25th, 1987.

31. Bo Yibo, a permanent vice chairman of the Central Party Rectification Guidance Commission, revealed on May 26th, 1987, that 33,896 party members had been formally expelled and another 90,069 not allowed to reregister during the three-and-a-half-year "rectification campaign." The party then had some 44 million members (*SWB* FE/8584/B2).

32. Document Number 10 also gave details of how to determine whether a party member should be refused permission to reregister. At the top of the list were "those who spread or advocated bourgeois liberal thinking or opposed the four basic principles [of Chinese communism] and had not corrected their mistakes." Also to be rejected were "those who opposed the party center's policies and decisions concerning the stopping of the turmoil and the suppression of the

counterrevolutionary rebellion and who failed to change their minds after receiving education." These extracts come from the journal *Zugong Tongxun* circulated by the party's Organization Department on May 24th, 1990, in an article entitled "Dangyuan Dengji Gongzuo Zuotanhui Jiyao." The journal is classified "internal" *(neibu)*.

33. The head of the party's Organization Department, Lu Feng, used this figure in the confidential version of a speech he made on June 30th, 1990, carried in the July 9th edition of *Zugong Tongxun*. The summary of his speech, published by Xinhua News Agency (*SWB* FE/0807/B2), omitted the figure.

34. "Dangyuan Dengji Gongzuo Zuotanhui Jiyao," *Zugong Tongxun*, February 24th, 1990.

35. From party sources interviewed by the author.

36. From "Zhongyang Lingdao Tongzhi Guanyu zai Bufen Danwei Jinxing Dangyuan Chongxin Dengji de Zhongyao Jianghua he Pishi," *Zugong Tongxun*, March 25th, 1990.

37. "Zhao Zongnai Tongzhi Tan Jinyibu Zuohao Dangyuan Chongxin Dengji Gongzuo," *Zugong Tongxun*, April 12th, 1990. Zhao Zongnai was speaking as the deputy head of the party's Organization Department.

38. "Fangzhi he Jiuzheng Zuzhi Chuli Pian Kuan de Qingxiang," *Zugong Tongxun*, August 27, 1990.

39. "Jinyibu Gaohao Ganbu Kaocha Gongzuo, Qieshi Jiaqiang Geji Lingdao Banzi Jianshe," *Zugong Tongxun*, March 6th, 1990.

40. "Tiananmen Square Dissident Vows to Fight on Just Hours after Release," Deutsche Presse-Agentur, June 19th, 1995.

41. "Jiang Qing Commits Suicide," Xinhua News Agency, June 4th, 1991. The brief announcement read, in part, "Jiang Qing, principal criminal of the case of Lin Biao-Jiang Qing counterrevolutionary clique, committed suicide and died in her residence in Beijing in the early hours of May 14th, 1991, Xinhua learned from related sources. Jiang Qing was sentenced to death with two years' reprieve and was deprived of all political rights for life in January 1981 by a special tribunal under the Supreme People's Court. In January 1983 she was resentenced to life imprisonment. Since May 4th, 1984, she had remained out of custody and obtained medical treatment."

The fact that Jiang Qing had been free for the last seven years of her life was, until Xinhua's belated announcement of her death, one of Beijing's best-kept secrets.

42. Bao Tong is due for release on May 28th, 1996.

43. See *Wenhua Dageming Shi Nian Shi*, Yan Jiaqi (Tianjin: Tianjin Renmin Chubanshe, 1986), 634–35.

44. Jiang Chunyun (Shandong Communist Party secretary), "Gongchandangyuan Yao Jiang Yuanze Shifei," *Zugong Tongxun*, December 31st, 1990. Jiang was promoted to the Politburo in 1992.

45. See chapter 3.

46. For a more detailed discussion of these problems, see chapters 4–7.

47. See *Wang Juntao Qi Ren, Qi Yan, Qi "Zui,"* Wang Juntao and Hou Xiaotian (Hong Kong: Dangdai Yuekan, 1992), 47.

Chapter 2

Epigraph from "We Are Confident That We Can Handle China's Affairs Well," *Selected Works of Deng Xiaoping,* vol. 3, 315–16. Deng was speaking to the American physicist Tsung-dao Lee of Columbia University.

1. *Ta Kung Pao,* June 4th, 1989. *SWB* FE/0474/B2.

2. *Beijing Ribao,* quoted by Reuters, October 8, 1989, "Hungary Gives Up Communism, China Proclaims Its Victory."

3. *Deng Xiaoping* (Beijing: Zhongyang Wenxian Chubanshe, 1988), 226.

4. "Romanian President Given Red Carpet Welcome in China," Reuters, October 7th, 1985.

5. "Qi'aosaiseku he Mengbotuo Biaoshi Zhichi Zhongguo Pingxi Fan'geming Baoluan," *Renmin Ribao,* September 23rd, 1989.

6. "Quan Li Fazhan Luo Zhong Youhao Hezuo Guanxi; Luomaniya Jianchi Shehuizhuyi Yuanze," *Renmin Ribao,* November 18th, 1989.

7. *Reference Materials (Cankao Ziliao)* is available, by subscription, to government departments and state-controlled units at the county level and above. The bulletin states that "the extent of circulation (within such departments) is to be decided by each unit according to work requirements on the basis that rules concerning the protection of secrets not be violated." It is classified "internal" *(neibu)*.

8. "Bulgaria to Further Socialist Reform," Xinhua News Agency, November 28th, 1989.

9. "Chinese Party Delegation Leaves Bulgaria for Home," Xinhua News Agency, December 2nd, 1989.

10. It never became clear why the jamming was not more effective. Perhaps it was simply too expensive to block every signal in a country as large as China. This was China's first ever attempt at jamming foreign radio stations, a task that requires transmitters as powerful as those beaming in the unwanted signal. In Mao's day, jamming was unnecessary since very few Chinese had access to short-wave radios and anyone who was caught listening to Western radio stations could be imprisoned. But in Deng's China, before 1989, very few efforts were made to stop people listening to foreign stations, except through negative publicity in the official media. One dissident in Sichuan showed me an official document that, among other things, accused him of having listened to "reactionary enemy stations" such as the BBC in 1989, but this was cited as one of several of his transgressions and apparently did not, unlike in Mao's day, constitute sufficient grounds in itself for punishment. Many people I met in the cities, including officials, relied more on the BBC and VOA than their own domestic media for news of events abroad as well as in China.

11. "Chinese Ordered to Carry ID Cards, Learn 40 Slogans," Reuters, September 10th, 1989. Wang Fang's remarks were quoted by *Fazhi Ribao*, September 9th, 1989.

12. "Beijing Protesters Beaten, Arrested; Demonstrators Proclaim Solidarity with Democracy Movement," *Washington Post*, December 14th, 1989.

13. "Qi'aosaisiku Fangwen Yilang," *Renmin Ribao*, December 21st, 1989.

14. "Qi'aosaisiku Huyu Quan Guo Tuanjie," *Renmin Ribao*, December 22nd, 1989.

15. The Xinhua story was published in *Renmin Ribao*, December 24th, 1989, under the headline "Luo Shoudu Bujialeisite Xianru Yanzhong Hunluan."

16. "Luo Dianshitai Xuanbu Luo Tebie Junshi Fating Panchu Qi'aosaisiku Sixing," *Renmin Ribao*, December 27th, 1989.

17. "China Expresses Concern to Soviets; Steps Up Security," United Press International, December 28th, 1989.

18. Xinhua News Agency, December 27th, 1989. *SWB* FE/0650/B2.

19. "With Stable Policies of Reform and Opening to the Outside World, China Can Have Great Hopes for the Future," *Selected Works of Deng Xiaoping*, vol. 3, 311.

20. *Ching Chi Jih Pao*, December 11th, 1989. *SWB* FE/0640/B2. The newspaper often reflects Chinese Communist Party thinking.

21. Li Peng was speaking to reporters at the end of a visit to Bangladesh, November 19th, 1989.

22. Beijing Television, May 26th, 1989. *SWB* FE/0468/B2.

23. In an interview with the Beijing correspondent of the *New York Times*, Patrick Tyler ("Deng's Daughter Opens a Long-Shut Door," *New York Times*, January 12th, 1995).

24. "Deng Xiaoping: Policies of Reform, Opening Won't Change," Xinhua News Agency, September 16th, 1989.

25. "We Are Confident That We Can Handle China's Affairs Well," *Selected Works of Deng Xiaoping*, vol. 3, 314.

26. The Fifth Plenum of the 13th Central Committee, November 6–9, 1989.

27. "China Can Have Great Hopes for the Future," *Selected Works of Deng Xiaoping*, vol. 3, 305 ff.

28. "Speech at First Session of CPC Advisory Commission," ibid., 17.

29. My translation. See *Deng Xiaoping Wenxuan*, vol. 3, 315.

30. Deng was speaking in the presence of foreign reporters.

31. Quoted by Reuters, February 8th, 1990, "Sino-Soviet Ideological Split Widens."

32. The following details of these documents were given to the author by Chinese sources.

33. "The International Situation and Economic Problems," *Selected Works of Deng Xiaoping*, vol. 3, 341 ff.

34. Author's sources.

35. "We Are Confident That We Can Handle China's Affairs Well," *Selected Works of Deng Xiaoping*, vol. 3, 315–16.

36. "We Must Adhere to Socialism and Prevent Peaceful Evolution Toward Capitalism," ibid., 333.

37. See *China to 2000; Reform's Last Chance*, by Simon Long (London: The Economist Intelligence Unit, May 1992), 74.

38. The Sixth Plenum of the 13th Central Committee, March 9–12, 1990.

39. Quoted by Xinhua News Agency, March 13th, 1990. *SWB* FE/0713/B2.

40. *Renmin Ribao Haiwaiban*, November 17th, 1989. *SWB* FE/0619/B2.

41. "On Opposing Bourgeois Liberalization," *Qiushi*, February 15th, 1990. Broadcast by Central People's Broadcasting Station, February 14th, 1990. *SWB* FE/0690/B2.

42. *Jingji Ribao*, November 3rd, 1989. *SWB* FE/0616/B2.

43. *Wen Wei Po*, October 6th, 1989. *SWB* FE/0583/B2.

44. *Xu Jiatun Xianggang Huiyilu*, by Xu Jiatun (Hong Kong: Lianhe Bao, 1993), 436. Xu said Jiang and Li argued for the clampdown at the Fifth Plenum of early November. A lot of people at the subsequent November 10th meeting of the Central Advisory Commission, of which Xu was a member, expressed private reservations about the two leaders' speeches, he said.

45. A rare public mention of the new regulation appeared in *Beijing Ribao* on November 24th, 1989. The newspaper said that at a meeting held on the previous day, the Beijing party secretary Li Ximing had announced the decision to bar heads of privately owned companies and entrepreneurs who "exploited" their employees from joining the party in the city.

46. "Guanyu Buneng Xishou Siying Qiyezhu Rudang Youguan Wenti de Wenda," *Zugong Tongxun*, March 22nd, 1990.

47. "Yingdang Jiji Xuanchuan Zhongyang Guanyu Buneng Xishou Siying Qiyezhu Rudang de Youguan Guiding," *Zugong Tongxun*, April 28th, 1990.

48. Chen Xitong was speaking to foreign and Chinese journalists at a news conference on March 7th, 1990—the first given by Chen since Tiananmen to which the overseas media were invited.

49. Xinhua News Agency, August 5th, 1990. *SWB* FE/0838/B2.

50. A copy of the document, marked "secret" *(jimi)*, was shown to the author by a Chinese source.

51. *Renmin Ribao*, October 7th, 1990.

52. *Beijing Ribao*, October 7th, 1990.

53. From the author's sources.

54. *Renmin Ribao*, quoted by Reuters, February 1st, 1991, "China Says Gulf War Exposes U.S. Bias Against Blacks."

55. "Jiang Zemin on Bolstering the Party's Theoretical Work," Xinhua News Agency, June 15th, 1991.

56. The swiftness of Xinhua's response aroused speculation among foreign observers that China might have been warned of the coup in advance. This rumor

was fueled by the fact that less than two weeks before the attempted coup, China's chief of general staff, Chi Haotian, held two meetings in Moscow with the Soviet Defense Minister Dmitri Yazov who later became one of the eight members of the State Committee for the State of Emergency, as the coup leaders described themselves. There is no firm evidence to suggest that the rumor was true.

57. "Review Your Experience and Use Professionally Trained People," *Selected Works of Deng Xiaoping,* vol. 3, 356–57.

58. "Guanyu Fan Heping Yanbian de Ruogan Sikao," *Dangdai Sichao,* August 20th, 1991.

59. "Correctly Understand the Situation of the Sudden Coup in the Soviet Union and Urgently Carry Out the Task of Party Construction." A copy was shown to the author by a Chinese source.

Chapter 3

Epigraph from "The 'Deng Whirlwind' Fills China with Vitality," *Beijing Review,* February 7–20, 1994.

1. *Zuoqing Ershi Nian,* edited by Yuan Yongsong and Wang Junwei (Beijing: Nongcun Duwu Chubanshe, 1993).

2. On January 28th, 1992, *Wen Wei Po* gave details of Deng's views on the media coverage of his activities following his retirement. It said that when he stepped down, Deng "proposed that he not meet foreign dignitaries again nor allow the mainland's mass media to report on his activities. . . . The practice of abolishing the lifelong tenure of leading posts for cadres is an important content of the reform of China's political system, its impact on history will be very profound, and it will be a great contribution to the promotion of China's advancement. The abolition of lifelong tenure of leading posts for cadres is a big thing, therefore Deng Xiaoping is very serious about not allowing the mainland's mass media to report on his activities." *SWB* FE/1290/B2 .

3. Whether Deng directly ordered that they be published, or whether, as some Hong Kong accounts had it, one of his daughters did so on her father's behalf is not known.

4. "Gaige Kaifang Yao You Xin Silu," *Jiefang Ribao,* March 2nd, 1991.

5. *Renmin Ribao,* December 17th, 1990, quoted in *Fang "Zuo" Beiwanglu,* edited by Zhao Shilin (Taiyuan: Shuhai Chubanshe, 1992), 50. Hard-liners tried to restrict circulation of this book, known in English as *Memorandum on Preventing Leftism,* which contains essays by several prominent liberal intellectuals attacking conservative viewpoints.

6. "Guangda Kaifang de Yishi Yao Geng Qiang Xie," *Jiefang Ribao,* March 22nd, 1991.

7. The Seventh Plenum of the 13th Central Committee, December 25–30, 1990. The plenum's main purpose was to discuss the eighth five-year plan, which

was to come into effect in 1991, as well as a development strategy for the coming decade. The plenum was repeatedly delayed, apparently because of the leadership's failure to reach consensus on the contents of the new plan. On December 24th, 1990, at a meeting with top leaders, Deng expressed satisfaction with the final compromise, but nevertheless the plenum failed to deliver a strongly proreform message.

8. "China Can Have Great Hopes for the Future," *Selected Works of Deng Xiaoping,* vol. 3, 307.

9. "Seize the Opportunity to Develop the Economy," *Selected Works of Deng Xiaoping,* vol. 3, 351. Deng himself did not attend the meeting. He did, however, make a public appearance during it, on December 26th, when he cast his vote in the Beijing municipal elections. Chinese television showed one of his daughters holding Deng's elbow as he walked slowly up to a table to receive his ballot form at a polling booth in Zhongnanhai, the party and government headquarters. He had obvious difficulty marking the paper, and his hand shook as he walked over to the ballot box with a fixed smile on his face. He then muttered the words, "that's that."

10. *Jiefang Ribao,* April 12th, 1991, *SWB* FE/1049/B2.

11. Chinese sources interviewed by the author.

12. "Gaige Kaifang Keyi Bu Wen Xing 'She' Xing 'Zi' Ma?" *Dangdai Sichao,* April 20th, 1991.

13. "*People's Daily* Editorial Calls for Further Reform," Xinhua News Agency, September 1st, 1991.

14. Quoted in *Lishi de Chaoliu,* edited by Liu Yaguang (Beijing: Zhongguo Renmin Daxue Chubanshe, 1992), 152. The banning of this controversial book, known in English as *Historical Trends,* is referred to later in this chapter.

15. The party was actually founded on July 23rd, 1921. But in 1941 when the party decided to celebrate the 20th anniversary of its founding, party leaders were unable amid the chaos of the anti-Japanese war to verify the exact date of the 1st Congress, which involved a mere 12 people. July 1st was therefore chosen as the best estimate. It was only after the establishment of the People's Republic in 1949 that the real date was discovered, but July 1st has remained the official anniversary.

16. Published in advance by Xinhua News Agency, July 18th, 1991. *SWB* FE/1129/B2.

17. Xinhua News Agency, September 24th, 1991. *SWB* FE/1188/B2.

18. China Central Television, October 9th, 1991. *SWB* FE/1200/C1.

19. "Zhengque Renshi Shehuizhuyi Shehui de Maodun, Zhangwo Chuli Maodun de Zhudong Quan," *Dangdai Sichao,* December 20th, 1991.

20. The Eighth Plenum of the 13th Central Committee, November 25–29, 1991.

21. See also *The Private Life of Chairman Mao,* by Li Zhisui (New York: Random House, 1994), 533–41.

22. *Fang "Zuo" Beiwanglu,* op. cit., 438.

23. The exact date of Deng's departure is not given in official accounts.

24. *Dachao Xinqi: Deng Xiaoping Nanxun Qianqian Houhou,* edited by Yu Xiguang, Li Liangdong et al. (Beijing: Zhongguo Guangbo Dianshi Chuban She, 1992), 181–82. Chinese sources told me that this account of Deng's southern tour and its aftermath, known in English as *Resurgence of the Spring Tide: The Inside Story of Deng's Southern Tour,* was also attacked by hard-liners who ordered bookshops not to stock it on the grounds that it contained typographical errors. The sources said the book's contents, however, were based mainly on information provided by Deng's office.

25. *Fang "Zuo" Beiwanglu,* op. cit., 107.

26. Zhongguo Tongxun She, November 25th, 1990. *SWB* FE/0932/B2.

27. Xinhua News Agency, July 22nd, 1992. *SWB* FE/1445/B2.

28. See "Make a Success of Special Economic Zones and Open More Cities to the Outside World," *Selected Works of Deng Xiaoping,* vol. 3, 61–62. Deng says of the proposed new open cities, "We wouldn't call them SEZs, but policies similar to those in the zones could be pursued there."

29. "Dongfang Feng Lai Man Yan Chun: Deng Xiaoping Tongzhi zai Shenzhen Jishi," *Shenzhen Tequ Bao,* March 26th, 1992. No foreign reporters were on hand to witness the scene.

30. *Ming Pao,* January 21st, 1992. *SWB* FE/1286/B2.

31. *SWB* FE/1285/B2.

32. For example, *Dachao Xinqi: Deng Xiaoping Nanxun Qianqian Houhou,* op. cit., 105–24, and "Deng Xiaoping Wei He Chongshen Fan 'Zuo?'" in the Beijing-controlled Hong Kong magazine *Bauhinia* (April 1992).

33. *Dachao Xinqi,* op. cit., 107.

34. Ibid.

35. Ibid., 106.

36. Zhongguo Tongxun She, September 6th, 1991. *SWB* FE/1172/B2.

37. *Guangming Ribao,* November 26th, 1991. *SWB* FE/1260/B2.

38. "Deng Xiaoping Wei He Chongshen Fan 'Zuo?'" *Bauhinia,* April 1992.

39. *Yangcheng Wanbao,* February 7th, 1992. *SWB* FE/1310/B2.

40. Xinhua News Agency, January 28th, 1992. *SWB* FE/1291/B2.

41. *Wen Wei Po,* January 31st, 1992. *SWB* FE/1292/B2. In his closing address at the 11th Party Congress in August 1977, when he was engaged in a struggle with Maoists led by Hua Guofeng, the then party vice chairman Deng Xiaoping had similarly told delegates, "there must be less empty talk and more hard work."

42. *Wen Wei Po,* January 28th, 1992. *SWB* FE/1290/B2.

43. *Shenzhen Tequ Bao,* March 26th, 1992. *SWB* FE/1345/B2.

44. *Wen Wei Po,* February 14th, 1992. *SWB* FE/1306/B2.

45. Ibid.

46. *Wen Wei Po,* January 28th, 1992. *SWB* FE/1290/B2.

47. This and the following quotations are taken from "Talks in Wuchang, Shenzhen, Zhuhai, and Shanghai," *Selected Works of Deng Xiaoping,* vol. 3, 358 ff. The official English translation omits the word *surnamed,* but the phrase Deng uses in Chinese clearly alludes to the "surnamed socialist or surnamed capitalist" debate that had been raging in the official press in the months preceding his trip.

48. According to the *World Development Report 1994* published by the World Bank, Hong Kong's per capita income in 1992 was $15,360. Britain's was $17,790.

49. Deng was clearly sensitive to possible criticisms of his strategy on the grounds that he was advocating another Mao-style Great Leap Forward. During his southern tour, Deng defended the period of rapid economic growth between 1984 and 1988, which had been attacked by hard-liners as inflationary and destabilizing. "What should be our overall assessment of the accelerated development in those five years?" Deng asked. "We might call it a leap, but unlike the 'Great Leap Forward' of 1958 it did not harm the structure and mechanisms of economic development as a whole. In my opinion, the accelerated development of that period was no small contribution." Hard-liners, however, had a very different assessment. A journal under their control, *Zhenli de Zhuiqiu (Pursuit of Truth),* argued in its June 1995 edition (p. 6) that the "overheating" that began in 1984 and again in 1992 was a manifestation of leftism, which it defined as striving for unrealistic targets. The implication was that it was Deng who was the leftist and not the hard-liners.

50. March 9–10, 1992.

51. *Shenzhen Tequ Bao,* March 12th, 1992.

52. "Fan Qingxiang de Zhongdian Gao Cuo le Hui Fan Chuan," *Dangdai Sichao,* February 20th, 1992.

53. "Dongfang Feng Lai Man Yan Chun: Deng Xiaoping Tongzhi zai Shenzhen Jishi," *Shenzhen Tequ Bao,* March 26th, 1992.

54. *Wen Wei Po,* February 18th, 1992. *SWB* FE/1310/B2.

55. "NPC Deputies Voice Opinions on Government Report," Xinhua News Agency, March 31st, 1992.

56. *Ta Kung Pao,* April 4th, 1992. *SWB* FE/1348/C3.

57. Ibid.

58. His speech never appeared in the Chinese press. It was, however, leaked to Hong Kong newspapers, and a part of it was published in *Dachao Xinqi: Deng Xiaoping Nanxun Qianqian Houhou,* op. cit., 191–92.

59. *Ta Kung Pao,* June 12th, 1992. *SWB* FE/1406/B2.

60. Others suffering a similar fate include *Fang "Zuo" Beiwanglu (Memorandum on Preventing Leftism)* and *Dachao Xinqi: Deng Xiaoping Nanxun Qianqian Houhou (Resurgence of the Spring Tide: The Inside Story of Deng's Southern Tour).*

61. Xinhua News Agency, July 22nd, 1992. *SWB* FE/1445/B2.

62. In official Chinese texts, quotation marks are almost invariably put around

the word "leftist" but not around the word "rightist." This is because "leftist" has two meanings. When it is used without quotation marks it means leftist in the Western sense, in other words, a supporter of socialism or communism. Within quotation marks, the word in Chinese strictly speaking means a radical communist who blindly pursues unattainable goals. Thus, the Great Leap Forward and the Cultural Revolution were leftist movements, with the quotation marks. In general speech, however, as well as in many official texts, the word "leftist" within quotation marks is loosely applied to any hard-line communist, not necessarily just those who are overhasty and irrational in the pursuit of their ideals. The ambiguity of the word thus provides an escape route for hard-liners who can correctly insist they are not leftist at all, by which they mean they are not supporters of Great Leap Forward–style campaigns.

63. *Renmin Ribao,* June 22nd, 1992. *SWB* FE/1417/B2.

64. *Renmin Ribao,* August 24th, 1992. *SWB* FE/1473/B2.

65. Yuan Mu speaking at a news conference, July 16th, 1992. At the National People's Congress held in March 1993 the GNP growth rate was formally revised to between 8 and 9 percent annually for the five-year plan period.

66. *Fang "Zuo" Beiwanglu,* op. cit., 50.

67. "The Man Who Makes History," *Beijing Review,* October 12–18, 1992.

Chapter 4

Epigraph: The Northern Expedition of 1926–27 was launched from southern China by Chiang Kai-shek's Kuomintang to overthrow the northern warlords.

1. "More Self-Employed Workers Appear in Beijing," Xinhua News Agency, September 1st, 1992.

2. In December 1994, the authorities sentenced nine of these dissidents who had played leading roles in underground groups to prison terms of between 3 and 20 years for "counterrevolutionary" activities. Others were released. In June 1995, the Beijing High Court rejected appeals by those convicted.

3. Xinhua News Agency, August 10th, 1992. *SWB* FE/1457/B2.

4. Quoted by Reuters, August 26th, 1992, "Puritanical China Stages Its First X-Rated Play."

5. "Theater of the Absurd Plays Enjoy Trial Runs," *China Daily,* January 25th, 1991.

6. *Jiefang Ribao,* quoted by United Press International, September 9th, 1992, "Chinese Official Paper Makes Bold Call for Press Freedom."

7. *Weilai Yu Fazhan,* October 1992. *SWB* FE/1581/B2.

8. Ibid.

9. Author's interview with Xu Liangying.

10. *Yangcheng Wanbao,* quoted by Reuters, September 3rd, 1992, "Strippers Bare All in China's Reform Drive."

11. Xinhua News Agency, October 27th, 1993. *SWB* FE/1853/G.

12. "Booming Outdoor Karaoke Rocks Northwest China City," Xinhua News Agency, August 7th, 1992.

13. In late 1994, the city government asked McDonald's to vacate the site to make way for the construction of a new shopping and office complex.

14. See "Shisida Jiang Wei Shichang Jingji Zuo Jielun," *Ta Kung Pao,* October 4th, 1992.

15. Ibid.

16. For example, "Market Economy Turns into Hot Topic in China," Xinhua News Agency, October 5th, 1992.

17. "Economic Policy 'One Key Issue of 14th Congress,'" *China Daily,* October 9th, 1992, quoting Tong Dalin, vice president of the China Society for Research on Economic System Reform.

18. "Talks in Wuchang, Shenzhen, Zhuhai, and Shanghai," *Selected Works of Deng Xiaoping,* vol. 3, 361.

19. The First Plenum of the 14th Central Committee, October 19th, 1992.

20. "We Must Form a Promising Collective Leadership That Will Carry Out Reform," *Selected Works of Deng Xiaoping,* vol. 3, 288–89. Deng was speaking to two top party leaders on May 31st, 1989.

21. The Ninth Plenum of the 13th Central Committee, October 5–9, 1992.

22. "Deng Xiaoping Yu Shisida," *Ban Yue Tan,* November 11th, 1992.

23. *Renmin Ribao,* quoted by Reuters, "China Hails Deng Xiaoping Theory as 'Magic Weapon,'" October 15th, 1992.

24. The 7th Congress, April 23–June 11, 1945.

25. *Wen Wei Po,* December 15th, 1992. *SWB* FE/1565/B2.

26. Zhongguo Xinwen She, July 6th, 1992. *SWB* FE/1438/B2.

27. State Statistics Bureau, quoted by Xinhua News Agency, December 30th, 1992, "China's Economy Jumps 12 Percent in 1992."

28. "'Go Gold-Rush in China': Chinese Vice-Premier," Xinhua News Agency, February 21st, 1992. Zhu was speaking to entrepreneurs in Auckland, New Zealand.

29. *Jiefangjun Bao,* November 15th, 1993. *SWB* FE/1856/G.

30. From "A Report of an Investigation into the Peasant Movement in Hunan," February 1927. This quotation is the source of the common phrase "revolution is not a tea (or dinner) party."

31. "Talks in Wuchang, Shenzhen, Zhuhai, and Shanghai," *Selected Works of Deng Xiaoping,* vol. 3, 363–64.

32. "Gong'an Gongzuo Bixu Genshang Gaige Kaifang de Bufa," *Shanghai Fazhi Bao,* June 11th, 1992.

33. "Hong Kong's Wharf Finalizes Mega-Port for China," Reuters, December 1st, 1992.

34. "Renovation of Existing Industries Going Smoothly in Wuhan," Xinhua News Agency, February 26th, 1995.

35. "State Enterprise Workers Become Private Businessmen," Xinhua News Agency, February 8th, 1992.

36. "Gong'an Gongzuo Bixu Genshang Gaige Kaifang de Bufa," *Shanghai Fazhi Bao,* June 11th, 1992.

37. Zhongguo Tongxun She, May 29th, 1992. *SWB* FE/1406/B2.

38. "Yifa Chachu Wugao Xianhai Gaigezhe de Anjian," *Zhongguo Jiancha Bao,* June 8th, 1992.

39. *Beijing Qingnian Bao* quoted by *Zhongguo Qingnian Bao,* September 5th, 1994. *SWB* FE/2100/G.

40. "Enterprise Reform to Smash 'Three Irons,'" Xinhua News Agency, March 25th, 1992.

41. "Sheng Tigaiwei Fuze Tongzhi Jiu Qiye Sanxiang Zhidu Gaige Da Ben Bao Jizhe Wen," *Liaoning Ribao,* June 8th, 1992.

42. According to "Urban Jobless to Receive State Aid," Xinhua News Agency, September 1st, 1993, an unemployed person would receive a monthly payment of 70 to 80 yuan from the unemployment fund. This is less than a quarter of the average monthly income for a worker in a state-owned enterprise. Xinhua quoted officials as saying the sum would be "enough to cover the minimum daily living expenses."

43. "Zou Jiahua Discusses Reform of Social Insurance System," Xinhua News Agency, December 12th, 1994.

44. "Labour Disputes in Beijing Up More Than 50 Percent," *China Daily,* May 31st, 1995, quoted by Agence France Presse.

45. "Second Jobs More Than a Fad for Many People," *China Daily,* August 19th, 1992.

46. "'Second Job Fever' Not a Crippling Disease," *China Daily,* March 8th, 1993.

47. *The East Asian Miracle: Economic Growth and Public Policy,* World Bank (New York: Oxford University Press, 1993).

48. *Renmin Ribao,* quoted by Reuters, June 20th, 1994, "China Warns of Crime Rise from Widening Wealth Gap."

49. See *1993–1994 Nian Zhongguo: Shehui Xingshi Fenxi Yu Yuce* (Beijing: Zhongguo Shehui Kexue Chubanshe, 1994), 51.

50. Ibid.

51. *Zhongguo Jingji Xingshi Yu Zhanwang (1994–1995)* (Beijing: Zhongguo Fazhan Chuban She, 1995), 242. The book was produced under the auspices of the Development Research Center of the State Council.

52. "Zhongguo Ren Jiujing Duo Fu?" *Beijing Qingnian Bao,* December 28th, 1993.

53. "Wo Lai Shuoshuo Qiong," *Yangcheng Wanbao,* June 20th, 1993.

54. Interview with author, June 1994.

55. Huang Da of the Financial and Economic Committee of the National Peo-

ple's Congress, quoted by Xinhua News Agency, March 14th, 1995. *SWB* FE/2253/S2.

56. For example, Jin Xin, director general of the State Tax Administration, quoted by Reuters, January 12th, 1994, "China Tax Reform Tackles Red Ink, Industry Losses."

57. Xinhua News Agency, March 20th, 1995. *SWB* FE/2259/S1.

58. *1993–1994 Nian Zhongguo: Shehui Xingshi Fenxi Yu Yuce,* op. cit., 33.

59. *Zhonghua Gongshang Bao,* January 27th, 1994, 1.

60. According to official figures, by 1986 less than 10 percent of the rural population enjoyed free health care, compared with more than 90 percent in 1978 when the economic reforms began. One-third of households living below the poverty line are reduced to that state by medical costs. See, for example, *1992–1993 Nian Zhongguo: Shehui Xingshi Fenxi Yu Yuce,* edited by Jiang Liu, Lu Xueyi, and Dan Tianlun (Beijing: Zhongguo Shehui Kexue Chubanshe, 1993), 191 ff.

61. Surprisingly, the World Health Organization reported in late 1993 that "most of the urban population has little financial constraints about seeking medical care." See "Health Care in China: A Rural-Urban Comparison after the Socioeconomic Reforms," *World Health Organization Bulletin,* November 1993.

62. "Pros and Cons of Private Schools Boom," Xinhua News Agency, March 23rd, 1994.

Chapter 5

Epigraph from "Jiang Zemin on China's Anti-Corruption Campaign," Xinhua News Agency, August 21st, 1993.

1. *Henan Ribao,* February 25th, 1991, translated in *Beijing Review,* July 1–7, 1991.

2. "Urgent Tasks of China's Third Generation of Collective Leadership," *Selected Works of Deng Xiaoping,* vol. 3, 304.

3. Deng Zhifang went on to become the chief executive of two Hong Kong–listed companies, Shougang Concord Grand and Hoi Sing Holdings, both subsidiaries of Beijing's largest steel company, Shougang Corporation. A close associate of Deng's in Shougang Concord, Zhou Beifang, was arrested in February 1995 on corruption charges, prompting speculation that Deng Zhifang might be in trouble too. Shougang officials, however, denied that Deng was being investigated.

4. Xinhua News Agency, July 24th, 1992. *SWB* FE/1453/B2.

5. Among them was the former head of Xinhua News Agency in Hong Kong, Xu Jiatun. Xu says in his memoirs that Li Peng sent a special plane to Hainan to bring Liang Xiang back to Beijing. The pretext he gave was that he wanted to discuss with Liang the development of Hainan's Yangpu port. Liang was detained, however, as soon as he got off the plane in Beijing. Li then sent a team to Hainan,

headed by the minister of supervision, Wei Jianxing, to investigate the sending of a telegram to Beijing in the name of the Hainan party and government expressing support for Zhao Ziyang during the Tiananmen Square protests. After three months, however, Wei found that Liang was not responsible and that accusations of corruption against him were implausible. Xu says he heard that Deng Xiaoping suggested to Li Peng and Jiang Zemin that Liang keep his job because of his contribution to reform, but the two proceeded to strip Liang of all his posts and accuse him of corruption. See *Xu Jiatun Xianggang Huiyilu,* op. cit., 451.

6. *Ta Kung Pao,* April 4th, 1990. *SWB* FE/0731/B2.

7. Xinhua News Agency, February 8th, 1990 (*SWB* FE/0688/B2), quoted the minister of supervision as saying that 22 out of the 40 "big and important cases" to which the ministry had paid "special attention" had been wound up. He said these cases involved 13 officials "at the provincial or ministerial level." But he said that only four of these top officials had been "dealt with," including Sabir and Liang Xiang.

8. *Renmin Ribao,* quoted by Xinhua News Agency, September 26th, 1989, "CPC a Leading Force Against Corruption."

9. Xinhua News Agency, July 4th, 1995. *SWB* FE/2347/G.

10. Ibid.

11. Xinhua News Agency, July 5th, 1995. *SWB* FE/2359/G.

12. Xinhua News Agency, June 30th, 1993. *SWB* FE/1730/B2. Jiang was speaking on June 25th at a forum marking the 72nd anniversary of the party's founding.

13. "Talks in Wuchang, Shenzhen, Zhuhai, and Shanghai," *Selected Works of Deng Xiaoping,* vol. 3, 361.

14. From *Zhongguo Jingji Xingshi Yu Zhanwang,* op. cit., 182. In 1993, real interest rates dropped to –3.7 percent and in 1994 to –10.72 percent, the lowest level since the high inflation year of 1988.

15. *South China Morning Post,* August 11th, 1992, dispatch from Kent Chen in Shenzhen.

16. "Police Beat Investors As Riots Hit Reform Showcase," Reuters, August 11th, 1994.

17. "Public Officials Punished Over Shenzhen Riots," *China Daily,* December 14th, 1992.

18. Ibid.

19. *Ta Kung Pao,* August 13th, 1992. *SWB* FE/1462/B2.

20. "Cong 'Changcheng' Fazhan Kan 'Wulao' Jiajie," *Renmin Ribao,* January 20th, 1993.

21. See "Entrepreneur Challenges China's Central Bank," Reuters, March 30th, 1993, and "China's Central Bank Sued Over Frozen Assets," United Press International, March 30th, 1993.

22. "One Billion Yuan Fraud Exposed," Xinhua News Agency, June 23rd, 1993.

23. "Company Head Executed for Corruption, Bribery," Xinhua News Agency, April 11th, 1994.

24. *Wen Wei Po,* June 8th, 1993. *SWB* FE/1714/B2.

25. "State Is Worried about 'Rampant' Raising of Funds," *China Daily,* April 24th, 1993.

26. *Wen Wei Po,* June 17th, 1993. *SWB* FE/1719/B2.

27. "Talks in Wuchang, Shenzhen, Zhuhai, and Shanghai," *Selected Works of Deng Xiaoping,* vol. 3, 360.

28. Beijing University economics professor Hu Daiguang in *Jingji Ribao,* September 2, 1994. SWB FE/2095/G.

29. *1992–1993 Nian Zhongguo: Shehui Xingshi Fenxi Yu Yuce,* op. cit., 31.

30. *Xiahai Kuangchao,* edited by Chen Ruying (Beijing: Tuanjie Chubanshe, 1993), 5.

31. Ibid., 28–29.

32. Jiang Xiaojuan in *Xiahai Kuangchao,* 76.

33. Usually defined as any business other than agriculture, industry, and construction. Tertiary industry includes education, culture, health, communications, commerce, and service trades.

34. *1992–1993 Nian Zhongguo: Shehui Xingshi Fenxi Yu Yuce,* op. cit., 300.

35. *Xiahai Kuangchao,* op. cit., 31.

36. Document Number 4.

37. "State Set to Combat Bribery, Corruption," *China Daily,* June 11th 1993.

38. *Xiahai Kuangchao,* op. cit., 104.

39. "China; RSVP, and Please Bring a Cheque," *The Economist,* July 17th, 1993, quoting the official magazine, *Ban Yue Tan.*

40. *Fanpai gongsi.*

41. Yuan Baoshan, quoted in *Lengxue Gongpu, Quan, Se, Li Chaoji Jiaoyi Beiwanglu,* by Yu Jian (Beijing: Hongqi Chubanshe, 1993), 188.

42. *Xinmin Wanbao,* November 10th, 1993, 12.

43. *Fazhi Ribao,* quoted by *China Daily,* November 27th, 1993, "What They Are Saying."

44. "Cases of Graft, Bribery More Severely Punished," Xinhua News Agency, August 27th, 1993.

45. Xinhua News Agency, October 28th, 1993. *SWB* FE/1834/G.

46. *Liaowang,* November 21st, 1994. *SWB* FE/2181/G.

47. *Renmin Ribao,* July 26th, 1993, quoted by Reuters, "China Warns Military to Stay Loyal to Communism."

48. *Baokan Wenzhai,* June 28th, 1993, 4.

49. Zhongguo Xinwen She, quoted by United Press International, March 21st, 1994, "Chinese Delegates Warn of Unrest Over Corruption, Prices."

50. Although foreign journalists were occasionally offered gifts by Chinese interviewees, they more often found themselves having to hand over money to rapacious officials. From the late 1980s onward, provincial governments began

to charge $20 or more a day for hosting visits by foreign correspondents. The charge was applied per head, and often quoted in U.S. dollars rather than the Chinese yuan. The sum far exceeded the cost incurred to the governments concerned of arranging interviews and assigning minders to accompany the journalists. But the authorities clearly believed that the foreign media served little useful propaganda purpose and were so desperate for news that they would be willing to pay the fee. In the latter assumption at least, they were usually right. The only (legal) alternative to paying the sum demanded was never to go on reporting trips outside the capital.

51. "Seven Obstacles Standing in Way of Rural Economy," *China Daily,* April 22nd, 1993.

52. "Four Still Held after Peasant Riot over Land Compensation," *South China Morning Post,* April 17th, 1994.

53. *Renmin Ribao,* January 14th, 1994, quoted by Reuters, "Grain Scam Left Hundreds of Thousands Starving."

Chapter 6

Epigraph from China Central Television, December 29th, 1992. *SWB* FE/1579/B2.

1. *Ming Pao,* March 9th, 1993. *SWB* FE/1638/C1.

Lena Sun of the *Washington Post,* one of the few foreign correspondents who visited Renshou without government approval soon after the first detailed official report came out in June, said villagers told her that only about 1,000 peasants were involved in the initial disturbance and one police car burned (*Washington Post,* June 20th, 1993).

2. Zhongguo Xinwen She, June 12th, 1993. *SWB* FE/1714/B2.

3. *Hsin Pao,* June 10th, 1993. *SWB* FE/1713/B2.

4. Xinhua News Agency, March 22nd, 1993. *SWB* FE/1644/B2. The circular was issued on March 19th.

5. *Hsin Pao,* June 10th, 1993. *SWB* FE/1713/B2.

6. *1993–1994 Nian Zhongguo: Shehui Xingshi Fenxi Yu Yuce,* op. cit., 125 ff.

7. Xinhua News Agency, December 26th, 1992. *SWB* FE/1579/B2.

8. China Central Television, December 29th, 1992. *SWB* FE/1579/B2.

9. *1992–1993 Nian Zhongguo: Shehui Xingshi Fenxi Yu Yuce,* op. cit., 302.

10. "Farmers Owed Cash by Postal Offices," *China Daily,* February 19th, 1993.

11. "Chendiandian de Lu Tiaozi," *Shoudu Jingji Xinxi Bao,* June 19th, 1993.

12. "Plan Is Devised to Cash Farmers' Overdue IOUs," *China Daily,* July 1st, 1993.

13. "Nongmin Fudan Mianmian Guan," *Beijing Ribao,* April 3rd, 1993.

14. *Xin Shiji,* June 10th, 1993. *SWB* FE/1719/B2.

15. "'Tian Guo' Meng, Yu Xi Qi An," *Minzhu Yu Fazhi,* December 1992.

16. Xinhua News Agency, quoted in *Renmin Ribao,* November 20th, 1992, "Yunnan Cuihui Pingyuan Diqu Fandu Fanqiang Tuanhuo."

17. *Fazhi Ribao,* quoted by Reuters, December 23rd, 1992, "China Mounts Military-Style Attack on Drug Lord."

18. *Nanfang Zhoumo,* January 15th, 1993. *SWB* FE/1598/B2.

19. "Nongcun Fazhan Dangyuan Gongzuo Bu Rong Hushi," *Zugong Tongxun,* June 7th, 1990.

20. "Gongchandangyuan Buneng Xinjiao," *Zugong Tongxun,* December 26th, 1990.

21. *Fazhi Ribao,* May 3rd, 1994. *SWB* FE/1990/G.

22. Zhongguo Tongxun She, October 6th, 1994. *SWB* FE/2140/G.

23. *Yangcheng Wanbao,* September 18th, 1993. *SWB* FE/1807/G.

24. *Renmin Ribao,* April 28th, 1992. *SWB* FE/1381/B2.

25. "Zongjiao Shili dui Nongcun Jiceng Zhengquan de Chongji he Yingxiang Bu Rong Hushi," *Zhenli de Zhuiqiu,* June 1995.

26. This was an unusual confirmation by an official report that coercive measures are used to force *(qiangzhi)* those who have had their quota of children to undergo sterilization. The article did not suggest that the authorities had done anything wrong, only the clan leaders.

27. *1993–1994 Nian Zhongguo: Shehui Xingshi Fenxi Yu Yuce,* op. cit., 131.

28. "Our Magnificent Goal and Basic Policies," *Selected Works of Deng Xiaoping,* vol. 3, 86.

29. "Socialism with a Specifically Chinese Character," *Selected Works of Deng Xiaoping,* vol. 3, 74.

30. These statistics are taken from official sources. Government reports often fail to point out that "rural incomes" include income from industry, making averages highly misleading. By 1994, more than 110 million peasants were working in village and township enterprises, earning as much as their urban counterparts. The gap between these "peasants" and those engaged purely in agriculture was phenomenal. Since many of those working in rural factories would send money back to their home villages, the wealth generated by rural industry is spread quite widely. But the official admission that half of peasant households suffered a decline in their incomes between 1989 and 1991 suggests that as many as half of all peasants derive little if any benefit from rural industry. In spite of the continuing rapid growth of rural enterprises, officials estimate that in the year 2000, there will be at least 520 million people in China relying solely on agriculture. Some of these figures can be found in *1992–1993 Nian Zhongguo: Shehui Xingshi Fenxi Yu Yuce,* op. cit., 289 ff.

31. *1993–1994 Nian Zhongguo: Shehui Xingshi Fenxi Yu Yuce,* op. cit., 145.

32. Ibid., 133.

33. "Many of Asia's Children Malnourished, UNICEF Chief Says," Reuters, October 7th, 1991.

34. *1992–1993 Nian Zhongguo: Shehui Xingshi Fenxi Yu Yuce,* op. cit., 278,

and *1993–1994 Nian Zhongguo: Shehui Xingshi Fenxi Yu Yuce,* op cit., 49. The figures quoted here are based on average incomes per capita.

35. *1993–1994 Nian Zhongguo: Shehui Xingshi Fenxi Yu Yuce,* op. cit., 49.

36. "Anhui Natives Settle into City," *China Daily,* March 15th, 1994.

37. Xinhua News Agency, July 14th, 1993. *SWB* FE/1759/B2.

38. "One Fifth of People in Shanghai Are Outsiders," Xinhua News Agency, November 25th, 1994.

39. "China's Capital Requires Transients to Register," Reuters, July 15th, 1995.

40. *Zhongguo Jingji Xingshi Yu Zhanwang,* op. cit., 275, 279.

41. Ibid.

42. Xinhua News Agency, July 11th, 1995. *SWB* FE/2361/G.

43. "Beijing Call to Pull Plug on Floating Job Seekers," *China Daily,* July 16th, 1993, and "First Census to Figure Out Beijing's Floating Population," Xinhua News Agency, October 27th, 1994.

44. *1993–1994 Nian Zhongguo: Shehui Xingshi Fenxi Yu Yuce,* op. cit., 60.

45. *SWB* FE/1965/S1.

46. Xinhua, June 15th, 1993. *SWB* FE/1728/B2.

47. "Millions of Job Seekers Cram Trains," *China Daily,* February 26th, 1992.

48. "Ba Qian Wan Liudong Renkou: Zhongguo Shehui Bu Wending Yinsu," *Wenhui Bao,* June 7th, 1993.

49. "Nongmin, Zhengfu, Nongye Wenti," *Jingjixue Zhoubao,* May 21st, 1989.

50. "Youmin: Daozhi Shehui Dongdang de Baozha Yuan," *Jingjixue Zhoubao,* April 16th, 1989.

51. "Vagrants a Threat to Social Stability," *China Daily,* March 23rd, 1989.

52. *Di San Zhi Yanjing Kan Zhongguo* by Luoyiningge'er, translated by Wang Shan (Shanxi: Shanxi Renmin Chubanshe, 1994).

53. See chapter 9 for a discussion of the political significance of the appearance of this book. It is widely believed that extreme hard-liners were among its chief backers, but even some radical dissidents in exile expressed approval of many of its arguments.

54. "'Jizhen' Nongcun Zhian; Baohu Chungeng Shengchan," *Zhongguo Jiancha Bao,* March 21st, 1994.

Chapter 7

Epigraph from interview with the author.

1. "Anhui Cracks Down on Corrupt Officials," Xinhua News Agency, January 4th, 1994.

2. He turned 26 two days before the tanks moved into Tiananmen Square.

3. Author's interviews with Zhang Lin, April–May 1994.

4. Anhui Provincial Radio, June 14th, 1989. *SWB* FE/0486/B2.

5. A relatively lenient sentence given the nature of the charges against him. Ding, whom I met before the verdict on Zhang became known, had predicted that Zhang would be imprisoned for at least eight years. He said he had heard rumors, however, that he would be treated leniently if he provided the police with information about his contacts. There is no evidence that Zhang did so, but Ding's suspiciousness, even of a close associate, was common to many of the dissidents I met in China, particularly those involved in underground groups.

6. See chapter 1 for more on the campaign.

7. The case referred to "Duzhe Lai Xin," *Wenyi Bao,* September 14th, 1991.

8. "Wo Ai He Xi Zhou," *Nongmin Ribao,* November 14th, 1991.

9. "Paroled Wang Retains Beliefs," *South China Morning Post,* February 4th, 1993.

10. The "four cardinal principles" of Chinese communism are adherence to (1) the socialist road, (2) the people's democratic dictatorship, (3) the leadership of the Communist Party, and (4) Marxism-Leninism and Mao Zedong Thought.

11. "Uphold the Four Cardinal Principles," *Selected Works of Deng Xiaoping (1975–1982)* (Beijing: Foreign Languages Press, 1984), 184. Deng was speaking on March 30th, 1979.

12. "Muqian de Xingshi he Renwu," *Xuexi Wenjian* (Beijing: Zhonggong Zhongyang Dangxiao Chubanshe, 1980), 170. This is an "internal" version of Deng's speech. Wei Jingsheng's name was omitted in the version that appears in *Selected Works of Deng Xiaoping (1975–1982):* "The Present Situation and the Tasks before Us," 224 ff.

13. Liu Qing was released in December 1989. He was imprisoned again for nearly six months in 1990. In 1992, he left China for the United States.

14. From a letter sent to the Central Committee and the National People's Congress on February 16th, 1989, signed by 33 intellectuals. See "Chinese Intellectuals Call for Prisoner Amnesty," United Press International, February 16th, 1989.

15. Wei told me that he did not regard Deng as particularly intelligent, far less so, in fact, than Mao Zedong. He said Deng was good at predicting some "big things," such as the dangers inherent in the Democracy Wall experiment. But he failed to take early enough action against the dissident astrophysicist Fang Lizhi, who as vice president of one of China's most prestigious universities, the Science and Technology University in Hefei, inspired students to take to the streets in 1986 to demand greater democracy. It was not until January 1987 that Fang lost his job and his party membership.

16. *Zhongguo Jingji Xingshi Yu Zhanwang (1994–1995),* op. cit., 260.

17. "Pinkun Zhigong Ji Xu Zuihou Pingzhang," *Beijing Qingnian Bao,* January 23rd, 1995.

18. *Zhongguo Bu Neng Luan,* edited by Hui Xiaobing, Chen Tianze et al. (Beijing: Zhonggong Zhongyang Dangxiao Chubanshe, 1994).

19. See chapter 3.

20. These figures come from Xinhua News Agency, September 10th, 1994

(*SWB* FE/2100/G); "House, Telephone, Computer—New Favors in China," Xinhua News Agency, August 11th, 1994, and "IBM Confident of Riding Booming PC Sales in China," Reuters, January 27th, 1995.

21. "China Dissident in Hospital after Tumor Operation," Reuters, September 7th, 1994.

22. "China Carries Out Full Scale Housing Reform," Xinhua News Agency, December 1st, 1993.

23. "Renyuan Wailiu Jiaju," *Wenzhai Bao,* April 22nd, 1993.

24. Other examples that Jiang reportedly cited were Wang Dan's birthday party in February, which was attended by some 100 relatives, friends, and dissidents—one of the biggest gatherings of former Tiananmen Square activists since 1989. He also mentioned the activities of Wei Jingsheng, including Wei's meeting in Beijing in March with the U.S. Assistant Secretary for Human Rights, John Shattuck, the first between a senior U.S. official and a high-profile Chinese dissident in China. Another manifestation of "hostile" activity in Jiang's view was the emergence of the league.

25. The following description of Chen Ziming and Wang Juntao's activities is based on the author's interviews with numerous associates, relatives, and acquaintances of the two men in China, Hong Kong, and the United States.

26. *Zhongguo Zhengzhi Wenhua: Minzhu Zhengzhi Nanchan de Shehui Xinli Yinsu,* by Min Qi (Kunming: Yunnan Renmin Chuban She, 1989).

27. *Renmin Ribao,* quoted by Xinhua News Agency, June 27th, 1988, "Opinions of National Legislators Surveyed"; *Zhongguo Qingnian Bao,* quoted by Xinhua, June 25th, 1988, "Survey of NPC Deputies Gives Good and Bad."

28. *Beijing Turmoil: More Than Meets the Eye,* by Che Muqi (Beijing: Foreign Languages Press, 1990), 97. The other two newspapers were the *Shijie Jingji Daobao* and the *Xin Guancha.* Both were closed down because of their coverage during the 1989 unrest.

29. "Zhongguo: Xuyao Pingxin Jingqi," *Jingjixue Zhoubao,* June 4th, 1989.

30. "Shehuizhuyi Guojia de Weiji yu Gaige," *Jingjixue Zhoubao,* July 18th, 1989.

31. The Tiananmen Square protests of April 1976, the Democracy Wall Movement of 1978–79, the student protests of 1986, and the antigovernment unrest of 1989. Chen and Wang, however, did not get involved in the 1986 demonstrations.

32. From the manuscript of Hou Xiaotian's account of Wang Juntao's trial, which she was allowed to attend. An abridged version appeared in the book *Wang Juntao: Qi Ren, Qi Yan, Qi "Zui,"* by Wang Juntao and Hou Xiaotian (Hong Kong: Dangdai Yuekan, 1992).

33. "China's Entrepreneurs—Stone's Wan Spells Time: Efficiency, Fortune, Success," Xinhua News Agency, March 31st, 1988.

34. "China's Entrepreneurs—'A New Breed,'" Xinhua News Agency, March 27th, 1988.

35. *Renmin Ribao,* August 17th, 1989. *SWB* FE/0539/B2.

36. Ibid.

37. For example, "Five Years of China's Bankruptcy Law: Problems and Prospects," *Beijing Review,* February 7–20, 1994.

38. The following information about Mu Qizhong and the Land Group comes from interviews with former employees, Land Group publicity materials, and official media accounts.

39. Quoted by the *New York Times,* August 30th, 1992, "A Tycoon Named Mu: Product of Old China Leading the New."

40. "Mu's Latest Mission: Making Millions in Moscow," *China Daily,* November 28th, 1993.

41. "Former Chinese Death Row Inmate Now Major Dealmaker," Reuters, August 3rd, 1992.

42. "Xiang, Cun Huanjie Xuanju Zhong Chuxian de Bu Zhengchang Xianxiang Zhide Zhuyi," *Zugong Tongxun,* November 1st, 1990.

43. "Jue Buneng Rang 'Hei Zi Hao' Zuoda," *Yangcheng Wanbao,* July 14th, 1993.

44. "'Hei Dao Er' . . . ." *Beijing Fazhi Bao,* October 17th, 1993.

45. "Triad Activity Spreading in China," Agence France Presse, November 28th, 1994.

46. "Public Security Reports Rise in Crime in 1993," *China Daily,* January 20th, 1994.

47. *1993–1994 Nian Zhongguo: Shehui Xingshi Fenxi Yu Yuce,* op. cit., 156.

48. The official magazine *Liaowang* said that in Guangxi and Yunnan Provinces, eight out of ten guns seized by the authorities originated from Vietnam. See "China Concerned on Gun Smuggling from Vietnam," United Press International, April 20th, 1993.

49. Zhongguo Xinwen She, September 30th, 1994. *SWB* FE/2125/G.

50. *Fazhi Ribao,* January 9th, 1995. *SWB* FE/2219/G.

51. Ibid.

52. "Jianjue Daji Daiyou Heishehui Xingzhi de Fanzui Tuanhuo," *Renmin Gong'an Bao,* August 6th, 1991.

53. "Jue Buneng Rang 'Hei Zi Hao' Zuoda," *Yangcheng Wanbao,* July 14th, 1993.

54. See chapter 9 on triad involvement in smuggling dissidents out of China.

55. *Zhongguo Banghui Shi,* by Zhou Yumin and Shao Yong (Shanghai: Shanghai Renmin Chubanshe, 1993), 494 ff.

56. After he came to power, Deng Xiaoping tried to rid the party of what were called "three types of people" involved in the Cultural Revolution, namely, followers of Lin Biao and the Gang of Four, those who practiced "serious factionalism," and people who engaged in acts of violence. Between 1982 and 1986, the party expelled more than 150,000 members in purges partly aimed at achieving this, but the authorities admitted in early 1987 that "major problems" remained.

In 1992, the Beijing-controlled *Wen Wei Po* in Hong Kong said that about 10 percent of candidates originally shortlisted for the new Central Committee due to be announced at the 14th Congress belonged to the "three types of people." It is impossible to know what the ideological inclinations of these people would be more than 15 years after the end of the Cultural Revolution. Some would probably be radical dissidents like Wei Jingsheng, others orthodox Maoists.

Chapter 8

1. See also chapter 3 for a description of differences between Guangdong's political atmosphere and that of the rest of China.

2. My interlocutors were all speaking English. For the sake of readability, I have tidied up some of their grammatical errors.

3. "Mainland Poll Backs Governor," *South China Morning Post,* November 1st, 1992.

4. "Maintain Prosperity and Stability in Hong Kong," *Selected Works of Deng Xiaoping,* vol. 3, 83.

5. "Speech at a Meeting with the Members of the Committee for Drafting the Basic Law of the Hong Kong Special Administrative Region," *Selected Works of Deng Xiaoping,* vol. 3, 220.

6. *Renmin Ribao,* July 21st, 1989. *SWB* FE/0515/A3. Xu Jiatun says in *Xu Jiatun Xianggang Huiyilu* (p. 397) that the article was written by the Hong Kong and Macao Affairs Office.

7. "Ji Pengfei Reaffirms Policies toward Hong Kong and Macao," Xinhua News Agency, June 22nd, 1989.

8. *Xu Jiatun Xianggang Huiyilu,* 394. Xu Jiatun's unauthorized departure for California in 1990 made him the highest-ranking Chinese official since Lin Biao in 1971 to flee abroad.

9. Lee stepped down from his post as deputy chairman of the alliance in 1990 and left its standing committee the following year. He, or rather his "office" in the Legislative Council, remained a member of the organization.

10. It was adopted on April 4th, 1990.

11. Article 18 of the Basic Law states that "in the event that the Standing Committee of the National People's Congress decides to declare a state of war or, by reason of turmoil within the Hong Kong Special Administrative Region which endangers national unity or security and is beyond the control of the government of the Region, decides that the Region is in a state of emergency, the Central People's Government may issue an order applying the relevant national laws in the Region."

Article 23 states that "the Hong Kong Special Administrative Region shall enact laws on its own to prohibit any act of treason, secession, sedition, subversion against the Central People's Government, or theft of state secrets, to prohibit foreign political organizations or bodies from conducting political activities in the

Region, and to prohibit political organizations or bodies of the Region from establishing ties with foreign political organizations or bodies."

12. *Xu Jiatun Xianggang Huiyilu,* 398.

13. *Experiences of China,* by Percy Cradock (London: John Murray, 1994), 230.

14. According to the 1988 draft of the Basic Law, out of the 60 Legislative Council seats there would be 10 directly elected seats in 1991 and 15 in 1997. In the 1990 version these figures were increased to 18 and 20, respectively, going up to 30 in 2003. China has never changed its stance, however, that the Legislative Council is and will remain an advisory body rather than a parliament in any Western understanding of the concept.

15. In a letter written by the then Political Adviser to the Hong Kong government, William Ehrman, to Xinhua News Agency's Hong Kong branch. The letter was later leaked to the Hong Kong press.

16. "Shi Goutong, Haishi Duikang?" *Wen Wei Po,* August 9th, 1995.

17. *Wen Wei Po,* May 30th, 1994. *SWB* FE/2012/F.

18. Sham refused to comment on this allegation.

19. Sham was speaking in an interview with Gavin Hewitt who made a documentary on Operation Yellow Bird for the BBC's *Panorama* program in 1991.

20. "China Chaos Would Mean Hong Kong Collapse—Deng," *Wen Wei Po,* quoted by Reuters, February 21st, 1992.

21. The first regular phone-in radio programs began on Pearl River Economic Radio in Canton in December 1986. The startup of a new look Radio Canton in early 1992 marked an even bolder step toward Western-style talk radio. Following Guangdong's lead, many cities around the country have adopted similar formats in recent years.

22. *Today's Hotline,* Guangdong People's Broadcasting Station, Canton, January 2nd, 1994. *SWB* FE/1889/G.

23. "One Country, Two Systems," *Selected Works of Deng Xiaoping,* vol. 3, 69.

24. Ibid., "Maintain Prosperity and Stability in Hong Kong," 83.

25. Xiamen SEZ gained similar powers in 1994.

26. The potential dangers of growing provincialism are discussed in the final chapter of this book.

27. In the official communist view of history, the Opium War of 1840–42, which ended with the ceding of Hong Kong to Britain, marked the degeneration of China into a "semicolonial and semifeudal society." The Portuguese, however, had established their colony in Macao in 1557.

28. "CPC 12th National Congress Opens in Beijing," Xinhua News Agency, September 1st, 1982.

29. "CPPCC Holds New Year Reception," Xinhua News Agency, January 1st, 1980.

30. Xinhua News Agency, October 9th, 1983. *SWB* FE/7641/C1. Hu was

speaking on August 15th, 1983, with Taisuke Yamaguchi, president of Japan's Mainichi Shimbun.

31. Xinhua News Agency, June 28th, 1987. *SWB* FE/8606/A3. Deng was talking to Japanese foreign minister, Tadashi Kuranari.

32. Xinhua News Agency, October 9th, 1983. *SWB* FE/7461/C1.

33. In 1989, the then finance minister, Shirley Kuo, took part in an annual meeting of the Asian Development Bank in Beijing, becoming the highest-ranking Taiwan visitor to the mainland since 1949. In late 1994, Taiwan permitted John Chang, a ministerial-level official, to go to Beijing to visit his sick brother.

34. Fujian Provincial Radio, May 18th, 1989. *SWB* FE/0464/B2.

35. Taiwan's hands-off stance toward Tiananmen did not, however, convince everyone in the Beijing leadership. As *Renmin Ribao* put it in its editorial of July 26th, 1989: "During the 40 years since the founding of the People's Republic of China, the KMT authorities in Taiwan have continuously dreamed of launching a counterattack on the mainland. With the change in the international situation and the consolidation of the socialist system, however, the 'military counterattack' has become difficult to realize. Regardless of the demand for the reunification of the motherland voiced by patriots of all walks of life, they have gradually shifted their strategy toward a so-called 'political landing' to carry out a 'soft offensive.' Never have they given up planned and organized activities to wage psychological war and instigate rebellions." *SWB* FE/0521/C1.

36. "Mainland Dissident Leader Meets ROC Political Leaders," Central News Agency, October 24th, 1990.

37. As opposed to Taipei's earlier stance that it alone was the legitimate representative of all China and that Beijing was simply a rebel government.

38. Xinhua News Agency, January 30th, 1995. *SWB* FE/2215/G.

39. *Renmin Ribao,* quoted by Xinhua News Agency, July 25th, 1995. *SWB* FE/2366/G.

40. *Renmin Ribao,* quoted by Xinhua News Agency, June 9th, 1995. *SWB* FE/2327/G.

41. Central People's Broadcasting Station (in a broadcast to Taiwan), July 19th, 1995. *SWB* FE/2364/G.

42. *Xu Jiatun Xianggang Huiyilu,* vol. 2, 324 ff.

Chapter 9

Epigraph from the talks given by Deng Xiaoping during his tour of southern China, January–February 1992. See "Talks in Wuchang, Shenzhen, Zhuhai, and Shanghai," *Selected Works of Deng Xiaoping,* vol. 3, 358. The generations referred to are stages in the party's political evolution rather than generations of age or party seniority. Even though there were several leaders before Chairman Mao, they were all "unstable and immature," according to Deng. Thus, Mao headed the "first generation" of a "truly mature leadership" that also included

Liu Shaoqi, Zhou Enlai, and Zhu De. Similarly, Hua Guofeng, who took over from Mao, did not represent a generation in Deng's view because he was "merely an interim leader" with "no ideas of his own." Deng himself, therefore, formed the "second generation" when he emerged as paramount leader in 1978, two years after Mao's death. By describing Jiang Zemin as the "core" of the "third generation," Deng was saying, in effect, that Jiang's leadership would be stable, long-lasting, and full of new ideas.

1. *Nanjie* literally means "South Street."

2. "Zhongyuan Dadi de Yi Mian Xianyan Hongqi," *Dangdai Sichao*, June 20th, 1994.

3. See chapter 3.

4. The term given to Deng's system of allowing peasants to farm their own plots of land on condition that they sell a contracted amount of their produce to the state.

5. *Zhong Yuan Feng: Nanjie Ren Jiang de Gushi* edited by Wang Hongbin, Yao Xilan, Liu Xiaoqing et al. (Henan), 2. The book was completed in 1993.

6. The "Three Articles" are "Serve the People," "In Memory of Norman Bethune," and "The Foolish Old Man Moves the Mountain." The five essays in the Nanjie collection include these three, plus another Cultural Revolution favorite, "Against Liberalism," as well as "Where Do Correct Ideas Come From?"

7. I saw these plaques during my trip, but the significance of them was explained by "Guoqu Shidai de Zhengzhi Yiji," *Yuegang Xinxi Ribao*, July 2nd, 1994.

8. "Zuotian de Meng, Jintian de Meng. . . ." *Zhongguo Qingnian Bao*, March 8th, 1994.

9. "Guoqu Shidai de Zhengzhi Yiji," *Yuegang Xinxi Ribao*, July 2nd, 1994.

10. "Nanjie Cun Fazhan Qishilu," *Zhongliu*, April 1995.

11. "Guoqu Shidai de Zhengzhi Yiji," *Yuegang Xinxi Ribao*, July 2nd, 1994.

12. "Nanjie, Ni Yao Gaosu Zhongguo Shenme?" *Yuegang Xinxi Ribao*, July 30th, 1994.

13. Fourth Plenum of the 14th Central Committee, September 25–28, 1994.

14. Official biographies say that during the Cultural Revolution, Jiang Zemin used to read Chairman Mao's *Selected Works* in the English version. While mayor and subsequently party secretary of Shanghai from 1985 to 1989, Jiang subscribed to the *Washington Post* and *Pravda*. His knowledge of Russian was refined during a year working as a trainee at the Stalin Automobile Plant in Moscow from 1955 to 1956.

15. "Urgent Tasks of China's Third Generation of Collective Leadership," *Selected Works of Deng Xiaoping*, vol. 3, 300.

16. "Speech to Comrades Who Had Attended an Enlarged Meeting of the Military Commission on the Central Committee of the Communist Party of China," *Selected Works of Deng Xiaoping*, vol. 3, 323.

17. Fifth Plenum of the 13th Central Committee, November 6–9, 1989.

18. Xinhua News Agency, November 21st, 1989. *SWB* FE/0622/B2. Jiang was speaking on November 9th.

19. *Xu Jiatun Xianggang Huiyilu,* 376.

20. *Zhongguo Qingnian Bao,* January 4th, 1994. *SWB* FE/1898/G.

21. See also chapter 6.

22. "'Luoyiningge'er' yu Ta de Yanjing," *Dushu Zazhi,* no. 9 (1994), 25–31.

23. See chapter 3 for more on Deng's attempts to emulate the "little dragons" of Singapore, Hong Kong, Taiwan, and South Korea.

24. Although Russia's economy was mired in deep recession at the time Wang's book appeared in 1994, its per capita GNP that year was still nearly five times that of China. Adult literacy in the former Soviet Union as a whole was 99 percent, compared with 68 percent in China. China's population, at 1.19 billion, was nearly eight times bigger than Russia's.

25. "Sulian Jubian zhi Hou Zhongguo de Xianshi Yingdui yu Zhanlue Xuanze." *China Spring,* a Chinese-language journal based in New York, published the essay in its January 1992 edition.

26. The Beijing-controlled Hong Kong news agency, Zhongguo Tongxun She, highlighted Chen's defeat in its December 17th, 1987, report on the elections, even pointing out in uncharacteristic style for an official dispatch that Chen is the son of Chen Yun (*SWB* FE/0032/B2). At the time of the elections, radical reformers were at the peak of their political influence.

27. This argument against neoauthoritarianism appeared in *Shijie Jingji Daobao,* January 16th, 1989, 12.

28. See chapter 4.

29. Zhu was speaking to *China Business Review* (U.S.-China Business Council, Washington, D.C.) 17, no. 5 (September 1990), 50.

30. Shanghai Radio, June 8th, 1989. *SWB* FE/0479/B2.

31. *Jiefang Ribao,* November 9th, 1991. *SWB* FE/1235/C2.

32. Xinhua News Agency, September 17th, 1991. *SWB* FE/1183/B2.

33. "Profile Zhu Rongji, Vice Premier," Xinhua News Agency, March 29th, 1993.

34. *Wen Wei Po,* November 14th, 1992. *SWB* FE/1540/B2.

35. Zhu was replaced as head of the People's Bank of China by his deputy Dai Xianglong in June 1995.

36. "Zhu Rongji's Smile of Confidence," *Nexus: China in Focus,* spring 1993 edition.

37. China Central Television, March 5th, 1995. *SWB* FE/2245/S1.

38. Beijing Radio, March 20th, 1989. *SWB* FE/0416/C1.

39. These quotations were put at the top of a biography of Qiao published on July 16th, 1993, by the official magazine *Zhonghua Yingcai* to mark his appointment as NPC chairman in March that year. The remarks, however, were attributed to an unnamed "Chinese Communist Party veteran." The book, *Zhonggong*

Xin Xuangui—Zui Xin Lingdaozhe Qun Xiang, by Ho Pin and Gao Xin (Hong Kong: Dangdai Yuekan and Zhongguo Jushi Fenxi Zhongxin, 1993), 52, ascribes the quotation to Li Xiannian.

40. *Xu Jiatun Xianggang Huiyilu,* 373.

41. Beijing Television, June 12th, 1989. *SWB* FE/0482/B2.

42. Xinhua News Agency, September 25th, 1989. *SWB* FE/0573/A2.

43. Beijing Radio, September 1st, 1989. *SWB* FE/0553/B2.

44. The remaining five are Yang Shangkun (b. 1907), Peng Zhen (b. 1901), Bo Yibo (b. 1908), Song Renqiong (b. 1909), and Deng Xiaoping (b. 1904). Different journalists, however, had different views on who should be included in the list. Some regarded Zhou Enlai's widow Deng Yingchao (b. 1904) as one of the immortals. She died in July 1992.

45. Quoted by Xinhua News Agency, November 10th, 1994. *SWB* FE/2165/G.

46. See chapter 4.

47. Xinhua News Agency, February 23rd, 1995. *SWB* FE/2237/G.

48. At a news conference at the end of the annual National People's Congress, April 4th, 1990. *SWB* FE/0733/C2.

49. *Wen Wei Po,* February 15th, 1993. *SWB* FE/1622/B2.

50. The *Wen Wei Po* reporter noted that "after speaking the three characters of Zhao Ziyang he stopped for a second and then added the two characters of 'comrade.' This little move remains fresh in my memory."

51. See chapter 2 for more on Xiao Yang and his unusually outspoken support of Zhao Ziyang.

52. *Hsin Pao,* June 4th, 1994. *SWB* FE/2018/S1.

53. The secret orders were issued on May 15th, 1992, by the chief of general staff, the General Political Department, and the General Logistics Department of the PLA. They replaced another set of unpublished regulations titled "Zhongguo Renmin Jiefangjun Suixing Fangbao Renwu Zhanxing Guiding," promulgated in July 1990. A copy of the new orders was leaked to foreign reporters.

Chapter 10

Epigraph from Xinhua News Agency, July 5th, 1993. *SWB* FE/1734/B2.

1. From Sun Yat-sen's first lecture on "The Principle of Nationalism," one of 16 lectures on the "Three Principles of the People," the guiding philosophy of the KMT. The Chinese Communist Party recognizes Dr. Sun's Three Principles as "revolutionary" but accuses the KMT of having twisted their meaning in order to oppose communism.

2. Bush was speaking in Hong Kong at a forum hosted by Citibank. His remarks were quoted by Xinhua News Agency, November 16th, 1993, "China's Development to U.S. Advantage: Bush."

3. "Kissinger Says China Key to Stable Asia," Reuters, March 21st, 1995.

4. Quoted by Itar-Tass News Agency, Moscow, June 28th, 1994. *SWB* SU/2035/B. Qian was speaking at Moscow University.

5. The poverty elimination target was included in China's 10-year development strategy adopted in 1991. It was restated by Li Peng in his address to the National People's Congress on March 5th, 1995. See *SWB* FE/2245/S1.

6. The illiteracy goal was included in the 10-year development strategy.

7. "China's Collective Leadership Strong and Stable: Li Peng," Xinhua News Agency, November 30th, 1990.

8. Zhang Shekui, head of the party Organization Department of Shanxi Province, quoted in *Qiushi,* October 16th, 1994. *SWB* FE/2159/G.

9. See also chapter 2 for a discussion of separatist tendencies in ethnic minority regions.

10. He Shengming and Liu Shangxi in *Zhenli de Zhuiqiu,* July 11th, 1995, "Caiquan Fensan Bu Li Yu Zhengquan Tongyi."

11. "Protectionism Hurts Economy," *China Daily,* September 13th, 1990.

12. "'Di Bi' de Beiju," *Xinmin Wanbao,* September 14th, 1990.

13. "Illegal Taxes on Rural Roads Must Stop," *China Daily,* April 6th, 1992.

14. Ibid.

15. Xinhua News Agency, January 11th, 1995. *SWB* FE/2202/G.

16. "Battles for Resources Rage in Western China," *China Daily,* August 7th, 1989.

17. "China Can Have Great Hopes for the Future," *Selected Works of Deng Xiaoping,* vol. 3, 309.

18. "Bu Wei Shang, Bu Wei Shu, Zhi Wei Shi, Jiaohuan, Bijiao, Fanfu," *Renmin Ribao,* January 18th, 1991.

19. *Jiefangjun Bao,* June 24th, 1992. *SWB* FE/1443/B2.

20. *Ta Kung Pao,* October 1st, 1993. *SWB* FE/1810/G.

21. The several thousand migrant workers in Daqiu did not enjoy such luxuries. They were accommodated in shabby dormitories, with several dozen people to a room sleeping in bunk beds.

22. Details of Yu Zuomin's alleged offenses come from Xinhua News Agency, August 27th, 1993. *SWB* FE/1788/G.

23. "Zai Baochi Shehui Zhengzhi Wending zhong Tuijin Gaige he Fazhan," *Zhenli de Zhuiqiu,* May 1994.

24. The word used for separatism is *fenliezhuyi,* the same term commonly used by Chinese officials to describe the views of those who support Tibet's independence from China.

25. In March 1989, shortly before the Tiananmen Square protests, Deng told party leaders that "over the last 10 years, our greatest mistake has been our failure in education. We haven't paid enough attention to the political and ideological education of young people and to the expansion of education." See "China Will Tolerate No Disturbances," *Selected Works of Deng Xiaoping,* vol. 3, 280.

26. *Jiaqiang Zhongyang Zhengfu Zai Shichang Jingji Zhuanxing Zhong De*

Zhudao Zuoyong by Wang Shaoguang and Hu Angang (Beijing: Chinese Academy of Sciences, May 1993).

27. See also chapter 4.

28. Hu Angang in *Jingji Ribao,* June 2nd, 1995. *SWB* FE/2361/S1.

29. Zhongguo Xinwen She, February 15th, 1995. *SWB* FE/2237/S1.

30. See chapter 9.

31. The report did not give the percentages of those holding these views.

32. "China's Special Economic Zones: Should They Remain Special?" *The Straits Times,* December 8th, 1994.

33. Article by Hu Angang in *Lien Ho Pao,* Hong Kong, November 7th, 1994. *SWB* FE/2166/G.

34. *Xizang Ribao,* June 13th, 1995. *SWB* FE/D2352/S2.

35. See "China Says No Need to Be Nervous in Leap Year," Reuters, February 24th, 1995.

36. *Yijiujiuwu Run Bayue,* by Zheng Langping (Taipei: Shangzhou Wenhua, 1994).

37. *Huang Huo,* by Bao Mi (Taipei: Fengyun Shidai Chuban Youxian Gongsi, 1991). The author's name, Bao Mi, is a pseudonym that means "Keep Secret."

38. *Tui Bei Tu Dian Zhu Ping Xi,* edited by Li Lianbin (Beijing: Beijing Shifan Daxue Chubanshe, 1992), 5.

39. *China in the Near Term,* Undersecretary of Defense (Policy), 1994 Summer Study, Newport, Rhode Island. The study was made public by the Department of Defense on January 24th, 1995. The Pentagon said the study did not reflect the official policy or position of the U.S. government.

40. "Keneng Fasheng zai 2000 Nian de Beiju," by Su Ming, reprinted in *Documents on the Chinese Democratic Movement 1978–1980,* edited by Claude Widor, vol. 2 (Paris: Ecole des Hautes Etudes en Sciences Sociales; Hong Kong: The Observer Publishers, 1984).

Bibliography

Bao Mi. *Huang Huo.*Taipei: Fengyun Shidai Chuban Youxian Gongsi, 1991.

保密： 《黃禍》 台北 『風雲時代出版有限公司』。

Che Muqi. *Beijing Turmoil: More Than Meets the Eye.* Beijing: Foreign Languages Press, 1990.

Chen Ruying, ed. *Xiahai Kuangchao.* Beijing: Tuanjie Chubanshe, 1993.

陳如穎編： 《下海狂潮》 北京 『團結出版社』。

China in the Near Term. Newport, RI: Under Secretary of Defense (Policy), 1994 Summer Study.

Cradock, Percy. *Experiences of China.* London: John Murray, 1994.

Deng Xiaoping. Beijing: Zhongyang Wenxian Chubanshe, 1988.

《鄧小平》 北京 『中央文獻出版社』。

Deng Xiaoping. *Selected Works of Deng Xiaoping (1975–1982).* Beijing: Foreign Languages Press. Beijing 1984

———. *Deng Xiaoping Wenxuan.* Vol. 3. Beijing: Renmin Chubanshe, 1993.

《鄧小平文選第三卷》 北京 『人民出版社』。

———. *Selected Works of Deng Xiaoping.* Vol. 3. Beijing: Foreign Languages Press, 1994.

Gao Gao and Yan Jiaqi. *Wenhua Dageming Shi Nian Shi.* Tianjin: Tianjin Renmin Chubanshe, 1986.

高皋、 嚴家其： 《文化大革命十年史》 天津 『天津人民出版社』。

Ho Pin and Gao Xin. *Zhonggong Xin Quangui: Zui Xin Lingdaozhe Qun Xiang.* Hong Kong: Dangdai Yuekan; Toronto: Zhongguo Jushi Fenxi Zhongxin, 1993.

何頻、 高新： 《中共新權貴： 最新領導者群像》 香港 『當代月刊』、 加拿大『中國局勢分析中心』。

Hui Xiaobing, Chen Tianze et al., eds. *Zhongguo Bu Neng Luan*. Beijing: Zhong-gong Zhongyang Dangxiao Chubanshe, 1994.

恚小兵、 陳天澤等編： 《中國不能亂》 北京 『中共中央黨校出版社』。

Jiang Liu, Lu Xueyi, Dan Tianlun, eds. *1992–1993 Nian Zhongguo: Shehui Xingshi Fenxi Yu Yuce*. Beijing: Zhongguo Shehui Kexue Chubanshe, 1993.

江流 、 陸學藝、 單天倫編： 《1992—1993 年中國： 社會形勢分析與預測》 北京『中國社會科學出版社』。

Jiang Liu, Lu Xueyi, Dan Tianlun, eds. *1993–1994 Nian Zhongguo: Shehui Xingshi Fenxi Yu Yuce*. Beijing: Zhongguo Shehui Kexue Chubanshe, 1994.

江流 、 陸學藝、 單天倫編： 《1993—1994 年中國： 社會形勢分析與預測》 北京 『中國社會科學出版社』。

Leng Quanqing and Miao Sufei, eds. *Jing Xin Dong Po de 56 Tian*. Beijing: Da Di Chubanshe, 1989.

冷銓清、 苗蘇菲編： 《驚心動魄的56天》 北京 『大地出版社』。

Li Lianbin, ed. *Tui Bei Tu Dian Zhu Ping Xi*. Beijing: Beijing Shifan Daxue Chubanshe, 1992.

李連斌編： 《推背圖點注評析》 北京 『北京師範大學出版社』。

Li Zhisui. *The Private Life of Chairman Mao*. New York: Random House, 1994.

Liu Yaguang, ed. *Lishi de Chaoliu*. Beijing: Zhongguo Renmin Daxue Chuban-she, 1992.

劉亞光編： 《歷史的潮流》 北京 『中國人民大學出版社』。

Long, Simon. *China to 2000; Reform's Last Chance*. London: The Economist Intelligence Unit, May 1992.

Luoyiningge'er. *Di San Zhi Yangjing Kan Zhongguo*. trans. by Wang Shan. Taiyuan: Shanxi Renmin Chubanshe, 1994.

洛伊寧格爾 （王山譯）： 《第三只眼睛看中國》 太原 『山西人民出版社』。

Ma Hong and Sun Shangqing, eds. *Zhongguo Jingji Xingshi Yu Zhanwang (1994–1995)*. Beijing: Zhongguo Fazhan Chuban She, 1995.

馬洪、 孫尚清編： 《中國經濟形勢與展望 1994—1995》 北京『中國發展出版社』。

Min Qi. *Zhongguo Zhengzhi Wenhua: Minzhu Zhengzhi Nanchan de Shehui Xinli Yinsu*. Kunming: Yunnan Renmin Chuban She, 1989.

閔琦： 《中國政治文化：民主政治難產的社會心理因素》昆明『雲南人民出版社』。

Walker, Anthony. *Hong Kong in China: Real Estate in the Economy.* Hong Kong: Brooke Hillier Parker, 1995.

Wang Hongbin, Yao Xilan, Liu Xiaoqing et al., eds. *Zhong Yuan Feng: Nanjie Ren Jiang de Gushi.* Henan: n. p., 1993.

王洪彬、 姚喜蘭、 劉小青等編： 《中原風： 南街人講的故事》 河南省南街村。

Wang Juntao and Hou Xiaotian. *Wang Juntao Qi Ren, Qi Yan, Qi 'Zui.'* Hong Kong: Dangdai Yuekan, 1992.

王軍濤、 侯曉天： 《王軍濤其人、 其言、 其 "罪"》 香港 『當代月刊』。

Wang Shaoguang and Hu Angang. *Jiaqiang Zhongyang Zhengfu Zai Shichang Jingji Zhuanxing Zhong De Zhudao Zuoyong.* Beijing: Chinese Academy of Sciences, 1993.

王紹光、 胡鞍鋼： 《加強中央政府在市場經濟轉型中的主導作用》 北京 『中國科學院』。

Widor, Claude, ed. *Documents on the Chinese Democratic Movement 1978–1980.* Vol. 2. Paris: École des Hautes Études en Sciences Sociales; Hong Kong: The Observer Publishers, 1984.

World Bank. *The East Asian Miracle: Economic Growth and Public Policy.* New York: Oxford University Press, 1993.

Xu Jiatun. *Xu Jiatun Xianggang Huiyilu.* Hong Kong: Lianhe Bao, 1993.

許家屯： 《許家屯香港回憶錄》 香港 『聯合報』。

Xuexi Wenjian. Beijing: Zhonggong Zhongyang Dangxiao Chubanshe, 1980.

《學習文件》 北京 『中共中央黨校出版社』。

Yu Jian. *Lengxue Gongpu, Quan, Se, Li Chaoji Jiaoyi Beiwanglu.* Beijing: Hongqi Chubanshe, 1993.

宇劍等： 《冷血公僕： 權、 色、 利超級交易備忘錄》 北京 『紅旗出版社』。

Yu Xiguang, Li Liangdong et al., eds. *Dachao Xinqi: Deng Xiaoping Nanxun Qianqian Houhou.* Beijing: Zhongguo Guangbo Dianshi Chuban She, 1992.

余習廣、李良棟等編： 《大潮新起： 鄧小平南巡前前後後》 北京 『中國廣播電視出版社』。

Yuan Yongsong and Wang Junwei eds. *Zuo Qing Ershi Nian.* Beijing: Nongcun Duwu Chubanshe, 1993.

袁永松、王均偉編： 《左傾二十年》 北京『農村讀物出版社』。

Zhao Shilin, ed. *Fang 'Zuo' Beiwanglu.* Taiyuan: Shuhai Chubanshe, 1992.

趙士林編： 《防 "左" 備忘錄》 太原 『書海出版社』。

Zhen Yuegang and Guan Shuguang, eds. *Gong' an Neiqin Gongzuo Shouce*. Beijing: Jingguan Jiaoyu Chubanshe, 1993.

甄岳剛、管曙光編：《公安內勤工作手冊》 北京 『警官教育出版社』。

Zheng Langping. *Yijiujiuwu Run Bayue*. Taipei: Shangzhou Wenhua, 1994.

鄭浪平：《一九九五閏八月》 台北 『商周文化』。

Zhou Yumin and Shao Yong. *Zhongguo Banghui Shi*. Shanghai: Shanghai Renmin Chubanshe, 1993.

周育民、邵雍：《中國幫會史》上海『上海人民出版社』。

Index